FIGHTER ACES OF THE LUFTWAFFE

With best personal wishes and
HORRIDO!
Raymond F. Toliver

and with my best wishes, too!
Trevor J. Constable

By the same authors

FIGHTER ACES

HORRIDO!

BLOND KNIGHT OF GERMANY

FIGHTER ACES OF THE LUFTWAFFE

Colonel Raymond F. Toliver, USAF (Ret.)

AND

Trevor J. Constable

INTRODUCTION BY
Lieutenant General Adolf Galland
General of the Fighter Arm, 1941–45

AERO PUBLISHERS, INC.

Fallbrook, California 92028

ISBN 0-8168-5790-3
Library of Congress No. 77-79516

Library of Congress Cataloging in Publication Data
Toliver, Raymond F.
    Fighter aces of the Luftwaffe.

    First ed. published in 1968 under title: Horrido!
Fighter aces of the Luftwaffe.
    Includes index.
    1. World War, 1939-1945—Aerial operations, German.
2. German. Luftwaffe—Biography. 3. World War, 1939-
1945—Biography.   I. Constable, Trevor J , joint author.
II. Title.
D787.C63   1977   940.54'49'430922   77-79516
ISBN 0-8168-5790-3

Printed and Published in the United States by Aero Publishers, Inc.

To

FRIENDSHIP

FAIRNESS

CHIVALRY

Without Which Man Descends Beneath the Beast

Acknowledgments

In the twenty years spent assembling this book, the authors incurred a vast debt to the German aces, historians, researchers, writers, and others who lent their strength to the work. If individual thanks were extended to all who have contributed, several pages of names would be necessary. To all these people the authors extend their heartfelt thanks. Special accolades go to the late distinguished air historian Hans-Otto Boehm, who was responsible for much early research guidance and also for introducing the authors to each other; Lieutenant General Adolf Galland, whose personal interest has been constant despite a busy business schedule; General Johannes "Macky" Steinhoff, a friend of this project since its inception; Colonel Erich Hartmann for numerous suggestions and research material; Lieutenant Generals Hannes Trautloft, Guenther Rall, Dietrich Hrabak, and Gerd Barkhorn and Colonel Willi Batz of the new German Air Force for their assistance; former Colonel Wolfgang Falck for his contributions to early night fighter history, for the loan of photographs and other help; former Major Hartmann Grasser for numerous suggestions and several rare photographs. Former Colonel Edu Neumann for his friendship and aid; former Major Georg-Peter Eder for the loan of documents and photographs; to the editors of *Fighter News (Jagerblatt)*, the most interesting publication of its kind in the world; historians Hans Hermann Schmidt, von Cajus Bekker, and Dr. P. R. Skawran for historical help; the late "Pips" Priller and his wife Johanna for valued material and memorable hospitality; Dr. Karl-Heinz Steinicke for his observations on Soviet aircraft and pilots; the late Heinz Baer for hitherto unpublished data on his war career; Heinz Nowarra, the eminent historian, and Ernst Obermaier of Munich for the loan of rare photographs; Mr. Hans Ring of Munich, documentation expert of the German Fighter Pilots' Association for important research assistance; to Miss Clare Amabile, for valuable assistance; to Mr. Charles Brooks and Eduard Schroeder for translations; to William Hess, the assistant historian of the American

Fighter Aces Association; to Christopher Shores, and to Lieutenant General Walter Krupinski, all of whom have contributed of their time and knowledge so unselfishly. Without the help of these people and *many* others, this book could not have been written.

The authors regret that they have been unable to obtain a complete list of the 5000-plus Luftwaffe fighter aces of WWII. Our sincere apologies to those aces who do not find their names on this list at the end of this book. We will be happy to add such names as come to our attention when revisions are printed.

Contents

Introduction

More than two decades have passed since the end of the Second World War, but this is the first comprehensive volume about the German fighter pilots written by anyone outside Germany. I therefore welcome this book as an international document, and something of a landmark in aviation history. Recognition for the relative handful of German fighter pilots who challenged the Allied air armadas on both fronts is long overdue. From my personal experience in writing history, I appreciate perhaps more than most people the magnitude of the task these two American authors have undertaken.

Colonel Raymond F. Toliver USAF (Ret.) and Trevor J. Constable have spent more than twelve years in the research and writing of this book. I know both of them personally. They have gained my complete trust and the respect and confidence of all former Luftwaffe pilots who have met them. Ray Toliver is a veteran fighter pilot, and we have been friends for years—in fact since he was Commanding Officer of the USAF 20th Tactical Fighter Wing at RAF Wethersfield in England. He is also the official historian of the American Fighter Aces Association, which makes this book all the more appropriate.

Trevor J. Constable has been my guest in Bonn, and his sincere good feeling for the German people is reflected in the fair and unbiased character of this book.

The authors have made an objective study of the Luftwaffe fighter force and most of its outstanding personalities. While I do not necessarily agree with all their conclusions, they have told their story with accuracy and close attention to technical detail. They have been able to capture the inner spirit of the Luftwaffe fighter force to a remarkable degree.

I regard this book not only as a worthy contribution to aviation history, but also as a valuable service to German-American friendship and mutual understanding.

ADOLF GALLAND, General der Jagdflieger a.D.

Bonn, West Germany

Foreword

Germany's fighter pilots did not create the Second World War, but they were caught up from first to last in its remorseless grind as were the pilots of no other nation. Most of the top-scoring German aces came from the prewar Luftwaffe as professional soldiers, but the majority of German aces as a whole were not professionals. They were volunteers drawn to the adventure of flying as were their forebears of the First World War.

Modern war opened the expensive and highly complex aviation field to these men. Without war, it was a line of work to which they would not have had access. Had the war not intervened, most of them would have become schoolteachers, bank clerks, managers, lawyers, and chemists, to which occupations many who survived have now returned.

Germany's fighter aces must be credited with outstanding and often astonishing achievements in the air. One purpose of this book is to record in the English language a sampling of their experiences, presented in many cases in their own words and often from contemporary accounts. This volume also seeks to illuminate the human side of the German aces; to present accurate biographies of outstanding pilots and to introduce many little-known German fighter leaders who helped give the Luftwaffe its characteristic spirit and vigor.

A quarter of a century after the end of the Second World War the time has come to dispel many myths and inaccurate views concerning the Luftwaffe fighter pilots which have their roots in wartime propaganda. The authors are not the first historians to marvel at the corrosive drivel published on both sides during the war. In cool blood and calm heart we should recognize that the German airman was a brave and fair opponent whose degree of professionalism is to be admired by all nationalities of fighter pilots.

Like their Allied counterparts, the German aces left families, wives, and loved ones behind when they went to war. Like all Germans of their generation they drank deeply from the cup of personal anguish as the consequences of the Hitlerian lunacy consumed their Fatherland. We need to recognize, too, that the German has as much right to love his Fatherland as we love America.

In their devotion to their country in the air, in their seemingly unquenchable courage, tenacity, and skill in the face of overwhelming Allied power, they were unsurpassed by any of the great warriors of history. They flew against the Allies to the final hour of the final day, but their historical misfortune was to be blamed by their own Supreme Commander for losing a war they had not conceived, but in the prosecution of which they had spent themselves to the limit of human endurance.

The patron saint of the German fighter pilots was St. Horridus, who had his origin in mess parties rather than the pantheon. During combat, the Luftwaffe fighter pilots would call *"Horrido!"* on the radio when they had scored a kill against an enemy aircraft. The distinctive cry alerted other pilots airborne to watch for a crash or a flamer, and also alerted ground stations. This practice helped confirm many victories. The night fighter pilots of the Luftwaffe used the cry *"Pauka! Pauka!"* for the same purpose, and most night victories were confirmed by ground stations and radar controllers alerted to watch for the crash.

The Allied pilots heard the cry *"Horrido!"* with disconcerting frequency, and it has since become a greeting cry among old German fighter pilots. The victory cry corresponded with "Tally Ho" on the Allied side, before the pilots locked themselves in the whirling maelstrom of aerial combat. Today Germany's aces sign their letters with a good-natured *"Horrido!"* as a link with their unforgettable past. *"Horrido!"* is the cry of the hunter!

Wartime antagonisms have been replaced by more worthy feelings. Dozens of German aces over the years have expressed the same sentiment to the authors in different ways, and it is adopted as the spirit of this book: May better understanding in the future unite with the terrible lessons of the past to prevent decent men with a common spiritual heritage ever going to war in the air again.

NOTE

German names have been anglicized in this book. Where German terms and ranks are used they have been italicized. Examples of anglicized pilot names are given below:

Bär	appears in this book as	Baer
Lützow	,, ,, ,, ,, ,,	Luetzow
Mölders	,, ,, ,, ,, ,,	Moelders
Schöpfel	,, ,, ,, ,, ,,	Schoepfel
Göring	,, ,, ,, ,, ,,	Goering
Günther	,, ,, ,, ,, ,,	Guenther
Göbbels	,, ,, ,, ,, ,,	Goebbels
Bölcke	,, ,, ,, ,, ,,	Boelcke

This procedure aids a more correct pronunciation of the names by those who do not understand German.

One further note of interest. The Messerschmitt fighter airplane known as the Me-109 is also known as the Bf-109. However, in America it has always been Me-109 so the authors have chosen to refer to it in that way.

1

Background to Sacrifice

"Our aces fought until they were killed."
ADOLF GALLAND

T HE German fighter pilots of the Second World War fought with surpassing valor from the first to the final day of the conflict. They began with everything in their favor—experience, better tactics than their foes, unexcelled combat leadership, well-tested weapons and a substantial technological lead in the development of the jet fighter. They also had a leader who was convinced they were invincible, and Goering, in turn convinced Hitler, a factor that led to over-commitment. They ended the war almost six years later heroically but vainly battling a veritable blizzard of Allied aircraft aloft, while their Fatherland fell into blazing ruin below.

The Luftwaffe produced the most successful and highest-scoring individual fighter pilots of all time, yet their formations were driven from the skies. The Germans were led in the air by their indomitable General, Adolf Galland, who must be deemed one of the two or three outstanding personalities of the air war on either side. Yet defeat, terror, and suffering swept in on the Reich from the air in spite of Galland's genius and the sacrificial devotion of his pilots. In a few short years the Luftwaffe fighter force was reduced from a dazzling ascendancy to a hunted and desperate collection of units struggling to get a handful of aircraft into the air.

Behind this dramatic change of fortune lies a well-nigh incredible story of courageous airmen repeatedly let down by their high command and by their political leaders. The careers of Germany's greatest aces cannot be accurately outlined or understood without this illuminating backdrop to the struggle in the skies. The derelictions, corruption, incompetence, failure and worse-than-failure of the significant personalities upon whom the fighter pilots depended for aircraft, training, and the general direction of their efforts are unprecedented at that time in modern military history. Soon afterward

American fighting men were to have two massive doses of the same kind of disheartening high-level failure in Korea and Viet Nam. The idea took root politically behind American servicemen in the lines of battle that there are acceptable substitutes for military victory.

The do-or-die valor of the Luftwaffe fighter pilots, and especially of the leading aces, never lost its devotional quality right to the end. This is a mantle of glory shared by all German fighter pilots, even though it was their own Supreme Commander and founder of the Luftwaffe who sought to strip it from them when the collapse of the Third Reich was imminent.

"THE FAT ONE" MEETS HIS FIGHTER LEADER: Reichsmarschall Hermann Goering, founder of the Luftwaffe and a Pour le Merite ace with von Richthofen in WWI, discusses a point of the new epoch with Adolf Galland (far right) during the Battle of Britain. Other Luftwaffe luminaries present were, from left, Joachim Huth, General Bodenschatz, and Walter Oesau. *(Galland Collection)*

When Hermann Goering blamed his fighter pilots for Germany's defeat, this bitter recrimination fell upon ears only too ready to accept it as the truth. The German populace, miserable, terrorized around the clock from the air, their lives and homes in ruins, largely accepted Goering's indictment as an accurate explanation of their woes.

The bulk of their miseries had come from the skies, as the result of Allied bombing raids. Was it not logical, therefore, that their country's main failure had been in the skies? And in particular, was it not the fault of those whose duty it was to sweep the enemy bombers from the skies—the fighter pilots? Dr. Goebbels had done a masterful job of distorting the truth about the war's course, and so Goering's great lie was in appropriate company.

The basic good sense of the German people soon enabled them to throw off these illusions. But even today, more than thirty years later, some Germans still believe their fighter pilots failed them. Their numbers today are small. In the immediate postwar period, however, the Goering lie was having its consequences. Some of Germany's greatest aces had doors slammed in their faces. Particularly if they belonged to the prewar Luftwaffe as active officers their civilian way was made hard.

These men had driven themselves to the limits of physical and mental endurance in defense of their country as soldiers. Yet they were often made scapegoats for the misery that came with defeat. Seeking employment, admission to trade unions or to universities they would be dismissed with the blanket condemnation: "You are a militarist!"

The blame belonged elsewhere, as history now clearly shows. Perhaps this book will help erase the stain placed on the honor of the German fighter pilots by their Commander in Chief—to his own eternal discredit.

Far beyond the inner circle of high command, the fighter pilots of the Luftwaffe were at once the instrumentality of Germany's stunning initial successes, and the Fatherland's main hope for averting final ruin. Despite all the will in the world on their part to rise to every challenge, they were never able to do so with the full force of German industry, German technology, the best military planning, and the political leadership united behind them. Had they been properly and loyally backed, the history of this century might have been different.

When there was a sufficiency of fighter aircraft, the years of criminal neglect in the training program resulted not only in a shortage of pilots, but in a steady and serious degradation of their training. When industry and military planning were capable on occasion of finding common ground, there was the aberrant decision-making of Hitler to disrupt this unity.

Opportunity after opportunity for sustaining and building up the Luftwaffe fighter force was presented to Germany's leaders. From the first major German failure of the war—the Battle of Britain—vital lessons were to be learned. The necessary shifts in emphasis in German air power, the vital need to boost production, introduce new fighter types, and expand the training schools were clearly discerned by the combat leaders and some members of the Luftwaffe General Staff, but rarely penetrated Goering's ego. In all fairness to Goering, by 1942 he was fully dominated by Hitler and was more often than not, afraid to press for what he thought was right in the face of a different Hitlerian viewpoint. In other words, Goering had become one of Hitler's "yes men". In reality, Goering was intelligent and forceful, but under Hitler's spell he became a nothing.

Even as late as 1943 the German position was not lost in the air. By that time it was evident that only a powerful fighter force could ensure

ME-262 IN 1945: This Me-262 twin-jet fighter was being concealed in the fringe of the Black Forest in 1945. Germans had great difficulty in keeping the handful of jets safe from attack by the marauding swarms of Allied fighters that sought them out in every part of Germany.   (*Obermaier Collection*)

the continuity of German industrial life and war potential. The opportunities presented for restoration of German aerial supremacy, chiefly in the form of the Me-262 jet fighter, went begging. The German fighter pilots continued to fly in fighters which were clearly on their way to eclipse. They were thus betrayed by forces, personalities, and factions far beyond their control and even further beyond their comprehension at the time.

Even the forceful, visionary genius of General Adolf Galland, combined with his brilliant combat record and the favor he enjoyed with Hitler, could not cope with the divisive activity and thinking that sabotaged German air power from within. In the air, where reality was confronted every blazing day and fiery night, the fighter pilots reaped the lethal consequences of these behind-the-scenes failures. A retrospective examination of the origin of these errors provides a quite different picture of the Luftwaffe from that projected during the war itself.

The Luftwaffe was founded by a fighter pilot—Hermann Goering. His faith in the air weapon was in inverse proportion to his technical knowledge, but his faith was backed with the enormous physical energy, drive, and personal forcefulness that were Goering's predominant traits in early middle life. These qualities, powered by sources only a political revolutionary can tap, made Goering the central figure in the rebirth of German air power.

Goering's aggressive personality exemplified one of the primary assets of the successful fighter ace. He scored twenty-two aerial victories in the First World War and rose to command the Richthofen Circus after the death of the famed Red Knight on the Western Front. He proved himself an aggressive rather than an intelligent leader, and he holds no historical position as a tactician and leader comparable with that enjoyed by von Richthofen or Boelcke. Losses of Richthofen Circus pilots and planes rose sharply under his command.

Expert knowledge was never Goering's personal strength, nor did he ever develop an appropriate respect for those who had earned such knowledge, either in the crucible of war or in the arena of industry. Given a choice between a technical expert and an individual of dominant personality, Goering would favor the latter.

He was in many respects a holdover from the age of chivalry. His interest in preserving the niceties of knightly conduct in the air remained undiminished. He was more interested in such relatively unimportant things than he was in realistic technical evaluations of equipment and tactics. He instructed his fighter pilots to fight an honorable battle. Shooting at a parachuting flyer was absolutely forbidden and so was strafing a bailed out pilot on the ground.

As an old fighter pilot who had hitched his destiny to a political star, Goering developed a politician's capacity to avoid or ignore confrontations with facts and situations inimical to his personal status. Under the Hitler regime, this status meant many things important to Goering—money, power, and position chief among them. Although provided with these in abundance, he failed to utilize them in a meaningful way for the Luftwaffe he had created.

He did not utilize his resources of leisure, for example, in acquiring the broad-based understanding of air power which he needed to effectively discharge his task as Commander in Chief of the Luftwaffe. Indeed, he was more like an actor flamboyantly playing out a role. This led to some signal errors of judgment which are exemplified by Goering's attitude toward air transport.

By the time he ascended to power, aircraft had conquered the oceans of the world. Air transport was fast becoming an obvious fundamental of modern war. In an era such as this, Goering indulged a First World War fighter pilot's contempt for the men who flew transport aircraft. In the First World War, the transport aircraft was a lumbering, easy target for the fighter pilot with his agile, well-armed machine.

Goering permitted this archaic contempt for transport pilots to color his thinking and warp his judgment on the whole question of German military air transport. Unfortunately, this attitude was shared by some of Goering's First World War associates in high Luftwaffe posts. Neglect of the Luftwaffe's air transport forces was the consequence, and it helped lose the war for Germany.

Fighter aircraft were given early attention in the National Socialist armament program, and in Goering they had an interested and eager supporter. Nevertheless the main developmental thrust was in bombers. The major controversies in the infant Luftwaffe were over the *kind of bombers* that should be developed. Fighters were never considered as other than a secondary element in German air power in the

WAR BIRD: An Me-109F-2 photographed in Russia in 1942. The aircraft belongs to JG-54. *(Boehm Collection)*

prewar period—a situation which was duplicated in the United States.

Because of the fame won by the Me-109 in the Second World War, there has been a historical tendency to regard the prewar Luftwaffe as fighter-oriented. Even though the Me-109 was the major fighter project of the thirties and set the world trend to the low-wing, all-metal monoplane,[1] fighters remained definitely secondary in high-level Luftwaffe thinking during this significant period. In any work dealing with the Luftwaffe fighter pilots and the burdens they bore during the war, it is important to establish this relationship.

New tactics suited to the era of the Me-109 were developed in the immediate prewar years. These significant tactical advances are detailed in Chapter Three, which is devoted to the career of Colonel Werner Moelders, the officer primarily responsible for the innovations.

Luftwaffe units which took part in the Spanish Civil War were known as the Condor Legion. This adventure provided modern experience to such outstanding German fighter leaders as Moelders, Galland, Edu Neumann, Trautloft, Oesau, Balthasar, and others. They were all of the new generation and we shall meet them in this book. This experience

[1]On 30 March 1939, a Heinkel He 100 V° set a new speed record of 463.9 mph. This record was broken 11 April 1939 when Captain Fritz Wendel flew a Bf-109R (Bf 209 V1) Messerschmitt at 469.24 mph. This stood as the world's record for reciprocating engined aircraft until August 16, 1969 when an American, Darryl Greenamyer, flew a Grumman F8F2 Bearcat to a new record of 483.041 mph (777.35 kmph).

in Spain gave them a substantial initial advantage over the foes they were to face later in the world conflict. The advantage was psychological as well as tactical.

In the higher commands, where air power was seen on an even broader canvas, such able leaders as General Baron Wolfram von Richthofen[2] and General Hugo Sperrle found the Spanish experience rich in lessons for the future. Some of these lessons, like the value and uses of tactical air power, were perhaps overlearned. Condor Legion operations were relatively modest in scale, but in many respects they were a rehearsal in miniature for the Martian concert that commenced in 1939.

With at least six years of preparation (four "official" years plus two "camouflage" years) and the experiential legacy of the Spanish Civil War, the Luftwaffe fighter force in 1939 was without doubt the best-finished, best-led, and most battle-worthy force of its kind in the world. America's Colonel Charles A. Lindbergh had tried to warn the United States of this fact, and was labeled "pro-Nazi" for his trouble.

The victories that followed were heady stuff, hardly destined to stimulate the capacity for review and analysis on the part of the German leaders. For the Germans it was the heyday of tactical air power, and in the words of Adolf Galland: "The success made everything right for

BATTLE PAINT: Focke-Wulf, with its wide landing gear, solved the ground-looping problem so many Luftwaffe pilots had with the Me-109. *(Bodie Collection)*

[2] General Baron Wolfram von Richthofen, Chief of Staff and then Commander of the Condor Legion, was a fighter pilot in World War I with eight aerial victories. He was a cousin of Baron Manfred von Richthofen, Germany's top World War I ace.

those who thought only in terms of tactical air power."

The rapid destruction of the air forces of Poland, Denmark, The Netherlands, Norway, and Belgium in 1939 and 1940 lent German air power a terrible aspect in the eyes of the world. The brilliantly efficient fighters secured air superiority at the least, and enjoyed air supremacy most of the time. The fighters thus set the stage for the full-scale use of their tactical air force—the main thrust of prewar air power doctrine in Germany.

In 1939–40 the Stuka dive bombers terrorized enemy armies and civilian populations alike. They operated without hindrance under the Me-109 fighter umbrella. The methodical shattering of armies and the surrender and occupation of a succession of independent nations that took place under this air umbrella not only invested the Luftwaffe with soaring morale but also surrounded it with an aura of invincibility. A succession of independent and ancient states was occupied in a few months. The world had never seen anything like it.

With one sweeping triumph crowding in on another with minimum losses, the fundamental conceptions which ruled prewar development of the Luftwaffe hardly seemed open to question. Lightning war— *Blitzkrieg*—was a brilliant success. The victories were so easy and complete that Hitler did not even deem it necessary to order full mobilization before crushing France!

War and easy victory against small, weak Continental nations such as Belgium and The Netherlands, and against the large, well-armed but poorly led and irresolute France, encouraged an over-estimation by Germany of its aerial strength—and to an over-reliance on its air weapon. The easy victories against neighboring states veiled some cardinal weaknesses in the structure of German air power for assaulting a less-accessible country. These weaknesses were exposed in the Battle of Britain.

The main deficiency in German aerial strength was rooted in the 1937 decision of the Luftwaffe High Command not to develop a four-engined bomber—the strategic weapon. German devotion to tactical, close-support air power rather than the sword-and-flail concept of a balanced strategic and tactical air force was a high-level blunder. The straitened economy of prewar Germany bulked large in this error. Smaller and cheaper tactical bombers appeared particularly attractive under these circumstances. The fighter pilots ultimately reaped the consequences of this over-reliance on tactical air power.

Controversies will continue to rage for decades over the significance of the Battle of Britain. The relative losses suffered by both sides are a perennial subject for argument among air history buffs. From the point of view of the Luftwaffe fighter pilots, the major consideration of this book, the Battle of Britain was a decisive encounter.

German fighters were suddenly elevated from their secondary role. As the Germans contemplated the problem of aerial assault on Britain, it was clear that the whole German effort would hinge on the Luftwaffe fighter force. Everything depended on their subduing the Royal Air Force fighters, for the Luftwaffe bombers could not survive over Britain while RAF Fighter Command maintained control of the air.

In the psychological sphere too, there lurked other decisive factors. The German fighter pilots had already tested the mettle of the RAF in the Battle of France. As hunters and sportsmen pursuing the grimmest game of all, the German fighter pilots looked forward to fully testing the mettle of the men they knew to be their toughest foes to date.

In terms of relative losses of fighter aircraft, it is generally agreed nowadays that the Luftwaffe did not suffer fighter casualties that were either disparate to the task or irreparable. Indeed, if the tangle of British wartime records of "lost" aircraft could ever be fully unraveled, there is a high probability that the Luftwaffe fighter pilots gave very nearly as good as they got.

In any event, the German defeat in the Battle of Britain was of a far more significant order than any sterile comparison of downed aircraft will ever indicate. For the Luftwaffe fighter pilots the Battle of Britain was a morale-shaking moment of truth.

For the first time since the invasion of Poland their superb fighter formations were frustrated. Inane high command directives robbed them of the power of the offensive. They were directed to fly formation with the bombers they were escorting. They found themselves grappling with an utterly determined enemy. And even when the Germans were released to the "free chase" of the RAF, they found that their beloved Me-109s, supreme in European skies, suffered now from a serious technical deficiency—lack of range.

The German fighter pilots could not sustain a fighter offensive over southern England because of Me-109 fuel limitations. The technological lead of the British in radar heightened the problem. When the Germans took off from their French bases and assembled in the air before crossing the English Channel, their every move was studied by British radar controllers. Most of the time, the RAF fighters were in the right position in time and space to disrupt the German attack. In reality, the time taken to assemble large fighter formations gave the British time to assemble their defense—thanks to radar.

Perhaps the most significant German failure of the whole battle was in not obliterating the RAF's radar sites on the south coast of England. Even continual strafing of the radar towers would probably have sufficed to blind Fighter Command, and this task lay well within the capacity of the German fighters.

At a serious disadvantage in the first stages with their old-fashioned, three-ship "vic" formations and tactics, the RAF quickly adopted the German tactical elements of *Rotte* and *Schwarm*, consisting of two and four ships respectively. RAF gunnery, initially poor, also soon improved with the daily practice provided by the incoming Luftwaffe bombers and fighters.

Galland has described the situation of the German fighter pilots as akin to that of a fierce dog trying to spring at the throat of his foes, only to find that his chain restricts the area in which he may attack his victim. When the RAF fighters did not succumb to the German fighters, this led to the direction of German bombers on to British fighter airfields. Serious weaknesses were soon revealed in the German prewar conception of the bomber.

The bomb loads carried by the Luftwaffe bombers were pathetically inadequate. The two-ton capacity of the He-111 and the one-ton load of the Dornier Do-17Z were far below the levels required for the elimination of fighter airfields and critical production centers. Suffice it to recall that even hundreds of RAF Lancasters swarming into Germany every night with up to *ten tons of explosives apiece,* and droves of USAAF bombers by day, were unable to substantially diminish fighter production in Germany even in 1944! That year proved to be the greatest year for the production of new German fighters—after three solid years of Allied bombing.

The British fighter defense, which envisaged progressive withdrawal to airfields farther inland in the event that south coast fields became inoperable, was thus conceived in depth. The German bombers fell between two stools—their inadequate bomb loads and their daylight vulnerability. In the confrontation the RAF outgamed its foes and never had to evacuate its best airfields.

The Ju-87 Stuka, fresh from an unbroken string of tactical triumphs all over Europe, was now unprotected. The Me-109 umbrella beneath which it had previously functioned could offer only ragged and occasional protection to the slow-flying Stuka. The RAF fighters blasted the Stuka from British skies. The losses of prime Stuka crews quickly became so serious that the Ju-87 was withdrawn from the assault on Britain. They achieved nothing of significance in the battle to justify their losses. Their very presence cramped the Me-109 pilots, who were at their best in the free chase of their RAF counterparts.

The cripplingly short range of the Me-109, the inadequate bomb load of the main Luftwaffe bomber force, and the Stuka failure against British targets were not the only German weaknesses exposed in the Battle of Britain. One of Goering's pet projects, the heavy fighter or *Zerstorer*—fighter-destroyer—also showed up poorly. Developed in accordance with prewar German aerial doctrine to provide close escort to the bombers, the Me-110 proved to be neither fish nor fowl.

Major Hartmann Grasser, 103-victory Luftwaffe ace recalls the wild dreams of Goering concerning the Me-110. As a young pilot in 1939 Goering told him: "The Me-110 and you who fly it will be like Hannibal's cavalry protecting the elephants; the bombers are my elephants." This concept of close fighter escort for bombers, naïve in retrospect, was theoretically difficult to refute in the nondynamic nineteen thirties. The Americans also entertained similar doctrines, but only the Germans developed and produced a heavy fighter for this task before the war.

The Americans, however, evidently learned little from the close escort disaster of the Me-110, because it was only with great reluctance that they eventually unleashed their own long-range escort fighters to the free chase over Germany. This reluctant step sealed the doom of the Luftwaffe fighters and of Germany itself.

The Me-110 could fly all the way to the target with the Heinkels and Dorniers. The *Zerstorer* units were not on a leash like the Me-109. But in the fires of combat the theory and conception of the heavy fighter were quickly melted down. The Me-110 was incapable of meeting even the Hurricane, the RAF's second-best fighter, on anything like equal terms. Hartmann Grasser, who became an ace against Spitfires in the Me-110, describes the hazards of combat in the heavy fighter:

"The RAF fighters could attack you always with an altitude advantage, and surprise was invariably on their side. The Me-110 was simply too heavy to contend with either the Spitfire or the Hurricane. You had to be lucky to survive."

The pilots for the *Zerstorer* formations had been obtained by raiding the elite Me-109 squadrons. Now these superior airmen died ignominiously in dozens, flying aircraft that could neither discharge their basic mission of protecting the bombers nor protect themselves against the heavily armed and more agile Spitfires and Hurricanes. If ever fighter pilots died in vain, it was the *Zerstorer* flyers of the Battle of Britain.

Considerable prewar German doctrine and a substantial amount of design and engineering development thus proved virtually valueless to Germany in the Battle of Britain. The Stuka and the Me-110 rendered yeoman service throughout the war in other ways and on other fronts. The short-winded Me-109 soon acquired drop-tanks, increasing its range, and it served with distinction on all fronts. German medium bombers did well on the Russian Front, in the Mediterranean, and in the Balkans. The Ju-88 became an efficient night fighter. Against Britain in 1940, however, the makeup of the Luftwaffe was inadequate for its mission—a mission which Goering eagerly sought in his thirst for new glories.

Thirty-five years later, it is not difficult to see how the Luftwaffe, as constituted in 1940, could not possibly blockade the British Isles, eliminate the Royal Navy from the English Channel, demoralize the civilian populace, paralyze British transport, wreck British war industry, and obliterate the RAF Fighter Command. Yet the invasion and conquest of Britain required air supremacy over the invasion beaches as a minimum condition. Not even air superiority was achieved. Goering had underestimated the task, and Hitler had believed him.

The Luftwaffe bomber pilots blamed the fighters for not protecting their formations better. The RAF fighters, natural foes of the Luftwaffe fighters, remained unquenchably aggressive. Stuka pilots, those who survived, reported that they had been set upon by RAF fighters and their formations blown to pieces. All these circumstances pointed in one direction for those who did not know the facts: failure of the German fighter pilots.

Hitler recoiled from "Operation Sea Lion"—the invasion of Britain —when minimum conditions could not be fulfilled by the Luftwaffe. Air superiority could not be wrested from the RAF. For the first time, German war aims were frustrated and the Luftwaffe fighter pilots became the scapegoats.

The German pilots shared to the last man in this bitter frustration. They had flown themselves to a frazzle day after day, drawing out their last reserves of endurance and ardor. Hundreds of RAF fighters had fallen to their guns. In the free pursuit of the RAF fighters they had done well, and aces like Moelders, Galland, Luetzow, Balthasar, and Schoepfel had rung up impressive strings of kills. Yet for the first time since 1939 they found large gaps in their ranks every day, including some of their best pilots and leaders.

The RAF could not be beaten over its own territory by Germany's existing equipment flown from Continental bases. Furthermore, the RAF fighters were being replenished with repaired and brand-new aircraft, and a steady stream of trained fighter pilots issued from their schools. The Germans felt and saw the growing strength of the RAF, while their own losses were made up all too slowly.

The impact of these events was considerable on German pilot morale. The dynamics of battle had elevated the fighters to primacy in German aerial affairs, even though this radical change from peacetime conceptions was not recognized at high level for a long time. The best efforts of the pilots had not been enough in a crucial struggle. Help was needed from higher up if the heroism and devotion of the pilots were not to be wasted.

FIGHTER CONFERENCE AT LE TOUQUET, 1940: Luftwaffe fighter leaders plan operations against the RAF in 1940. From left they are Adolf Galland, Guenther Lützow, Werner Moelders, Carl Viek, Theo Osterkamp, Guenther Maltzahn and General Teichmann. Battle of Britain was in process at the time, one of the most critical encounters of the Luftwaffe fighters in WWII.(*Boehm Collection*)

Men of intelligence and integrity, had they been directing the Luftwaffe, would have sought with all their strength to make up deficiencies, shift emphasis, and make changes. No such rational activity supported the Luftwaffe fighter pilots. The inertia on the German side is revealed by 1941 fighter production, which averaged only 250 machines a month. This was *after* the Battle of Britain had impressed its clear warning on the future!

Sharply criticized within the German defense establishment for the Luftwaffe failure against England, Goering began to go sour on his fighter pilots. A man of his makeup naturally sought scapegoats for failures that were essentially his own. He adopted this attitude from the time it became obvious that the air war against Britain was not going to be another lopsided German victory.

Goering complained to Galland, Moelders, and other young leaders about the German fighter pilots' lack of aggressiveness. He promoted these two young leaders quickly to Wing Commander and removed all First World War pilots from group and wing leadership. These steps did not reach the roots of the problem.

Germany's unprecedented aerial assault on Britain had been a failure of doctrine, planning, and equipment. In today's terminology, it was an abortive effort to conduct strategic aerial warfare with an essentially tactical air force.[3] Failure was inherent in the whole venture away from the Continent to try to conquer an island power from the air.

CHANNEL FRONT PLANS: Göring discusses plans with Lt. Col. Adolf Galland at Audembert, France, during the Battle of Britain. Far left is General Bodenschatz and on the right is Göring's Aide 1st Lt. Rothenberger. *(Galland Collection)*

When Goering's first measures failed to significantly change a situation ruled by more massive factors, "The Fat One" resorted to carping criticism of the fighter pilots. From this theme he seldom sub-

---

[3]In 1967 the United States was following a similar pattern in Viet Nam. B-52 strategic bombers attacked tactical targets in South Viet Nam, while tactical fighter-bombers were bombing strategic targets in the North. History teaches only that we learn nothing from history!

sequently departed. His main response to Germany's aerial failures was
thenceforth mainly limited to this negative activity. His tactical and
strategic ideas were usually devoid of value, overrode the analyses and
recommendations of fighter leaders, and literally wasted thousands of
fighter pilots' lives. Some of Goering's gambits are detailed in Chapter
Two, dealing with the career of Adolf Galland.

Germany's aerial warriors proved the validity for 1940 of von
Richthofen's classic 1917 maxim: "Find the enemy and shoot him
down—anything else is nonsense." The Germans had shown up best
in the free chase of RAF fighters—the aggressive role. But the
beginning of 1941 saw JG-26, JG-2, and JG-51 assigned by their per-
plexed high command to the static defense of Channel coast targets in
France. The German fighter pilots had suffered a come-down.

This dramatic switch to the defensive drove home to the German
fighter pilots their loss of air superiority in the West. They were never
again able to sustain the offensive role, except locally, briefly, and
nondecisively. Hitler's decision to conquer Russia and then deal with
Britain later meant that the RAF had won the first round. As it turned
out, it was also the final round in the Battle of Britain.

The manifold problems arising on the German side from the Battle
of Britain, including production, training, and technical development,
were serious and far-reaching in their implications. Inadequate
attention to these issues led ultimately to the ruin of the Luftwaffe
fighter force. Grave as these problems were, they were soon forgotten
in a new blaze of glory as the Luftwaffe roared into the Balkans and
then into Russia as the primary striking arm of the German forces.

Weak forces were again confronted in the Balkans. Once more the
Luftwaffe fighters swept the skies and gave full scope to tactical air
power. The string of ensuing victories was marred only by the savage
Allied defense of Crete. Conducted by the New Zealand General
Freyberg, the Battle of Crete resulted in heavy losses to Germany's
elite paratroops.[4] Nevertheless, the German sweep through the
Balkans was a dazzling victory made possible by air power, and by the
obliteration of fighter opposition in particular.

In the invasion of Russia, through their dash and skill the German
fighter pilots again knew the intoxicating feeling of air supremacy.
In the first week of "Operation Barbarossa," in concert with the German bomber and ground-attack units, they cut the Soviet Air Force to
pieces. Almost five thousand Russian aircraft of various types were
destroyed, virtually eliminating Soviet air power in the vital first month
of the invasion.

In the Russian fighter pilots the German veterans of Poland, the
Low Countries, and the Battle of Britain found a far easier prey than
the valiant British, who had sent them home so often with holes in

---

[4] German paratroops never fought "on the drop" again in any major operation of the Second
World War. The losses suffered in Crete turned Hitler decisively against the invasion of Malta in
the spring of 1942, and thus cost the Axis victory in North Africa.

their aircraft and gaps in their ranks. In these early air battles the Soviet pilots were no match for the experienced and habile Germans. Soviet aircraft of all types were shot down in droves. Kill totals on the

"LIKE SHOOTING DUCKS . . . " is how Johannes "Macky" Steinhoff described early fighter campaigns against Red Air Force in 1941. This photograph of Steinhoff was taken before his fiery 1945 crash in a Me-262 jet which left him with a badly burned face. Up to that time, the handsome Steinhoff carried only a saber scar from his student duelling days. (*Steinhoff Collection*)

Eastern Front rose more rapidly than at any other time in the history of aerial warfare. In the words of Colonel (now General retired) Johannes "Macky" Steinhoff, "It was like shooting ducks."

Thus in the early days of the Russian campaign the German pilots drank deeply once again of the heady wine of victory. The Russian fighter pilot, product of a system that sought to extinguish individuality, was unable to meet his German foe on equal terms. The superiority of the German fighter pilots was not only technical, but psychological. Even after the Russians later redressed their technical disadvantage, the Germans retained their psychological edge.

The often astonishing facts about the Second World War Soviet Air Force—its size, development, and technical status—are detailed in the chapters devoted to the Eastern Front. Those who continue to entertain complacent attitudes concerning Soviet technology will not find the truth about the Russian air effort, including fighter production, in any way conducive to smugness. German aviators who fought in Russia have much to teach the West.

The German pilot gained and retained the ascendancy over his Russian counterpart mainly because of his superior *ego* factor. All the qualities of individual intelligence, independence, initiative, and enterprise which fitted him temperamentally for the highly individualized art of aerial combat were encouraged and developed in his training. The Soviet system with its leveling tendencies and opposition to individualism was less than an ideal environment in which to breed fighter pilots.

Even as the Russians got steadily better with the passage of time, the individual German fighter pilot never lost the inner conviction that he was a better man than his foes. Even when the Russians enjoyed a staggering numerical superiority through their own production and massive lend-lease aid, the Germans continued to hurl themselves on their enemies with amazing and continued success. The capacity of the German fighter pilots to sustain themselves in the air under such adverse conditions shows that what a fighter pilot *thinks of himself* will manifest itself in what he achieves.

On the Russian Front, the Luftwaffe produced the highest-scoring fighter aces of all time. They are Erich Hartmann, with 352 kills; Gerhard Barkhorn, with 301 kills; and Guenther Rall, with 275 kills. Other leading German aces of the Russian Front were Otto Kittel with 267 aerial victories, Walter Nowotny with 258 kills, and Wilhelm Batz with 237 victories. These men are but the top scorers. There were also numerous lower-scoring but eminent pilots such as Johannes "Macky" Steinhoff with 176 victories, Tony Hafner with 204 kills, and Hermann Graf with 212 victories.

HIGHEST SCORING ACE OF ALL TIME: Erich Hartmann with 352 victories was highest scoring ace of all time. 345 of these vic- against the Red Air Force. The 7 remaining kills were P-51 Mustangs of the USAAF. (*Hartmann Collection*)

SECOND HIGHEST SCORING ACE OF ALL TIME: Gerd Barkhorn scored 301 victories in WWII, a tally exceeded only by that of Erich Hartmann. Barkhorn flew 1105 combat missions. *(Boehm Collection)*

THIRD HIGHEST SCORING ACE OF ALL TIME: Guenther Rall flew from 1939 to 1945 in an epic career that included 275 victories scored on all fronts against Russian, British and American aircraft. In an air battle over Berlin, an American fighter pilot shot off his left thumb, which he nurses here shortly after the encounter in May 1944. *(Boehm Collection)*

These scores are enormous by the standards of the contemporary USAAF and RAF. As a consequence, there has been a reluctance for more than twenty years to accept the German scores as valid. Only in recent years, as Western historians have taken the time and trouble to investigate thoroughly the German records and procedures, has the magnitude of the German achievement found acceptance in Allied countries.

The authors have spent sufficient time interviewing numerous German aces, examining records, logbooks, wing histories, and other official documents in the past twenty years to entertain no doubt whatever as to the thoroughness and rigidity with which German fighter pilots' victories were claimed, recorded, and credited. Their system was far more rigid than either the British or the American scoring procedures, and avoided such mythical accreditation as one half, one third, or three quarters of a victory—the so-called shared kill.

The German penchant for precision could not abide the concept of a pilot shooting down one third or one half of an aircraft. This fiction was eliminated by a simple set of rules. Where more than one pilot was involved in the downing of an aircraft, the pilots had to decide between themselves who was to get the kill credit. In the event of an impasse, the confirmed kill was credited to the pilots' *unit*, with no individual pilot credit awarded.

A case in point may be cited from 22 March 1943, when First Lieutenant Heinz-Wolfgang Schnaufer, later to become the top-scoring night fighter ace of the war with 121 victories, claimed a victory over an RAF Lancaster. Captain Wilhelm Herget, later Major Herget and credited with fifty-seven night kills and fifteen day kills by war's end,

TOP SCORING NIGHT FIGHTER ACE OF ALL TIME: Major Heinz-Wolfgang Schnaufer scored 121 victories against the Allies in WWII, all of them at night. He won Germany's highest decoration, the Diamonds of his Knight's Cross, and also survived the war. He was killed in an automobile accident in 1950. *(Boehm Collection)*

SECOND HIGHEST SCORING NIGHT FIGHTER ACE OF ALL TIME: Lieutenant Colonel Helmut Lent scored 102 aerial victories at night in WWII, and another 18 day victories before he entered the difficult art of night fighting. He was awarded Germany's highest decoration— the Diamonds to his Knight's Cross—but was killed in a flying accident late in 1944. *(Boehm Collection)*

claimed the same Lancaster. Both pilots had shot at the same bomber. General Kammhuber ordered the two aces to draw lots and Herget was the winner.

Under the USAAF system by contrast, it was possible for a fighter pilot to become an ace without ever scoring a clear victory of his own. A mathematical abstraction could, under the USAAF system become a substitute for genuine achievement. The USAF continues this questionable tradition even today. Late in 1966 the USAF further adulterated its already suspect victory credits system by announcing that kills scored by USAF aircraft manned by a pilot in the front seat and a radar operator or "guy in back" (two persons in the same aircraft) would be accredited by giving *both* pilots credit for a kill. Thus, five enemy aircraft downed creates *two* American aces!

The Luftwaffe system was clearly more rational and realistic. "One pilot—one kill" was the invariable scoring rule, straightforward and logical. Confirmation procedures were similarly direct in the Luftwaffe. Without a witness, a Luftwaffe fighter pilot had no chance to have his victory claim confirmed. Such a claim, even if filed, would not pass beyond group level.[5]

The final destruction or explosion of an enemy aircraft in the air, or the bail-out of the pilot, had to be observed either on gun-camera film or by at least one other human witness. The witness could be the German pilot's wingman, squadron mate, or a ground observer of the encounter.

There was no possibility, as with some RAF and USAAF pilots, of having a victory credited because the claiming officer was a gentleman and a man of his word. The German rule was simply "no witness—no kill." The rule applied all the way up to the General of the Fighter Arm himself, Adolf Galland. The authors have a photostatic copy of one of Galland's own wartime combat reports of a downing. The report concludes with the following simple statement: "I resign the confirmation of this victory for lack of a witness."

The German system was impartial, inflexible, and far less error-prone than either the British or the American procedures. German fighter pilots frequently had to wait several months, a year, or sometimes even longer for kill confirmation to reach them from the German High Command. Examples from German records appear in various places in this book.

The Germans differed radically from the Allies with their complicated "points" system, instituted solely for the award of decorations.

[5] Antithetically, the *Pacific Stars and Stripes* of Tuesday, 25 April 1967, reported that during a recent battle with MIG fighters over Viet Nam, the pilot and radar operator of an American F-4 Phantom had each been accredited with a "probable" because an air-to-air missile they had fired at a MIG disappearing into a large cloud bank just after the missile was fired also disappeared into the same cloud. The airmen were unable to confirm a hit but an Air Force spokesman at Da Nang said the crew was credited with a *probable kill*. This method of accreditation will, no doubt, revolutionize air-to-air combat scoring procedures but it also renders suspect all combat claims not documented on film or by witnesses.

The purpose of the points system was to introduce a modicum of uniformity into the bestowal of higher German decorations. The points system had no counterpart in the Allied air forces.

The authors previously described the German points system in their book *Fighter Aces*.[6] For the sake of clarity, this summary of the points system is now quoted here again:

"The German points system was in effect on the Western Front only, and for the purposes of decorations points were awarded in the following manner:

Single-engined plane destroyed	1 point
Twin-engined plane destroyed	2 points
Three-engined plane destroyed	3 points
Four-engined plane destroyed	3 points
Twin-engined plane damaged	1 point
Three- or four-engined plane damaged	2 points
Final destruction of a damaged twin-engined plane	$\frac{1}{2}$ point
Final destruction of a damaged four-engined plane	1 point

"The Germans also set great store by the ability of a fighter pilot to separate individual Allied bombers from the box formations in which they flew. Thus, a German pilot could not win points for damaging an Allied bomber unless he separated it from the box—that separation known to the Germans as *Herausschuss*.

"That this 'points for decorations' system, with all its ramified and intricate rules, has been confused with the normal victory confirmation procedures is obvious from much inaccurate material previously published about German fighter pilots' scores—most of it critical. A practical example of the two systems as they worked during the war will show how the confusion has arisen.

"Suppose it is early 1943, at which time forty points were required to qualify a fighter pilot for the Knight's Cross of the Iron Cross. Our hypothetical pilot, Captain Fritz Flugmann, has already shot down and confirmed twenty-two single-engined fighters (twenty-two points), five twin-engined bombers (ten points), and two four-engined bombers (six points). Captain Flugmann is an ace with twenty-nine kills, but he has only thirty-eight *points*—not enough for his Knight's Cross.

"Next day, Flugmann takes off and damages a B-17, separating it from its box formation, and accomplishes the final destruction of a second B-17 damaged previously by another German pilot. Captain Flugmann now has forty-one points, enough for his Knight's Cross, but he is credited with thirty kills after reconciling the aerial battle with other pilots and getting victory credit for one of the bombers.

"This point-decoration system was used only on the Western Front, because the Germans believed it was easier to shoot down Russian

[6] *Fighter Aces* by Colonel Raymond F. Toliver and Trevor J. Constable. The Macmillan Company, New York, 1965.

fighters and bombers on the Eastern Front than to down Mustangs, Thunderbolts, and Mosquitos in the West. They considered the mighty Allied bomber streams, with their lethal volumes of protective fire and hordes of accompanying fighters, to be a far tougher proposition than Soviet air power.

"Although the point-decoration system for the Russian front was therefore not in effect, the kill-confirmation rules were the same. Late in the war, there were pilots on the Russian front with over one hundred confirmed victories who had still to receive the Knight's Cross awarded for forty points won in the West."

The quality of the German fighter pilots, and of the equipment they flew, was a dominant factor in the destruction of Soviet air power during June and July 1941. The surprise element must also be given due weight, at least in the first few days when the Russians were taken unawares, and enormous losses inflicted on their parked aircraft.

Throughout the next two years the quality of the German pilots and aircraft kept Soviet air power in check. But in a battle of attrition, quantity will nearly always win out over quality. By 1944 the battle of attrition had tipped in favor of the Russians in the air, and they had long since tipped the scales in the ground fighting.

The important thing to remember is that in the invasion of Russia the German fighter pilots accomplished everything that could conceivably have been asked of them. They won air supremacy as a cardinal element of the *Blitzkrieg*. The depth of the Russian defense and the early, severe and sudden winter of 1941 laid the basis for Germany's defeat.

The German failure in Russia was not a failure of its fighter force.

The Russian struggle again bared the primary deficiency in German air power, an element without which Germany could not prevail against a geographically large or remote country—the strategic bomber. In 1941 the Luftwaffe again desperately needed its four-engined "Ural Bomber"—the project killed in 1937—to throttle Soviet industrial potential. Russian war potential, like that of Britain, remained beyond the reach of German air power and thus assured the eventual recovery of the Soviet Union.

The German aces who made their names and scores in Russia fought under conditions of great privation and hardship. They operated from primitive grass airfields with minimal facilities. Rarely did they enjoy the "luxury" of life in a wooden barracks building. Tents or dugouts with tents over them were their living quarters for most of the war. In winter particularly, these grim conditions had no counterpart in the war against the Western powers. In comparing Western and Eastern Front scores it is worth remembering that Eastern Front pilots fought not only against numerical odds, but also against a savage environment.

In more pleasant Mediterranean climes and under the African sun, other German fighter pilots were flying their hearts out. In North Africa JG-27 and JG-77, together with one *Gruppe* of JG-51, flew in support of the Axis armies, but without the strength to sustain aerial superiority other than locally and briefly. German air power in North Africa was also misused and frittered away in many respects by the Germans, so that attrition of pilots and planes was out of proportion to achievements.

The North African war nevertheless produced one of the most colorful German aces and folk heroes, Hans-Joachim Marseille. The theater also gave scope to some outstanding German ace-leaders, including Joachim Muencheberg, Herbert Ihlefeld, and Johannes Steinhoff, all of whom served as *Kommodore* of JG-77 at various times.

"STAR OF AFRICA": Captain Hans-Joachim Marseille with 158 victories was Germany's greatest combat hero of the war in North Africa. All his victories were against British and American aircraft. Marseille destroyed more R.A.F. aircraft than any other pilot in history. He was killed in a flying accident in North Africa while at the height of his fame. *(Neumann Collection)*

ACE AND TUTOR: Colonel Herbert Ihlefeld was a 7-victory ace with the Condor Legion in Spain, and went on to become one of the Luftwaffe's leading tutors. He commanded JG-77, JG-52, JG-11 and JG-1 at various times, had 130 aerial victories all told and won the Swords to his Knight's Cross. *(Boehm Collection)*

North Africa tested and proved the exceptional command and leadership talents of Edu Neumann, who distinguished himself as *Kommodore* of JG-27.

The supply problem to North Africa, as well as the insufficiency of German fighter production during the critical period of Rommel's campaigns, prevented an adequate build-up of German air power in North Africa. Their British foes in that theater recall the Luftwaffe fighter pilots as fair and hard opponents. Against high-quality RAF opposition, which fought its own supply battle successfully, the Germans found their African fortunes steadily declining. Aerial warfare in North Africa ended with the eviction of the Luftwaffe from Tunisia in early 1943.

Against the island of Malta, the German fighters once more accomplished all that could be asked of them in behalf of combined operations. Flying from Sicilian airfields, the Luftwaffe fighters struggled mightily to subdue the RAF bombing operations from Malta which were crippling the flow of spares, new aircraft, and gasoline to JG-27 and JG-77 in North Africa. The German failure to invade Malta in the spring of 1942, when the Axis had the troops, gliders, and aerial superiority over the island to ensure success, must be accounted one of the German High Command's major failures in the Mediterranean.

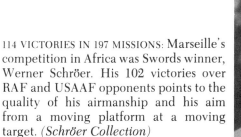

114 VICTORIES IN 197 MISSIONS: Marseille's competition in Africa was Swords winner, Werner Schröer. His 102 victories over RAF and USAAF opponents points to the quality of his airmanship and his aim from a moving platform at a moving target. *(Schröer Collection)*

Significantly the Luftwaffe fighter pilots provided the all-important air superiority necessary for such an operation. They harassed the RAF fighters on Malta endlessly. Frequently they reduced British fighter operations to token resistance. When in due course on their second attempt the British reinforced Malta with an all-new force of Spitfires flown from the U.S. carrier *Wasp*, air superiority over Malta was regained by the British.

From this time on, the Luftwaffe had to abandon its daylight raids, and all possibility of invading Malta evaporated. The balance of air power swung steadily back to the Allies, and German supply lines to North Africa were again pinched off. The higher direction of German strategy again had thrown away opportunities won for the Wehrmacht by the German fighter pilots. Malta was the last occasion on which they were able to open such grandiose possibilities to their high command.

By the spring of 1943 the Luftwaffe fighters had their backs to the wall on all fronts. American air power was moving into the conflict with increasing weight. The stunning reverses of Stalingrad and El Alamein had triggered wholesale processes of decline in Germany's war effort. In Italy the German Army was settling down for a war of attrition under a frayed air umbrella. On the Channel coast, the pilots of JG-2 and JG-26 watched with mounting concern the build-up of Allied air power. Their own capacity to significantly damage enemy air strength diminished every month.

By the end of 1943 German military realists no longer doubted that Germany's defeat was inevitable. Slowly the realization seeped into high German circles that the country's only means of maintaining industrial capacity and war potential was through vast fleets of protective fighters. By March 1944, Allied bombing raids were making production extremely difficult, and it seemed almost too late to make any decisive move.

Field Marshal Erhard Milch, Goering's deputy, chose this moment to set up the Fighter Staff to reorganize aircraft production. Under the energetic direction of Saur, the Fighter Staff dispersed production centers, developed and expanded underground workshops and assembly centers, and coordinated these measures with Albert Speer, then Germany's war production chief.

A veritable flood of new fighter aircraft resulted from these measures, despite Allied bombing. Ten new training schools were opened in 1944. By September the same year, *monthly* production attained the astonishing level of 3129 new fighter aircraft. These were the measures which should have been launched right after the Battle of Britain, when they might easily have changed the course of world history.

Earlier derelictions on the part of Germany's air power architects now began to have serious consequences. The basis of German fighter pilot training at the beginning of the war—the Luftwaffe had only *one* fighter pilot training school in 1939—was far too narrow to sustain the massive expansion demanded at the eleventh hour. There were not sufficient skilled instructors, and dozens of highly skilled training specialists had been peremptorily moved to the Eastern Front during the Stalingrad emergency. They never returned from this disaster. Training was further harassed by a perpetual shortage of gasoline. And there was the inexorable enemy—time.

Pilots could not be produced quickly enough in 1944 to fill the thousands of fighters being delivered from the factories. The average German fighter pilot went into action with less than one third the flying training hours of his American counterpart.[7] He was given only minimum instruction in such advanced aspects of his art as blind flying. These boys were shot down in dozens before they scored even their first kill.

Galland and other ace-leaders could reflect bitterly on their years of urging, proposing, pleading, suggesting, and demanding that such expansion of the fighter force be undertaken. By November of 1944

[7] Less than 150 hours for the German, versus 450 hours for the American.

there were almost seven hundred day fighters and seven hundred night fighters at operational readiness in Germany. Thus, the peak was reached as ruin was approached, for it was now too late.

The night fighters of the Luftwaffe must be credited with outstanding achievements. While the scores of the great night fighter aces do not approach those of the leading day fighter pilots, they must be assessed on a different scale of values.

Heinz-Wolfgang Schnaufer's 121 kills as the top night fighter ace of the war is three times as many victories as the leading British and American aces were able to record during the day. Schnaufer's tally is almost twice that of the top-scoring Allied day ace of the war, Colonel Ivan Kojedub of the Soviet Air Force.

Helmut Lent's 102 night kills against Western-flown bombers assure him of a historical niche with the outstanding pilots of the war. Werner Streib, sometimes called the "Father of Night Fighting," scored sixty-five aerial kills in a first-to-last career as a night fighter. We shall meet all these incredible characters in Chapter Ten, "Knights of the Night."

The jets and rocket-powered fighters which Germany made operational in the Second World War showed the clear technical advantage held by German designers over the Allies. The Me-262 and Me-163 went on operations in spite of the difficult conditions prevailing in Germany during 1944. Bad management and high-level ineptitude once again failed Germany's fighter pilots. They were deprived by their own high command and irrational political leaders from use of the technical superiority German aeronautical research, development,

NIGHT FIGHTING PIONEERS: Werner Streib (1) and Wolfgang Falck were two leading pioneers of the new art of night fighting, which was subject of much early ridicule by Goering. Falck pioneered ground control methods and Streib pioneered airborne attack techniques at night. Both ended the war as Colonels. *(Falck Collection)*

and ingenuity made possible. The full story of the jet fighter and the men who flew it will be found in Chapters Fourteen and Fifteen.

High-level vanity and purblindness undermined Adolf Galland's efforts to make best use of the fighter force. Typical of this high-level "sabotage" was the Hitlerian edict on 20 June 1944 that all available fighters be sent to France to help stop the invasion. This decision came just as the effects of the Fighter Staff–Speer combination were becoming evident. Fighter production was soaring, and pilots were being trained to replenish losses and build up reserves.

Convinced of the efficacy of large-scale fighter assaults on the Allied bomber streams, Galland watched with keen anticipation the growth of the reserves which had so long eluded him. His aim: morale-shattering attacks on the bombers, such as those driven home on 17 August and 14 October 1943. Each time, sixty or more American bombers were brought down and hundreds damaged over Schweinfurt.[8]

In the interim, the Americans had exploited the 1943–44 winter, damaging German fighter production and utilizing the bad weather in which the poorly trained German fighter pilots could not operate adequately. The Americans had also added the long-range escort fighter.

Keeping all these factors in balance, Galland was almost ready for more massed attacks on the bombers when his fighter force was peremptorily ordered to France. The heavyweight punch of which the young General had dreamed was subsequently dissipated in an ineffective and worthless effort to contend with Allied air power over the Normandy battleground. The Allies enjoyed virtual air supremacy in this area. The German pilots, operating from unfamiliar, makeshift, and continually harassed airfields became a vain sacrifice to another of Hitler's all-or-nothing operational fiats.

During the Ardennes offensive, a repetition of this profligate waste of aerial strength occurred. Between June and November 1944 the indomitable Galland and his devoted staff had again built up a reserve of planes and pilots. Galland's plan was to hurl a blizzard of two thousand fighters in one mighty blow at the American bombers. He visualized the destruction of at least four hundred of the heavies. He felt certain it would shake the morale of the Allied airmen and their generals.

Hitler intervened. He ordered this powerful fighter force hurled into the close-support mission in the Ardennes offensive. Under appalling weather conditions and with its striking power again dissipated, the Luftwaffe fighter force was expended against nondecisive tactical ground targets. Losses of planes and pilots were severe, and out of proportion with the results obtained. The American bombers meanwhile still kept coming with their daily loads of misery for the German populace.

The final major blow that the Luftwaffe fighters mounted was

[8] U.S. statistics.

"Operation Bodenplatte," on New Year's Day 1945. Fifteen Allied airfields were subjected to low-level surprise attack in strength by the remaining Luftwaffe fighter formations. The Germans lost approximately one hundred and fifty fighters. In exchange, they destroyed or severely damaged over eight hundred Allied aircraft.

At this stage in the war, the Allies could easily absorb such a one-time loss. For the Luftwaffe, it was the last blow. All that remained were the few final, defiant sorties from scattered airfields, and the glorious but vain operations of JV-44, Galland's "Squadron of Experts" flying the Me-262 jet.

On a microcosmic scale, the great German aces like Galland, Baer, Luetzow, Steinhoff, and Rudorffer, who flew the jets in the Luftwaffe's last days, had traveled a full circle from air supremacy in 1939–40. In the Me-262 they took on and defeated all their arch-foes: the hated Mosquitos, nemesis of the Luftwaffe; the American heavies—vulnerable at last to a superior machine with the armament to tear them apart and shatter their formations; the ubiquitous Mustangs and Thunderbolts, whose presence had allowed the Allied air offensive to reach full potential.

As the crack veteran aces of the Luftwaffe flew the Me-262 to victory over the best the Allies could produce, they had a glimpse of what might have been. Better than any men alive, they knew how different the course of history could have been had their efforts and skills been directed rationally by their top leadership. The professionalism and dedication of the German fighter pilots was never reflected in the Luftwaffe High Command. That was the good fortune of the Allies, who made their own quota of blunders. Again we come to Goering's defense. There is no doubt he was an intelligent and capable leader, but during the early days of the war he was forced to knuckle under to Hitler's will or be banished or executed as were so many of Der Fuehrer's aides. Hitler's early decisions and audacious military moves were so successful in the 1938-1942 time period that Hitler and the German populace were convinced he must be receiving guidance from Providence. Goering was one of the few who argued with Hitler and lived until the end of the war. To do so, Goering had to prostitute himself. He discovered it was wisest to find out what the "old man" wanted and then put his shoulder to the wheel to make the decision work out correctly. By 1942 Goering was afraid to argue with Hitler for the benefit of the Luftwaffe.

Wars take their decisive turns from the human element rather than the technical. The advance in weaponry stands mute before *the man who must decide*. The Germans produced superb air leaders and fighter aces of unprecedented achievement. But like the Light Brigade at Balaclava, "theirs was not to reason why." Today, their do-or-die achievements stand in almost irreconcilable contrast to the defeat Germany suffered in the air.

Because of this almost incredible anomaly, the authors feel that the careers of Germany's aces need to be seen against the backdrop of almost constant high command and political failure. The devotion, skill, and achievements of the German aces as soldiers in the service of their country were nullified by a leadership history will say was not fit to shine their shoes.

RAF Air Vice-Marshal Raymond Collishaw, 59-victory ace of WWI, gives another fair and learned viewpoint. In a letter to the authors he divines it this way:

"It is wrong to place all the blame on the bad decisions made by the German Air Staff. The chief causes of failure were Hitler and Göring who failed to perceive the consequences of the war potential of America. Göring was too open-handed in offering unlimited air help to the German Army in Russia. He actually believed German industrial capacity was enough to replace a lost Air Force, but when it became necessary to do it, the Allied bombers had crippled the industrial potential.

"By late 1941, it was obvious that British heavy bombers would be supplemented by American bombers and within a year would reach a dominating stage. The German Air Staff knew by this time, that an adequate radar-controlled fighter defense could overwhelm bomber intrusives. The British had proven that fact, and German planners should have known the best bet lay in defense.

"Air historians are fully aware of the German blooper in not using its jet aircraft as a fighter at the outset. This was another manifestation of Hitler's passion to bomb England. Imagine what would have developed had the Germans ordered 10,000 jet fighters in 1942!

"It has become fashionable for Air Historians to blame all German failures on Hitler. HE, more than anyone else, passionately wanted to win the war. Unfortunately for Germany, he became surrounded by "yes" men who tended to encourage him to embark upon unwise courses of action. Göring, too, tended to become a "yes" man and his attitude from the outset that the GAF could do anything was a major factor in the ultimate defeat of Germany. For instance: Hitler's decision to stand fast at Stalingrad was made because Göring told Hitler the Air Force could meet the army requirement of a besieged Stalingrad in the face of an adverse opinion by General Wolfram von Richthofen who adamantly insisted the Air Arm could not meet such requirements.

"No country can expect success from the employment of airpower when a civilian Dictator over-rides the professional advice of an air staff. The speculations made about the wisdom of Germany on the offensive in Russia while remaining on the defensive in the west were subject to the temperament of Hitler and Göring. We have to remember that in 1941 and 1942, Germany had yet to meet any real defeat in the air or on the ground, and therefore Hitler and Göring would certainly agree to any policy of air defense in the west.

"By 1943 it was too late to build that needed defensive force. The writing was on the wall indicating Germany's eventual defeat and from then on it really did not matter much what decisions were made by those two.

"May I also state that Air Power is a relative term. Bomber personnel are apt to think of it as a power vested in the bombers. Fighter personnel think of it in terms of air superiority. The truth is that bomber air power cannot develop where enemy fighters have an air superiority. We had two examples of this in WWII when German fighter·s forced the RAF to abandon daylight bombing and bomb only at night. The second example was when the USAF was forced to abandon long-distance bombing raids until the long-range escort fighters were plentiful.

"I mention the above factors to emphasize the difficulties that would have emerged in WWII had Germany prepared a vast air defense force from early in 1941."

From the far and frozen North, where the Polar Wing JG-5 functioned under incredible hardships, to the scorching desert of North Africa, where JG-27 fought as hard for gasoline as it did for Germany, the Luftwaffe fighter force produced some memorable pilots, leaders, personalities, and "characters." It is time to meet some of them.

2

Adolf Galland – Fighting Genius

*"The most important branch of aviation is pursuit,
which fights for and gains control of the air."*
U.S. BRIGADIER GENERAL WILLIAM MITCHELL,
1920

By far the best-known of Germany's Second World War fighter pilots and air leaders, Lieutenant General Adolf Galland is a multi-faceted personality. He is one of the most unusual men to reach high rank on either side during the conflict. Galland's major role in the ebb and flow of Germany's aerial fortunes makes him an absorbing subject for study by air power historians, and he will undoubtedly receive their attention for generations to come. He is also a fighting pilot who has earned his place as one of the immortal aces.

Shrewd, perceptive, courageous, and prescient, Galland was exposed to the burdens of high command while still in his early thirties. Despite the demands of his post as Inspector of the Fighter Arm, loosely called "General of the Fighters," he continued to fly fighter combat throughout the war. Opportunities for aerial combat were not lacking over Germany, even for a General. He ended the war fighting.

This intimate personal involvement with the problems facing his fighter pilots made Galland the most realistic of air generals. His pilots were asked to do nothing that he had not already done. History has verified the accuracy with which he analyzed the trends of the air war—both strategically and tactically. He may go down in history as the Billy Mitchell, the Douhet, and the aerial Clausewitz of the Second World War all embodied in one man. Because of the magnitude of his achievements, his career needs to be examined in detail.

World War all embodied in one man. Because of the magnitude of his achievements, his career needs to be examined in detail.

A brilliant pilot, exceptional marksman, and top tactician, Galland was able to marry these battle talents to a capacity for the larger strategic

TWO GENERATIONS: Major Adolf Galland (left) discusses fighter operations in the Channel area with Major General Eduard Ritter von Schleich. Meeting took place at Wissant, in 1941. von Schleich had 35 aerial victories in WWI, and also briefly flew combat in WWII as Kommodore of JG-26, the wing later commanded by Galland. Both von Schleich and Galland led formations of the Condor Legion in Spain. Galland had profound respect for von Schleich, who served with the higher commands of the Luftwaffe throughout WWII and died in 1947. *(Galland Collection)*

factors involved in command of the Luftwaffe fighter force. Few men in the history of air power have been able to make the transition from outstanding fighter ace to successful high commander. There are many notable failures, including both Goering and Udet.

The forceful personality that led Goering to acedom in the First World War and later made him a successful political revolutionary was quite unable to meet the challenge of Luftwaffe command. Similarly, Ernst Udet was a brilliant fighter ace who could not cope with the pressures and intrigues underlying the development of German air power. In both these instances the personalities had the tempering effect of maturity to aid them.

Galland, by contrast, became General of the Fighter Arm before he was thirty. He meets the two basic criteria of genius: capacity to probe deeper and see further than his contemporaries and ability to give effect to this insight in a practical way. He will be as long remembered for his battles on the ground as the advocate of the fighter pilots in high councils as he will for his 104 confirmed aerial victories—all of them scored against British- and American-flown aircraft. Only a few German pilots lived to score one hundred victories on the Western Front.

Galland is of Huguenot ancestry, as indicated by his French name. He is of middle height, with a large, well-shaped head and thick, black hair going straight back from a high forehead. A scarred right eyebrow is a souvenir of an early crash. His heavy black eyebrows, well-trimmed

MAGNETIC PERSONALITIES — 30 YEARS LATER: Five great dynamos of the WWII Luftwaffe meet again in 1976. Lt. General Walter Krupinski beams from the extreme left, flanked by Lt. General Adolf Galland, Colonel Wolfgang Falck, Maj. General Dieter Hrabak and Lt. General Guenther Rall who is facing away from the camera. Krupinski, Hrabak and Rall all became major figures in the new Luftwaffe, but Galland and Falck stayed out and pursued successful business careers. *(Credit: Jagerblatt)*

mustache, and strong, square chin form an appropriate setting for his salient physical feature—his eyes.

Fiction writers often attribute penetrating eyes to fighter pilots. With Galland, it is no fiction. His eyes have a penetration and sharpness that set him aside from ordinary men. They are truly the mirrors of a tenacious and comprehending soul—perhaps even a visionary. They are eyes that can smite like hammers, dance engagingly at the prospect of a party, or freeze a phony or a pretender. They are also the eyes of a master marksman and hunter, and the supreme expression of a driving personality—a man born to achievement, to be seen and heard.

Looking at Galland today it is hard to believe that more than thirty years have passed since he was General of the Fighter Arm, with the outcome of the world's greatest aerial battles depending on his qualities and skill. Now in his mid-sixties, he is an astonishingly young-looking man. There are flecks of gray in the dark mane. But he retains all his verve and dash and on 7 November 1966 became a father for the first time at the age of fifty-four. He is the classic example of a magnetic personality.

Galland's personal magnetism is something quite exceptional in the experience of the authors, for the impact even of a social meeting with him lasts for several days. After a conversation with him, his image and his words return again and again to the mind, long after he has departed. One may have contact with a wide range of dominant personalities— high military officers, business tycoons, top scientists—and never encounter the like of the sheer, polarizing force of Adolf Galland.

He earnestly and honestly tries to be unobtrusive. He is the most modest man concerning himself that could be found. Because he is a social lion, and also because he is esteemed by his old comrades-in-arms, he is always invited to their parties. He prefers and tries to slip into these affairs unobserved.

He will seat himself in a corner with one or two friends, sometimes turning his back to the room so that as few people as possible will recognize him. These efforts invariably fail. Within minutes, his magnetism pulls the center of interest to his table. He then remains the center of the gathering until he departs.

His black cigars were an ever-present trademark until he quit in 1963. Gerhard Schoepfel, forty-kill ace who flew in Galland's group in JG-26, recalls the special cigar holder installed in his leader's Me-109 so Galland could park his cigar when he had to go on oxygen. Relinquishing the stogies he loved was not easy. Today, a toothpick is a frequent substitute, and as he guns his Beech Bonanza down the runway at Cologne–Bonn airport, the toothpick twirls between his lips like a second propeller.

His sharp wit and exceptional sense of humor are particularly evident at the social level. These qualities are a balancing force to the tigerish energy he brought to both combat and command. He is thus a man of exceptional equilibrium, an aspect of his character that served him well during the war when he was the focus of many conflicting forces that would have shattered a lesser man.

Born in 1912, Galland wanted to become a pilot early in life and began with gliders in the nineteen twenties. After graduating from the Gymnasium at Buer/Westphalia, where he studied the Humanities, he was given a glider of his own. Before his final school examination he stated on his papers that he wanted to be a commercial pilot.

One of Germany's most famous First World War pilots, Oberst Keller, was managing the German Commercial Air Transport School at Brunswick in 1932 when Galland became a pupil there. Under the guidance of Keller, who had led heavy bomber strikes against London during the war and emerged from the conflict wearing the Pour le Mérite, many of Germany's most famous fighter pilots received their first training. Keller[1] of course was at this time in mufti, but the prestige of his "Blue Max" and war career was not lost on his pupils.

During the "camouflage" period when German military pilots were being trained under various subterfuges to avoid Versailles Treaty limitations, Galland was sent to Italy for air force pilot training. This arrangement had been set up by Goering and Balbo, the Italian air minister. It was scheduled as a replacement for the agreement under which German military pilots and crews were trained in the Soviet Union at Lipetsk during the preceding period.

Due to Goering's way of doing things, a misunderstanding developed as to the purposes of the training. Galland was sent to an airfield at Grotaglie in southern Italy. He was a member of a group of about thirty other German pilots, and virtually all of them except Galland were veteran professionals or "camouflage" pilots trained in the USSR. They averaged about ten years of flying experience each.

Goering had left the Italians under the impression that they were

---

[1] In the Second World War, Generaloberst Keller, Air Fleet Chief, I Air Fleet, Northwest Russia.

LUFTWAFFE TRAINER: Alfred Keller, seen here in the uniform of a Colonel-General late in WWII, was director of the German Air Transport School at Brunswick in the early nineteen thirties. The school served as a training base for future Luftwaffe pilots and leaders, including Adolf Galland, who looked up to Keller as a leading WWI bomber pilot and Pour le Merite winner. *(Nowarra Collection)*

students or hard-case, problem pilots. In an effort to educate their bad habits out of them, the Italians launched the highly skilled Germans on elementary flying training, including taxiing and similar introductory maneuvers. The fiasco was soon straightened out, but not before Galland and his compatriots had many moments of merriment.

The training in Italy proved invaluable. "We had the opportunity to fly all the major modern types of Italian aircraft, plus a lot of aerobatics, gunnery and shooting practice that we could not have obtained in Germany," Galland says of this period. The Italian military aircraft were not impressive, but they were better than none.

By the end of 1934 Galland's formal transfer to the still-camouflaged Luftwaffe had been made. He was an accomplished pilot and instructor at the Fighter Pilot School at Munich-Schleissheim. The school was conducted entirely along First World War lines as far as aerobatics and gunnery were concerned. Galland had many misgivings about it, but by April 1935 he had been transferred to the first Luftwaffe fighter wing, JG-2 *Richthofen*.

Two years later he volunteered for service with the Condor Legion in Spain. He was called the "guide" of four hundred Germans on their way to Spain—an ominous-looking group of "tourists" who sailed from Hamburg to assist Franco's rebellion. He had his introduction to aerial warfare in the uniform of a Captain, since Condor Legion personnel wore Spanish-looking uniforms of special design and officers were formally promoted to the next grade.

Galland's war career began as it ended eight years later in 1945—in a position of aerial inferiority to the enemy. His Jagdstaffel 3 was flying the obsolescent Heinkel 51 biplane, while the Loyalist forces were equipped with vastly superior American Curtiss and Russian Polikar-

OFF TO MEET THE R.A.F.: Adolf Galland snugs down the canopy of his Me-109 as he prepares to take off on a fighter sweep over England during the Battle of Britain. In addition to the "S" insignia of the Schlageter wing (JG-26), the fuselage carries the Mickey Mouse caricature favored by Galland. A born hunter and fighter, Galland found that high command diminished his opportujnities to enter combat, but he still managed to do so frequently until the end of the war, He ended the war with 104 victories, all of them against aircraft of the Western Allies. (*Haussmann/Obermaier*)

CIGAR LOVER: Adolf Galland muffles himself up in the cockpit of his Me-109 before taking off on a sortie over England in 1940. He had his fighter fitted with a special cigar holder so he could park the stogie securely when he went on oxygen. Such things contributed greatly to the Galland legend. Today Galland is not allowed his beloved cigars. (*Galland Collection*)

VICTORY MARKS: Tail of Galland's fighter shows 57 victory marks during a visit made to Finland by the ace-leader. (*Foto: Dolling*)

pov I-15"Chato and I-16"Rata" fighters. Aerial combat was therefore avoided at this stage by Galland's squadron. The unit confined itself to close support of Franco's ground troops.

Other Me-109 squadrons of the Condor Legion's Fighter Wing 88 were cleaning up the sky at this time, but Galland had no opportunity for scoring aerial kills in Spain.[2] His He-51s were occasionally brought to battle by the superior Loyalist fighters, and in these encounters Galland had his baptism of fire. These rare dogfights were insignificant in Galland's career by comparison with his advocacy of close-support flying—which arose out of the Spanish Civil War and first brought him to the attention of the Luftwaffe High Command.

Galland had his first meeting in Spain with Werner Moelders. Staffel 3 had its problems with unsatisfactory squadron leaders to replace Galland, who personally relieved the first replacement and sent him back to Germany. A second replacement died in a mid-air collision. This set the stage for Werner Moelders to go to Spain as Galland's successor, with all the historic significance that this was to have in the careers of both great ace-leaders.

The German command noted Galland's desire for superior material. Determined not to keep supplying replacements indefinitely, the command accordingly advised the C.O. of Fighter Squadron 3: "This is the last replacement you will get. Moelders is the best man we have, and you are expected to make do with him."

Galland recalls that he was not too happy with this advice from Germany. "I didn't like the idea of being compelled to keep this man Moelders," Galland recalls. "The recommendations he had from the high command also seemed like a sort of challenge." This is the origin of the coolness with which Galland received the new arrival when they met in the famous Christine Hotel in Seville. He did not know it then, but he was sizing up the man who was to become his greatest rival as well as his friend—a man who would walk into history with him.

Galland's early coolness soon was replaced by an enthusiastic acceptance of the new squadron leader, who proved himself to be all that the high command had claimed. When Galland left Jagdstaffel 3, the 88th Fighter Wing, and Spain in 1938 his successor was Werner Moelders. Apocryphal yarns have had it through the years that Moelders was a student of Galland at Munich-Schleissheim and that they knew each other then or later, but the truth is that Galland and Moelders did not meet until the Spanish Civil War, under the circumstances just described.

During his stay in Spain, Galland wrote a continuous series of perceptive reports on direct ground-support operations. In these reports, which formalized his experience in over three hundred operational sorties in Spain, he had compiled virtually a manual on the subject.

---

[2] Nine Spanish fighter pilots scored ten or more victories in the Spanish Civil War. Top scorer was Colonel Joaquín García Morato, who scored forty kills before a fatal crash 4 April 1939. Several Spanish aces later fought with the Germans against Russia in World War II.

His work was well received in high Luftwaffe circles. His experience reinforced the main line of tactical thinking behind the new direct-support bomber force.

Johannes Jeschonnek, already influential as Commander of a special test wing, and soon to become Chief of the Luftwaffe General Staff, had an almost obsessive devotion to dive-bombing and the dive bomber. Jeschonnek was heavily influenced along this line by Udet, who had imported the dive bomber from America. Jeschonnek regarded the dive bomber as the key to small-target bombing success. He typified an already large and growing body of officers who were shaping German air power.

Galland's immediate prewar work in direct-support flying brought him to the attention of the Luftwaffe hierarchy. His reward for his work was not what he expected, and not what he wanted. He found himself flying a desk in the German Air Ministry. He was told, in effect: "You have written these significant reports, now implement them." This meant working out directives for the organization of fighter units and the training of fighter pilots in direct-support operations.

The dynamic young airman loathed the confinement of his new job. He yearned to be back with a squadron. When he was subsequently assigned to organize, train, and equip two new ground-support wings to assist in the Sudetenland invasion in 1938, he was glad to be back in a more practical job.

The new wings would consist of obsolescent aircraft, Heinkel 45s,

ROUND TABLE CONFERENCE: Adolf Galland (center) uses a hand gesture to make a point during a conference of fighter leaders at Le Touquet during Battle of Britain. Werner Moelders, Galland's friend and rival, listens with arms akimbo. Lt. Gen. Theo Osterkamp is on Moelders' left and the officer with his back to the camera is Guenther Lutzow. At the left hand end of the table, General Paul Deichmann listens to the discussion. *(Boehm Collection)*

Henschel 123s and Heinkel 51s. They had to be welded into modern *Schlachtgeschwader*, capable of going to battle with the Czech Army if need be. The hard-driving Galland whipped the ragged leftovers into some semblance of fighting units, with special training for the pilots in the new techniques. The Munich Pact of 1938 eliminated the need to throw these old machines into combat.

The following year he was serving as a squadron leader (*Staffel-kapitan*) with a *Schlachtgruppe* in Silesia when his unit was ordered to action in the invasion of Poland. From the original six *Gruppen* he had formed the previous year into two *Schlachtgeschwader* only one *Gruppe* now remained, the others having been disbanded. Equipped with the HS-123 (biplane Stuka) Galland's unit took part in the first live test of the direct-support use of air power as a vital element in the *Blitzkrieg*.

The effects were devastating. Polish air power was obliterated on the ground, leaving the Polish infantry, cavalry, and transport at the mercy of the Luftwaffe. For nearly a month at rooftop height the Luft-waffe fighters and direct-support units wreaked havoc on the Polish forces. Polish Army transport, much of it horse-drawn, was strangled by the deadly strafing. Unhindered by the Polish Air Force, Stuka dive bombers and low-flying Luftwaffe direct-support fighters broke the morale of the Polish forces. The lessons of the Spanish Civil War had been well learned.

Galland was both a witness to the success of the close-support tech-niques he had advocated and a lively participant in the battles. In the twenty-seven days of the Polish campaign he flew incessantly, up to four sorties a day. For his efforts he was awarded the Iron Cross, Second Class. The very success of this campaign made a critical personal decision necessary for Galland.

There was now a high probability that he would spend his flying days with direct-support aviation. He was an acknowledged expert in this field. He had become too valuable for his own good, because he was utterly determined to fly fighters. He recognized that unless he did something drastic to break himself free of direct-support flying, he would continue to fly second- and third-rate aircraft and never get to grips with the enemy in the air. His blood was that of a hunter; his instinct was for the chase.

Galland reached down into the old soldier's bag of tricks for his answer. After the Polish campaign, he feigned rheumatism. His *Gruppe* physician sent him to Wiesbaden for treatment. Here, the doctor on his case was a friend, who understood the young pilot's problem. The medical verdict: "No more flying in *open* cockpits." This ruling took Galland out of direct-support and into regular modern fighter piloting. History may note with a smile how large a role in Galland's career was played by a little act of lead-swinging which diverted him to glory!

His Wiesbaden interlude had a second fortunate aspect for Ger-many's future fighter commander. He met Werner Moelders there

HUNTER'S HOLIDAY: A consummate hunter aloft as a fighter pilot, Adolf Galland had a lifelong passion for hunting as a sport. His contemporaries from Battle of Britain days, including Gerd Schopfel, testify to Galland's uncanny ability to find his foes as well as to shoot them down. Here Galland takes time out from the war for a shooting party on the Belgian coast in the winter of 1940. (*Galland Collection*)

for the third time. They had met previously in Spain, and at a parade of the Condor Legion in Berlin after the end of the Spanish War. Moelders was now operating with conspicuous success around the "Four Borders" area—the region where the national borders of France, Luxembourg, Belgium, and Germany meet.

Moelders had there already downed numerous Allied aircraft. He was a recognized master of air-to-air dogfights. Galland took lectures from his former subordinate and today frankly states: "Werner Moelders taught me how to shoot in the air and bring down aircraft." Shortly afterward, Galland was posted to JG-27 at Krefeld, commanded by Colonel Max Ibel. He looked forward eagerly to getting into action.

Galland was sadly disappointed. As Captain Galland, he served as Operations Officer to Ibel, the Wing Commander and a participant in the First World War. His battles were once again with paper work. He was irked to watch his comrades taking off on operations while he waded through administrative work on the ground. He says of this period: "I had to literally steal away on any combat sortie I wanted to make. What others regarded merely as a daily duty was for me something I had to get by tricks and ruses."

On 12 May 1940, west of Liège in Belgium, Galland scored his first aerial kill. Two more followed on the same day. All three victims were Hawker Hurricanes of the Royal Air Force, indifferently flown and shot down like clay pigeons. For years, Galland was under the impression that these first victories were aircraft of the Belgian Air Force. Subsequent contacts between Galland and RAF fighter pilots of the squadron involved have established beyond doubt that his first three kills were British.

He confesses to a twinge of conscience over the ease with which he scored these kills. In his epic book *The First and Last*, he contrasts them with later savage combats against British and American fighters, when every victory was just cause for elation. More British and French aircraft fell to Galland's guns during the Battle of France, and then in June 1940 he was transferred to JG-26.

He was assigned to command the 3rd Group of JG-26, which is expressed in German form as III/JG-26. JG-26 *Schlageter* later became an elite formation, and was variously known to the Allies as "The Yellow Nose Boys," "The Abbeville Boys," and "The St. Omer Boys." JG-26 fought only on the Western Front throughout the war, although many Allied pilots encountering yellow-cowled Me-109 and FW-190 fighters elsewhere swore they had met "Germany's best—the Yellow Nose Boys."

Galland made an impressive entry to his new post, downing two enemy fighters on his first day. Gerhard Schoepfel, who was one of Galland's squadron leaders in the 3rd Group of JG-26, has a very vivid memory of this time:

"With Galland, a totally new era began. He replaced von Berg, a First World War pilot, as *Gruppenkommandeur* and everything from then on changed. Galland was throughout the war a fighter, and especially a *hunter*. He had a good nose for the enemy, probably because hunting has always been one of his favorite sports, which he enjoys to this day. Galland led us down from altitudes above six thousand meters, at which we were accustomed to fighting through nothing more than habit.

"Thenceforth we did our hunting at lower altitude with success. But he was not easy to fly with. He flew over Dover and the south of England at one thousand meters and the flak was terrible. The close

---

✻ Galland's famous "nose for the enemy" was greatly enhanced during his JG-26 days and thereafter, by a remarkable intelligence adjunct that Galland himself originally distrusted and opposed. Starting before the war, Captain Horst Barth of the Engineers had begun assembling and training a special intelligence unit centered around outstanding linguistic ability and superior radio operating skill. This unit was designed to give German air operations a valuable new dimension.

By penetrating completely the R/T traffic of the RAF, Barth's unit became so familiar with the operation of RAF bases and units, and with the voices of the British controllers, commanders and pilots, that RAF fighter operations were as clearly known to them as those of their own Luftwaffe. The German unit penetrated all the R/T codes, both formal and informal, used by the British, and all the RAF slang that was a distinctive language all by itself.

Galland the Hunter initially feared that introduction of data from this strange, obscure listening unit — set up on the upper floor of a dilapidated farmhouse near a JG-26 airfield—would mean more control from the ground of what he wanted to do in the air. To Galland it meant less hunting, less of the free chase at which his fighters excelled, and he viewed it all in a face-to-face encounter with Barth with unalloyed distaste and skepticism.

When Major Galland took off soon afterwards with his wingman to sweep the English skies, Barth's unit immediately heard the RAF send fighters up on intercept. Climbing high above the incoming Galland, they would be able to bounce him out of the sun. The astute Germans listening in the old farmhouse in France even knew who the British pilots were in the now frantically climbing RAF fighters.

Word was flashed by radio to Galland. Warned in time, he turned the RAF bounce into two victories for himself. Returning to France, he sought out Barth and held up two fingers with a contrite expression on his face — a double kill. "But I didn't know they were there, and wouldn't have seen them but for you," said the chastened Major Galland. Thereafter, the future General of the Fighter Arm integrated the priceless information pouring out of Barth's unit into his fighter operations.

The full story of Captain Barth's unit — so secret in wartime that even Goering and high Luftwaffe generals were surprised to find it in existence — is told in Colonel Raymond F. Toliver's forthcoming book *The Interrogator*, an account of German intelligence operatives and their influence on the fighter war.

detonations of the flak were hard on the nerves, but he was the leader and the teacher and we followed him. He was the outstanding fighter leader in my experience.''

Schoepfel's experience includes a highly successful record in the Battle of Britain with twenty-nine kills confirmed by December 1940. We will meet him again later.

Promoted Major on 18 July 1940, Galland remained with JG-26 through the most critical phase of the Battle of Britain. By September of 1940 he had forty confirmed kills and was one of the leading aces of the Luftwaffe. He won the coveted Knight's Cross to his Iron Cross on 1 August 1940, and on 25 September 1940 was awarded the newly instituted Oak Leaves (*Eichenlaub*) to his Knight's Cross. When he received this decoration personally from Hitler, only two soldiers in the German armed forces had preceded him in its award—General Dietl, and his friend Werner Moelders.

After his fiftieth kill, Galland was promoted to Lieutenant Colonel (*Oberstleutnant*) and given command of JG-26 on 1 November 1940. He replaced Gotthardt Handrick, the German Olympic champion of 1936. Galland's promotion was part of Goering's plan to replace the older wing and group commanders of First World War vintage with successful members of the new generation.

Goering wanted his new wing commanders to be top-scoring combat pilots. This policy led to high rank and heavy responsibility early in life for Galland, Moelders, Trautloft, Schoepfel, Balthasar, Luetzow, Nordmann, Oesau, Hrabak, and Wilcke, among others. All and more reached *Kommodore* in their twenties.

GALLAND RECEIVES HIS SWORDS: On 1 July 1941 Adolf Galland receives the Swords to his Knight's Cross decoration personally from Adolf Hitler. Galland went on to win highest order of the decoration—the Diamonds—then fell from grace with Germany's irrational leadership. As a Lieutenant General, he ended the war in command of a squadron of Me-262 fighters. (*Carlson Collection*)

BADER IN GERMAN HANDS: Wing Commander Douglas Bader of the RAF is greeted by JG-26 officers at the Schlageter wing's HQ in France. The famed legless ace of the Battle of Britain was an intriguing prize of the Germans, who treated him with great courtesy and respect. Bader here meets Colonel Joachim Huth, a first world war pilot who lost a leg in that conflict. Note Huth's gloves held in his left hand. German pilots from left are Adolph, Schopfel, Galland, Causin, and to the right rear of Colonel Huth stands Eschwege, and at Huth's right shoulder is Horst Barth. (Boehm Collection)

GUN OR GLOVES?: Douglas Bader is allowed by his German captors to sit in the cockpit of an Me-109 at a JG-26 airfield. The legless RAF ace later interpreted Colonel Joachim Huth's gloves—jutting into the bottom center of this picture—as a pistol butt, with Huth presumably ready to shoot Bader. The one-legged Huth had to constantly brace himself, and on this occasion, his gloves are in the hand he has resting on his lap. Horst Barth stands at Huth's right. (Boehm Collection)

SPARE LEG FOR WINGCO DOUG BADER: A Luftwaffe NCO holds the artificial leg belonging to POW Douglas Bader of the RAF. Box was dropped by an RAF plane to replace one lost when Bader abandoned his plane and was captured. (Eder Collection)

Galland was a chivalrous soldier, like the vast majority of German professionals. He was and is a passionate believer in fair play. Much of the knightly tradition ruled his thinking and his actions toward his foes in the air and on the ground. Like most German air fighters of the Second World War, he was a hard but fair opponent. When Goering felt him out in 1941 regarding a hypothetical order to shoot at parachuting enemy pilots, Galland exploded with indignation. Even the idea was revolting to him.

"I should regard such an order as *murder*," he told Goering, "and I would do everything possible to disobey such an order."

His reaction exemplified the aversion to such barbaric acts felt by German fighter pilots as a whole. It is doubtful indeed if a German pilot ever strafed a parachuting enemy, although in the heat of battle anything can happen. The instructions issued to German fighter pilots were never to shoot a parachuting flyer. Unfortunately the same assurances cannot be given concerning the American fighter pilots, who offended this tradition of aerial combat all too often, and were actually ordered to do so in the case of parachuting Me-262 pilots.

Galland's chivalry is typified by his wartime encounter on the ground with Wing Commander (later Group Captain) Douglas Bader, the legless Royal Air Force ace. Shot down with several of his squadron mates in a wild melee over the Pas de Calais, Bader fell into German hands. Galland was one of the German pilots scoring kills in this action, but the confusion of the battle made it impossible to precisely identify Bader's conqueror.

Like many professional British military men of his era, Bader was evidently quite rank-conscious. The British ace was anxious to know the *rank* of the German pilot who had taken his measure. Both the British and the Germans had NCO pilots in the fighter forces, and the idea that one of these noncommissioned men might have shot him down made Bader curious as to his identity.

The Germans were delighted to have brought the infamous "Stationmaster" of Tangmere to earth, and they were intrigued with their prize. Even across the havoc of war, the chivalrous Galland took account of Bader's feelings. The Englishman was assured that he had not been downed by an NCO. One of the victorious commissioned German pilots was selected as the "fall guy" and was introduced to Bader as his conqueror.

When Bader asked for a spare set of artificial legs to be flown across from England (the legs he was wearing had been damaged in his crash), Galland forwarded his request with a recommendation for HQ approval. Goering also approved, and offered safe conduct for the aircraft bringing the legs. The British concept of chivalry had been worn a little thin by the bombing of London, so the RAF dropped Bader's legs along with some bombs targeted on the airfields of JG-26.

Some British sources deny that bombs were dropped. The Germans who were on the airfields at the time are in no doubt about what was dropped. History cannot give an ironclad verdict on the affair, which is really a teacup tempest.

There is an interesting sidelight to Bader's meeting with his foes of JG-26. He was allowed to sit in the cockpit of an Me-109, and even asked permission to fly it around the field a couple of times. Galland was compelled to courteously decline this request. Bader later alleged that a German officer had his hand on or near a pistol while he, Bader, was sitting in the Me-109. The impression of the British ace was that any attempt on his part to escape would have resulted in his being shot at point-blank range. A photograph was even widely published showing an alleged pistol butt on the hip of the officer in question, who was presumably ready to draw the weapon in an instant.

The officer was Colonel Joachim Hueth, a First World War veteran who had already lost a leg in that conflict. Poor old Hueth had to constantly brace his wooden leg, and in the picture in question was resting his hand on his hip—the hand containing his gloves. These *gloves*, jutting into the bottom of the picture which shows Bader in the Me-109 cockpit, certainly resemble a pistol butt. Nevertheless, examination of numerous full-length photos of the incident by the authors leave no doubt that Hueth's gloves were mistaken for a pistol. Had Bader gunned the aircraft, the one-legged Hueth, far from demonstrating a quick draw, would have been the first man on the airfield to fall over! The British version of the incident is one of those stories which, once started, proves very difficult to stop.

Galland's victory record mounted as his opportunities for combat

BUSMAN'S HOLIDAY: Captain Joachim Muncheberg (R.), one of the Luftwaffe's most successful and promising leaders, scored 135 victories before his death in 1943 in North Africa as a major. In the calmer days of 1941 he sharpens his marksmanship in the company of 1st Lieutenant Graf Erbo Kageneck (67 victories in WWII) and veteran World War I pilot Colonel Joachim Hüth. *(Credit: Haussman)*

increased. On one occasion, when he was close to seventy kills, the young Wing Commander was himself a victory and underwent what he calls "the most terrifying experience of my life."

On 21 June 1941, Galland had blasted a Spitfire out of formation northeast of Boulogne. The British fighter was in flames and Galland was following him down to accurately register the crash because he was flying alone. He made the neophyte's error of paying too much attention to the British flamer and too little to his own tail. He was jumped. He tells it in his own words:

"Hell broke loose in my crate. Now they've got me . . . Something hard hit my head and arm. My aircraft was in bad shape. The wings were ripped by cannon fire. I was sitting half in the open . . . the right side of the cockpit had been shot away. Fuel tank and radiator were both leaking heavily. Instinctively I banked away to the north. Almost calmly I noticed that my heavily damaged fighter still flew and responded tolerably well with the engine cut off. My luck had held once more, I was thinking, and I will try to glide home. My altitude was eighteen thousand feet.

"My arm and head were bleeding. But I didn't feel any pain. No time for that. Anyhow, nothing precious was hurt. A sharp detonation tore me out of my reverie. The tank, which up to then had been gurgling away quietly, suddenly exploded. The whole fuselage was immediately aflame. Burning petrol ran into the cockpit. It was uncomfortably hot. Only one thought remained: Get out! Get out! Get out! The cockpit-roof release—would not work—must be jammed. Shall I burn alive in here? I tore my belt open. I tried to open the hinged top of the roof. The air pressure on it was too strong. Flames all around me. I must open it! I must not fry to death in here! Terror! Those were the most terrible seconds in my life. With a last effort I pushed my whole body against the roof. The flap opened and was torn away by the airstream . . . I had already pulled her nose up. The push against the joystick did not throw me entirely clear of the burning coffin, which a few minutes before was my beloved and faithful Me-109. The parachute on which I had been sitting was caught on the fixed part of the cockpit roof. The entire plane was now in flames and dashing down to earth with me. With my arm around the antenna mast I tugged, I pushed against anything I could find with my feet. All in vain! Should I be doomed at the last moment although I was already half-freed? I don't know how I got free in the end. Suddenly I was falling.

"I turned over several times in the air. Thank God! In my excitement I nearly operated the quick harness release instead of the ripcord handle. At the last moment I noticed that I was releasing the safety catch. Another shock! The parachute and I would have arrived separately . . . slowly and softly I floated down to the earth.

"Below me a column of smoke marked the spot where my Messerschmitt had crashed. By rights I should have landed in the forest of Boulogne like a monkey on a tree, but the parachute only brushed a

CONCEALED EAGLE: An Me-109 pokes its nose from a hangar camouflaged as a farmhouse in France during the Battle of Britain. The fighter is a unit of JG-26 Schlageter, commanded at various times by some of the Luftwaffe's most famous aces. *(Galland Collection)*

poplar and then folded up. I landed rather luckily in a soft, boggy meadow. Up to now I had been under high tension of nerves and energy. I collapsed. I felt as wretched as a dog. Shot and bleeding profusely from head and arm, with a painfully twisted ankle which started to swell immediately, I could neither walk nor stand up."

The clanked and bleeding Galland was picked up by car. After a session with Dr. Heim in the naval hospital at Hardingham and a few jolts of cognac he was on his way to recovery. Before long he was up and around again, this time wearing the Swords (*Shwertern*), another newly created degree of the Iron Cross. The Swords were instituted to recognize valorous deeds beyond the level of the Oak Leaves. Galland was the first officer in the German armed forces to win the Swords,[3] and his rivalry with Moelders is well illustrated by the award of the Swords to Moelders the following day.

During the war, and perhaps because of Dr. Goebbels' extravagant propaganda, the British nicknamed Galland "The Fighting Fop." His taste for epicurean delights and fine cigars had created in British eyes the image of a dandy. His arresting appearance in uniform, immaculate and with his decorations at his throat and breast, contributed to this impression through widely circulated photographs.

Galland enjoys the good things in life, including a sauna bath with a swimming pool on the lower level of his home in Oberwinter, a suburb of Bonn. But he never allowed his tastes for good things to interfere with his war-making. Sometimes he even mixed the two with rare élan, thus generating the stuff of which legends are made.

Such an occasion was Theo Osterkamp's birthday on 15 April 1941. The veteran ace with the outstanding accomplishment of acedom in

[3] 21 June 1941.

both world wars was then Fighter Leader (*Jafü*)[4] at Le Touquet. A party was arranged for "Uncle Theo," whom we will meet in Chapter Thirteen, and Galland was invited. "The Fighting Fop" stuffed a huge basket of lobsters and champagne in his Me-109 at Brest. With First Lieutenant Westphal as his wingman, he set out for Le Touquet, the party site, *via England*—an audacious detour for a fighter pilot flying a plane loaded with champagne and lobsters.

Fortune favors the brave, and did so on this occasion. The party-bound Germans intercepted a flight of six Spitfires over Kent, which obviously had been sent against the incoming bandits. Galland

EXTRAORDINARY ACHIEVEMENT: Acedom in each of the two world wars was the remarkable record of Generalleutnant Theo Osterkamp. In WWI, Osterkamp downed 32 Allied aircraft, and won the Pour le Merite, top German decoration of that conflict. In WWII, flying against pilots young enough to be his sons, the redoubtable Osterkamp scored 6 more victories. He also won the Knight's Cross. Counselor, inspiration and friend to younger pilots in WWII—in which he rose to Generalleutnant—Osterkamp was affectionately known until his 1976 death as "Onkel Theo"—Uncle Theo. *(Credit: Jagerblatt)*

downed one British machine in flames west of Dover after an approach which caught the Englishman by surprise. Fortune then smiled again.

"The Fighting Fop" then attacked a second Spitfire, not realizing that his wingman, with technical trouble, was not in a position to help him. Galland got the message quickly enough when the Spitfires turned on the Germans, who immediately broke off the action and raced balls out for the French coast. The champagne-laden Me-109 was sluggish on the controls as British cannon shells and bullets whistled around him. He began to think how smart it would have been to fly straight to Le Touquet.

A few anxious minutes later, Galland gradually pulled out of range of the angry RAF pilots. Westphal was nowhere to be seen, and the overdue Wing Commander prepared to land at Le Touquet. There was no radio at the field, and as "The Fighting Fop" roared in at low altitude he was startled to see red flares shooting up and an agitated ground staff frenziedly waving him off.

He made another approach. More red flares. The implication of the frantic wave-offs slowly seeped into Galland's mind. His under-carriage was now up, while during the frantic escape it must have been down. He had come close to landing wheels up, no way for a Wing

[4] *Jafü* is an abbreviation of *Jagdführer*. These were separate fighter commands established in each air fleet (*Luftflotte*). *Jafü* originally was concerned primarily with policy matters in the beginning, but later controlled operations. It was an HQ unit.

OLD ACES HUDDLE: Two winners of the Pour le Merite in World War I enjoy a joke during World War II, in which both served as generals in the Luftwaffe. Ernst Udet (l.) with 62 victories in WWI later committed suicide over political problems that plagued German fighter production. Gen. Karl-Friedrich Christiansen scored 21 aerial victories in WWI. Photo was taken during Battle of Britain. (*Galland Collection*)

Commander to arrive with a cargo of champagne.

The dark-haired fighter ace was undeniably one of Lady Luck's favorite sons. By his own admission, he often didn't deserve her favors. One such instance occurred on 2 July 1941, shortly after he was seriously wounded as previously related.

Strict orders from both Hitler and Goering had him grounded. These orders were superfluous for a time, because he was physically unable to fly. The moment he got mobile, however, he started taking fighters up on "test flights."

His ground crews were completely devoted to him. Sergeant Meyer of his personal crew had been mortified by his Wing Commander's head wound. Meyer diligently installed a special sheet of armor plate on top of the cockpit, to prevent any repetition of the near-fatal wound. When Galland violated orders on 2 July 1941 and led his wing against heavily escorted RAF bombers at St. Omer, he was unaware of Meyer's addition to the cockpit.

Jumping into his fighter, Galland promptly thumped his already sore head on the new armor plate. Furious, he was still cursing Meyer as he roared off into the air to battle the bombers. He downed a Blenheim and was hurling himself on the Spitfire escort when another British fighter bounced him and caught his Me-109 in a withering torrent of cannon shells.

A searing blow on the head and blood pouring down his face told him he had been badly hit. His instrument panel was a shambles, but the Me-109 still flew soggily. Petrified lest he black out, Galland dove away from the fight and was able to land his crippled fighter safely at the JG-26 airfield.

An examination of the battered machine showed that Meyer's modification had proved its value. The armor plate had absorbed the main force of a 20mm cannon shell—which would otherwise have decapitated the future General of the Fighter Arm. A contrite and grateful Galland gave Meyer one hundred marks and special leave, after being again sewn up and bandaged by the long-suffering Dr. Heim.

Shortly afterward, Ernst Udet committed suicide, and Galland was ordered to Berlin to stand in the Honor Guard with five other leading

German fighter pilots: Oesau, Falck, Schalck, Muencheberg, and Luetzow. Moelders was also to be present, but was delayed. It was a grim proceeding—a farewell to an old fighter who had been something of a hero as well as a comrade to the new generation.

The new generation was about to suffer an even heavier blow. Werner Moelders, rushing to Udet's funeral from the Crimea as a passenger in an He-111 bomber, was killed in a crash. Galland did not even have time to get back to his unit on the Channel after the Udet funeral. He was summoned back to Berlin from a small station in Lippe, and within a few days was standing once again in an Honor Guard—this time for his friend.

Overborne by a grim intuition as he stood at the graveside, Galland's worst fears were realized when he looked up and saw Goering beckoning him from the Honor Guard. On the spot the Reichsmarschall named him General of the Fighter Arm. He was to be his friend's successor.

Dramatic changes followed in Galland's life and career. Gone was the day-to-day excitement of combat with JG-26 on the Channel. A hater of desks, paper work, and red tape, Galland had a front line soldier's aversion to staff work. He was first and foremost a fighter. Yet in the next three years he was involved in the fight of his life—a running fight against intrigue, corruption, political interference, and the fatuous misdirection of Germany's air power by his superiors.

After his promotion to General of the Fighter Arm and before the

SHOOTING PARTY: Generalleutnant Adolf Galland loved to hunt, in the sky and on the ground, as in this 1941 hunting party in France. Accompanying Galland are: Left rear, Wilhelm "Wutz" Galland, his brother; flanking "Wutz" are two beaters; with cigar is Johannes Seifert (57 victories); next to Seifert is Gerd Schöpfel (40 victories); the man with his hand raised is a flak officer; far right and smiling is Joachim Müncheberg (135 victories); front and center with back to camera is Major Wick and in the left front with back to camera is Captain Janke. *(Credit: Haussman)*

really serious degeneration of German aerial strength set in, Galland had one outstanding opportunity to prove his generalship under reasonably balanced conditions. The planned escape of the German battleships *Scharnhorst* and *Gneisenau*, and the heavy cruiser *Prinz Eugen*, from Brest through the English Channel was dependent primarily on fighter protection. Galland rose to the challenge with tigerish determination.

Without constant fighter cover, the German ships would certainly fall victim to do-or-die attacks by the British Fleet Air Arm and RAF. Only JG-2 and JG-26 were available on the Channel coast. Combined with night fighters and fighters scraped together from Operational Training Units, Galland's protective force totaled only 250 first-line machines.

The Luftwaffe would be numerically inferior to the British air strength that could be sent against the warships. Sensitive about control of the seas, the British could be relied upon to hurl everything into the battle. By cunningly juggling arrival and departure times of the successive fighter waves over the ships, Galland hoped to have at least thirty-two fighters over the naval force most of the time. The plan required not only navigational precision, but protracted maximum effort by the fighter pilots.

Hitler had personally resolved on the effort to get the ships back from Brest. Swearing everyone to secrecy at a Wolf's Redoubt conference of the commanders involved, he demanded a detailed discussion of the plans. The participants were unanimous that operational success depended upon the efficacy of the air cover.

Hitler took his twenty-nine-year-old fighter General aside and asked for a frank assessment of the chances. He got an honest and prescient answer:

"It all depends on how much time the British have to mobilize the RAF against the ships. We need complete surprise and a bit of luck into the bargain. My fighter pilots will give their best when they know what is at stake."

"Operation Thunderbolt" thus went forward with Hitler's full endorsement. Its success undoubtedly did much to enhance Galland's status with Hitler as an independent and forthright young leader. Certainly "Thunderbolt" was an example of what Germany's military and naval professionals could accomplish when unhindered by astrological strategy.

Every man involved was caught up in the spirit of fighting for something larger than himself. This spirit also permeated the fighting squadrons, on whom so much was to depend. Under Galland's inspired leadership the pilots of JG-2 and JG-26 were able to throw off the morale handicap imposed by months of grinding struggle against the superior RAF on the Channel coast. They went into "Thunderbolt" with soaring spirits.

Aided by inclement weather, poor visibility, and an incredibly slow British reaction to the breakout, the Germans brought off the daring operation. At 10 A.M. on 12 February 1942, an RAF fighter spotted the battleships and the whole convoy of about forty vessels. The fighter radioed the position of the German force to its base.

Galland's radio crews intercepted the message, so the German leader knew that the jig was up. With that presence of mind that distinguishes the great tactician, Galland kept radio silence on his own side. This was a rare feat, for the Luftwaffe pilots were notoriously voluble in the air, and almost impossible to control in this respect. But for "Thunderbolt" they shut up.

By keeping the radio lid on, Galland won an extra thirty-five miles of unmolested passage for the big formation, right when the ships were at the narrowest part of the Channel. Approximately two hours elapsed between the RAF sighting and the first British air attack.

Battles raged around the warships for hours. The Luftwaffe pilots and the formidable shipboard flak downed more than sixty British aircraft of all types. The battleships made good their escape, and despite striking several mines arrived safely at Wilhelmshaven on 13 February 1942.

A command triumph that portended well for the fortunes of Germany's fighter force, "Thunderbolt" proved Galland's mettle. He had played a significant and perhaps even a decisive role in passing the first major naval force through the English Channel in two and a half centuries. It humiliated the British and gave German morale a lift.

"Thunderbolt" was probably the high-water mark of Galland's career as a commander—in terms of really stinging blows against the Allies. He was never again to experience the thrill of such large-scale operational success, despite odd days and weeks when his fighters were successful against Allied air power. Henceforth, his major struggles were against the ineptitude of his own side, and his main antagonist was Goering.

By the end of 1942 the trend of the war had been reversed. Stalingrad turned the tide in Russia, and El Alamein ruined Rommel. The Luftwaffe had suffered hammer blows in these events, not only equipment and pilots, but in terms of the status it previously enjoyed in Hitler's eyes. Hitler had reached the stage where he was blaming the Luftwaffe for the larger failures of his own strategy.

Derelictions extending over almost a decade caught up with Goering, and those who shared his disdain for air transport, in the Stalingrad disaster. Efforts to supply the encircled Germans from the air failed. The available lift was inadequate. Jeschonnek, Chief of the Luftwaffe General Staff and apostle of tactical air power, had made Hitler his god. The shattering tragedy not only exposed the falsity of the god, but turned the all-or-nothing gamble on tactical air power into a loss.

Jeschonnek committed suicide. His demise shook the fighting squadrons, where he was well liked as an ex-pilot, whatever his other failings. The Luftwaffe was entering a critical period when high-level decisions could afford no more errors.

Galland clearly divined these massive reversals in German fortunes as the "hour of the fighter." Defending German conquests, supporting the retreating German armies, protecting the Fatherland itself against Allied bombing—all reduced themselves in essence to the correct employment and deployment of fighter planes. Galland had no use for passive defense. Fighters in his view had to be employed aggressively even when in the defensive role, and "Thunderbolt" was a classic example. The fighter pilots defending the German battleships had hurled themselves furiously on the attacking British—and had won.

Galland's aim was to defend Germany in the air by these same aggressive tactics. The RAF thousand-bomber raids and the growing daylight strength of the USAAF bombers were a powerful incentive to build up the Luftwaffe fighter force even if other circumstances were excluded. There could be no doubt that the main thrust of the Allies in the west would be in the air.

Rational men like Albert Speer, the production genius, had no difficulty in seeing the essential nature of the problem as Galland outlined it. The production and technical problems were amenable to solution. But the fighter General was not dealing with rational men at the level where the big decisions were made.

Hitler's early successes had been supplanted by a steady parade of defeats. His response showed not only the magnitude of his neurosis, but the utter futility of trying to meet such an individual with rational arguments. In the face of the Allied bombing threat, Hitler's response was to irrationally insist on primacy for the Luftwaffe *bomber* force. Reprisal bombing of English cities was his goal and his obsession as far as air power was concerned.

RAF and USAAF fighter strength over the United Kingdom was by this time so enormous that any large-scale Luftwaffe bombing attack was sheer suicide. Pinprick attacks, which were the only possible "bombing" offensive against British targets, had no power to arrest the growth of Allied strength. These facts, obvious enough to junior fighter pilots on the Channel coast, were totally ignored in Hitler's direction of German air operations and aircraft production.

This was not the only irrationality with which Galland had to deal. Goering insisted for political reasons on peripheral air defense of the Reich. He was primarily interested in vindicating his earlier assertions that no Allied bombs would fall on Germany. Matching Luftwaffe strength to its tasks was to him an academic, secondary consideration. Galland by contrast advocated a central fighter defense, strongly aggressive and capable of shattering raiding bomber formations by concentrating its strength at decisive points.

He advocated the heavyweight punch. He held that if fighter strength could be increased to four times the numerical strength of the bombers, bombing could be made too expensive for the Allies. On rare occasions Galland was able to achieve these concentrations. The effects were devastating.

In February and March 1944 on several different occasions the USAAF lost over sixty heavy bombers in daylight raids—a loss of almost six hundred highly trained men on each occasion. By night, a similar success was attained on March 30–31, when massive concentrations of German night fighters clawed down over ninety RAF bombers from a force of approximately eight hundred machines attacking Nuremberg.

Galland's Clausewitzian ideal of concentration also paid off on occasions even against heavily escorted USAAF bombers. On 10 February 1944, 169 B-17s were sent to the Brunswick area but bad weather upset the accuracy of their bombing. Bad weather also caused rendezvous problems on the withdrawal with the escort fighters. An estimated 350 German fighters found the bombers and took advantage of the thick and persistent contrails from the heavies. Using the contrails as cover, the Germans launched attack after attack on the Fortresses. Eight escort fighters and 29 bombers were destroyed, and 111 of the returning B-17s had battle damage.

These battles in the air will be extensively dealt with in the appropriate chapters dealing with the various German fighter pilots who flew the missions. Galland's main fight continued to be with Goering, who gradually lost all his independence from the Fuehrer and degenerated into an abject lackey of the dictator. Goering's own command decisions resulted in crippling losses to the Luftwaffe fighters and the Allied bombing was not in any way diminished.

Goering continually accused the fighter pilots of cowardice—a savage accusation only a man who had never tackled the bomber boxes could afford to make. Galland risked not only his career but his life in vehemently defending his pilots against these unfounded charges. For

FIGHTING GENIUS: Lt. General Adolf Galland became General of the Fighter Arm at age 29. He provided outstanding leadership not only to the fighter force, but also against the irrational interference of German political leaders. A brilliant strategist and tactician, Galland managed to fly combat until the end of the war. He is credited with 104 aerial victories, all of them against British and American-flown aircraft.
(*Galland Collection*)

Goering, these successive confrontations with Galland must have been bitter experiences.

For years Goering had asserted the desirability of strong personalities in command, regardless of expert knowledge. In his young fighter General Goering confronted a strong personality and a technical expert in one dynamic package. Galland was gifted with the forthrightness one might expect in an aggressive fighter, and he also had considerable power of expression.

When it came to fighting in the air, Goering was dealing with a young General with an impressive string of kills—and one who continued to enter combat with the enemy whenever the opportunity offered. As an aerial tactician, he was unsurpassed. In strategy, the failure of Goering's peripheral defense, which Galland had predicted, led to such incredible horrors as the Hamburg fire raids. By contrast, whenever Galland got a free hand the fortunes of the Luftwaffe fighters would rise—as would the Allied losses.

Crowning all these facts of life in the wartime Reich, so devastating for an egomaniac like Goering to contemplate, was the anomaly that Galland had been hand-picked for his job by the Reichsmarschall himself. He had been selected on account of the very abilities and skills which Goering now found so irksome to his vanity and so difficult to counteract.

Goering's reactions could follow only one channel—railing against the fighter pilots. Occasionally he blamed the poor dead Udet, forced into his job by Goering. But most of the time the fighter pilots were accused of everything from lying about their kills to lacking in will and courage. Like his master Hitler, whose voice he continued to accept as though under hypnosis, Goering had long lost the capability for rational thought and deed. One of the tragedies of modern times is that the German nation was dragged to war and ruin by these sick individuals, whose position remained impregnable in a police state they had created.

Galland's soul-searing destiny was to occupy a front-row seat at these events, with no power to change their course. In the end, he was publicly blamed by Goering for the failure of the Luftwaffe to defend Germany. By December 1944 almost five thousand Allied bombers were available to pound the Reich around the clock. Sharp differences of view with Goering, mainly over the Me-262[5] jet fighter, led to Galland's dismissal as General of the Fighter Arm in January 1945.

Hitler finally intervened in the Galland-Goering controversy with a decision that brought some satisfaction to the young General. His dismissal had been a coordinated act of Hitler, Himmler, and Goering. But now it was the Fuehrer who insisted that Galland be allowed to form a fighter unit with the Me-262, lead it into battle, and prove his contentions about the new aircraft . . . "or die in the attempt." This ruling led Galland back into combat and probably saved his life.

[5] See Chapter Fourteen, "The Coming of the Jet."

He led his elite unit, JV-44, until 26 April 1945, when he was forced down and ended the war crouching in a foxhole with cannon fragments in his leg. The story of JV-44 is dealt with in Chapter Four by Steinhoff, and also in Chapter Fifteen. The most elite fighter unit of the Second World War, and possibly of all time, it was a fitting place for a fighting soldier like Galland to end the greatest drama of his life.

He began the war in 1939 as a First Lieutenant and squadron leader. At the end in 1945 he was again a squadron leader—with the rank of Lieutenant General. No other fighter General of the war on either side could claim a comparable up-and-down career.

Galland was taken POW and held in military custody for two years. After his 1947 release he lived in northern Germany near Kiel for about a year, and was then offered a four-year contract by the Argentine Government in October 1948. He was to assist in the building of the Argentine Air Force by using his war experience.

A second contract for three years followed the first. He was thus engaged in consulting work with the Argentine Air Force from 1948 to the end of 1954, mainly concerned with organization, training, and operations. His vast experience of the war years was put to good use, and he avoided the doldrum years after the war when most of his German contemporaries were completely out of touch with aviation.

Returning to Germany in 1955, he did not join the new German Air Force. The general view in Germany is that he was favored by one faction in politics while Kammhuber was the choice of the other faction.

TIGER AT BAY: Galland exhibits tigerish energy while hanging on the crib of his first child, Andreas Hubertus, born in 1966 when Galland was fifty-four. A daughter followed the son. Galland today is a successful businessman in Germany in the aerospace field. *(Photo: Toliver)*

Great efforts have been made to bring his genius back to top command, and he is still regarded in high German circles as that country's best military man.

Today he still flies a great deal. His Beechcraft Bonanza is not as hot as an Me-262, but as he puts it, "I am older now." He is an aerospace industry consultant and has his office in Bonn in a rambling old building on the Koblenzerstrasse—handy to the Defense Ministry and all important military and political nerve centers. He is the German representative for a number of leading American firms.

His high-ceilinged office is lined with stag-heads, trophies of the hunter and sportsman. There are only a few mementos of the war, including photographs of his deceased brothers Paul and Wilhelm, both of whom were killed in action as fighter aces during the war. In an anteroom there is a huge and compelling oil portrait of Galland painted by Leo Poeten in 1940. Only a few people get to see the painting, but one day it must surely find its place in a more handsome gallery.

He is successful in business and last married to his former secretary after several previous forays into marital *blitz*. Adolf and Hannelies Galland were blessed with their first child, Andreas Hubertus, in November 1966. To all outward appearances Galland is a typical, successful German businessman, even to producing sheafs of photographs of his son to show to friends and old comrades.

High in the hills in nearby Oberwinter he has a comfortable, pleasant home, with a bar in the basement adjoining his swimming pool and sauna bath. Fighter pilots and visitors have scrawled greetings all over the walls. He commutes to Bonn in his Mercedes and in general resembles businessmen the world over.

He is different in one salient aspect. There arises in all who know him well the idea that perhaps there is another chapter to be written in his biography. He is like a well-tuned engine waiting for the right touch of the throttle.

Galland is a living legend. In the twentieth century on either side of the two great world conflicts he is unsurpassed as a fighter ace, commander, tactician, strategist, and apostle of air power. Indeed, it is doubtful if he has an equal. The Luftwaffe fighter force would not have been the same without him. He was the embodiment and expression of its spirit, and he enjoys a permanent historical association with Germany's aerial destiny.

Few men living have had greater insight into the consequences of demented minds in control of national power and with unlimited authority. He saw it all at first hand. Having survived these ordeals on the ground, as well as fire in the air, Adolf Galland has earned the undisturbed tranquillity of his autumn.

3

They Called Him "Daddy"

*"We were just fighter pilots. Werner Moelders
was something more."*
GENERALMAJOR DIETRICH HRABAK

"**Y**OU suffer from acute motion sickness — you will never make an airman."

The German doctor's words rang in the foggy consciousness of Werner Moelders like a death sentence. Trembling and deathly pale, the twenty-two-year-old German Army Lieutenant slumped groggily in the centrifugal test chair. The device had stopped spinning, but Moelders' brain was still reeling violently. He leaned forward and retched.

The doctor shook his head and clucked his tongue.

"You will do much better to stay in the Army, Leutnant Moelders. You are not fit to fly."

This disastrous end to his first attempt to enter the Luftwaffe in 1935 was something young Moelders had not anticipated. Great leaders are not easily put off from pursuit of their goals, and he was no exception. He failed only this once, in 1935.

Six years later in 1941, he was Germany's top-scoring fighter ace, with 115 kills to his credit.[1] He had become an ace in each of two separate wars, and was the first man to exceed von Richthofen's First World War record of eighty victories. Also, Moelders was the first man to down one hundred enemy aircraft in aerial combat.

Brilliant as this combat record is, it nevertheless tells only half the Moelders story. With outstanding gifts for command and organization, as well as for tactics and instruction, he rose at the incredibly early age of twenty-eight to General of the Fighter Arm. Forbidden to fly any further combat, he was destined for a significant career in high com-

---

[1] Moelders had fourteen victories in Spain, 101 in World War II. At one time, Major Helmut Wick led him in the scoring race, and when Moelders had sixty-five kills, Hermann-Friedrich Joppien of JG-51 scored his seventieth victory on 23 April 1941. Wick and Joppien were both killed in action.

"DADDY": Werner Moelders was a brilliant, serious-minded leader of outstanding quality and character. A few years older than the pilots he led, they called him "Daddy" Moelders because he also taught them how to stay alive in the maelstrom of aerial combat. General of the Fighter Arm at age 28, he was killed in a bad weather crash while flying from Russia to the funeral of Ernst Udet. He scored 115 aerial kills. (*Boehm Collection*)

mand. Yet before he reached his twenty-ninth birthday he was buried in Invaliden Cemetery in Berlin, not far from the grave of Baron Manfred von Richthofen.

An air crash in bad weather robbed Germany of Werner Moelders long before his unique talents had fully unfolded. Perhaps it is as well for the Allies that he was removed from the scene. Be that as it may, Moelders was probably the most highly respected fighter pilot and leader in Germany as far as his contemporaries are concerned. Galland is his only equal, and even a quarter century after Moelders' death the two great ace-leaders are still rivals in the affection and esteem of the men they led.

Intent on a military career from boyhood, Moelders changed the focus of this ambition when an indulgent uncle took him on an aerial joyride. Thenceforth he never wavered in his determination to become a military pilot. His progress toward this goal suffered only a temporary setback when it was found he suffered from motion sickness.

Following his initial medical rejection, Moelders began training himself to master his motion sickness. On his second attempt in the centrifugal chair he did not vomit, although he felt as sick and groggy as ever. He won conditional permission to begin flying training. He soon found that there was more to conquering his difficulties than just squeaking past the doctor.

Flying training was carried on at this time in so-called civil training schools, such as the *Deutsche Verkehrsflieger Schule* in Brunswick run by Keller. For the first month of his flying training, vomiting became a way of life for Moelders. Plagued by fierce headaches and giddiness, flying for him was sheer misery—self-torture in an almost unendurable form. He could have given up at any time he wished and thereby avoided this steady program of physical distress.

Moelders would not give in. Slowly but surely he accomplished a triumph of the will. The retching and headaches became less frequent and their violence diminished. Complete mastery of these conditions soon followed and from then on Moelders never looked back as an airman and leader.

A year after his entry into the Luftwaffe he was instructing at Wiesbaden, and the new Luftwaffe was no longer camouflaged. During two years of successful instructing, Moelders yearned for real combat experience. The Spanish Civil War provided the opportunity.

The conflict became a "curtain raiser" for the Second World War, and a trial ground for new weapons and tactics. Germany's most important contribution to Franco's cause was the Condor Legion, made up of volunteers from the Luftwaffe. The Condor Legion's Fighter Wing 88 was a highly successful unit and gave firsthand experience of modern aerial warfare to such future aces and leaders as Wilhelm Balthasar, Edu Neumann, Herbert Ihlefeld, Walter Oesau, and Hannes Trautloft, among others.

As has been previously recounted, Fighter Squadron 3 needed a new squadron leader to replace Adolf Galland, who was determined that only a top-quality man would fill his shoes. After the death of one substitute in an aerial collision and Galland's action in relieving another replacement and sending him back to Germany, the German command selected Moelders as the best man available.

In April 1938, carrying a cardboard suitcase and thinly disguised as a "strength through joy" tourist, Moelders arrived in Spain for his first taste of aerial combat. Galland's initially stony reaction to Moelders was soon replaced with warm approval as the newcomer demonstrated his flying and leadership capabilities. By the time Galland departed in May 1938 his reports on the man were glowing with enthusiasm. "Lieutenant Moelders is an excellent officer and splendid pilot, with brilliant and precise leadership," wrote Galland to his superiors.

Two months after Moelders took over Fighter Squadron 3 the unit's conversion to the latest model Me-109 fighters commenced. These superb aircraft were fit weapons for an aerial warrior of Moelders' caliber, and he made good use of them. In the process, he began his spectacular rise to his place among the immortals of the air.

The slow He-51 biplanes which Fighter Squadron 3 had previously flown were no match for the Polikarpov I-15 and I-16 "Rata" fighters supplied by Russia to the Loyalists. The situation now changed dramatically in favor of Moelders and Fighter Squadron 3.

On 15 July 1938, Moelders sighted a formation of I-16s and began the chase. The young German reveled in the splendid response of his new fighter as the Me-109 quickly closed the distance. Eyes bulging, stomach churning, heart pounding, young Werner had a classic case of "buck fever." His first burst fell far astern of the Russian-built machine.

Fuming at his own ineptitude, Moelders pulled off the first I-16 and quickly closed on another. All the strict injunctions in the fighter pilot's manual were racing through his head as he closed in to point-blank range. With the I-16 filling his windshield, Moelders pressed his gun buttons.

The Polikarpov fighter sagged under the impact of the Me-109's four machine guns, then disappeared in a shroud of fire and smoke. Moelders watched as the enemy plunged earthward, tracing its course to final impact. He had scored the first of fourteen victories in the Spanish Civil War. He emerged from the Spanish conflict as Germany's most successful fighter pilot.[2]

The Me-109 was blooded in Spain, and many modifications followed which were of advantage when the Second World War came. Moelders was largely responsible for improving the armament of the famed fighter, the most important modification being the substitution of a 20mm cannon for the centrally mounted 7.9mm machine gun.

His greatest achievement with the Condor Legion lay in the field of tactics, to which he made a revolutionary contribution. The leap forward in aerial fighting for which Moelders was primarily responsible left the other world powers behind. Only a few men in military life, in any country, have the vision, insight, and force of personality to make the comprehensive innovations to fit new tactics to new technology. Moelders was such a man.

Goering had established the Luftwaffe as an independent service branch—his main contribution to the renaissance of German air power. Although a new force, the Luftwaffe had strong roots in the German Air Service of the First World War. These connections were far from being exclusively traditional, although all due homage was extended to the famous aces and leaders of the earlier conflict. Right down to wing, group, and even squadron level, former First World War pilots and aces were *in command* of the new Luftwaffe.

Eduard Ritter von Schleich (thirty-five WW I kills), Karl-August von Schoenebeck (eight WW I kills), Theo Osterkamp (thirty-two WW I kills), and Werner Junck (five WW I kills) were just a few of the old aces actively flying with or instructing the Luftwaffe fighter force in the nineteen thirties. These distinguished men all later had splendid careers in the high echelons of the Luftwaffe. Nevertheless, in the pre-war years their presence tended to keep aerial tactics within the First World War frame of reference. Moelders was able to remove the tactical strait jacket.

He felt the dead hand of the past lying heavily on the present, and saw it blocking the way to the future. In Spain the new dynamics of war in the air demanded changes. The combat advent of the all-metal, low-wing monoplane required that aerial tactics undergo a substantial metamorphosis. Moelders initiated and directed a new era in fighter tactics, just as Galland had added new dimensions to tactical air power.

[2]Moelders downed his fourteen aircraft between 15 July 1938 and 3 November 1938. All were single-engined fighters. He downed two I-15s on 31 October 1938, his best day. His tally consisted of four I-15s and ten Polikarpov I-16 "Rata" fighters.

BLACK KNIGHT: In WWI, Eduard Ritter von Schleich became known on the Western Front as the "Black Knight" of the German Air Service. He won the Pour le Merite. In WWII, first as a wing commander who again flew combat, and later as a general, von Schleich added to his laurels the Knight's Cross of the Iron Cross. He led the famous JG-26 *Schlageter* from 1 Nov 1938 until 9 December 1939. von Schleich died in 1947. (*Galland Collection*)

Boelcke and von Richthofen had introduced and developed formation flying on the German side in the First World War. Their innovations had ousted the lone-wolf fighter pilot and began the era of aerial battles between formations. The close formation of fighters had been gradually introduced on both sides until scores of machines were involved in some of the mass dogfights toward the end of the war.

The tendency to cling to close formation had persisted in the new Luftwaffe. Close formation was the most recent actual combat experience of the old aces who were now leading Me-109 formations. Aided by other German pilots, Moelders developed and proved in Spain what has since become known as the "Finger Four" formation, because of its similarity to the extended fingers of the human hand. Today in the USAF it is called the Double Attack System, but the Germans actually invented this tactic.[3]

Fighter pilots now flew in pairs. Each pair was called a *Rotte* in German. Large intervals were maintained between the two aircraft in each *Rotte*, and two *Rotten* made up a *Schwarm*. In each *Rotte* one pilot undertook the primary attacking role, with his wingman protecting his tail. The leader of each *Rotte* would ideally be the ablest and most experienced pilot, the best marksman and spotter. This pilot was free to give all his attention to the enemy. Similarly, when in *Schwarm* formation, one *Rotte* assumed the attacking role while the accompanying *Rotte* protected against attack, as the occasion demanded.

By staggering the altitudes of the airborne units, the nerve-wracking

[3] USAF Colonel E. E. Riccioni is the outstanding proponent of the Double Attack System in the USAF.

distraction of keeping precise formation was eliminated. This had been a hazardous proposition even in the First World War. In the earlier conflict the fighter pilot's attention was divided between keeping formation and spotting the enemy. In those days this division of attention was not as significant as it became on the eve of the Second World War.

Aircraft in the first war did not have the necessary speed to close an enemy sighted at a great distance. But at 350 mph in a modern fighter it was possible to bring an enemy machine to battle even if it was a distant speck in the sky. To this end, the vision of every pilot in the new Moelders formation was maximized. No longer were huge sectors of the sky cut off from view by the wings of dozens of other friendly aircraft flying in close formation. Initiative—one of the cardinal attributes of the successful fighter pilot—was given the fullest possible rein in the Finger Four formation.

Formations so constituted "swept" a far larger expanse of sky both physically and ocularly than First World War formations. They were thus many times more efficient in the all-important task of finding the enemy so that he could be shot down. By spreading out his formations Moelders also reduced their vulnerability. The devastating power of multiple batteries of aerial machine guns and cannons meant that close formation would very likely be suicidal. Radiotelephones made it unnecessary for the aircraft to be within close visual range, thus completing the essentials of the new era.

Since all these factors united to increase the fighting efficiency of the formations, the new tactics were tantamount to an increase in numerical strength. If formations of modern enemy fighters clung to the old methods, they would be outclassed. Moelders' prescience as

EASTERN FRONT FIGHTER LEADERS: The redoubtable Werner Moelders, center, is flanked in Russia by two other German fighter leaders, Carl-Gottfried Nordmann (78 victories) left, and Guenther Luetzow (108 victories). Nordmann was Kommodore of JG-51 *Moelders*, survived the war, and became a top executive of VW-America in the nineteen seventies. Luetzow was killed in the Me-262, Moelders in a flying accident. (*Boehm Collection*)

a tactician is well illustrated by the caliber of his imitators. Both the RAF and the USAAF subsequently adopted the Finger Four formation in the Second World War, and their first encounters with it were a nasty surprise to the British.

The old ideas did not die easily. They were derived from authentic aerial combat and had been tried and true in their own era. All this, however, had slipped into the limbo even while some of its most accomplished practitioners were still on active flying duty. The time of the new ideas had come, and it was Moelders who opened the door.

His success as a fighter pilot in Spain gave him the individual status which, in spite of his youth, helped the general introduction of the new tactics. He upgraded tactics to fit the new technological realities. Armed with these tactics, the Luftwaffe was ahead of the rest of the world in 1939 when the Second World War commenced.

Returning from Spain late in 1938 Moelders enjoyed a status in the Luftwaffe out of all proportion to his age and rank. His personal fighting record had made him one of Goering's favorites, but even this could not account for the legendary personality that was now emerging. He had other qualities as a man which reinforced his piloting and leadership talents.

He had been raised as a strict Roman Catholic. From this religious foundation he never departed. He was thereby equipped with a moral and ethical anchorage missing from those who embraced the National Socialist polemic as their religion. Moelders deplored in open arguments with his young fellow pilots what he considered the excesses of the Hitler regime. He was opposed to all doctrines rooted in materialism and hatred and was fearless in his defense of the good and true in all men—friends or foes.

Moelders was therefore an exceedingly well-balanced man, whose attention to his inner life played a dominant role in shaping his personality. He was mature far beyond his years, and it was in 1939 while he was squadron leader of No. 1 Squadron of JG-53 that his pilots began calling him "Daddy" Moelders. The nickname came naturally as the expression of the respect and admiration his pilots felt for the old-young man who led them.

In German, Daddy is written "*Vati*" and pronounced "fatty." This has led to his being called "Fatty" Moelders in many apocryphal English-language books and articles. He was a dark-haired man of lean build and middle height, who weighed about 155 pounds. A physician friend of the authors who knew Moelders well in 1940 describes him thus:

"He was a very beautiful man, almost too beautiful to be a man. His features, very finely chiseled, were perfect and he had a profile which caused people to stare at him. His complexion, skin texture, and coloring were not surpassed by the most beautiful of women. But there was nothing else feminine about him in any way. His piercing gaze and his unmistakable acceptance and exercise of authority caused subordi-

103 VICTORIES: Major Hartmann Grasser served on all fronts in WWII, amassing 103 kills over Russian, British and American-flown fighters. He was adjutant to Werner Moelders in JG-51 and at one time commanded a fighter wing that was set up to train Russian dissidents to fly against the Soviet Union. He won the Oak Leaves to his Knight's Cross and survived the war.
(*Steinhoff Collection*)

nates, contemporaries, and superiors alike to listen and to obey."

That was the physical side of Moelders. Major Hartmann Grasser served as Moelders' adjutant in JG-51 during the Battle of Britain and in Russia. Himself an ace with 103 kills, Grasser retains a warmly admiring recollection of his former C.O.:

"Werner Moelders was a very well-educated and a highly intelligent man with an exceptionally good character. His character was such that it guaranteed everything else about him. He had a direct line of thought, was brilliantly analytical, and he was especially a man with good leadership. He had an ear and an eye for everybody in his *Geschwader*. He had a good discipline without harshness, and an understanding for the mistakes of others—but he had no understanding of anything that went against discipline in fighting the war.[4]

"He was an outstanding teacher and instructor. He could teach you to fight in the air. His special personal attention was given to every new pilot who came to the wing. He would take these young men to himself and introduce them to the conditions and demands of aerial fighting. His credo was, 'The most important thing for a fighter pilot is to get his first victory without too much shock.'

"He had a gift for tactics, an outstanding tactical imagination. He was mature beyond his years, an analytical thinker, a practical man and with it all a humanist. I owe my life entirely to Werner Moelders. He not only showed me how to fight in the air, he showed me how to stay alive and come back from a fighter operation. His men were devoted to him.

"I think that if Moelders had lived then he was a man with the character and intellectual capacity to get his ideas through against the leadership—against the politicians."

[4] Moelders' chivalrous, soldierly code is exemplified by his reaction when he saw Joppien, leader of I/JG-51 attack a train during the Battle of Britain. Moelders was horrified, summoned Joppien and admonished him with a blistering lecture on the difference between military and civilian targets.

Moelders' first aerial victory of the Second World War came on 21 September 1939 when he downed a Curtiss fighter of the French Air Army. The following week he was made *Gruppenkommandeur* of III/JG-53.[5] Part of JG-53's assignment was the final destruction of French air power. On 5 June 1940, with two victories already under his belt for that day, Moelders was leading a fighter sweep over Chantilly Forest when he met his match.

A French fighter pilot who had not forgotten the first principles of air fighting brought off a perfect bounce out of the sun. The German ace's Me-109 caught the full force of the Frenchman's armament. In a few shocking seconds cannon shells and machine gun bullets had riddled Moelders' aircraft from nose to tail. Miraculously unwounded, a startled "Daddy" found his machine going soggy in his hands.

Smoke belched back into the cockpit from the stricken engine. There was only one way out—jump! Praying that the hail of French fire had not also riddled his parachute pack Moelders bailed out. He floated down in French territory and was taken prisoner by the French Army. He had scored his twenty-fifth kill that same day.

His internment was brief. Two weeks later the French surrendered, and he was released for return to Germany. A significant promotion awaited him. He was the new *Kommodore* of JG-51 and the youngest Wing Commander in the Luftwaffe.

JG-51 was called *Geschwader Moelders*, the Moelders Wing, and its insignia was the head of a condor in a circle on a shield. With this unit from the collapse of France onward, Moelders was engaged in almost incessant operational activity against the RAF. On the German side, he was one of the leading figures of the Battle of Britain.

Daily sorties against the south of England and fighting at the limit of their operational range against the redoubtable RAF took heavy toll of JG-51. Moelders shone both as a fighting pilot and as a formation leader. He also had the satisfaction of seeing the RAF desert its old-fashioned tactics and adopt his. By 12 October 1940 he had forty-five kills in the Second World War and had flown 196 combat missions. JG-51 was credited with over five hundred kills at this time.

During this period of intense and prolonged strain, Moelders was seen to lose his head for the only time in his career. Medically grounded with severe influenza on 11 November 1940 it was a profusely sweating and distraught young Wing Commander who listened to the radio communications of JG-51 on a sweep over the Thames Estuary.

His friend First Lieutenant Claus had been shot down. The returning pilots confirmed that Claus had gone down in the drink. Feverishly Moelders barked impossible orders to air–sea rescue units. When they declared themselves unable to execute his orders, he commanded his own fighter be made ready.

His staff could not reason with him. Accompanied by Lieutenant Eberle he roared off across the English Channel and conducted a futile

[5] III/JG-53 means the third *Gruppe* of *Jagdgeschwader* 53 (Fighter Wing 53).

FIRST TO 40 VICTORIES: Major Helmut Wick was one of the Luftwaffe's best leaders and aces in the bitterly fought Battle of Britain. He was the first pilot of WWII to reach 40 aerial victories. He was shot down on 28 November 1940, with 56 victories to his credit. He was awarded the Oak Leaves to his Iron Cross. (*Nowarra Collection*)

sweep of the Thames Estuary, looking for an Me-109 that must long ago have sunk. On this perilous flight so close to British shores, the pride of the Luftwaffe, sick and dispirited, was a very vulnerable target for the RAF, but he returned.

When Hitler turned his attention to Russia, JG-51 was sent to the Eastern Front. Moelders' score rose to 101 and he was the first man to crack the magic century mark in aerial combat. He was forbidden to fly combat on the personal order of Goering, but he continued to do so from time to time. He was made General of the Fighter Arm at the age of twenty-eight.

He was commanding a Battle Group consisting of Stukas, fighters, and ground-attack fighters when Ernst Udet committed suicide. At the time, the Germans were trying to force their way south to the Crimea and the fighting was extremely heavy both on the ground and in the air. Major (who rose to the rank of Lieutenant General and was the Chief of the German Air Force and has now retired) Gunther Rall, the third-ranking ace of Germany and the world with 275 kills, recalls this period:

"Every morning Moelders was flying a Fieseler Storch right over the front. He had his own radio. He would land and hide in a foxhole and then talk to the pilots in the air. He became a Forward Air Controller, in effect, pioneering this technique, and directing us accurately on to enemy positions. Then in the evening he would fly back and hold a commander's conference. He would review the day's operations and tell us what we had done right and show us where we had gone wrong.

"This was a period of heavy, critical fighting. Three days before he left for the Udet funeral he had serious support troubles. He didn't get enough ammunition, fuel, or spares and he wanted to fly back to Germany and tackle the high command—'I need support,' he said, and he meant it."

It was in these circumstances then that Moelders was advised of Udet's death and was ordered by Goering to return to Berlin. He was to be in the Honor Guard. Moelders took off in an He-111 in vile weather from Chaplinka Airport, glad of the opportunity to personally redress the shortages and deficiencies that were hampering air operations in the Crimea and leading to a loss of German lives.

TACTICIANS IN RUSSIA: Major Herman-Friedrich Joppien opens a map to discuss situation with Colonel Werner Moelders during 1941 operations of JG-51 on the Russian Front. Comrades in Battle of Britain operations, Moelders and Joppien moved east with Operation Barbarossa. Joppien was killed in action in Russia on 25 August 1941, with 70 victories to his credit, including 25 in the Battle of Britain. (*Obermaier Collection*)

At the controls of the He-111 was Oberleutnant Kolbe, a thoroughly competent pilot and like Moelders a veteran of Condor Legion service. Kolbe had to use every trick in the book to get the bomber back to Germany through the appalling weather. The anger of the elements served only to deepen Moelders' determination to get to Berlin as soon as possible.

When the He-111 was forced down at Lemberg by the weather, Kolbe urged Moelders not to continue the flight. Weather reports told of even worse conditions between Lemberg and Berlin. The young fighter General would not agree to abandon or delay the flight. They piled back into the bomber.

A terrific headwind pummeled the machine unmercifully and Kolbe poured fuel to the engines to keep making headway. The gas gauges sank lower and lower. Near Breslau an engine quit and Kolbe nursed the stricken aircraft down through dense cloud and lashing rain. His approach was low and short.

Frantically the pilot gunned the one good engine, only to find it quite dead. A cable railway beside the airfield came rushing up at them through the murk. Kolbe hauled back on the stick and the Heinkel lifted soggily. Staggering over the cables the bomber stalled and crashed thunderously to the ground.

Moelders and Kolbe were killed. The bomber's radio operator and Moelders' aide-de-camp were pulled out of the wreckage and lived to reconstruct the last moments of "Daddy," who died an airman's death. The pursuant demise of Moelders was probably the most unfortunate sequel to Udet's suicide, although he may well have flown back from the front without the order from Goering in view of the military situation.

The authors have had access to Moelders' logbook and have found it a marvel of precise record-keeping. The ace's handwriting is almost like engraving, and reflects the well-ordered personality of the man. The logbook also provides an extremely interesting parallel with the career of American ace Robert S. Johnson,[6] and should further assist in vitiating any assertions that German kill claims were exaggerated simply because their totals are larger than those of the Allied aces.

A comparison between Bob Johnson's twenty-eight victories in ninety-one sorties and Werner Moelders' victory tally as recorded in his logbook is interesting and illuminating:

ROBERT S. JOHNSON

Mission	Victory	Date	Type	Area or Mission
11	1	6.13.43	1 FW-190	Dunkirk
30	2	8.24.43	1 FW-190	Paris (claimed probable—was confirmed)
42	3	10. 8.43	1 FW-190	Bremen
43	4	10.10.43	1 Me-110	Munster
	5		1 FW-190	Munster
45	6	11. 3.43	1 Me-109	Wilhelmshaven
50	7	12.22.43	1 Me-109 (or 209)	Osnabruck
53	8	12.20.43	1 FW-190	Ludwighaven (claimed damaged, was confirmed as destroyed)
54	9–10	12.31.43	2 FW-190	Kerlin-Bastard (Brest)
56	11	1. 5.44	1 FW-190	Elberfeld
59	12	1.21.44	1 FW-190	Rouen, France
62	13	1.30.44	1 Me-210	Brunswick
	14		1 Me-109	Brunswick
64	15–16	2.20.44	2 Me-110	Hanover
70	17	3. 6.44	1 Me-109	Berlin mission nr. Brunswick
71	18–19	3. 8.44	2 Me-109	Berlin mission nr. Brunswick
73	20–21	3.15.44	2 FW-190	Brunswick

[6] Robert S. Johnson, who, with twenty-eight victories over Europe, tied with American Colonel Francis S. Gabreski for top honors in the United States Army Air Corps in the European Theater of Operations.

AMERICA'S BEST: Lt. Colonel Robert S. Johnson scored 28 victories in the European Theater of Operations in WWII, which made him the top scoring ace in Europe in a tie for that honor with Colonel Francis Gabreski. A fair comparison of Bob Johnson's combat record with that of Werner Moelders, indicates that their scoring rate was approximately the same under similar conditions. The matter is fully discussed in the text. German aces however, flew until they were killed, and were not withdrawn from combat to train other pilots, sell war bonds or make morale-building tours as were Allied aces. *(Photo: USAF)*

	22		1 Me-109	Brunswick
80	23	4. 9.44	1 FW-190	Kiel
83	24–25	4.13.44	2 FW-190	Strasburg
88	26	5. 4.44	1 Me-109 (or 209)	Berlin mission (claimed damaged, confirmed as destroyed)
91	27–28	5. 8.44	1 FW-190 1 Me-109	Berlin mission (claimed damaged, confirmed as destroyed)

Johnson was one of the quickest and deadliest of the American aces, and Werner Moelders was one of Germany's best. The portion of his logbook herein reproduced deals with his victories over French-, British-, and Belgian-flown aircraft of all types, with RAF Spitfires and Hurricanes making up the largest portion of his bag.

Werner Moelders' Logbook 26.8.39–8.5.41

Date	Hours	Type A/C	Combat Mission	Victory	Location
21. 9.39	1310–1433	1 Curtiss	6	1	
30.10.39	1020–1135	1 Blenheim	19	2	
23.11.39	1435–1700	1 Morane	35	3	
22.12.39	1415–1540	1 Morane	41	4	
2. 3.40	1135–1245	1 Hurricane	53	5	
3. 3.40	1334–1445	1 Morane	56	6	
26. 3.40	1405–1535	1 Morane	68	7	
2. 4.40	1130–1250	1 Hurricane	71	8	
20. 4.40	1125–1235	1 Curtiss	74	9	
23. 4.40	1030–1155	1 Hurricane	78	10	
14. 5.40	1545–1708	1 Hurricane	94	11	
19. 5.40	0845–0955	1 Curtiss	104	12	
20. 5.40	1835–2050	1 Vickers	107	13	
21. 5.40	1603–2005	3 Moranes	110	14, 15, 16	
22. 5.40	1750–2250	1 Potez 63	111	17	
25. 5.40		1 Morane	114	18	
27. 5.40		2 Curtiss	116	19, 20	
31. 5.40		1 Leo 45	119	21	
3. 6.40		1 Spitfire	123	22	
		1 Curtiss		23	
5. 6.40		1 Potez 63	127	24	
		1 Bloch		25	
28. 7.40		1 Spitfire	129	26	
26. 8.40	@1255	1 Spitfire	140	27	
28. 8.40	@1040	1 Curtiss	142	28	
28. 8.40	@1840	1 Hurricane	143	29	
31. 8.40	@0950	3 Hurricanes	146	30, 31, 32	
6. 9.40	@1440	1 Spitfire	161	33	Over Folkstone
7. 9.40	@1830	1 Spitfire	165	34	Over London
9. 9.40	@1845	1 Spitfire	166	35	Over London
11. 9.40	@1705	1 Hurricane	167	36	Over SE London
14. 9.40	@1740	1 Spitfire	169	37	SW London
16. 9.40	@0850	1 Hurricane	173	38	Over London
20. 9.40	@1234	2 Spitfires	179	39, 40	Near Dungeness
27. 9.40	@1700	1 Spitfire	180	41	Near Maidstone
28. 9.40	@1500	1 Spitfire	181	42	Near Littlestone
11.10.40	@1230	1 Spitfire	193	43	Near Folkstone
12.10.40	@1040	1 Hurricane	195	44	Liquizue
	@1045	1 Hurricane		45	Cauberberg
	@1412	1 Hurricane	196	46	Dungeness
15.10.40	@0915	1 Hurricane	197	47	Kneleig
17.10.40	@1625	1 Spitfire	201	48	London
22.10.40	@1540	3 Hurricanes	204	49, 50, 51	Maidstone
25.10.40	@1045	1 Spitfire	205	52	NW Dover
	@1310	1 Spitfire	206	53	Margate
29.10.40	@1355	1 Hurricane	208	54	Dungeness
1.12.40	@1515	1 Hurricane	220	55	Ashforth
10. 2.41	@1729	1 Hurricane	227	56	5 km NNE Calais
20. 2.41	@1656	1 Spitfire	239	57	
	@1659	1 Spitfire	239	58	

25. 2.41	@1520	1 Spitfire	242	59	N. of Dravelines
26. 2.41	@1822	1 Spitfire	245	60	SW Dungeness
12. 3.41	@1915	Unknown	259	61	Near Dungeness
13. 3.41	@1522	1 Spitfire	261	62	SW Boulogne
15. 4.41		1 Spitfire	273	63	Boulogne
16. 4.41		1 Hurricane	274	64	S. of Dungeness
		1 Spitfire	274	65	S. of Le Touquet
4. 5.41		1 Hurricane	286	66	E. of Canterbury
6. 5.41		1 Hurricane	290	67	Dover
8. 5.41		1 Spitfire	292	68	Dover

This statistical summary has been selected from a large number of such collections in the possession of the authors because it provides a *fair* comparison of two leading fighter pilots. The accomplishments of each were attained under conditions of attack, on the Western Front in each case.

Johnson required ninety-one missions to score twenty-eight confirmed kills. Moelders required 142 combat missions to record his first twenty-eight kills. Johnson emerges very favorably from the comparison, especially considering that Moelders was already a fighter ace of the Spanish War, with fourteen kills, long before Johnson ever learned to fly. Moelders began the Second World War as an accomplished ace.

Moelders' pathway to his first sixty kills is revealed as a long, hard grind. Some 245 combat missions were needed to register this score, mainly against the RAF. His logbook is an effective counter to the notion of many American writers that German aces counted the engines of their downed foes' aircraft in tallying their kills, or that the

A RARE MOELDERS SMILE: Werner Moelders was a serious-minded and high-minded man of war who was rarely ever heard to laugh or seen to smile. Hence the rarity of this photograph showing that Moelders, one of the two greatest fighter leaders produced by the Luftwaffe, did have the capacity for humor. He was made General of the Fighter Arm at 28 years of age. (*Obermaier Collection*)

squadron leader took personal credit for all the victories of his pilots. Moelders' victories are his own.

Johnson was in action less than eleven months from his first kill to his last. He was then forbidden to fly any further combat. If his performance is projected over five years, assuming that kill rates can be subjected to this abstraction, it is evident that he would have scored over one hundred victories—as did many Luftwaffe aces who flew from 1939 to 1945. The "projection" assumes of course that Johnson would have survived and found sufficient combat opportunities.

By comparison, Moelders in his first year of Second World War action recorded forty kills in 179 combat missions. He thus flew more often in that year than Bob Johnson did in 1943–44. Had Johnson doubled his missions in the eleven months he flew, his score would project to fifty-six, or rather more than Moelders scored in the same time span.

The German scores resulted from greater exposure to aerial combat, over a longer time period, than was either possible or permissible for Allied aces. The great experience of the Germans produced fighter pilots with masterful skills, so that a large number of the top Luftwaffe aces were able to survive the war—in spite of the hordes of Allied fighters sent against them.

Moelders pioneered the hundred-plus scoring of the Luftwaffe, but his contemporaries generally agree that his gifts as an administrator were at least equal to his talents as a fighter pilot. Consequently, much was expected of him when he was named General of the Fighter Arm. Not long before he received this important appointment, he had discussed the future with his friend, rival, and fellow ace Adolf Galland.

In an energetic argument, the two young leaders had compared the relative contributions of Germany's two leading First World War airmen—von Richthofen and Boelcke. Galland admired von Richthofen, the consummate aerial hunter and fighter. Moelders had greater admiration for Oswald Boelcke, who had dedicated himself to providing technical superiority for Germany's First World War pilots. Moelders ended the discussion by saying, "You can be the Richthofen of the Luftwaffe, Adolf. I will be its Boelcke."

As long as the history of air power is studied, buffs will take pleasure in speculating what might have happened had Moelders lived through the war. The history of the Luftwaffe High Command is not a happy one, mainly because of the constant political interference in technical matters. Moelders might have fared better than did Galland, but no one can say for sure.

Galland and Moelders would probably have to rank as the two outstanding personalities of the Luftwaffe fighter force in the Second World War. Perhaps the worthiest tribute to Moelders is the respected place he occupies in the minds and memories of his contemporaries, and the posthumous fame he still enjoys. The authors, as externes to German wartime affairs, have had abundant opportunity to meet in recent years numerous German aces and fighter leaders. From this it has been possible to build up an objective comparison of Moelders and Galland which may prove of interest to the reader.

Moelders actively sought and desired the challenges inherent in following in Boelcke's footsteps. Galland by contrast was the archetypal aerial hunter—a fighter first, last, and always to whom the thrill of the chase and victory in a fair fight was the elixir of life. Moelders approached the problems of high command with zeal and zest. Galland never wanted high command, hated paper work and desk flying, and resisted being taken off operations; he returned to aerial fighting whenever possible.

Moelders was serious and quiet, a man who seldom smiled and rarely laughed. He took his responsibilities right to heart and poured his energy into his work. Galland was an ebullient young leader, dashing, gallant, and arresting in appearance. Galland has a superb sense of humor; he is a wit and a man who can laugh.

Moelders maintained his equilibrium and sustained his seriously energetic approach to life from a strong religious base. He was in no sense a religious propagandist, but he lived with a quiet Christian dignity that no inferior individual could breach. Moelders' inner strength, combined with his formidable flying, tactical, administrative, and leadership skills, made him a practical man in the true sense of the term.

RIVALS AND FRIENDS: Adolf Galland (1.) and Werner Moelders confer on fighter tactics during the Battle of Britain. Rivals in the race for achievement, they worked out together the tactics that sharply reduced the loss rate of Me-109's in combat with Spitfires in the Battle of Britain. Galland later succeeded Moelders as General of the Fighter Arm. There is unanimous agreement among those who lived through the period and who knew both Moelders and Galland that they were the two finest leaders produced by the Luftwaffe fighter force in WWII. *(Galland Collection)*

Galland's equilibrium stems from his sense of humor. Yet his amiability, friendliness, and warm heart in no way diminish the razor-sharpness of his intelligence. He was a far better General than he himself thought he was. Moelders was perhaps more of a humanist, but Galland had to steel himself to ruthless decisions involving men's lives from which Moelders may have recoiled.

Both were immensely strong men in mind and heart. For Germany the ideal situation would have been for the two great rivals to work together. That is the view of Major Hartmann Grasser, who served on the staff of both men; and numerous other German ace-leaders feel similarly. In any event, Galland was presented with the Boelckian challenge while Moelders got an airman's death, like von Richthofen.

The two men came together at least once to the detriment of the Allies. In 1940 the Germans were losing their Me-109s to the Spitfires in combat at an alarming rate. Galland and Moelders put their heads together to find the tactical answer.

The Me-109 enjoyed a climb, dive, and top-speed superiority over the more maneuverable Spitfire. In a lively discussion they reflected on these facts and asked themselves why they should dogfight the Spitfire where it was in its best element. They decided to adopt a tactic of hit-and-run at high speed, thus nullifying the turning advantage of the Spitfire.

Orders were issued to the squadrons on the Channel Front and the prohibitive loss rate of Me-109s was arrested. The situation was similar to that between the Curtiss P-40 Warhawk and the Japanese Zero in the Pacific two years later. Once the Americans learned it was almost certain death to dogfight the Zero, and that hit-and-run meant success, American losses slowed and Japanese losses increased.

Although Moelders was killed 22 November 1941 he was throughout the war and remains to this day one of the best-known German aces to the English-speaking world. His tactical innovations and achievements were well recognized, even by his late foes. Perhaps the most significant aspect of "Daddy" Moelders is that he is remembered as much for his many attributes of character as he is for his feats in the air. He is one of the surpassing figures of the Luftwaffe, and history will mark him large as an officer and man.

4

From Biplane to Aerospace – Johannes Steinhoff

"The aeroplane is good sport, but worthless for use by the Army."
FERDINAND FOCH,
1911

TWO years after the illustrious Marshal Foch assigned aviation to sportsmen rather than soldiers, a boy was born in Thuringia to whom the air was life itself and the airplane civilization's most fascinating development. Johannes "Macky" Steinhoff, true to Foch's dictum, turned out to be a sportsman. He was also an outstanding soldier and is by every measure one of the most able commanders produced in his generation.

Although less famous than either Galland or Moelders, a special place among the leaders and tutors of the Luftwaffe must be accorded Steinhoff. With a varied and colorful combat career and 176 confirmed aerial victories, he is the twenty-second-ranked ace of Germany and the world. On active service as one of the elite "first-to-last" aces from 1939-1945, he survived a terrible crash at war's end to later become one of the major organizing brains behind the new German Air Force. Steinhoff rose to become the Chief of the German Air Force, the first fighter pilot and ace to occupy the post, then two years later was promoted to full General and assigned to represent Germany on the NATO staff at Brussells. He retired in 1972.

He spans the historical spectrum from biplane to aerospace, yet his pathway to the pilot's seat was somewhat devious. A youthful interest in languages led him to study philology at the University of Jena from 1932 to 1934. In 1934 he entered the German Navy for officer's training.

An aviation enthusiast, he transferred in 1936 to the rapidly expanding Luftwaffe. He took fighter pilot training, and by the outbreak of war in 1939 he was a twenty-six-year-old squadron leader, already showing leadership capacity and a penchant for independent decision. He is among the few successful and experienced German fighter pilots of 1939 to survive the Second World War, and subsequently rise to

STEINHOFF IN RUSSIA: Johannes "Macky" Steinhoff made an outstanding command record with JG-52 in Russia, later flew with Galland's "Squadron of Experts," JV-44 in final days of war. Steinhoff flew 993 combat missions between 1939 and 1945, was himself shot down 12 times. He ended the war in a hospital with a badly burned face, 176 aerial victories and the Swords to his Knights Cross. *(Steinhoff Collection)*

FAMOUS DUO: Lt. Gen. Johannes Steinhoff, 176 victories, and Erich Hartmann, 352, pose for author in Steinhoff's home in Wachtburg/Pech on 4 Dec. 1967. Behind them hangs the painting showing Steinhoff before his face was disfigured by the flames from the Me-262. *(Toliver)*

high command in the new German Air Force.

His war career includes service with some of Germany's most famous fighter units—JG-26 (the "Abbeville Boys"), JG-77, JG-52, and Galland's JV-44 jet unit, the "Squadron of Experts." Steinhoff was also a foundation member of NJG-1, and only his independent spirit kept him from becoming a night fighter permanently. He saw service in the Battle of Britain, on the Eastern Front, in North Africa and the Central Mediterranean, and again on the Western Front in the final defense of Germany. Twenty-seven of his aerial victories were scored against the Western powers, 149 in Russia.

Steinhoff's youthful interest in philology has certainly paid off as far as his many American friends are concerned. He is one of the greatest raconteurs, in English, about the Luftwaffe. With an engaging personality and a sense of humor that is more British than German, Steinhoff has more good yarns about the Luftwaffe and its personalities than almost any other German aviator known to the authors.

He is about five feet eleven inches tall and weighs about 180 pounds, maintaining this weight carefully. He has a very athletic build and his vigorous dynamism makes him stand out in any group of men. He insists on being combat-qualified on current jet aircraft, and has flown over a hundred different types of aircraft ranging from the biplanes of the early Luftwaffe to the fringe-of-space jets of today.

A story he likes to tell concerns his Battle of Britain days. A formation of battered German fighters was returning to France after a daylight escort mission over England. The badly clanked pilots flying with Steinhoff were maintaining radio silence, since they were not anxious for any further encounters with the RAF. In their headphones came a pitiful wail from some hapless, wandering German fighter pilot:

"I'm all alone . . . I'm all alone," moaned the lost German.

After several minutes of this dolorous caterwauling, Steinhoff heard one of his formation's R/T transmitters switch on.

"Shut up, you stupid bastard," barked Steinhoff's squadron mate. "You are *not* alone. There's a Spitfire on your tail."

The moaning stopped abruptly. The air went dead. Steinhoff reflects that it was a terrifying but effective way to prevent an overwrought pilot from committing suicide—in retrospect, not without its humor.

As a Group Commander in Russia, he ran up an impressive string of kills. Today, he says that by comparison with combat on the Western Front, aerial warfare in Russia was more like shooting down ducks than airplanes during the time he was there. After many months of this kind of combat, Steinhoff was transferred to North Africa.

"I took along a lot of bad habits with me which I acquired in Russia," he says. Chief of these was a certain carelessness or even a disdain for the enemy—the result of battling the low-caliber Soviet pilots of 1941-42.

"In Africa, you just couldn't get away with that sort of thing," he says. "The RAF promptly shot me down and in the process snapped me back to the realities of war in the air."

STEINHOFF - 1970: General Johannes "Macky" Steinhoff in 1970. The gallant Steinhoff endured many surgical operations on his burned face, overcame every handicap connected with it, and became one of the most respected NATO leaders. He was also one of the architects of the new Luftwaffe. He was a popular figure in Washington DC for many years while stationed in the U. S. Capitol. *(Steinhoff Collection)*

Later, Steinhoff commanded JG-77 in Italy after the loss of North Africa. While in this command he displayed great initiative and independence, frequently giving only nominal obedience to the streams of often absurd orders emanating from Goering and the high command.

As a product of both the naval and Luftwaffe officer training schools before the war, Steinhoff exemplifies the "officer and gentleman" concept of professional military service in that period. Fairness, chivalry, and decency were taught and expected along with military skills and prowess. An officer's word was his bond. Steinhoff's acceptance of such a code was complete, and led to an interesting incident during the Italian campaign in the fall of 1943.

Steinhoff shot down a P-38 and, landing immediately, found the American pilot and put him up for the night in his own tent. Steinhoff's men wanted to tie up the American with rope and attach a string to their *Kommodore's* toe. The German Wing Commander turned to the American.

"Will you give me your word that you will not run away?"

The American agreed.

SEPTEMBER 1941: Johannes "Macky" Steinhoff photographed against a sheepskin and a pile of firewood in his quarters on the Eastern Front. Steinhoff served in the Battle of Britain, Russia, North Africa and the Mediterranean and in the final air defense of Germany against the Allied bomber streams. 176 aerial victories in 993 combat missions. *(Steinhoff Collection)*

Two enemies who only a few hours before had been trying to blast each other from the air with batteries of cannon and machine guns lay down and slept side by side in the same tent, bound only by the ancient military tradition of parole.

Next morning, the two men had breakfast together. They both had bad hangovers and consumed a large amount of black coffee.

"I have to hand you over now to the guards who will take you to the prison camp," said Steinhoff.

The American pilot was obviously upset.

"Couldn't I stay with you, Colonel Steinhoff?" he said. "I am afraid they will not have *Schnaps* and good coffee in POW camp."

Before the beginning of the Second World War, Steinhoff was assigned an experimental night fighter squadron. By training, preference, and instinct a day fighter pilot, he approached night fighting with extreme skepticism. He was unconvinced of its efficacy and aware of its dangers and shortcomings.

A few days after the outbreak of the Second World War he was ordered to participate in a high-level conference at Berlin on night fighter tactics. Goering was chairing the gathering of a few generals, among them Ernst Udet, the First World War ace. Steinhoff had to sit at the tail end of the table.

Goering paced up and down pompously, elaborating on night fighter tactics. He developed a mixture of First World War and Space Age ideas, and talked for over an hour. The only night fighter and active pilot in the group, Steinhoff raised his finger in a humble way and asked if he could comment.

GRUPPENKOMMANDEUR 1941: "Macky" Steinhoff issuing orders on the Eastern Front in September of 1941. He won the Swords to his Knight's Cross, but in the final days of the war was appointed to "command" one aircraft—an Me-262 jet—by Goering who sought in this way to demean Steinhoff. *(Steinhoff Collection)*

When Goering gave a curt nod, Steinhoff stood up and said: "Things have changed considerably since the great days of von Richthofen—"

Goering immediately interrupted.

"Sit down on your little ass, young man," said the Reichsmarschall. "Before talking you must first gain a lot of experience."

Steinhoff sat down.

Later on, Steinhoff was squadron leader in an Me-109 Group that was incorporated into NJG-1, the first Night Fighter Wing in the Luftwaffe. Experiments in attacking British bombers at night, co-operating with searchlights, had proved highly unsatisfactory. There had been many losses of Me-109 fighters and no kills of the night invaders.

Wolfgang Falck, as a Captain, was given command of Night Fighter Wing No. 1 (NJG-1) with orders to build up the unit. Falck was given *carte blanche* in the selection of officers. Goering specified that the Major commanding Steinhoff's Group was to be fired. As his replacement, Falck chose Steinhoff. The two men had been successful squadron leaders in the December 1939 Battle of the German Bight against RAF bombers—Falck as a squadron leader of Me-110s and Steinhoff as a squadron leader of Me-109s.

FALCON'S PROFILE: The artist who made this drawing of Wolfgang Falck at the controls of his Me-110 captured this bird-man beak to perfection. Falck ended the war looking for his command in the Rhineland, as German formations melted away with the Allied Advance. (*Falck Collection*)

Even after his appointment as *Gruppenkommandeur*, Steinhoff was still expressing his vigorous opposition to night fighting. He asserted that new equipment and technological developments were necessary to make night fighting reasonably safe for the pilots, and effective against the enemy. In accordance with his independent outlook, Steinhoff gave frank and frequent voice to his objections.

His new Wing Commander, Wolfgang Falck, is today one of his closest friends. Falck says of this period:

"'Macky' Steinhoff was and is a sensitive man. He could not bear to see the loss of good men to no good purpose. It was this that primarily disturbed him about night fighting."

The objecting Steinhoff was stationed in Krefeld, and Falck in Düsseldorf decided that it was time for a conference. Steinhoff was becoming something of a problem. Falck intended delivering an ultimatum—Steinhoff would change his attitude or get the axe.

The perceptive Steinhoff was well aware that he might be fired when he was ordered to report to Falck. Philosophically stuffing his bags into his Me-109 he took off from Krefeld in vile weather. He was scheduled to appear before the Wing Commander at noon sharp at Düsseldorf Airport where HQ for NJG-1 was then located.

At about eleven-thirty Steinhoff began his approach into the weather. He broke out beneath ragged clouds at five hundred feet. As he did so, an alarming report crackled in his headphones. The base was under attack! An RAF Bristol Blenheim bomber was pounding the base with bombs and strafing the buildings and parked aircraft.

The report was still rasping in when Steinhoff sighted the Blenheim skimming in and out of the ragged cloud base. He set off in hot pursuit. The British machine was swallowed in the murk, but Steinhoff swept after it, mentally calculating how the bomber would maneuver for another bombing run. Half a minute later, peering through his wet windshield, he glimpsed the Blenheim going in on its run.

He cursed quietly. The British plane was too far away for him to attack. He winced as the bomb flashes pierced the gloom. Someone down there was really getting it! Then the Blenheim shot up into the cloud cover again, Steinhoff hot after it.

In the soup, there was nothing to see but a fleecy white wall. In vain he stared through his streaming canopy, angrily frustrated by his inability to attack the invader. After a couple of minutes of blind circling, he pulled back on the stick. Upstairs there might be some clue to the bomber's whereabouts. All he needed was a glimpse.

In his climb, he broke out between cloud layers. Directly in front of him was the climbing and departing Blenheim!

The German fighter's superior speed ate up the distance between the two aircraft. Closing in to "barn door" range, Steinhoff fired a couple of cannon bursts into the Blenheim. The bomber belched fire and plunged down to the earth. Well satisfied, he approached the base again and landed right at noon.

A HELPING HAND—AALBORG 1940: The two pilots who did most to establish night fighting in the Luftwaffe—Wolfgang Falck and Werner Streib—join forces here to help Falck into his parachute harness at Aalborg in 1940 where the night fighter drama began. Streib was outstanding at night tactics, and Falck excelled at the overall techniques of control and command. (*Falck Collection*)

The aerial battle had cost him at least twenty minutes. Quickly dismounting from his fighter, he was furnished with transportation and made it to Falck's office—late for his appointment. Psychologically geared to deal with a troublemaker, Falck was now additionally miffed by Steinhoff's tardiness. Testily the Wing Commander lectured him on the virtues of punctuality.

There was a flurry at the door and several of Falck's staff entered, begging forgiveness for the intrusion. The British bomber which had been pounding the base half an hour ago had been shot down. It had crashed a couple of miles away.

Falck's face lit up. This was good news. It must have been flak that got the Englander.

"Who else in hell would have been flying in such lousy weather?" said Falck.

"I was, sir," replied Steinhoff. "I shot down the bomber just before I landed. That is why I am late."

The exultant Falck, all smiles, quickly recovered himself and put on a stern expression.

"Well, Steinhoff, you have to be on time for appointments with me, in spite of the British."

The two men piled in a car and drove out to the wrecked Blenheim. Falck tells the story:

"The bodies of the crew were there. There was also a big, fat, pompous policeman and some civilians. They started touching the bodies of the dead Britons with their feet. I blew my top. 'These are dead people,' I shouted. 'They are soldiers and they do the same thing we have to do every day. If you don't take proper care of these bodies, I will kill you.' I lost my head and my temper while Steinhoff looked on quietly."

We will meet Wolfgang Falck as "The Happy Falcon" in Chapter Eight. A man of exceptional character, he could maintain no further appearance of antipathy toward Steinhoff after this kill. The two men had a long discussion about Steinhoff's dislike for and disquiet with night fighters. Falck could see his forthright squadron leader's viewpoint, and later arranged for his return to the day fighter force. "The Happy Falcon" thus opened the way for Steinhoff's distinguished future career. Transfers were not always easy to come by in the Luftwaffe.

For a time during the Battle of Britain, Steinhoff was the commanding officer of a sharp-featured Berliner named Joachim Marseille.

HOLOCAUST: This is the flaming wreckage of "Macky" Steinhoff's Me-262, after it crashed and burned on takeoff on 18 April 1945. Steinhoff was pulled from the flames more dead than alive, spent months in the hospital. He recovered to become one of the leading architects of the new Luftwaffe, *Inspekteur* of the force he helped rebuild, and an internationally respected NATO leader. *(F. Stigler Collection)*

Fame came to this young pilot later as "The Star of Africa" and we will meet him in the next chapter. To Steinhoff, he was a problem:

"Marseille was extremely handsome. He was a very gifted pilot and fighter—but he was unreliable. He had girl friends everywhere, and they kept him so busy that he was sometimes so worn out he had to be grounded.

"His sometimes irresponsible way of conducting his duties was the main reason I fired him. But he had irresistible charm."

Steinhoff got rid of Marseille before the persuasive youngster could infect more of his squadron with his lighthearted ways. So it was that Steinhoff, diverted himself from a night fighting career through Falck's assistance, was mainly responsible for the change of units that led Marseille to North Africa and glory.

Like Galland, Steinhoff's career went from first to last, or almost to last in Steinhoff's case. On 18 April 1945, just a few weeks from Germany's surrender, he was a Colonel and member of JV-44, "The Squadron of Experts," flying the Me-262 jet and commanded by Adolf Galland. On this day he was taking off in formation in what was probably the most elite *Kette*[1] in the history of the Luftwaffe—Steinhoff (176 kills), General Galland (104 kills), and Gerhard Barkhorn (301 kills)—three pilots with a total of 581 kills between them.

Steinhoff's Me-262, fully loaded with forty-eight rockets, had its left gear torn off in a shallow crater. The aircraft scraped both engine nacelles, setting them on fire. The machine became momentarily airborne, but Steinhoff was unable to maintain flight and the aircraft crashed and exploded.

Steinhoff was badly burned, especially his face. Many skin grafts and much delicate plastic surgery were required over a period of two years. "The handsomest man in the Luftwaffe," as Falck called him, would henceforth make his way in the world without the aid of a striking and memorable face.[2]

Discharged from hospital in 1947, Steinhoff found, as did many others, that former active officers were unwelcome in the atmosphere of defeat that pervaded Germany. Nothing daunted, he plunged into the advertising agency business. He was successful in this transition from high command to huckstering, and stayed in advertising until 1952 and the birth of the new German Air Force.

At that time, he was summoned to the Chancellor's office, where he began the staff work that preceded the formal advent of the *Bundesluftwaffe*. In 1955, ten years after his devastating crash, and aged forty-two, he came to America for refresher training on jets. Again he made a successful transition to a new way of life, becoming Deputy Chief of Staff, Operations, German Air Force, in 1956.

Promoted Brigadier General in 1958 and Major General in 1962, the jet ace served for several years as German Military Representative to the Military Committee of NATO in Washington, D.C. When he was assigned to this post, there was a conviction among his detractors in Germany that his badly scarred face would seriously impair his effectiveness with NATO in America.

The reverse proved to be true. Steinhoff's dynamic personality proved more than equal to the challenge. His friends in America are

---

[1] A flight formation of three aircraft.

[2] Several years ago, Falck discovered some propaganda film made after the Battle of the German Bight. Falck and Steinhoff were two of the "stars." In a typical gesture, Falck had a copy made of the film and presented it to Steinhoff's children, who had never seen what their father looked like before his 1945 accident.

legion, and it is doubtful if any German in Washington since the war has done more for Germany in winning friends. Certainly no German is more admired in the American capital than "Macky" Steinhoff.

His scarred face, far from being a handicap or an impediment to his work, was regarded by his late foes as a badge of courage—a symbol of Steinhoff's strength of character. Many American fighter aces are his friends. To a man, they respect and admire him.

In addition to contributing much material from his personal experience to this book, as well as many suggestions, General Steinhoff offers the following thumbnail sketch of the Second World War in the air, written by himself:

<h1 style="text-align:center">They Had Forgotten the Roof
by
Lieutenant General Johannes Steinhoff</h1>

GERMAN AIR FORCE

"The fifteenth of September 1940 was the day of our Victory."

These words of Churchill, spoken after the breakdown of Germany, might be hard to understand at the first appraisal by many people, but for us fliers who had a part on that important fifteenth of September it contains a great truth.

Throughout one long, hot summer during the so-called "Battle of Britain" we flew over the island and in the fight for air superiority had used up the best part of our fighters, and even more so our bombers.

STEINHOFF PORTRAIT: This oil painting was made in the Caucasus in 1942 during Johannes "Macky" Steinhoff's service with JG-52. (*Steinhoff Collection*)

FROM BIPLANE TO AEROSPACE: The U.S.A. had to make a near-quantum jump from the biplanes to aerospace in the same period as the Luftwaffe. In 1932 the US Army Air Corps front line fighters included the Boeing P-12 as shown in this photo. (*Credit: USAAC*)

CURTIS P-36: In 1938, the U. S. Army Air Corps had adopted the Curtis P-36 as its first line fighter. It was to prove no match for the German Messerschmitt Me-109, often designated Bf-109. (*U. S. Army Air Corps*)

BELL P-39 *AIRACOBRA*: In 1940, the Bell P-39 fighter appeared in the American USAAC inventory. Powered by an Allison V-1710 engine mounted behind the pilot, the aircraft proved marginally satisfactory. Many of them were given to the Soviets in the Lend-Lease program and the Russian "Red Guards" flew them with some success. (*U. S. Army Air Corps*)

For a month it seemed as though our objective, air superiority, had been reached. We flew with the assurance of owning the airspace from Calais to London. But this enormous exertion led to the almost complete expenditure of our physical and moral reserves. The fact remains that by the end of July the English fighter force was sharply reduced.

But then, the situation changed. Literally out of the blue sky came the surprise, and we found ourselves saying, "They are here again!" They hadn't slept on that island. No, exactly the opposite.

On the fifteenth of September we escorted a bomber formation to an attack on the southern railroad terminals of London. At the same time, for demonstration purposes, everything that we had in the way of bombers and fighters was thrown into the air. Then our formation, after assembling, began the flight to England. At that time we had no idea that three years later the "other side" would show us the practical application of the theories of the great air tactician Douhet—pioneer of air power. General Douhet's demand for a "strong formation of flying fortresses" was demonstrated for us by the Allies, with terrible consequences for Germany.

While flying over the Straits of Dover we already saw an unusually large number of Spitfires (the best English fighter) high above us. They were shadowing us at what was for us an unreachable height. The sky was streaked with a great number of white contrails. Suddenly we understood! The English had started their counterattack. When we reached our target, we knew it would all go wrong, for the number of our "silent companions" became uncontrollably large.

On the way back we had to leave the bombers behind. We did it with the feeling that everything would have to take its course now. The fighters' fuel was almost used up. For an hour we had flown without orientation and there was the danger that we, the entire fighter force, would not reach the French coast. We might run out of fuel and crash in the Channel.

On the evening of that day, the English radio reported the downing of ninety-nine German bombers. That was the revenge they took for the defeat they suffered in the air battle over the German "Bucht" in December 1939.[3] This crushing result of irresponsible conduct of an aerial war had a devastating effect on us pilots. But it is doubtful if it had the same effect on Hitler and Goering. The fifteenth of September should have caused Hitler to begin planning defensively, at least in the air.

The English had ingeniously found a way to defend their island. Every pilot, except a small group of night flyers and bomber pilots who were the nucleus of the coming night bomber fleet, was retrained as a fighter pilot. It made no difference if he was a liaison plane pilot, a bomber or fighter-bomber pilot, he was retrained. Industry was instructed to concentrate on fighters. And in this way it was possible to

[3] As Captain Steinhoff, the author of "They Had Forgotten the Roof" took part in this battle as squadron leader of an Me-109 squadron.

seal the gap—and more! In one stroke, the lost air superiority was regained, and henceforth we did not own the airspace from Calais to London.

The Decline of the Fighters

Like a red thread, a series of bad decisions and compromises weaves its way through every action in the planning and production of the German aircraft industry. The leaders would not admit that "the strongest air force in the world," after such an auspicious beginning, had now lost the lead. The subsequent mass victories on the Russian Front contributed to the delusions of the leaders, as it did to the units active there with such success. Hitler seemed determined to remain oblivious to the air struggle on the Channel coast, where the three and then two wings left there were fighting a hard and eventually hopeless battle.

Then it seemed for a time as if Hitler had seen the need for planning new fighter wings. It gave us renewed hope at the front. But if fighter production was given top industrial priority today, then it was usual that tomorrow this program would be cut or changed. Not only we fliers at the front, but also the economic planners could not understand this catastrophic lack of planning and foresight. Eventually they just resigned themselves and carried out orders. Often on their own initiative, they tried to prevent the worst.

Then came the inevitable. It happened sooner than expected, and was disastrously underestimated. The first formation of four-engined American bombers flew over the Channel coast—an ominous development which Goering made into a bagatelle! The advent of the four-engined "heavies" hit the German fighters a devastating blow, and unsettled the fighter leaders.

The time of mass attacks and saturation bombings began. This decisive weapon within the space of a year reduced us fighters to the role of a fire department in perpetual action from one call to the next. Ultimately the big bombers raced through all Europe, including Hitler's fortress, to the total exhaustion of men and machines.

Churchill said in 1944: "Hitler did make Europe into a fortress, but he forgot the roof."

In the spring of 1943 a rumor ran like wildfire through the front. Industry was reported to have developed an all-new aircraft. This machine did not propel itself with the old method of piston engine driving a propeller, but used the air compressed by turbines to fly. It had reached speeds never previously attained.

The rumor proved to be the truth. The chief pilot of the Messerschmitt works had made the first flights in this machine, and soon afterward the General of the Fighter Arm, Galland, tried it and enthusiastically talked of the fighter of the future. Endless technical problems had to be solved before production could commence and the machine find its way to combat. But before this stage could begin, the means for further production had to be authorized. And that needed the approval

REPUBLIC P-47 *THUNDERBOLT:* U. S. Army Air Corps pilots called it the "JUG." This is a P-47C model and was the first series of the *Thunderbolt* to go into combat over Europe. *(Republic Aviation Corp.)*

FORK-TAILED DEVIL . . . THE P-38 *LIGHTNING:* America may have "forgotten the roof" but it recovered quickly. The Lockheed P-38 was the first fighter with the range to escort the four-engined bombers from bases in England to targets deep in Europe. This cut bomber losses to enemy fighters by 75 percent. *(Lockheed Aircraft Corp.)*

of Hitler!

Neither the builder, Professor Messerschmitt, nor the leaders of the Luftwaffe had for even one second thought that this new aircraft would be anything but a fighter plane. The later misuse of this Me-262 type, which we knew for short as "Turbo," proved incredible. It was used for everything *except* as a fighter. The situation demonstrated how little Hitler and Goering understood the possibilities. It also shows how, in the last three years of the war, with Hitler's blind hitting-out, even the best thoughts and ideas had to be lost.

In the autumn of 1943, at the air base at Insterburg in East Prussia there was one of those displays of new weapons so beloved by Army and industry notables. Among the new weapons was the Me-262. After an impressive flying display, we fliers, defense-production leaders, members of the General Staff, escort officers, and engineers thoughtfully admired the machine and waited for the all-highest verdict.

After Hitler asked Messerschmitt about the flying performance, range, and fuel consumption, he further inquired if the aircraft could carry bombs. When this was reluctantly admitted, Hitler turned to the Luftwaffe leaders with a dramatic gesture.

"This is the bomber with which I will fight off the invasion—this is my revenge bomber. Of course, none of you thought of that."

With these words all Galland's hopes were destroyed. Hitler's edict meant forgetting the idea that fighters could once again play the role of strong defenders. The bomber pilots were now in the foreground, as were the bombers in 1940, except that now all possibility of their conducting effective attacks against England had vanished. The Luftwaffe went into a deep sleep after the end of the Battle of Britain—a sleep out of which it was now cruelly awakened.

The Great Tug O' War

Thus the bomber wings sat at home and waited for the birth of the new bomber Hitler had promised them. But the bomber did not come.

After the Insterburg display a tug o' war began over the Me-262 which was disgraceful not only for the leaders, but also for the combat pilots. Bitter fights and rancor existed between bomber pilots and fighter pilots to get the awaited, longed-for new type. In the meantime, Galland, as Udet before him, tirelessly tried to convince Goering that the morale of the fighter pilots alone was not enough in the aerial battle to stop the attacks of the four-engined heavy bombers. He asked for a better aircraft—demanded the "Turbo."

Squadron of Experts

In the last months of the war our dream of forming a team of fighter aces was realized. There is no connection now to HQ. Berlin has enough to do with itself and so has Goering. Word gets around that we need "great guns." Those who do not volunteer we retrieve from rest homes and hospitals, where most of the people wait for the war's end. "Galland" and the miracle word "Turbo" galvanize every pilot. Once again air superiority—The Great Aviation—will be experienced.

There are no dreams of great victory or turning the tide, as some fools may believe, but it is an opportunity to show once more what flying experience and technical superiority are able to do. This prospect lures even men who, from the flight surgeon's standpoint, are everything else but able to fly.

Those officers who came to visit us during those last days at Riem, whether they came from HQ or elsewhere, were dazzled by the array of high war decorations accumulated in one spot. The Knight's Cross was almost our squadron badge. The unique composition of the outfit also evoked surprise:

One General (a General as a squadron leader is certainly unique)
Two Colonels
One Lieutenant Colonel
Three Majors
Two Captains
Eight Lieutenants

Combined with a similar number of noncommissioned officers, these were our pilots.

There was Colonel Guenther Luetzow, exiled until now from Germany because of his courageous opposition to Goering. Major Heinz Baer came to us, a brilliant sharpshooter and outstanding fighter. And Gerd Barkhorn, who had 301 kills to his account on the Eastern Front. With Barkhorn came Hohagen, Schnell, and Krupinski, whom we enticed to come from the hospitals. All were in the war from

GÜNTHER LÜTZOW—COURAGEOUS LEADER: "Franzl" Lützow stood eyeball-to-eyeball and argued with Reichsmarschall Göring when the latter accused the fighter pilots of cowardice when they were not able to wrest air superiority from the Western Allies. Lützow was the spokesman in the "Revolt of the Kommodores." Lützow, an ace with 5 victories in Spain and a total of 108 kills, lost his life in an Me-262 jet April 24th, 1945. (*Obermaier Collection*)

the first day. All were at least once wounded, some many times. All had high decorations.

Each one of them wanted to know once more the feel of air superiority after years of flying under oppressing circumstances. They wanted this experience even if they had to pay for it with their lives. Such was the spirit of the "Squadron of Experts."

With nervous activity, preparations go forward for the mission. Our actions are ruled by urgency. The Americans are fighting near Crailsheim, but there is no clear battle line. Everything is in flux.

The evening after arrival in Riem we discussed the mission against the four-engined bomber stream. The jet fighters which remain in Brandenburg have already had this experience. Under the leadership of Weissenberger this squadron was successful—indicating the damage that could be done with a planned mission at the right time.

However, Galland said: "Let the Mustangs and Thunderbolts go by, don't tangle with them even if they are right in front of your gunsight. I want to know what chance we have against the Flying Fortress, which brings death to thousands of helpless people on the ground."

The next morning from the ten available jets, three are ready for operations. With those three, I am supposed to fly the first mission. With me goes Faehrmann, my wingman for two years, a very elegant, natural pilot who is able to follow instinctively all my decisions. Also with me is a third man, Krupinski, who has been wounded five times and burnt severely. With enviable nonchalance he climbs again and again into the cockpit.

"Lightnings coming across the Alps," blares the radio.

Mustang invasion starts and Operations reports, "Many Mustangs are coming from the west."

Galland: "This looks like a fighter invasion, but I think the four-engined bombers will follow."

Nuremberg reports: "Bombs dropped by two-engined airplanes. Keep your nerve, they are coming for certain."

By noon the situation is clear: "Long-range bomber formation near Frankfurt flying east."

Now they are there. An hour later Galland orders Steinhoff: "Take off!"

The first formation is reported directly north of Munich and between Munich and the Danube. Then Faehrmann reports a large formation at nine o'clock. There the stream straggles between six and eight thousand meters. While we are flying over the first bombers we cannot see the end of the formation. At the tip, the Liberators are flying, a bomber of older type somewhat more vulnerable than the Forts and therefore flying ahead of the formation. Then come the B-17s, for which we have some respect from experience.

At the end of the formation I make a large, wide turn which carries me up to nine thousand meters altitude and brings me to the head of the bomber formation. I call "get ready," then we dive for the attack on the last small formation. The airspeed indicator shows 900 km per hour when I recognize the little dots ahead of me moving at an incredible speed.

A short burst from my four cannons, fired at the left airplane, and then I have to jerk my stick back to avoid a collision. Looking back, I see black smoke and flames leaping out of the bomber's engines.

At the same time, the airplane in the center is burning. That's the one Faehrmann attacked. Approach and kill! It is all over in seconds. Krupinski, our third man, works alone and in his own particular way. He picks a Boeing. Mustangs and Thunderbolts which are above the formation in the correct attack position prepare to dive on us from all directions. It is a grotesque picture. They look like balloons standing still in the air, since we have a speed margin of at least 400–500 km per hour. Literally we ride through the bombers. Still I do not know how many kills we had—the ride was too fast. Then my guns jam while Faehrmann kills another bomber. While in a chandelle he radios, "My right engine is dead."

Faehrmann slows down more and more and there is a new emergency call: "My left engine is also dying." With that, he is chased by a lot of Thunderbolts. When I turn around to help him, my right turbine stops. Now I have to think of myself, and I take off heading for Munich. I report to Operations on the way, telling them of my condition. Back comes the ominous reply: "If possible, do not land in Riem. The field is under surveillance by Mustangs."

I still have enough fuel, and therefore I would like to convince myself if the situation is really precarious. Then I see the polished wings of four Mustangs as they fly across the field in absolutely perfect formation.

I cannot miss this chance, even with one engine dead. None of the Mustang pilots sees me coming. Only one of my 30mm cannons is operational, but it goes through the wing of the Mustang like a buzz saw. The other three Mustangs drop their tanks and disappear.

After I land, Faehrmann calls the base and reports that he parachuted into the Danube. Krupinski is already home and says jauntily, "That was a lot of fun. Why don't we refuel and go again? We could still catch them."

The Proof

During the middle of April we finally receive additional weapons for our jets. This looks promising. Under each of the wings, twenty-four rockets can be mounted. The trajectory of these rockets is practically straight up to a distance of twelve hundred meters, and during this distance their velocity rises to 15×30 meters. According to our estimates one could not miss if all rockets were fired simultaneously into a bomber formation.

Only a few aircraft can be fitted with this equipment. The rockets are manufactured in northern Germany while the factory for the launchers is in Czechoslovakia. There is no possibility of proper logistic support. During the night a transport plane brings ammunition from the Baltic coast, but there is only one such flight before the airfield in the north is in enemy hands.

During the first trial to fire the rockets into a close formation, Galland demonstrates that at Germany's dying gasp we finally have the means to destroy the bomber formations, which up to this point seemed to be untouchable.

The rockets roar among the bombers like a shotgun into a flock of ducks. Two of the bombers move close to each other and then fuselage hits fuselage. Both dive together into the ground. The bomber formation is in a state of confusion and as two more rockets burst two other Flying Fortresses are destroyed.

We work day and night to patch up our wounded jets. We also receive hits, but we don't lose one pilot. We do not have spare parts, and during the night the familiar drone of the well-feared Mosquitos can be heard circling our airfield.

We fight to see who will be permitted to fly next. The few airplanes we have are not able to stand the continuous use, and if we have six jets flying we are very proud. Near Nuremberg, near Augsberg, above the Danube and the Alps we shoot the Flying Fortresses from the sky. Maybe there are only two or three during each mission, but we know before we take off that we will not return without a kill.

The supply problem is suddenly solved. In mid-April we receive jets from all quarters as presents. The reconnaissance squadrons, bomber squadrons, and the fighter-bombers park their airplanes next to ours. "Here's a present for you," they say, "you can use it."

If only the Americans did not make our lives so miserable. It is a perpetual race between the bomb shelter and the airplane. The harassment is nerve-wracking. You always hope you will have sufficient time for an undetected takeoff. You are not safe until the airspeed indicator shows 500 km per hour.

Four Me-262s land. They are special machines, fitted with a 5cm cannon. This is one of Hitler's ideas. There were many fights regarding the merits of this cannon and its role in air defense, but we prove in the meantime that this weapon's time has passed.

Soon we have seventy jets on our airfield. Only a month ago we had to beg for one on our knees. We reflect bitterly on these events.

Crash

On 18 April 1945 we are ready to take off with six jets. The weather is ideal. For an hour we sit in our cockpits and cannot decide which of the many incoming formations we should attack. Finally Galland loses patience. He is the leader of our little formation. We start our engines and in a tremendous dust cloud I see the airplanes disappear which take off ahead of me.

I give full power and start my takeoff roll. The heavy jet rolls along the grass with painful slowness. All my tanks are full, and as an additional load under my wings are forty-eight rockets. Yesterday's air raid pocked the field, and as I pass over some of the scarcely filled craters my speed is reduced. In the final third of my takeoff run I reach nearly 200 km per hour when suddenly my left wing drops. The airplane starts to yaw. This will end in a crash.

I lose my left gear. I lose direction. My speed doesn't increase and is not enough to get airborne. The road at the end of the airfield looms closer. I know now that a crash cannot be avoided due to the heavy load. In this doomed airplane I am an impotent prisoner. There is the road. The airplane runs into the incline and is propelled fifty meters into the air, then it lands on a bare field on the other side of the street with a thunderous crash.

Now I am sitting amid leaping flames. These flames will leave marks on me forever. To this day, I can still hear the consuming roar of the fire. I know only one thing, as I see everything through red glasses, wedged as I am in the jet I wanted so much: "Get out!" "Get out!" I don't know how I got out, but I ran away from the airplane blindly, knowing that any moment the ammunition and the rockets would explode. In unbearable agony from burns, the last thing I knew was the explosion.

In the hospital at Tegernsee the last phase of the war passed in a haze for me. On 26 April 1945 a new patient is carried into my room— Galland. A shell fragment went through his knee. For him, too, the war is over.

The end comes to the "Squadron of Experts" in Riem like a tornado. The Americans came to Munich, so another retreat is made, this time the seventy jets were flown to Salzburg. There on 3 May 1945 they were blown up. The first American tanks rolled onto the airfield as one jet after another burst into flames.

Thus ended the greatest drama of Steinhoff's combat career. He flew 993 combat missions between 1939 and 1945. He was shot down twelve times, enough to create at least two Allied aces. He crash-landed all twelve times and never bailed out once. He commanded everything from a fighter wing down to the one jet fighter to which Goering "appointed" him in an effort to belittle him.

After his postwar service in Washington, he became Chief of Staff of

SOME STORY!: Josef "Pips" Priller, left, makes a point. The varied reactions are from American Arthur Thorsen, Germans Edu Neumann, Werner Panitzki and American Jim Brooks. (*USAF-Giuliano*)

the NATO Air Force in Central Europe, with his headquarters in Paris. In 1966, during the controversy in the German Air Force which led to the resignation of General Panitzki as Inspector, Steinhoff was offered the top job. After a ten-day period in which he completely considered the appointment, which has politico-economic as well as military aspects, he agreed to take the job.

When he took up his new appointment in August 1966, he brought the German Air Force full circle. The old Luftwaffe, bomber and dive-bomber oriented from its inception, eventually was forced to become fighter-oriented—but not until it was too late. Neither Josef Kammhuber, the first Inspector of the new German Air Force, nor General Panitzki, his successor, was a fighter pilot. Steinhoff is a fighter pilot, but with a breadth of vision not usually found among fighter pilots.

For the first time since its inception the German Air Force is under the guidance of a man who helped pioneer the jet fighter, as well as make an outstanding record as a commander and combat pilot. Germany today has few men at its disposal of Steinhoff's ability and brilliance. You cannot find an old fighter pilot in Germany or an American friend of Steinhoff's who doesn't wish him well. You also cannot find one who would like his job.[4]

He is one of America's warmest friends and admirers. Once he said

---

[4] Which brings to mind the comment of boxer Joe Louis, "Everybody wants to go to heaven but nobody wants to die."

after speaking on his war experiences to a group of American aces in Washington:

"It is a strange world after all, where it is possible for a man who fought for years against you to be invited here to talk about his experiences. If someone had told me twenty years ago that this would happen today, I would have considered him insane.

"I have always been impressed by the tolerance, humanity, and openmindedness that is so characteristic of this great nation, America. We Germans owe it primarily to the United States that we were received again as equals in the community of free nations."

The airmen of the Allied nations had no worthier opponent than "Macky" Steinhoff in war, and in peace it is hard to find a firmer friend.

5

Marseille – "Star of Africa"

"Real combat in the air, such as journalists and romancers
have described, should be considered a myth.
The duty of aviation is to see and not to fight."
THE GERMAN STAFF,
October 1914

IF Hans-Joachim Marseille had lived on the earth before the advent
of gunpowder, it is certain he would have found that romantic era of
knights, fair ladies, and chivalrous fighting a comfortable environment
for his personality. Instead, he was thrust into a fast-moving, highly
technical world war and made a part of a tightly disciplined fighting

MARSEILLE HERO IN THE SUN, 1942:
Despite a shaky start as a fighter pilot in
the Battle of Britain, Hans-Joachim
Marseille went on to become one of Germany's greatest heroes. From a flippant,
irresponsible and mediocre fighter pilot,
he turned into a serious and deadly
marksman and consummately skillful
aerial warrior. Many of his contemporaries believe him to have been the
Luftwaffe's best aerial marksman.
(Obemaier Collection)

force that cramped his romantic spirit. In spite of these modern strictures, Marseille earned his place among the immortal knights of the air.

As General Adolf Galland states in *The First and the Last*, his career was meteoric. Marseille enlisted in the Luftwaffe at eighteen and a half. By twenty-two he was dead, with a spectacular skein of achievements to his credit. In the final year of his life he not only won Germany's highest war decoration—the Diamonds to his Knight's Cross—but also became one of his country's eternal heroes. The passage of over a quarter century since his death has subtracted nothing from the fame and glory that he won in North Africa. On the contrary, he is more famous than ever.

His historical status has become such that no book dealing with German aces of the Second World War can omit him and be complete. Twenty-eight other German aces brought down more Allied aircraft than Marseille, yet only Galland and Moelders enjoy wider fame. Everywhere aerial combat buffs meet and talk, the name Marseille electrifies the conversation. What and where are the sources of the Marseille magic?

His rise to glory as a soldier forms part of a fascinating character study, for although born in Berlin in 1919 to a military family, he had a built-in aversion to military ideals. Raised amid Army traditions, he developed into the most easy-going and informal of military officers.

His father was an Army officer, and his parents were legally separated most of his life. This may help explain part of Marseille's attitude to discipline. He was probably the most unmilitary of all Germany's top aces. But his informal attitudes are justified by his formal achievements.

A youthful passion for flying led him to enlist in the Luftwaffe at eighteen and a half. He thus had the benefit of a peacetime training, complete and unhurried. He seems to have accepted military life as the necessary and inseparable handmaiden of flying. He endured one in order to enjoy the other. During his training, he distinguished himself only by disciplinary infractions. As a cadet pilot, Master Sergeant Marseille was sent to help conquer the RAF in the Battle of Britain.

His record in combat in 1940, when he was under Steinhoff's command, did not presage a career of distinction as a fighter. Although he downed at least seven British aircraft, he had witnesses for only three of these kills. This illustrates his "lone wolf" tendency in those days. He had a penchant for hunting alone and he was a perpetual violator of flying discipline. He was forced to bail out six times, producing a ratio of victories to losses hardly destined to turn the tide of the air war.

At the end of his first year in the Luftwaffe, his conduct record was littered with entries describing his unmilitary ways and general recalcitrance. If Marseille had been alive in the past decade, he would have been termed a "beatnik" by his contemporaries. It so happened that he came along a little before that era, but he showed many of its characteristics.

THE "STAR" STRAPS HIMSELF IN: Captain Hans-Joachim Marseille straps himself into his Me-109 in North Africa before taking off on a sweep above the Afrika Korps. With 158 victories against the Western Allies, Marseille wrote a brilliant but brief chapter in aerial history. He was killed in a crash at the age of 22, but already the wearer of Germany's highest decoration — the Diamonds to his Knight's Cross. *(Edu Neumann Collection)*

He wore his hair long. His way was the way of the Bohemian. His lean, handsomely chiseled features made him a favorite with the girls. Since Marseille liked female company, during this period he was more a lover than a fighter. Indeed, as Steinhoff has already recounted, his romantic exertions were such as to necessitate his being taken off operations on occasions, until he recovered.

In January 1941 he was sent to join JG-27 at Döberitz near Berlin. Shortly afterward, the wing was assigned to North Africa, with one Group diverted to participate in the German air assault on Yugoslavia. Complaints of the German pilots that they were not seeing enough action were soon heard no more.

Reaching Africa in the spring of 1941, JG-27's role was to provide air support for the *Afrika Korps*, soon to make an immortal record under the command of Field Marshal Erwin Rommel, the "Desert Fox." As history now reveals, only the illustrious Rommel, Hitler's hand-picked "Hero in the Sun," outshone Marseille among the German soldiers of the African campaigns.

As the Rommel campaigns seesawed across the Western Desert, Marseille's name became increasingly featured in German news releases. Dr. Goebbels' Propaganda Ministry in Berlin saw to it that Marseille's feats were given adequate publicity—and for good reason. Rommel's fortunes ebbed and flowed. He was at the mercy of his supply lines. With inferior force but surpassing guile he outmaneuvered and frequently defeated the more stolid British. But because Rommel's forces were smaller than the enemy, he had almost as many reverses as triumphs.

Regardless of the fortunes of the *Afrika Korps* struggling on the desert below him, for Marseille it was always victory. Triumph followed triumph. Kill followed kill. Marseille was accentuating the positive and Goebbels' organization knew the value of an upbeat story.

The German newspapers called him "African Eagle" and "Star of the Desert." Fan mail arrived by sack and bundle from breathless German females, asking for everything from a lock of Marseille's hair to more tangible gestures of his interest. These fan letters generated much merriment among the pilots of Marseille's squadron.

Mussolini's Italy conferred on the slender-faced Berliner its Gold Medal for Bravery. This decoration was awarded only twice to Germans in the Second World War. The other German recipient was also a fighter pilot, Captain (later Major) Joachim Muencheberg, *Kommodore* of JG-77 and a protégé of Galland. Even Rommel had to be content with the inferior silver version of this decoration, as did his courageous subordinate in the *Afrika Korps*, General Nehring.

Like numerous other leading fighter aces of all nations, Marseille's real rise to fame commenced when his shooting eye came in during his early days in Africa. Numerous aces frankly admit today that at a certain moment, which most of them can pinpoint quite accurately, their aerial marksmanship made a sudden and dramatic improvement. Frequently this point came only after a long period of mediocre and frustrating performance.

THREE AGAINST BRITAIN: Adolf Galland, center, as Kommodore of JG-26, the famous "Yellow Nose Boys," links arms with two of his stellar fighter pilots, Gerhard Schöpfel left, and Joachim Müncheberg. Schöpfel and Galland survived the war, but Müncheberg died in Tunisian air combat in March 1943. Müncheberg and Marseille were the only two German recipients in WWII of the Italian Gold Medal for Bravery. *(Credit: Haussman)*

When Marseille got his shooting eye, it proved to be one of the most remarkable in the history of aerial combat. Uncanny in its gift, deadly in its application, it lifted Marseille to the level of the unforgettable.

He was in effect a human computer. He was able in the twinkling of eye, and while moving in three dimensions, to determine the exact moment at which to fire and the precise point in the heavens at which to aim, to make a lethal rendezvous between his bullets and the enemy plane, also moving in three dimensions. No one who saw him shoot in the air will ever forget his deadly precision.

Marseille was much more, however, than just a superlative marksman. Since his shaky beginning as a cadet pilot, he had developed an aerobatic ability so pronounced that he could thrill even veteran German aces with his flying. In this respect, he resembled Nishizawa, "The Devil," Japan's leading ace of the Second World War. "The Devil" could enthrall even the hardened aces of the famed Lae Wing in New Guinea with his aerobatics.

Marseille's portfolio of talents also included eagle eyesight, fearlessness, and an aggressive spirit in the air that frequently unnerved his foes. To speak of an "aggressive spirit" may seem like an abstraction. Combat pilots know otherwise.

For the nonflying layman, an aggressive spirit in the air may be accurately equated with the sometimes frightening determination and ruthlessness of the "road hog"—the kind of driver who forces his way through traffic, imposing his will on others by the determined and aggressive way he drives his car. Both aggressiveness and timidity stand out far more sharply in the air than they do in traffic, but the analogy is an accurate one.

"YOU'LL NEVER FLY AGAIN": Doctors told third-ranking Guenther Rall in 1941, after he broke his back in a crash, that he would never fly again. The indomitable Rall made it back to combat, returned to the scoring race, and ended the war with 275 victories as the third-ranking fighter pilot of all time. He flew on both fronts, and was on occasion Erich Hartmann's C.O. (*Rall Collection*)

In combat, it was as though the aiming and the firing of Marseille's guns were under the control of a supernatural force. The precision with which he sent shells and bullets smashing into his target from almost incredible angles, was only exceeded by the damage his pinpoint hits inflicted. Those who flew with him, and the armorers who serviced his aircraft in North Africa, state that he often landed with less than half his ammunition expended. And this from missions on which he had scored as many as six kills!

For the skeptics, there is the experience of Major Guenther Rall (now Lt. General Rall) on which to draw. With 275 kills in the Second World War, Rall is the third-ranking ace of Germany and the world. During the war, he was for a period on Galland's staff, when the exhaustive German pilot combat reports were being evaluated. He has this to say:

"The wartime combat reports of the Luftwaffe fighter pilot were highly detailed. Every evening you had this business to go through. Witness, air witness, ground witness, your account of the combat, the type of enemy aircraft, the kind of ammunition you fired, the armament of your aircraft, and how many rounds of ammunition. These reports were a nuisance to us, but when I was on the staff of Galland I saw how valuable they could sometimes be.

"We found that Marseille needed an average of only fifteen bullets per kill—which is tremendous. No other fighter remotely approached him in this respect. Marseille was the real type—an excellent pilot and a brilliant marksman. I think he was the best shot in the Luftwaffe."

In tackling British formations above the desert, Marseille was completely fearless. His technique was to hurl himself on the enemy so that the fury of his assault would cause confusion and uncertainty among the British pilots. Separating an obviously shaken pilot from the enemy formation, Marseille would shoot him down with one of his short, deadly bursts, then hurl himself again on the enemy. His long-time wingman, Reiner Poettgen, has recounted how difficult it was to keep up with the mercurial Berliner.

Properly confirming and position-fixing the ace's multiple kills was a taxing task for any wingman. To this burden was added the back-breaking aerobatics of Marseille and the nerve-wracking responsibility of somehow keeping the ace's tail clear of enemy fighters. He was a hard man to fly with.

In his combat tactics, Marseille frequently violated one of the classic principles of aerial warfare—that combat must be carried on at full power. Poettgen, his wingman, and others who flew with the ace report that he would frequently throttle his Me-109 back almost to nothing, and even use his flaps to tighten his turns and thus find a firing position below his foe.[1] From there, he would squirt a short but lethal burst into

---

[1] It was a similar maneuver that cost the life of America's number two ace in combat during World War II. Major Thomas B. McGuire (38 victories), in an attempt to shoot a Japanese airplane, turned too tightly and his P-38 snapped into a spin at low altitude.

its belly. Then he would slam his throttle all the way open again and plunge after other enemy planes.

The role of the German fighters in North Africa was not easy. Month after month the murderous grind went on, with Allied air superiority continually mounting. Despite his passion for combat and the vitality of his extreme youth, Marseille began to show the strain of his grueling weeks in the air. His thin features became markedly thinner, and his whole expression tired and drawn as continual combat took its toll.

He was sustained to a high degree by his unorthodox, Bohemian attitudes to life—an outlook that his soaring status as hero did nothing to change. His prestigious new position did, however, allow him to indulge these tastes.

His quarters, save for the canvas tent walls, might have been lifted bodily out of Paris. Couches fashioned out of sandbags were draped with salvaged canvas. Supply crates and boxes served as tables and chairs. There was no formality. High-ranking German and Italian officers were his frequent guests, and found themselves cheek-by-jowl with Marseille's squadron mates. To have "visited with Marseille" became something of a status symbol among the Axis staffs.

The cafe atmosphere in Marseille's quarters was completed with the installation of a roughly made bar. Well stocked to the envy of all who visited, the bar was tended by Matthias, a Negro from the Transvaal. Thus, hard-core advocates of Hitler's racial theories visiting Marseille had to endure Matthias's color in order to qualify for the fabulous Marseille hospitality.

In 1942 Marseille had a distinguished visitor from Germany, the General of the Fighters, Adolf Galland, who recalls the occasion thus:

THREE ACES:James L. Brooks of Los Angeles, 13-victory ace with the 15th Air Force in WWII, left, and Eugene A. Valencia, 23-victory U.S. Navy ace, right, chat with Eduard Neumann on 11 May 1961 in Augsburg, Germany. Neumann was wartime Kommodore of JG-27 in Africa and scored 13 aerial victories. (*USAF-Giuliano*)

"Shortly after I became General of the Fighters I made a visit to JG-27 in North Africa, commanded by Eduard Neumann. Marseille was one of his squadron commanders.

FRONT LINE ENTERTAINMENT 1942: Pilots and other personnel of JG-27 relax from the nearby desert war while entertained by an Italian conjurer. Hans-Joachim Marseille appears in the front center, with fellow ace Werner Schröer on his left. Hard-pressed flyers of JG-27 got little relaxation in the see-saw desert war against the heavy numerical superiority of the RAF and later, the USAAF. Arrows point to Marseille on left, Werner Schröer on right. *(Schröer Collection.)*

"The airstrip was located on top of a hill and the squadron was nestled in a small valley not far away. As I approached Marseille's bivouacked squadron in a jeep with Neumann, we began to see small signboards, nailed on trees and hung on bushes, which pointed the way to 'The World's Best Fighter Squadron.' They were all humorous or semi-humorous, but they indicated the high morale of Marseille's unit.

"He greeted me with grace and enthusiasm, and it was not long before I felt the full impact of his charm and recognized his natural bent for leadership. We talked far into the night. I told him that I needed to perform a vital natural function before I could have a nightcap and go to sleep.

"Marseille immediately produced a small spade and said: 'Proceed sixty paces straight away from the tent, then turn right twenty paces, and use the spade, sir.' I duly followed his instructions.

"In the morning upon awakening, I stepped out of my tent to use the spade again. I was flabbergasted to find signs pointing the way now. One final sign had a huge, downward-pointing arrow and said: 'At This Spot, on 22 September 1942, the General of the Fighter Arm Answered Nature's Call.'"

Marseille was the complete reverse of the classical German military hero. He was a good comrade aloft and on the ground gay and romantic. Even when overhung by the portent of his own doom he was yet eager to live life to the full, his gaiety undiminished. In the whole North African campaign there was nobody quite like him in the Axis forces.

His career reached its zenith on 1 September 1942, during the heavy air activity attending the Battle of Alam El Halfa—sometimes called the "Stalingrad of the Desert." It was a cruel stroke of fate for the Marseille family that Hans-Joachim's father, an infantry General, was killed at Stalingrad even as his hero-son added new laurels to the family's military tradition.

The story of Marseille's most remarkable day in combat is best told by quoting a contemporary German document. The book *Die Wehrmacht (The Armed Forces)* was published by the German High Command in 1942. This account has a sense of immediacy to it, and faithfully records some of the feeling of those days on the German side:

MARSEILLE IN NORTH AFRICA: A skinny, fine-drawn Hans-Joachim Marseille clowns in this rare photo of JG-27 pilots in North Africa, resting himself on fellow ace Werner Schröer. Schröer ended the war with 114 kills and is today a Messerschmitt executive in Germany. *(Schröer Collection)*

A Single Man Fights a Battle
The Biggest Day in the Life of Captain Marseille

The accomplishments of the Luftwaffe in the North African campaign will require a special page of glory when the history of this war is written someday. They are equal in greatness to the deeds of the men fighting on the ground. But without the Luftwaffe—the fighter pilots, bomber pilots, local and long-range reconnaissance pilots, the transport flyers— much if not all that was achieved by Rommel's men and the soldiers of Italy would have been unthinkable.

We must consider that they found themselves in a very different land and in an unaccustomed climate. One must add the indirect support for the Axis soldiers fighting in the desert sand and rocks of Libya—that is, the fight against the Mediterranean convoys which were to supply the enemy with ammunition, material, and provisions; or the neutralization of Malta, the island aircraft base from which tactical aircraft threatened to disrupt the German and Italian supply system.

Below, the war correspondent First Lieutenant Fritz Dettman tells us about one of them, the most successful one, Captain Hans-Joachim Marseille, squadron commander in the fighter wing. He gave his life for Germany after 158 aerial victories. Only a single day in the life of this flyer will be described: 1 September 1942, the day on which Marseille succeeded in shooting down seventeen enemy aircraft by himself, an achievement unparalleled in the short history of aerial war, and one that probably will not be equaled for some time.

The following pages comment appreciatively on this feat, and it

LUFTWAFFE'S DEADLIEST MARKSMAN: Captain Hans-Joachim Marseille was considered by virtually all the top aces of the Luftwaffe to be Germany's most deadly aerial marksman. Statistical analysis of ammunition expended for kills credited put Marseille well ahead of his closest rivals. He was killed in a crash while returning from a combat mission near El Alamein in North Africa in 1942. *(Boehm Collection)*

should be said that even though no one else has equaled this achievement, it is typical of the spirit prevailing in the Luftwaffe. The Luftwaffe has to fight under conditions which, like those in North Africa, make great demands on each individual.

Before us lies an official document. It provides a silent testimony of the greatest fighter pilot feat of this war to date. The document tells in dispassionate terms of the action of a squadron on 1 September 1942, when twenty-two-year-old Hans-Joachim Marseille took off three times and destroyed seventeen British and American enemies, all of them fighter aircraft. We leaf through the document, and it takes us only a few minutes to feel the impact of the silent text. Here is the case of one man alone fighting a battle, a soldier in the sky above El Alamein who flew into the swarms of his enemies like a winged Mars.

When Captain Marseille, at the time still a First Lieutenant. drove out to the parked aircraft at 0730 on 1 September, there was nothing to indicate that this would be a special day. Marseille had been full of energy for days; the weather was as clear as ever this North African summer. By early morning, the sun shone with almost uncomfortable warmth, and only a light breeze blew in from the sea.

The squadron had orders to provide escort for a Stuka mission headed for a target south of Imayid. At 0750 the squadron had joined the Stuka unit not far from the field. The planes flew away eastward into the clear blue sky of the combat area.

Near the target, they climbed to thirty-five hundred meters when the Chief reported the approach of enemy fighters on the radio. He counted ten planes, tiny dots which were approaching rapidly. When they were close to the target the Stukas prepared to attack.

Marseille pulled up in a short right-hand curve. Then the others heard him say: "I'm attacking!" Three seconds later his wingman watched the squadron commander swing out of a left turn to get behind the tail-end Curtiss fighter of the formation that was now veering away. He fired from a distance of one hundred meters.

As if a fist had suddenly grabbed it and torn it from its rapid flight, the enemy plane tipped over on its left wing and plunged to the ground almost vertically, like a rock. It burst into flame on impact. The pilot had not been able to save himself. Marseille's wingman looked at the clock when the smoke mushroom rose from below. It was 0820. Then he checked the map section: 18 km SSE of El Imayid.

The wingman didn't have to look long for his Chief. Right after the first attack, Marseille had changed from the left turn from the Curtiss he shot down to the next one. Two kilometers farther east, a plane was plunging, leaving a black trail. It was 0830. The flames of the second crash fire flared up only a few hundred meters from the plane destroyed two minutes earlier. This time, too, the bullets scored a direct hit in the cockpit.

By now, the Stukas have dropped their bombs. The comrades have already turned away for home and are flying back at an altitude of about one hundred meters. The squadron, which had assembled in the meantime, plunged down in a steep dive. It is high time. An unnoticed Curtiss had turned north, and, flying low, was trying to get near the German dive bombers.

At 0833, as the enemy machine was getting ready to attack, it was the Captain's chance. Out of a sharp left turn, his burst of fire hit the target with millimeter precision. Only a hundred meters down, the earth's surface was suddenly illuminated by a giant flash and the fire consumed man and plane. This was 1 km SE of Imayid.

Just as the squadron wanted to turn away westward, the cry of "Spitfire!" blared over the radio. The other crews were already in front with the Stukas. Alone with his wingman, Marseille seemed vulnerable as the six enemy planes, close as a phalanx, came at him from six o'clock high. But Marseille knew the right moment to break. He held for that perfect moment. Head cocked backward to the left, he watched the leading enemy plane, which had separated from the rest, approach almost within firing range.

He could clearly see the muzzles of the cannon and machine guns. But as he said: "As long as I look right into the muzzles, nothing can happen to me. Only if he pulls lead am I in danger." Flames spurt from the muzzles and the fine, silky smoke trails lance downward, then float in the air. The Englishman, firing constantly, had approached to within 150 meters of the young Captain. At that moment, Marseille suddenly made a sharp left turn. The Spitfires soared away under Marseille and his wingman at tremendous speed. This was their chance.

The Germans could now turn the tables—taking advantage of the big radius of turn the British had to fly in order to get into attacking position again. Marseille figured correctly. He pulled to the right and within seconds was eighty meters behind the last Englishman, fired and hit him. The enemy plummeted to the ground, fluttering a trail of black smoke behind him. This time too the defeated pilot did not have time to remove his canopy and bail out.

It was 0839 and the wreckage of a crashed Spitfire was burning itself out 20 km ESE of El Imayid.

At 0914 Marseille's squadron landed. The flight mechanics and armorer approached and congratulated the Chief. Without any excitement though, because it was nothing unusual for Marseille to shoot down four adversaries on a mission. The armorer replaced the ammunition belts. The flight mechanics were already busy with the engine. Electricians and radio mechanics checked circuits. When the armorer refilled the belt, he found that the Chief had consumed twenty rounds of cannon shells and sixty rounds of machine gun ammunition. That too was nothing special. It was normal ammunition consumption for Marseille.

Alam El Halfa is neither a city nor a settlement. A dot in the desert thirty or forty kilometers southeast of the coast, it has a well and a few native huts battered by the winds. Here, hardly two hours later, Marseille was to experience his greatest triumph.

His squadron was again ordered to escort a Stuka strike in this area. At 1020 hours the Chief had taken off with only one flight. Just before the Stuka's objective, only eight to ten kilometers south of his position, Marseille suddenly caught sight of two British bomber formations— fifteen to eighteen aircraft in each—and two formations of escorting fighters each with twenty-five to thirty aircraft.

Numerical superiority of his foes never impressed Marseille. He had been familiar with British numerical superiority ever since he came to Africa. Marseille knew that it is not the number of aircraft that decides the outcome, but the better man. He waited now for a few moments, until he saw what he was anticipating.

A squadron of the British escort fighters with eight Curtiss P-36s[2] peeled off from their escort duties and went after the Stukas. Marseille and his wingman met them halfway. The British saw what was coming. They turned and formed a defensive circle. This tactical measure would normally suffice, but not against Marseille.

Adjusting his speed, he was suddenly sitting in the middle of the enemy merry-go-round and shot down a Curtiss from fifty meters, out of a sharp left turn. Half a minute later the second enemy dropped from almost the same maneuver. Abruptly the aircraft that had held together the defensive circle were dispersed. Their leader had lost his nerve.

The remaining British fighters split into two-ship elements and flew off to the northwest. Two minutes later, Marseille had again approached to within one hundred meters. A third plane plunged down. The other five Curtiss fighters turned east and drew close together again. Marseille raced after his foes.

When they took a northwesterly course toward the Mediterranean in a shallow dive from thirty-five hundred meters, there were only four left. Two minutes later, at 1101, the fifth P-36 went down. Direct hits by Marseille's guns exploded the British machine in mid-air. The sixth fighter went down at 1102 when the tenacious Marseille from a left-hand climbing turn shot down the remaining aircraft.

The combatants had meanwhile worked their way eastward. Marseille's two-ship formation was close together and climbing when more Curtiss fighters appeared below, flying east. They had not seen the Germans. Flying straight, Marseille plunged toward them like an arrow, taking them from the right rear. Under the impact of Marseille's guns, the fuselage of a Curtiss exploded.

Now the young Captain led his two-plane element north, to return to the field. Again, a Curtiss appeared a few hundred meters below them, flying eastward with a white trail of smoke. Marseille attacked immediately, firing from a distance of eighty meters, and saw the fuselage and tail assembly disintegrate. The fuselage spun downward and when he flew past, the victor could see the pilot dead in his seat.

Eight enemy aircraft had been downed by his fire. Marseille had been victorious over a whole squadron in an aerial battle of ten minutes. Not till we place the downing times next to each other do we get a real picture of this amazing achievement: 10:55, 10:56, 10:58, 10:59, 11:01, 11:02, 11:03, 11:05.

Half an hour later Marseille appeared in the squadron's operational HQ. Field Marshal Kesselring had come. Marseille reported the return of his squadron from its mission with twelve victories.

"And how many of these twelve did you get?" asked the Field Marshal.

[2] The aircraft referred to in this wartime article as P-36 fighters were probably P-40s.

"Twelve, sir!"

The Field Marshal shook hands with the young officer, took a chair and sat down without saying a word.

The day had now become hot and oppressive. Anyone else would have called it a day. Marseille too, perhaps, on some other day. But this day he felt full of energy—strong enough to go up again. He waited for the next mission in the bunker of his squadron. But at the 1358 takeoff he had to stay behind. His plane had a flat tire.

It was almost 1700 when he took off again with his squadron on his third mission. Once more the fighters would escort bombers, Ju-88s this time, to Imayid. What now happened was similar to the morning action.

A formation of fifteen Curtiss P-40s tried to attack the Ju-88s while the big bombers were diving on their target. Marseille cut into the British fighters with his squadron and dispersed the enemy formation. The aerial combat that followed lasted six minutes. In this time, at altitudes between fifteen hundred and one hundred meters Marseille shot down five British aircraft.

The first four went down at precise one-minute intervals between 1745 and 1750 hours. The fifth one was shot down at 1753. The victory sites were 7 km south, 8 km southeast, 6 km southeast, 9 km south-southeast, and 7 km south-southwest of Imayid.

With a total of seventeen victories in one day (sixteen were reported in the Wehrmacht report, because one downing was not confirmed until twelve hours later, through the statement of a witness) Captain Marseille had established something that is without comparison. A performance of singular greatness, a magnificent victory, it was enhanced by the squadron's lack of losses. In a day filled with fighting, they lost no men or aircraft.

⊗

Marseille's accomplishment was excelled by only one pilot. Major Emil Lang, flying on the Russian Front, is credited with eighteen confirmed victories in one day. Against the RAF, Marseille's feat is an all-time record.

This tremendous bag of British aircraft has been the subject since the war of much skeptical comment. In 1964 the authors exhaustively investigated the German records of the event, in Germany, as part of a long and comprehensive review of German aerial victory claims.

The record of the kills was accurately kept at the time, as indicated in the *Die Wehrmacht* account. The crediting of the kills was accurate and meticulous. Evidence of this kind should settle the question of Marseille's great day in favor of the amazing ace from Berlin.

After this blazing opening to September, the young German fighter made the final month of his life one of savage brilliancy. He added a further forty-four kills in the next four weeks, for a total of sixty-one kills in September 1942. His victory record in September is as follows:

Sept.	1	17 victories	Sept.	11	2
Sept.	2	5	Sept.	15	7
Sept.	3	6	Sept.	24	Promoted Captain
Sept.	5	4	Sept.	26	7
Sept.	6	4	Sept.	28	7
Sept.	7	2			61

Following his 125th kill, Marseille was awarded his Diamonds decoration. The jeweled award was to have been made to the special order of the Fuehrer. Hitler had decided to present it to Marseille personally, at a special investiture to be held later in the year. These plans were never realized due to the ace's death. His Diamonds were never conveyed to his family as far as the authors have been able to determine.

With these four fierce September weeks behind him, and the added distinction of being the youngest Captain in the Luftwaffe, Marseille clambered into his "Yellow 14" for a sweep over the Cairo area. The aircraft was an Me-109. The *Afrika Korps* had reached the end of its rope on the ground and was awaiting the inevitable Allied assault before El Alamein. JG-27 was trying to stay aggressive in the air.

Marseille's aircraft had been specially modified for extra performance, and with this edge in power the young ace was hopeful of even more victories. This time, no RAF fighters rose to the challenge. The thirtieth of September 1942 looked like a blank day for the aggressive young German Captain. A disappointed Marseille reluctantly turned around and began leading his flight back to base.

At 1135 Marseille's fellow pilots noticed a wisp of black smoke trail-

DESERT FIGHT LINE—JG-27: Lt. Franz Stigler's Me-109 stands ready on the flight line in Africa. Stigler, a 28 victory ace, survived the war and now lives in Surrey, British Columbia, Canada. *(Stigler Collection)*

ing from his machine. Simultaneously Marseille's radio transmitter came on.

"There's smoke in my cockpit," he said, ending his report with a sharp cough.

Smoke began pouring out more thickly. Marseille shoved open the cockpit vent on the port side of his fighter. Big, black billows of smoke came rushing out.

Inside the cockpit, Marseille could be seen writhing in his seat, turning his head frantically from side to side. His face was stark white. He seemed to be losing control. His alarmed squadron mates tried guiding him, calling directions for steering over the radio.

"I can't see . . . I can't see," came the choking response.

Just east of El Alamein, German ground control was listening with growing consternation to the radio conversations of Marseille and his pilots. Colonel Eduard Neumann, *Kommodore* of JG-27, arrived at ground control in the middle of these cryptic indications of tragedy. Neumann took the microphone and tried to ascertain the nature of Marseille's problem, directing his questions to "Yellow 14."

Marseille ignored this communication. Probably he was gambling that he could somehow struggle with his stricken fighter into German-held territory. To be taken prisoner by the enemy army would be an unfortunate end to the career of the "Star of Africa." He probably considered this.

Whatever his reasons, Marseille's decision to stay with his machine was to cost him his life.

The suffocating Marseille rolled the aircraft over on its back to dump the canopy. Off it came, whirling and flashing out of the smoke. Now the slender boy from Berlin was trying to clamber out, but with the canopy gone, the slipstream kept him pinned in the cockpit. He had been weakened by his near-asphyxiation.

In a shallow dive at almost 400 mph, his Me-109 would be his coffin if he could not get clear. While his anguished comrades watched, Marseille's slim figure gradually forced its way clear of the cockpit. The cheer that rose in the throats of his comrades as the ace came free was choked back in sudden shock. Marseille's body slammed into the fighter's tailplane. He went tumbling down to the desert floor like a bundle of rags. His comrades, looking for the life-saving white umbrella of his parachute, watched in vain.

The body of the unconquered young eagle was found seven kilometers south of Sidi Abdel Raman—a white tomb in the desert used as a landmark by airmen of both sides. He was buried where he fell. A small monument erected in the desert marks the final resting place of the "Star of Africa." He was two months short of his twenty-third birthday.

He is the twenty-seventh-ranked German fighter ace, in terms of his tally of aerial victories. In one special respect he excelled them all, including von Richthofen of the First World War. Hans-Joachim Marseille shot down more British aircraft than any other German

KOMMANDEUR TO COMMODORE: Eduard Neumann was Kommandeur of I Gruppe, JG-27 in Africa during the early days of the war. When the remaining Gruppes arrived from Germany, Neumann was promoted to KOMMODORE of JG-27. He was considered one of the Luftwaffe's ablest and most effective leaders. This picture taken in Africa in 1941. (*Neumann Collection*)

fighter pilot who ever lived.

General Adolf Galland coined the name "Virtuoso of the Fighter Pilots" for Marseille, a rare tribute from the man who personally led Germany's greatest aces. Yet it should be observed that Marseille found his way to immortality as much for personal qualities as for his fighting skills and victories. Without his distinctive personality, he would be as obscure as fifteen or twenty other German aces who downed more enemies than he did.

Marseille was an anachronism. He was a knight born a few centuries too late, a beatnik born fifteen years too soon. He was human enough to resent military discipline and exhibit many attributes of a poor soldier, in the classical sense. These traits, contrasting sharply with his gift for aerial combat, have made him seem in retrospect perhaps a little more human and a little more comprehensible than many of his German contemporaries.

Colonel Eduard Neumann,[3] who was *Kommodore* of JG-27 during Marseille's days of glory, saw the ace from an unusual perspective. Neumann's status as one of the Luftwaffe's most important leaders and tutors, and his experience dating back to the Spanish Civil War, lend added force to this tribute:

"When Marseille came to JG-27 he brought a very bad military reputation with him, and he was not at all a sympathetic fellow. He tried to show off, and considered his acquaintance with a lot of movie stars to be of great importance.

"In Africa, he became ambitious in a good way, and completely changed his character. After some time there, it became a matter of some importance to movie stars to know *him*.

"He was too fast and too mercurial to be a good leader and teacher, but his pilots adored him. He thanked them by protecting them and bringing them home safely.

"He was a mixture of the fresh air of Berlin and French champagne— a gentleman."

Marseille the man thus walks into history along with the warrior, and few aces under any flag are likely to outshine him in the annals of combat flying.

[3] Edu Neumann, still very much alive, lives in Munich, where he is in the commercial elevator business.

6

The "300 Club"

"Fighter piloting is the acme of all piloting."
MAJOR GENERAL BARRY GOLDWATER,
USAF RESERVE

THE most exclusive club in the world has only two members, and it is unlikely that anyone else will ever qualify to join. Nepotism, wealth, and heredity cannot force the club's doors. The two exclusive members are Erich Hartmann and Gerhard Barkhorn, the only two fighter pilots in history to down more than three hundred aircraft in aerial combat.

Hartmann is credited with 352 kills, and his bag includes seven American-flown Mustangs. He shot down five Mustangs in two missions over Rumania in one day, and downed his other two American fighters in one mission in southern Czechoslovakia shortly before the war's end. His other 345 victories were against the Soviet Air Force.

Barkhorn's 301 kills were all Russian-flown aircraft downed on the Russian Front. He flew on the Western Front in the Battle of Britain and also during the final months of the war, but was unable to confirm a victory against the Western Allies.

For a long time, the two most successful fighter pilots of all the wars flew together with JG-52 in Russia. In 1944 Hartmann became a squadron leader in II/JG-52, which was under Barkhorn's command. When the latter left JG-52 to become *Kommodore* of JG-5, Hartmann succeeded him as *Gruppenkommandeur* of II/JG-52. They both survived the war, and have been friends for almost a quarter century. They are also mutual admirers.

Hartmann and Barkhorn have many parallels in their careers, but they are contrasting personalities. Each has a distinctive, individual approach to life, duty, and the world around him. Both would stand out in any group of men, but for different reasons. The two members of the "300 Club" exemplify the high quality of manhood which was a primary element in the makeup of the Luftwaffe fighter force.

Erich Hartmann in his physical appearance epitomizes the German man as he is conceived of in Britain and America. He has a thick thatch of blond hair and ruggedly handsome features with a strong Nordic cast. He is about five feet seven inches tall, a well-muscled, nuggety 150-pounder who moves with a vigor belying his fifty-four years—more than ten of them spent in Russian prisons after the end of the war.

THE BLOND KNIGHT OF GERMANY - 1943: When this photograph was taken of Erich Hartmann on 29 October 1943, shortly after his 148th victory on the Eastern Front, he was relatively undistinguished among the numerous German pilots with more than 100 aerial victories. Perfection of his special tactics and techniques, however, sent him rocketing ahead of all his contemporaries to the unprecedented total of 352 victories at war's end. He was never wounded in more than 1400 combat missions. (*Hartmann Collection*)

CHIVALROUS SOLDIER: Gerhard Barkhorn had 301 aerial victories in WWII, but was frequently seen to encourage pilots of riddled Russian aircraft to bail out rather than kill them in the air as most other fighter pilots would have done. Ace of aces Erich Hartmann described Barkhorn as "a leader for whom every fighter pilot would gladly kill himself." Barkhorn survived the war and is retired from the Bundesluftwaffe. This photograph was made in April 1943. (*Obermaier Collection*)

To his friends and comrades he is "Bubi," which means "boy" or "lad" in German. As a fair-haired, slender, boyish cadet pilot, the nickname was a natural one in the early nineteen forties and it has stuck with him ever since. Today he looks at least ten years younger than his contemporaries, and they still call him "Bubi." But when you shake his hand you are clearly not meeting a boy.

His blue eyes look directly at you, and you can feel the whipcord strength in his arms—a wiry power that he used to good effect in wrenching his Me-109 on to the tails of Russian aircraft. He was strong enough to frequently overstress his machine during the war, and as all experienced pilots of that conflict know, physical strength was vital to successful fighter piloting—on an even basis with good eyesight.

He is a man who does not waver, but weighs and decides quickly and then bores in. Whether it is organizing a dinner party or giving his views on the present German Air Force, Hartmann is direct, blunt, decisive, and not given to compromise. He is from head to foot and in his heart and mind, as well as by instinct and training, a *fighter*.

In the American vernacular, he "calls 'em as he sees 'em," and while he is basically a friendly, affable man, he does not suffer fools gladly. He was probably the most forthright officer in today's German Air Force, where frankness is perhaps sometimes a liability. Hartmann typifies the breed of which he is the world all-time champion.

"Gerd" Barkhorn is about two inches taller than Hartmann and weighs perhaps ten to fifteen pounds more than "Bubi." If fighter pilots came in sizes, Barkhorn would be the next size larger than the President of the 300 Club. Barkhorn is as dark as Hartmann is blond, and his olive complexion forms a contrasting setting for a pair of penetrating, steel-blue eyes. Born in 1919, Barkhorn is three years older than Hartmann, but like "Bubi" does not look his age or show his ordeals.

Gerd Barkhorn too is a friendly man, but he is a more reserved personality than Hartmann. Trained in the prewar Luftwaffe, Barkhorn bears to this day the hallmarks of that training. In the experience of the authors, such men exhibit a remarkable balance in their personalities, and Barkhorn is a typical example.

He is bilingual, interested in and well acquainted with the world beyond Germany. He meets and mixes well with men and women of any nationality and his social and professional conduct is exemplary. He is more than modest about his amazing achievements as an aerial fighter, but he is cooperative with sincere historians. He is quiet, a solid family man, and a gentleman.

Hartmann is a down-to-earth personality who can talk all day about his experiences, if drawn out and properly questioned. But he speaks about himself almost clinically. He discusses his old Luftwaffe contemporaries fairly and dispassionately, as one professional speaking of others. About the only time "Bubi" really warms up is when he talks about Gerd Barkhorn, and then sincere admiration and enthusiasm come to light. The President of the 300 Club is probably his Vice-

President's warmest admirer.

Stuttgart-born in 1922, Erich Hartmann spent part of his boyhood in China, where his physician father practiced during the nineteen-twenties. His mother, Elisabeth Machtholf, was a pioneer airwoman in Germany, and she was responsible for his early contact with aviation. Frau Hartmann was originally a sport flyer, but after Hitler's advent, glider clubs were encouraged. She helped establish a glider club at Weil im Schoenbuch, near Stuttgart, in 1936.

Young Erich learned to fly gliders in his teens, and by 1938 he was a fully qualified glider instructor. He says today that this early contact with flying helped him develop a sixth sense about aircraft mal-functions:

"If there is something wrong with an aircraft when I fly it, I *know* there is something wrong even before the instruments tell me or I get some other direct physical evidence of trouble." This intuition saved him many times during the war, and was an asset to him when he was a Tactical Evaluation Expert for the German Air Force.

As a fifteen-year-old schoolboy in 1937, flaxen-haired Erich took notice of a dark-haired thirteen-year-old schoolgirl named Ursula Paetsch. The future ace was not as aggressive then as he subsequently became. Two years later, in September 1939, he was ready to strike.

Ursula and a girl friend were walking down a street toward the school in Korntal-Stuttgart when Erich came rushing up on his bicycle. Jumping off beside the two girls and looking directly into Ursula's eyes, he shyly said, "Erich Hartmann!" This incident launched a love story which, if it were presented as fiction, would be thrown out

FATHER AND SON: October 1942 at Weil in Schoenbuch, Dr. Alfred Hartmann and his neophyte fighter pilot son, Erich, watch an airplane fly over the village. Erich had just graduated from the com-bat fighter pilot school and was being posted to the Russian front. (*Hartmann Collection*)

ENGAGED ACE: In June 1943, Erich Hartmann became engaged to his childhood sweetheart, Ursula Paetsch, whom he later married. "Usch" Hartmann waited ten years for the world's leading fighter pilot, who was a prisoner of the Soviet Union until 1955. *(Hartmann Collection)*

of the publishing houses and movie studios as the product of an old-fashioned imagination.

"Usch," as Hartmann calls her, became his steady girl friend. But it was not until 10 September 1944, after Erich had shot down his 301st enemy aircraft, that they were married. Aces Gerd Barkhorn and Willi Batz were witnesses at the ceremony. During their periods of separation he would paint a bleeding heart on the fuselage of his Me-109—symbolic of his anguish. A worse separation was to come.

In April 1945, after the collapse of the Reich, Hartmann marched westward with his *Gruppe* into the arms of an advanced tank unit of General George Patton's 3rd U.S. Army. He became a prisoner of war, but under the agreement between Roosevelt and Stalin he was in a short time transferred by the Americans to Russian custody. He was incarcerated in Russian prisons for ten and a half years, stripped of even the most rudimentary rights.

He received only sporadic mail from Germany, occasional postcards and sometimes a letter. These letters were frequently used in subtle Soviet efforts to break his will. In 1948, while he was a prisoner, his three-year-old son Peter Erich died in Germany. Hartmann never heard of this loss until 1950. When he was finally released in 1955, almost one third of his life had been wasted in this illegal confinement. His son and his father were both dead. But his beloved Usch was waiting.

Her faith that he would survive and return never deserted her. He says today that it was his confidence in her that sustained him. Decent German men confined in these bestial Russian jails were often reduced to broken shells by word that their wives had divorced them *in absentia*. In the late nineteen forties and early nineteen fifties, with the war over for half a decade or more, there was no guarantee that any imprisoned

German would ever see his family or Fatherland again. Their women could hardly be blamed for trying to start new lives, but Usch Hartmann provided an inspiring example of faith.

Despite the huge bite out of their lives, Erich and Usch Hartmann began over again. Their second child is today a lovely 18-year-old named Ursula after her mother, but nicknamed "Little Usch" or "Boots." As this is written, Hartmann has retired as a full colonel from the German Air Force. His life's ambition was to become a doctor like his father, but the long prison years left him too old to commence such a demanding study.

WEDDING BELLS PEAL: Flanked by his best and most stalwart friends, Gerhard Barkhorn (left) and Willi Batz (right), *Brilliants* winner Erich Hartmann took his childhood sweetheart and darling Ursula Paetsch to be his lawfully wedded wife. Erich made many good judgments in his career but this one was perhaps the best of his entire life. *(Hartmann Collection)*

The love between Erich and Usch is the backdrop to his exciting combat career, and the epic story of his decade in Russian jails. Hartmann's career is not being dealt with in any detail in this book since the authors have written his official biography titled "The Blond Knight of Germany". In Germany the book title is "Holt Hartmann Vom Himmel." For the present, the following brief outline of his war career will have to suffice.

Hartmann was the fortunate recipient of a full-time Luftwaffe fighter pilot's training, which started on 15 October 1940, when he joined the Luftwaffe Military Training Regiment 10 at Neukuhrn near Koenigsberg in East Prussia. Flying training did not begin until March 1941, at the Air Academy School at Berlin-Gatow. His instructors decided at this time that he was best suited to become a fighter pilot.

Graduating almost a year later, he rushed back to Stuttgart to be sure no one had run off with his sweetheart. Reassured on his return that she was still his girl, he asked Usch to wait for him. Things would perhaps soon settle down, and conditions would be more suitable for marriage. The dark-haired young lady agreed.

He was then sent to Fighter School No. 2 in Zerbst, which is now in the Eastern Zone of Germany. On his twentieth birthday he checked out in the Me-109. In August 1942 he was posted to JG-52 in Russia.

SPECULATION: Erich Hartmann and Helmut Lipfert in a serious moment. Perhaps they were wondering where it was all going to end . . . and when. *(Hartmann Collection)*

This wing was operating west of Mostock on the northern side of the Caucasus Mountains, under its redoubtable *Kommodore*, Dietrich Hrabak, whom we will meet in Chapter Twelve.

Hartmann was impressed by Hrabak, one of the Luftwaffe's outstanding wing commanders, who assigned him to the 7th Squadron. Familiarization with front-line conditions and practical tactics followed. For this, Hartmann was assigned to the care of Master Sergeant (later Leutnant) Edmund "Paule" Rossmann, recognized as one of the best *Schwarmfuehrers* on the Eastern Front. He scored ninety-three aerial kills before a forced landing in Russian territory made him a prisoner of war.

On his third mission with Rossmann, wingman Hartmann saw action. Rossmann called out some enemy fighters on the R/T and led the *Rotte* in a five-thousand-foot power dive. Recollecting this action, Hartmann says:

"I could not see any enemy aircraft myself. When we leveled off at high speed, however, I saw two dark green aircraft in front and a little higher than us at about three thousand meters' distance. My first thought was, 'Now I must have my first kill.' I put on full power, overtaking my leader to get in front of him for firing position.

"I closed very fast and opened fire within about one thousand meters

ACE OF ACES: Most successful fighter ace of all the nations and all the wars, Erich Hartmann here clambers out of his Me-109 on the Russian Front in 1943. Bleeding heart insignia with his wife's name "Ursel" can be seen on the fuselage with the legend "Karaya" underneath. (*Hartmann Collection*)

range. I watched all my ammunition whiz over and to the left of the target without scoring a hit. The target grew so big so fast that I quickly pulled back on the stick and zoomed upward. Immediately I was surrounded on all sides by dark green aircraft which quickly turned behind me. I started feeling pretty bad. I had lost my leader. I climbed through a cloud layer and was all alone.

"Then came Rossmann's voice on the R/T: 'Don't sweat it. I watched you. Now I've lost you. Come down through the cloud layer so I can pick you up again.'

"I dropped down through the cloud layer and saw an aircraft head on to me at about four or five thousand feet. I was scared stiff and went split-essing downward, heading west and yelling for my leader, telling him that an unknown aircraft was on my tail. Rossmann's voice came back: 'Turn right so I can close you.' I turned right, but the machine following me cut across my turn. Now I really panicked. Full power down to low level and head west. I couldn't understand Rossmann's words any more. I kept pulling my head in behind the cockpit armor plate like an ostrich, waiting for and dreading the crash of enemy projectiles into my aircraft.

"The aircraft stayed behind me and after a short time I once more heard Rossmann's voice telling me that the aircraft on my tail had gone. I climbed again to fix my position, spotted Mt. Elbrus to my left and reoriented myself. Then I saw the red fuel warning light glowing in front of me. Five minutes' more flight, then the engine went bang, bang, bang, and quit. I was out of gas.

"There were huge sunflower fields below me and a road with military trucks. The ground was coming up fast. I bellied in amid a monstrous dust cloud. I opened the canopy and took out my personal equipment. Army soldiers took me back to the base at Soldatskaja, twenty miles away.

"That evening there was a big, noisy, and uncomfortable debriefing by Major von Bonin, the *Gruppenkommandeur*, and then by Rossmann about *Rotte* tactics. I had committed all the cardinal sins of a tyro fighter pilot, and these were impressed on me with emphatic precision:

1. I separated from my leader.
2. I flew into his firing position instead of protecting him while he did the firing.
3. I climbed through the cloud layer.
4. After descending through the clouds, I escaped from my leader— it was *Rossmann* who was in the aircraft on my tail.

CONDOR LEGION VETERAN: Lt. Colonel Hubertus von Bonin flew with Germany's Condor Legion in Spain, gaining valuable experience of modern combat and 4 aerial victories against Russian flown aircraft. An outstanding leader and tutor, he was the first *Gruppenkommandeur* under whom Erich Hartmann served in Russia, and a radical departure from spit-and-polish officers in the training schools. With a lifetime tally of 70 aerial victories, von Bonin was awarded the Knight's Cross. He was killed in aerial combat in Russia in 1943. (*Hartmann Collection*)

5. I didn't follow his orders.
6. I lost orientation.
7. I destroyed my own aircraft with nothing to show for it.

"I was grounded for three days and had to work with the maintenance people during this time. I felt terrible."

This assignment to a maintenance job probably enriched his knowledge of mechanical support. Years later, as *Kommodore* of JG-71 *Richthofen* at Ahlhorn in 1959–62 Hartmann presided over the development of an outstanding maintenance system. The "Blond Knight," however, credits the assistance of "my old friend Colonel Toliver of the 20th Fighter Bomber Wing at Wethersfield" for his widely reputed JG-71 maintenance set-up.

The combat career of the pilot who was to become the world's most successful ace thus began on a negative note. This experience was sobering as well as humiliating. When Hartmann returned to the fray he was determined not to repeat his mistakes.

For two and a half weeks he continued flying as a wingman, waiting his chance and steadily improving his feel for combat flying. His chance came on 5 November 1942. At noon, the *Schwarm* of four fighters in which he was flying as a wingman was scrambled against ten Lagg-3 fighters and eighteen IL-2 fighter-bombers.

The Russian force intended attacking the forward roads of the German Army. East of the town of Digora the German fighters sighted the intruders. Hartmann recounts the battle:

"Our position was behind and above our enemies. We split the *Schwarm* into two two-ship elements (*Rotten*) and attacked in a steep dive, firing through the fighters and attacking the bombers. I attacked the aircraft on the extreme left, closing in very fast and opening fire at about two or three hundred feet. I saw numerous hits, but the bullets and shells ricocheted off the IL-2. The heavy armor plating on those IL-2s resisted even 20mm cannon shell hits.

"I began my second attack on the same machine, starting with a steep dive and coming up on him from behind and below. This time I closed in even closer before opening fire. A hit in the oil-cooling system! Black smoke belched from the IL-2 followed by rapidly lengthening tongues of flame. The fire swept back under the fuselage. I was alone at this time because the aircraft I attacked had pulled out of formation and was trying to escape to the east.

"I was still sitting behind him and we were both in a shallow dive. Then there was an explosion under his wing, and simultaneously there was a heavy explosion in my own aircraft. Smoke billowed back into the cockpit, and I could see fire glaring redly under the engine doors. There wasn't much time for action.

"Quickly I went through the drill. Altitude: low level, and still on the German side of the lines. Fast, power back, fuel master switch off and ignition switch off in quick order. None too soon. I bellied into a

ACE AND CREW CHIEF: Erich Hartmann sits on the wing of his Me-109, "Karaya One" and chats with his faithful crew chief Heinz "Bimmel" Mertens. Hartmann said that Mertens's work was flawless. Mertens was devoted to Hartmann, once went looking for him when he crashed behind Russian lines. (*Hartmann Collection*)

field, raising a huge shower of dirt and dust which quickly extinguished the fire. Just as I clambered out of the cockpit, my first kill crashed thunderously three kilometers away."

Two minutes later Hartmann was picked up by an Army car and taken back to his base. In this encounter, he was a greatly improved pilot, but he had nevertheless lost his own aircraft in downing the IL-2. Two days later he was stricken with fever and hospitalized for two weeks.

He did not score again until 27 January 1943, when he downed a MIG fighter and returned safely to base. By the end of April 1943 he had eleven kills and had scored his first multiple kill, two Lagg-3 aircraft on 30 April 1943. He had conquered his buck fever, was making fewer and fewer errors, and quietly developing his own fighting techniques.

On 7 July 1943 he scored seven kills in one day—four La-5s and three IL-2s. The days when he scored only one kill were becoming increasingly rare. He was consistently flying up to four missions a day and often more. Action with the enemy came just a few minutes after takeoff, and there were numerous fifteen-minute scrambles to intercept Soviet aircraft approaching the front line.

During the early months of his combat experience, Hartmann was flying in the company of some outstanding aces, all of whom were well ahead of him in the scoring. JG-52's III *Gruppe* in early 1943 was under the command of Major Hubertus von Bonin, a veteran of the Spanish Civil War. Von Bonin had four kills in that conflict, and when he was killed in action in December 1943 he was credited with seventy-seven confirmed kills for both wars.

EASY GOING ACE — 1943: Erich Hartmann was never the standard military type, wore a battered hat and affected a relaxed drawl. Spit and polish officers tended to dislike Hartmann, but in the air his expertise was such as to reduce all such ideas to the ridiculous. His 352 aerial victories were gained in over 1400 combat missions. He survived 10 1/2 years of illegal imprisonment after WWII. (*Hartmann Collection*)

A leading light of JG-52 was Guenther Rall, busy piling up kills with numerous multiple victories. On 29 August 1943, Rall downed his two-hundredth enemy aircraft, the third Luftwaffe pilot to reach this tally. At this time, Hartmann had eighty-eight victories.

Another luminary of the same *Gruppe* was Walter Krupinski, with whom Hartmann had flown as wingman during his first break-in period. Hartmann scored his first ten kills as wingman to Krupinski and Rossmann. Krupinski stood well ahead of Hartmann in the scoring, and JG-52 was the unit of Gerd Barkhorn, who had reached two hundred kills by 30 November 1943 as *Gruppenkommandeur* of II/JG-52.

Hartmann's scoring was consistent, sometimes brilliant, but always steady once he conquered his buck fever. Rall, Krupinski, and Barkhorn were all later transferred to the Western Front where the missions were not as numerous and kills harder to come by.[1] All these men were wounded, which removed them from the scoring race for varying periods.

Young, strong, and tireless, Hartmann flew about fourteen hundred missions, entering combat over eight hundred times before the end of the war. He was never wounded. He was one of the "flyingest" German fighter pilots. His victories nevertheless were rooted in something other than repeated exposure to combat.

His approach to gunnery was different from that of Rall, Marseille, Rudorffer, and other deflection-shooting artists of the Luftwaffe. Hartmann himself absolutely denies that he was any kind of marksman at long range, which he considered a chancy way of attack. His approach was to get as close to the other aircraft as possible before opening fire— a throwback to von Richthofen which bears some elaboration. Hartmann explains it this way:

"CRIMINAL" GENTLEMAN: A lean, young Walter Krupinski was a dashing fighter pilot in the classic mold with an inexhaustible love for the good life. Erich Hartmann, who was tutored by Krupinski when he arrived on the Eastern Front fresh from training, called the Krupinski of those days "a criminal" type. "Criminal" in this sense is a kidding term used by the Germans. In the air, Krupinski did not kid around, scoring 197 aerial victories and winning the Oak Leaves. He finished the war in JV-44, flying the Me-262 and later became a Lt. General in the new German Air Force. (*Krupinski Collection*)

"My only tactic was to wait until I had the chance to attack the enemy and then close in at high speed. I opened fire only when the whole windshield was *black* with the enemy. Wait!—until the enemy covers your windshield. Then not a single shot goes wild. The farther you get away from the enemy the less impact and penetration your projectiles have. With the tactic I have described, the enemy aircraft absorbs the full force of your armament at minimum range and it *doesn't matter* what your angle is to him or whether you are in a turn or any other maneuver. When all your guns hit him like this, he goes *down!* And you have saved your ammunition."

Hartmann emphasizes how important it is for a fighter pilot to learn to close in without fear of collision.

"When you begin flying combat and you are a hundred meters from the enemy machine, you get jittery because you are too close to him. That is what you feel in the beginning. By experience you come to know that when you are a hundred meters from the other machine you are still too far away. The inexperienced pilot breaks away for fear of mid-air collision. The experienced pilot brings his machine in much closer . . . and when he fires, the other machine goes down."

Hartmann is aware of the innumerable yarns told about his gunnery

---

[1] Rall and Krupinski were transferred to the Reich Defense in the west on 18 April 1944. Willi Batz replaced Rall as C.O. of III *Gruppe* and Hartmann replaced Krupinski as operations officer of the *Gruppe*.

[2] Hartmann reputedly had the finest airplane crew chief in JG-52, Sergeant Heinrich "Bimmel" Mertens, who lives today in Kapellen/Erft in Germany. Hartmann pays tribute to Bimmel by quickly admitting that he was the real secret to success. In addition, when Hartmann was shot down and captured by the Russians, Bimmel spent four days and nights behind Russian lines searching for him. Mertens says "the happiest moment of the war for me was when I returned to our base after those four days and Erich was there to meet me!"

ACE OF ACES: What pilot with 200 aerial victories would not smile? Here is Leutnant Erich Hartmann in the spring of 1944, standing in front of his Me-109 on the Russian Front. He was awarded the Oak Leaves in March 1944, subsequently earned the two higher orders of the decoration before war's end. His final victory tally: 352 confirmed kills. (*Hartmann Collection*)

wherever fighter pilots and buffs gather. He discounts them all, and denies that he was the possessor of such magical skills as have been attributed to him.[2] Other aces have a different view of air-to-air shooting, and in the next chapter, Guenther Rall will present a contrasting approach to the subject.

"Bubi" found his views vindicated, of all places, in the United States. During refresher training in America, the visiting German pilots were shown gun camera film of successful U.S. fighter missions. Hartmann found that these combat films not only confirmed kills, but also his distinctive approach to gunnery.

"The big successes of World War II, and in Korea as well, are when you see only a big enemy aircraft filling the screen. Then you see how, when you shoot, pieces of the other aircraft are blasted away and the machine explodes. All the other movies, from a long way away, show you only a few hits, but you can never see that he goes down. You can have computer sights or anything you like, but I think you have to go to the enemy on the shortest distance and knock him down from point-blank range. You'll get him from in close. At long distance, it's questionable."

America's top ace of the European Theater of Operations, Colonel Francis S. Gabreski,[3] believed strongly in Hartmann's tactic. He scored twenty-eight kills against the Germans, and he regarded the computer sight as a nuisance.

The *modus operandi* of the Blond Knight was not without its hazards. At least eight of the sixteen times Hartmann was forced down, his

[3] Gabreski shares top honors with Robert S. Johnson, USAAF ace who also scored twenty-eight aerial victories in World War II.

AMERICAN ACE WHO WAS A "FIGHTING IRISH": Colonel Francis Stanley Gabreski, who attended Notre Dame University at South Bend, Indiana, became the top American ace against the Luftwaffe. He shared the honor, 28 victories, with Capt. Robert S. Johnson. "Gabby" shot down 28 over Europe and added another 6 1/2 aerial kills in the Korean War, for a total of 34 1/2 victories. He is America's top living ace today. Richard Bong (40) and Thomas B. McGuire (38) were killed in crashes. (USAF)

aircraft was brought to earth by flying into the debris of the Russian aircraft he had exploded at point-blank range. Despite this risk, he went through the war unwounded. His narrowest escape from death came when he was almost shot by a German infantryman, the bullet passing through his trouser leg.

Forced down behind the Russian lines on 20 August 1943, Hartmann was captured by Soviet troops but feigned injury until he could make good his escape. Lying low by day and walking only by night, the young ace slowly worked his way back toward the front. Stumbling up a hill in darkness, he was petrified when a black shadow loomed in front of him, yelled, "Halt," in German and fired a rifle at the same time.

"For God's sake," shouted Hartmann, "don't shoot your own people."

The sentry already had a second cartridge in the chamber. Again he shouted, "Stop!" Hartmann could hear the soldier's voice cracking with nervousness.

"Damn you, I'm a German pilot."

The sentry was quaking with fear. The rifle trembled in his hands, but fortunately he never fired again or there would have been no Blond Knight to pass into history.

Hartmann takes pride in one aspect of his war career. He regards as a genuine achievement his fourteen hundred missions without losing a wingman. He took pains with the education of young pilots coming to the front straight from the schools, most of them with far less training than he had when he made his first disastrous operational errors.

The only casualty among the dozens of wingmen who were introduced to combat flying by Hartmann was Major Kapito, a bomber

TOP BRITISH FIGHTER ACE: Group Captain James E. "Johnny" Johnson of the RAF was the top-scoring British ace of WWII. After the war, he wrote two books on his experience as a fighter pilot and on the evolution of fighter combat tactics. *(Toliver Collection)*

pilot transferred to JG-52 late in the war. He was not yet accustomed to the greater maneuverability of the Me-109, as compared with the bombers he had previously flown, when he and Erich were involved in a dogfight with Airacobras. Hartmann tells it in this way:

"We were attacked by a higher Russian element. I let them close until they were in firing range, and called to Kapito to stay very close to me. As they fired, I pulled a steep turn, but Kapito could not stay with me. He made a standard-rate *bomber* turn. After a 180-degree turn, he and the attacking Airacobras were opposite me. I called to him to turn hard opposite so that I could sandwich the enemy, but in his standard-rate bomber turn he got hit. I ordered him to bail out immediately, which he did. I got behind the Airacobra and downed it with a short burst. The Soviet aircraft went in burning, crashing with a tremendous explosion about a kilometer from where Kapito had landed. I flew back to the base, got a car, and picked him up unhurt. This was the only occasion in all my operational flights in which I lost my wingman, but fortunately he was not hurt and is alive today in Germany."

The worst sin of a combat pilot in Hartmann's estimation was to

NEAR MISS: Erich Hartmann shows his crew chief Bimmel Mertens a bullet hole in his windshield. Mertens is holding the replacement plexiglas ready for installation. In more than 1400 combat missions and over 800 aerial battles, Erich Hartmann was never once wounded. (*Hartmann Collection*)

GRUPPENKOMMANDEUR HARTMANN: In 1944, Hartmann has a few words with his squadron personnel on the Russian Front. Informality of unit may be assessed from sloppy garb of personnel. Eastern Front fighter units bore little resemblance to the traditional spit and polish of German armed forces in the past, but were the most successful fighter units in the history of aerial warfare. (*Hartmann Collection*)

GOOD NEWS: Ace of aces Erich Hartmann had already clambered out of his Me-109 in March 1944 after scoring his 150th aerial victory, when crew chief Bimmel Mertens informed him he had been awarded the Oak Leaves. Hartmann had to clamber back into his aircraft for this publicity photo while crew chief Mertens perched beside him. (*Hartmann Collection*)

win a victory and lose a wingman:

"It was my view that no kill was worth the life of a wingman, many of whom were young and inexperienced boys. Pilots in my units who lost wingmen on this basis were prohibited from leading a *Rotte*.[4] They were made to fly as wingmen, instead."

Hartmann met Hitler personally three times during the war, the occasions being the awards of the Oak Leaves, the Swords, and the Diamonds. The young ace was aware of the dramatic changes in Hitler's manner and bearing as the war lengthened. On the first occasion he met the Fuehrer at the latter's house in Salzburg:

"Hitler knew all the details about the Luftwaffe and was well informed. He told us to believe that we would win the war. He presented the decoration and asked me about my family life, and if there was anything I wanted of a personal nature. In our later meetings, things were different."

Hartmann received both the Swords and the Diamonds at Hitler's HQ in East Prussia. When he received the Diamonds, it was shortly after the assassination attempt of 20 July 1944:

"HQ was detailed into three areas. Nobody was allowed to enter the third zone without a thorough body search by an officer of Hitler's HQ guard. I told the officer of the guard that he should tell Hitler I didn't want the Diamonds if he had no faith in his front-line officers.

"After this, Hitler's Luftwaffe adjutant, Colonel von Below, told me I could pass into the third zone without being searched, and I could take my pistol with me. During my talk with Hitler, my pistol hung outside the conference room. Had I wished, I could have taken it with me in my pocket."

Hartmann's fearless, head-on approach to problems is exemplified by this incident. The Blond Knight's attitude was simply, let Hitler keep his Diamonds if he does not trust me. Hartmann is not a man who locks such prickly thoughts inside himself. He brings them out in the light of day and is fearless in voicing them. During the war he once wrote a steamingly angry letter to Goering about the slaughter of young, inexperienced pilots in bad weather conditions through Goering's orders.

So it was that when everyone else was forbidden to carry a pistol in Hitler's presence, the young ace stalked in wearing his sidearm in the normal way. He took it off while they had coffee in the first conference room, then put it back on when he and Hitler walked into an adjoining building for lunch. Hartmann makes light of the much-publicized and overglorified attempt of Count von Stauffenberg to kill Hitler with a clumsy bomb.

"Before the July revolt, everybody could wear his normal weapons

---

[4] *Rotte* consisted of a flight of 2 aircraft;
2 *Rotten* made up a *Schwarm*—4 aircraft;
3 *Schwarms* made up a *Staffel*—12 aircraft;
3 *Staffeln* made up a *Gruppe*—36 aircraft;
3 *Gruppen* (or more in some cases) made up a *Geschwader*, or Wing.

necessary for the uniform. It would have been easy for Stauffenberg at this time to kill Hitler personally and directly in his room. Nobody was looking at what was in your pockets in those days."

When Hartmann received his Diamonds from Hitler, the Fuehrer was no longer thinking of victory. He told the young pilot that the war was lost in the military sense. The dictator's view was that the differences between America and Britain on the one hand, and the Soviet Union on the other, were completely irreconcilable. His hope was for a rapprochement between Germany and the West, so that all might turn united against The Bear.

These dreams never came true, and as JG-52 withdrew step by step from Soviet territory Hartmann and his men knew that their greatest danger lay in being taken prisoners by the Red Army. As Major Hartmann, the most successful fighter ace of the war was *Gruppenkommandeur* of I/JG-52 as all hope of further resistance faded. Only a handful of flyable aircraft remained.

On 8 May 1945 Hartmann flew his final combat mission and scored one kill. He knew it was the end. The airfield was under Soviet artillery fire. Reports came in that an American armored unit had been spotted ten miles to the northwest. The Americans were advancing toward the base.

Hartmann gave the order to burn the remaining aircraft with all munitions. The entire *Gruppe* would march toward the advancing Americans. Due to the large number of women and children with the unit—wives and families of group personnel who had escaped from the advancing Russians—Hartmann gave up his chance to fly into American territory. He was walking across the fields two hours later, leading his unit and their families to what he thought was safety. Smoke palls behind him and the popping of exploding ammunition marked the end of one of the most successful fighter units of the war.

The 90th U.S. Infantry Division accepted the surrender of Hartmann and his unit, at the town of Pisek in Czechoslovakia. At 1300 hours on 8 May 1945, Erich Hartmann's war was over. His troubles were just beginning.

Sanity was lacking in the world in those times. History will characterize as insane barbarism the high-level transactions under which German soldiers and their families in Anglo-American hands were turned over to Soviet custody. The Russians fully intended to slake their hatreds against these now defenseless people. Their masses of brutish soldiers, swarming over the German countryside, were being egged on by Ilya Ehrenburg, the "Russian Goebbels," to "take the blond German women who will make you forget the hard fighting."

On the morning of 16 May 1945, Hartmann was told that his entire unit, women and children included, would have to be delivered to the Russians. They were delivered in trucks to the Red Army. Hartmann's soldiers were stripped of any items that could conceivably be of utility or plunder value. Clothes, boots, food, maps—everything was taken.

OAK LEAVES FROM THE FUEHRER: On this occasion, Erich Hartmann and onetime aerial warfare tutor Walter Krupinski received their Oak Leaves personally from Adolf Hitler. There ceremony was at Obersalzberg on 4 April 1944. The officers at the investiture are from left, Dr. Maximilian Otto, Reinhard Seiler, Horst Adameit, Walter Krupinski, Erich Hartmann and Walter Möse. *(Obermaier Collection)*

GENERAL AND MAJOR HARTMANN: General Seidemann conversing with Major Erich Hartmann near the end of WWII. Seidemann later ordered Hartmann to leave his *Gruppe* in Czechoslovakia and fly in his fighter to surrender to the Western powers. Seidemann feared for the fate of Hartmann in Russian hands . Hartmann ignored Seidemann's order so that he could stay with his men and the extensive family entourage the unit had with it. His surrender was to the U.S. Army in Czechoslovakia, but he was later turned over to the Soviets by the Americans and held illegally as a prisoner for 10 1/2 years. *(Hartmann Collection)*

EPIC MOMENT: Erich Hartmann has just returned to base in Russia after downing his 301st enemy aircraft — an unprecedented feat in the history of aerial warfare. On 24 August 1944, Hartmann's squadron mates hang an improvised victory wreath around him and chair him across the field to the waiting champagne. *(Hartmann Collection)*

HIGHEST AWARD: Chancellor Adolf Hitler congratulates 1st Lieutenant Erich Hartmann after presenting him with the Diamonds to his Knights Cross on 26 August 1944. Only 27 German servicemen won the Diamonds between 1939 and 1945. Hartmann was the 18th recipient of the award. Investiture was at the Wolf's Redoubt, Insterburg, East Prussia, where Hitler nearly lost his life in a bomb plot not long before this photograph was taken. Hartmann noted the deteriorated appearance and morale of the German dictator when they had lunch shortly afterwards. *(Obermaier Collection)*

The Russians separated the women and girls from the men. Beside the road and in nearby fields the Russians then gave terrible effect to propagandist Ehrenburg's urgings. The women, teenagers and even younger girls were stripped of their clothes and raped while the Germans watched in anguish. A force of thirty Russian tanks surrounded the POW area to keep order during these proceedings. The hell endured by the German men as their wives, sweethearts, and daughters were raped in broad daylight defies description.

Many women were driven away in Red Army vehicles and never seen again. The rest were "returned" to their shocked and shattered husbands and fathers. Families committed suicide during the night, for the Russian troops came again and again to the compound. The following day, a high-ranking Red Army officer arrived and immediately forbade these excesses. But Hartmann calls this incredible first day in Russian captivity "the worst memory of my life."

For more than ten years he engaged in a constant battle of will and wits with his Soviet captors. He went on hunger strikes and was force-fed by the Russians to keep him alive. Solitary confinement in total darkness was frequently his lot. When he was forced to work on construction details, Hartmann constantly baited his guards and instigated sabotage against the projects.

While the best years of his life wasted away, Hartmann's main source of sustenance was his faith that Usch would not fail him. That faith was not only fulfilled, but returned. This book will presently outline other experiences of German officers in Soviet confinement, but Hartmann's faith in his wife was the foundation of his resistance to the Russians. He will always be honored among that desperate fraternity of former prisoners of the Soviet Union as one of their outstanding leaders.

When Chancellor Adenauer went to Moscow in 1955 to make a general rapprochement with the Soviet Union, the release of German

HUMAN CONTACT: All-time leading ace of the world, Erich Hartmann reached the heights of glory in WWII with 352 victories, but followed this with ten and a half years of illegal imprisonment in Soviet Russia. His Russian captors censored or blocked all his mail, confining him at times to ten words per month on a postcard to his wife. One of the greatest moments of his prison career is recorded here, as Hartmann joyously is allowed a photograph of his wife. Russians permitted him only 50 of more than 400 letters written him from Germany in 1945-55. (*Hartmann Collection*)

BACK FROM HELL: Major Erich Hartmann photographed in 1955 at the border between East Germany and West Germany upon his return from 10 1/2 years in Russian prisons. Gaunt, emaciated Hartmann at this time had spent almost one third of his life in prison, illegally confined by Soviet government who used the P.O.W.'s as a bargaining tool with the Western Powers. *(Hartmann Collection)*

REUNION: Still gaunt from his 10 1/2 year ordeal in Russian prisons, Erich Hartmann meets his former school teacher in Weil in Schoenbuch in 1955. School years of the ace of aces exerted powerful formative influence on the young man's character, and enabled him to withstand diabolical cruelties of Soviet confinement. *(Hartmann Collection)*

THE BLOND KNIGHT AND HIS BIOGRAPHERS: Ace of aces Erich Hartmann stands between the two American authors of his official biography, Trevor J. Constable (left) and Colonel Raymond F. Toliver, USAF Ret. Meeting was at Luke AFB in Phoenix, Arizona in 1969. An active duty colonel in the German Air Force at the time, Hartmann gave the graduation address to a class of German fighter pilots trained at Luke by the USAF. *(Toliver Collection)*

prisoners of war was one of the concessions he sought. Adenauer was successful. The release of men who had been illegally incarcerated for more than a decade began. The Soviet Union had circumvented the Rules of the Geneva Convention concerning POW treatment and release by reclassifying thousands of Germans as common criminals and sentencing them to 25 and 50 year prison terms. It was men, and women, in this category whose release was effected by Adenauer. One must wonder, however, how many thousands of German POWs still languish in the Soviet prison system.

1104 VICTORIES: These four German aces in WWII destroyed the incredible total of 1104 Allied aircraft. They are from left, Gerd Barkhorn (301), Erich Hartmann (352), Johannes Steinhoff (176) and Guenther Rall (257). The four met in 1962 at a German Air Force base. Steinhoff and Rall both rose to become Inspekteur of the Bundesluftwaffe, while Hartmann retired as Colonel and Barkhorn as a Major General. *(Toliver Collection)*

When the Blond Knight returned to West Germany, his beloved Usch was waiting. There was a period of adjustment to a free life, which included building up his physical strength. Hartmann's amazing resilience brought him through it all. Two weeks after he arrived home, the ebullient Walter Krupinski was on the phone urging Erich to come with him and Gerd Barkhorn for refresher jet training in England. As Hartmann dryly puts it, "This was a little too much to ask right after ten years in prison."

Old comrades, including Hrabak, urged him to return to the new Luftwaffe. He was too old to begin a new career, and he eventually agreed. He was given refresher training in the United States and was selected to command the Richthofen Wing in the new Air Force, the first fighter wing to be rebuilt since the war. He filled this post with spirit and distinction and was then transferred to Porz Wahn as a Tactical Evaluation expert. He retired from the GAF in 1973.

"THERE I WAS AT 30 THOUSAND FEET, FLAT ON MY BACK": USAF Colonel Hubert Zemke, American 18-victory ace and commander of the famous "Wolfpack" in WWII, holds Walter Krupinski (15th ranking ace of the world) and Erich Hartmann (number 1 ace of the world) spellbound with his account of an aerial rhubarb over Germany. Photo was made at Buchel Air Base in Germany in May 1961 during a visit by members of the American Fighter Aces Association. Right center is American ace Walker M. "Bud" Mahurin, 25 victories. *(Credit: (USAF Giuliano)*

WEDDING GUEST: This snapshot of Gerd Barkhorn was made at Erich Hartmann's wartime wedding on 10 September 1944 in Bad Wiessee. Barkhorn was official witness at the ceremony, along with another JG-52 ace, Willi Batz. Barkhorn and Hartmann, acedom's two top scorers, have remained close friends to this day. *(Hartmann Collection)*

"AND THAT'S THE WAY IT WAS!": James L. Brooks, President of the American Fighter Aces Asso. tells top ace Lt. Col. Erich Hartmann all about World War II from a different view point at Buchel Air Base in Germany in May 1961. Brooks, 13-victory American ace, is married to the former "liltin'" Martha Tilton, famous songstress of the 40's. *(USAF Giuliano)*

Contrary to what might be expected, Erich Hartmann is not one of this world's Russia-haters. He has more kindly and authentic friendly feelings for the Russian people than you will ever find expressed in an American newspaper. He well remembers how the Russian people on occasion would crowd around their prison compounds, abusing the Soviet guards for keeping the Germans confined and urging that they be returned to their homes.

Hartmann's contacts with these Russian civilians and with the numerous villagers he knew during the occupation days form the basis for his views on the Soviet people—not his bitter battles with the Russian secret police. He knows more from a practical viewpoint of Russian psychology than do numerous academic theorists on the subject. He speaks English, Russian, and German, and is thus able to penetrate the language barriers between his own country, the West, and Russia.

Today he describes himself as "Not a tiger any longer, but an old tomcat." Surrounded by his happy little family, he lives an active life as headmaster of a flight training school and flight examiner. He reserves his exuberant moments for special occasions, such as the 1966 promotion to Brigadier General of Guenther Rall, his old friend and wartime C.O., or for the promotion to Inspector of the German Air Force of Macky Steinhoff.

Few people in Germany today even know his name. He is rarely recognized in public by anyone outside the old Luftwaffe. In the presence of the authors he was once subjected to a petty indignity by the arrogant headwaiter of a Cologne restaurant. The headwaiter had not the remotest inkling that he had slighted one of his country's twenty-eight most highly decorated soldiers, or that he had been rude to the world's most successful fighter ace. Hartmann doesn't look old enough to be associated with such remote events, for one thing.

Erich Hartmann was a sixteen-year-old schoolboy in March 1938 when Gerd Barkhorn was beginning his flying training, which culminated with the Me-109 in October 1939. Barkhorn flew in the Battle of Britain with JG-2 *Richthofen*, but was not successful during this period. He was a long time on operations before confirming his first kill.

In August 1940 Barkhorn began his association with II/JG-52, which was to last until January 1945. In the Battle of Britain he flew in this unit with Marseille. He had 120 missions under his belt on 2 July 1941 when he scored his first kill on the Eastern Front, and he scored steadily thenceforth, until he reached three hundred victories on 5 January 1945.

Gerd Barkhorn was never among the large single-mission scorers on the Eastern Front, his best single sortie, on 20 July 1942, resulting in four kills—a modest tally by Eastern Front standards. Seven kills in one day was his best effort, and required several missions. His busiest day saw him fly eight missions in one day from makeshift airstrips in Russia, entering aerial combat on all eight of these missions.

He had an abiding faith in the Me-109, which he preferred to the FW-190 and in which he was happier than in the Me-262 jet. The Me-109-F was in his view the best of all the numerous variants produced, but he emphasizes the personal nature of such preferences.

"The Me-109-F could climb and turn like hell. It was lighter than other Me-109s and was especially good when fitted with the 15mm Mk 151 gun. I felt I could do anything with it."

In 1104 combat missions and at least 1800 starts, Barkhorn met and conquered every type of fighter used by the Russians, including British-built Spitfires and Hurricanes, as well as the U.S.-built Airacobras. The Soviet Yak-9 was the best Russian aircraft in Barkhorn's experience, but he stresses the importance of individual pilot quality in his battles in these terms:

"Some of the Russian pilots flew without looking to either side of them or back behind their tails. I shot down a lot of them like this who didn't even know I was there. A few of them were good, like other European pilots, but most were not flexible in their response to aerial fighting.

"Once I had a forty-minute battle in 1943 with a hot Russian pilot and I just couldn't get him. Sweat was pouring off me just as though I had stepped out of the shower, and I wondered if he was in the same condition. He was flying a Lagg-3, and we both pulled every aerobatic maneuver we knew, as well as inventing some new ones as we went. I couldn't nail him, nor could he get me. He belonged to one of the Guards Regiments, in which the Russians concentrated their best pilots, and his aircraft had its whole nose painted red. We knew the names of some of the Russian aces, the *Stalinfalken* (Stalin Falcons or Hawks), but I have no idea who this pilot was who fought me to a draw."

Barkhorn's amazing 301 victories were not all easily won or gained without cost. He was shot down nine times, bailed out once, and was wounded twice. As a man who took off over eleven hundred times in search of the enemy, Barkhorn admits he was lucky to come through the war.

On one occasion in May 1944, Gerd flew escort for the redoubtable Stuka pilot Hans-Ulrich Ruedel,[6] and spent four months in hospital as a result. The Stuka strike went off smoothly and Barkhorn was on his way home. The time was 6 P.M., and it was his sixth mission in a day that had commenced at 2 A.M.

"I got a message that there were Russian fighters about, but I was very tired and negligent. I didn't look behind me. I had 273 victories at the time, and I remember thinking about getting 275, and perhaps later, 300. Unfortunately, the next victory was *me*."

A Russian fighter bounced him from behind, shot him down and put him out of action for four months. But for this misfortune, Barkhorn

---

[6] Ruedel was credited with eleven air-to-air victories (nine Russian fighter planes and two IL-2 dive bombers) during his more than twenty-five hundred combat sorties. Ruedel says, "Squadron Leader Barkhorn knew his job from A to Z."

THE BARKHORN'S AT EASTER, 1944: Gerd Barkhorn and his wife Christl and baby daughter, home for the Easter Holidays after being awarded the Swords to the Ritterkreuz and Eichenlaub (Oak Leaf). (*Barkhorn Collection*)

might well have emerged as top ace of the war. Hartmann was at this time well behind him in the scoring race with about two hundred kills. In the four months between Barkhorn's crash and his return to operations, "Bubi" leaped into the lead and subsequently never lost it.

Apocryphal stories about various aces of all nations frequently depict the hero giving away numerous victories to his squadron mates. Objective investigation of such cases almost invariably reveals that the ace in question was after every kill he could get for himself, without giving any away, and rightly so. Among the exceptions is Gerd Barkhorn.

Rather than flip a coin or argue over a kill that could belong either to him or to another pilot, Barkhorn always awarded the victory to the other man. If he shot down an enemy plane and there was no witness, his smiling reaction was to say, "Give this one to the poor people." The universal respect for Gerd Barkhorn among all his contemporaries is a fair guide to his character and personal qualities, aside from his achievements as an airman.

Lieutenant General Johannes "Macky" Steinhoff says of him:

"Gerd Barkhorn is my choice of all the fighter pilots of the Second World War. He was best or among the best, and was extremely reliable. Whenever he made a claim for a victory there was no doubt about it. I never knew of a single claim of Barkhorn's that was not confirmed."

Others confirm Steinhoff's view of Barkhorn. He could conceivably have scored many more kills had he not been transferred to JG-6 in the West, and subsequently to Galland's JV-44 flying the Me-262 jet. He flew only two missions in the jet after conversion training, without scoring kills on either sortie.

On the second mission he was attacking a bomber formation when his right jet engine failed. He broke off the action, and started to return to

#2 ACE AND HIS TEACHER: Gerd Barkhorn flew 1800 missions in WWII and entered aerial combat on 1104 occasions in winning his 301 victories in the air, but he was a student pilot when this photograph was taken at RAF Valley in Wales in 1956. Barkhorn flew against the British in the Battle of Britain but Flight Lieutenant Albert Wallace RAF, seen here with Barkhorn checked out the great combat pilot on jets in an amusing historical turnabout. Barkhorn is highly esteemed amongst international fighter pilot fraternity. (*Toliver Collection*)

base. Mustangs from the bomber escort jumped him. The Me-262 had approximately 100-mph advantage over the Mustang when both jet engines were operating, but with one engine out, it was marginally slower than the American bird. Furthermore, the Me-262 so crippled was not maneuverable enough to evade the Mustang.

These crucial facts raced through Barkhorn's mind as he saw the Mustangs attacking. Diving for a small clearing, he prepared for a crash landing. He pulled his cockpit canopy back ready for a quick dash from the doomed jet. Plunging into the clearing, the jet went bumping and lurching across the uneven surface. This motion, combined with the sharp deceleration, bounced Barkhorn up out of his seat and slammed the canopy forward on his neck. He joined other members of JV-44 in the hospital. For Major Gerd Barkhorn the war was over.

Married in 1943, he has three daughters. He joined the new Air Force in 1955 and was given refresher training in Great Britain, at RAF Valley in Wales. He is retired after becoming a Major General and heading up one of the German Tactical Air Forces.

His warmest admirer is probably Erich Hartmann, the only man to down more aircraft in combat. Hartmann likes to relate a story about Barkhorn which illustrates from life's experience how Gerd is able to evoke the loyalty and affection of his men.

Hartmann was flying with Barkhorn on the Eastern Front and the latter closed in on a Russian fighter. His point-blank fire set the Soviet machine ablaze underneath. Seeing that the Russian aircraft was doomed, Barkhorn flew alongside the stricken enemy ship, pulled back his canopy and gestured to the Russian pilot to bail out. The Russian seized his chance and his parachute took him safely to earth.

On the ground, Hartmann asked Barkhorn why he had not just simply shot the Russian fighter to pieces even if it meant killing the pilot. Barkhorn's reply is something Hartmann will never forget:

"Bubi, you must remember that one day that Russian pilot was the baby son of a beautiful Russian girl. He has his right to life and love the same as we do."

Says the Blond Knight of his erstwhile commanding officer:

"Gerd Barkhorn could really enjoy it if someone else was successful. Few men were like this. When I overtook him, he congratulated me with all his heart. He was a man and leader who really could take his men into Hell itself. Everybody would be proud to kill himself for this leader. He was the fighter commander of whom every fighter pilot dreams—leader, friend, comrade, father—the best I ever met.

"He is too honest for today's Air Force, but he is one of the few commanders whose men, ten and even twenty-five years later, still speak of him with respect and affection. Gerd Barkhorn is an unforgettable man."

Such then is the nature of the 300 Club, whose two members fairly earned their places among the immortals of the air.

EAGLES GATHER: Colonel Raymond F. Toliver, USAF, second from left, was C.O. of 20th Tactical Fighter Bomber Wing in England in 1956 when these elite birdmen from Germany were taking jet transition training in Wales. Gerhard Barkhorn (left) is world's second ranking fighter ace with 301 victories. On Colonel Toliver's left are Herbert Wehnelt (36 victories) and Walter Krupinski (197 victories). (*Toliver Collection*)

FABULOUS FIGHTING MAN: Colonel Gerhard Barkhorn survived six years of aerial combat and many wounds in WWII, serving subsequently in the Bundesluftwaffe until his retirement in 1976. Here he enjoys the Paris Air Show in June 1973 with his wife Christl. Barkhorn is one of the most admired fighter pilots produced by the WWII Luftwaffe. 301 aerial victories in the big war. (*Toliver Collection*)

7

The Third Man –
Guenther Rall

"Aerial gunnery is 90 percent instinct and 10 percent aim."
CAPTAIN FREDERICK LIBBY,
first American to shoot down five enemy aircraft

THE flyingest General in the GAF, until his retirement in 1975, was its erstwhile commander Lieutenant General Guenther Rall. He is a slender, quick moving and quick smiling pilot whose happiest moments in life are when he is at home with his lovely family or when he is at 30,000 feet at the controls of an airplane.

A spectacular career between 1939 and 1945 brought Rall 275 victories. He fought in the invasion of France, the Battle of Britain, in the Balkan campaign and over Crete. He had a long career on the Eastern Front and ended the war in the final defense of Germany against the air fleets of the Western Allies. He was the second fighter pilot after Walter Nowotny to reach 250 victories, and only Hartmann and Barkhorn, both of whom served with him in JG-52, surpass him in the final totals.

Rall scored his two-hundredth kill on 29 August 1943, while flying from Makeevka. He had an excellent chance of emerging from the war as the top-scoring German ace, but bad luck and wounds dogged him throughout the remainder of the war. He began the conflict as a young Second Lieutenant, and was a Major and *Kommodore* of JG-300 at the surrender.

Guenther Rall is a fair-haired man in his late fifties whose smooth complexion and youthful zest make him seem more like a typical Californian in his late thirties. He spent several years at Palmdale, California as F-104 Project Officer and he considers southern California, *"Der Grosse"*—the greatest. This American interlude has given him a brilliant command of English, including contemporary slang and such subvariants of the tongue as "aviation English."

Standing about five feet nine inches and weighing around 155 pounds, he is a mass of nervous energy in perpetual motion—a vital, intense personality unmatched among present-day German Air Force generals for sheer vigor. When he speaks of the old days, the movements of his limbs and his expressive face are like visible speech. Even if you could not hear him, you would know pretty well what he is saying.

He makes wings out of his hands, as do all fighter pilots to explain maneuvers. Rall goes further. When he describes a forced landing or the pursuit of an enemy machine, he holds an imaginary stick, pushes an unseen rudder, and presses phantom triggers as he talks. He is transported through time and space to the actual scenes he is describing, and his photographic memory makes him a historian's delight.

Rall has the piercing eyes of a master marksman and the soaring zest for life that is classically attributed to the fighter ace. But this is the Guenther Rall who is almost sixty years old. You wonder what kind of tiger he must have been a quarter century ago at the height of his career.

Born in the small village of Gaggenau in the state of Baden 10 March 1918, he is by preference and by nature a southern German. He has the fun-loving traits which distinguish Bavarians from their fellow Germans. His father was a merchant, and young Guenther grew up during the hard years of the nineteen twenties and early thirties. Life was grim, but had its compensations.

A keen member of the Christian Boy Scouts in his boyhood, the young Rall poured his energy into this branch of YMCA activities. He was indistinguishable from hundreds of thousands of boy scouts the world over, absorbing woodcraft, going camping, and learning self-reliance and a decent code of conduct toward one's fellow men. Aviation was inaccessible during his young years, so he had no chance for youthful contact with flying.

Finishing school in 1936, he joined the German Army as a cadet. He still had no thought of aviation as a career. His training was that of a typical future infantry officer. The change of direction came in 1937 when he was attending the War College (*Kriegschule*) in Dresden.

A young officer from the Luftwaffe Officers' School in Dresden was one of Rall's friends. This man kept telling him on weekends how good life was in the Luftwaffe. Flying was a thrilling adventure—a young man's game. Rall was sold. He recalls it in these terms:

"I was just a grasshopper—an infantryman. Flying seemed to have a future, as well as getting you out of the mud. So I said to myself, 'Flying is going to be *my* game,' and transferred to the Luftwaffe."

Entering the pilots' school at Neu Dieburg in the summer of 1938, he had finished all his courses by the early summer of 1939. He graduated as a pilot, and was sent to the Fighter Weapons School at Werneuchen, north of Berlin. All the famed aces and leaders attended this school at one time or another. Guenther Luetzow, already an ace with five kills

BRIGADIER GENERAL: Guenther Rall ended WWII as third ranking ace of the world with 275 victories. He was wounded and shot down many times in epic combat career. In postwar Germany was one of many aces treated with gross unfairness by both businessmen and union officials. He survived all this, found a niche with the Siemens combine, and later joined the new German Air Force. He rose to become *Inspekteur*, the title the GAF accords its chief. This 1967 photo shows him as a Brigadier General. (*Rall Collection*)

in the Spanish Civil War, was Rall's Group Commander at Werneuchen in 1939.

The flaxen-haired young Second Lieutenant was then posted to II/JG-52 at a base near Stuttgart. He was the youngest officer in the wing. French capacity and will to continue in the war were uncertain at this time. JG-52 units therefore flew patrol missions along the Franco-German border, but were forbidden to violate French airspace.

A taste of combat would sometimes come tantalizingly close, as French reconnaissance planes occasionally overflew German territory and were attacked. The eager Rall missed out on these encounters. He had to listen to other pilots talking of these rare downings. He remained an unblooded member of the border patrol.

A third *Gruppe* for JG-52 was subsequently organized, and Rall was transferred to the 8th Squadron in the new formation. Operating from Mannheim in the Battle of France, on 12 May 1940 the ambitious, fair-haired youngster scored his first kill. His unit was detailed to pick up a German reconnaissance plane returning from France. The German aircraft was spotted at 8000 meters over Diedenhoven, just as twelve Curtiss P-36 fighters of the French Air Army began their attack on the lone machine.

The German fighters bounced the P-36s and in the ensuing melee, Rall downed one of the American-built machines:

"Looking back on it, I was lucky in my first dogfight, but it did give me a hell of a self-confidence."

As "Daddy" Moelders always insisted, "The most important thing for a young pilot is to get his first kill without too much shock." So it was with Guenther Rall, who got off on the right foot as a young pilot in the first days of the war.

More missions and more successes against the French followed. Then his unit was transferred to a German base on the North Sea, where the Me-109s were modified for over-water flights. Among other things, they were equipped with dinghies for operations over the North Sea. The Group was given intensive training in the fine art of ditching and survival. The moment of truth soon followed—the hot missions against England.

From a base near Calais, III/JG-52 joined the German effort to throttle British air power. Rall tells it thus:

"Now we had to face Spitfires and rough dogfights every day of our lives. We had many wrong techniques, including being ordered to stay as close escort for the bombers. This was particularly rough with the Ju-87 Stuka, a murderously slow aircraft. It was deadly. They might just as well have set our fighters on fire on the ground. The Spitfires would always bounce us with an altitude advantage, and shoot us up."

These bitter battles with England's best saw JG-52 hit hard. III/JG-52 lost in quick succession its C.O. as well as two squadron leaders, including First Lieutenant Erich of the 8th Squadron. After four missions to England, the unit was running short of officers, since in those days the Germans maintained a ratio of perhaps four NCO pilots to each officer pilot. With no other officer pilot available, Rall became a squadron leader. He was twenty-two years old.

Rall continued with the 8th Squadron until the Group was withdrawn in October 1940 to rebuild personnel losses. As the unit began to shape up again and fill the gaps in its ranks, the pilots were eager to get back to the Channel coast and tangle once more with the RAF. They were doomed to disappointment.

Secret orders moved the unit to a base near Vienna. From this base Rall's squadron flew down to Bucharest in Rumania. Mission: Protection of the derricks, refineries, and oil installations in Rumania, and protection of the bridges across the Danube to Bulgaria. The air defense of Constanza Harbor was also Rall's operational responsibility.

These two months rolled the war away from the minds of the young men who had previously been absorbed in fighting to the exclusion of all else. Rumania was at that time a neutral country, yet a belligerent power was defending portions of its industry and harbors. The young Germans stayed in a hotel, and in the night club found British, French, Russian, and American military personnel sitting at adjoining tables. Supervising everything was the Rumanian Secret Service, but after a time everyone knew everyone else and their business and the war seemed remote and unreal.

This interlude terminated with the assignment of Rall's squadron to support the attack on Crete—history's first opposed landing by parachute troops. From bases in the Peloponnesus Islands, Rall and his pilots flew close-support missions against the New Zealand, British, and Australian troops, the RAF having been eliminated from Crete early in

GUENTHER RALL (left): gets a happy handshake from JG-52 Kommodore Dietrich Hrabak after returning from a successful fighter mission against the Red Air Force in 1942. Rall's adjutant, 1st Lieutenant Funke, shares in the smiles, and was an ace himself. With 275 victories scored on all fronts, Rall was third-ranked ace of Luftwaffe, and survived to become Inspekteur of the Bundesluftwaffe. Hrabak also survived the war with 125 victories, and became one of the architects of the new German Air Force in the nineteen fifties. *(Rall Collection)*

the battle. Rall describes these missions:

"The struggle for Crete was a grim battle. A deadly fight—horrible even from the air. Some of the most bitter fighting of the war took place on that island. Working with the troops was exceedingly difficult. Together with the paratroops our planes also dropped boxes with guns, supplies, and ammunition. In every box there was a German flag. The idea was for our men to lay these flags out on the ground, so we could see where they were and get an idea of the front lines. The New Zealanders got these flags from many of the containers they captured and spread them out on *their* positions. It was wonderful protection for them, and caused total confusion in the air on our side. You could not see where the lines were, which made ground attack very difficult."

After Crete fell, Rall and his squadron returned to Rumania via Athens. They were switched to the Me-109-E with the new engine and the round wingtips. After a brief training period with the new variant the unit was ordered to the Constanza region on the second day of the Russo-German war. Soviet bombers were already hammering the Rumanian refineries, and against them the Rumanians had only flak.

Rall flew his squadron down to a bare grass field near the refineries and set up a fighter "base." His assets were a few drums of fuel flown down in a Ju-52 together with a handful of spare parts. Buildings and facilities at the field were nonexistent. Despite the primitivity of the operation, Rall and his pilots downed between forty-five and fifty Russian bombers in the ensuing five days, and brought Soviet strikes against the oilfields to an abrupt end.

He says of this series of events:

"We had nothing to eat, practically no fuel, no shelter, and after a few sorties, no spares. But in this meager environment, we were nevertheless heroes to the Rumanians. Antonescu came and congratulated us, and we even felt a bit like heroes."

When JG-52 was charged with the fighter role in southern Russia, Rall took part in the offensive in the Crimea and to the Sea of Azov. In the big battle around Rostov he was steadily scoring kills when the winter of 1941 clasped the Germans in its frozen grip. He will never forget that winter.

"The savage cold started like hell. We had no outfits or equipment

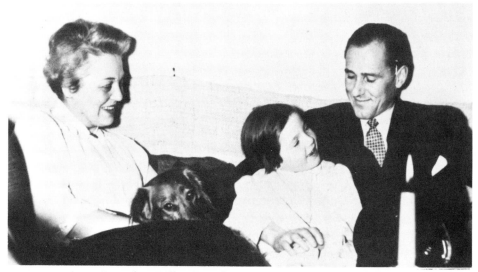

ACE AND FAMILY: Guenther Rall survived severe wartime injuries and a hectic 1939-45 career to take up family life with his wife Hertha, a medical doctor who nursed him through one of his worst wartime crashes. Rall retired from the Bundesluftwaffe in 1976. *(Rall Collection)*

for contending with it. The temperature skidded from the mildness of autumn to 30–35 below zero Centigrade in a couple of days. Once down, the temperatures stayed down.

"Just getting our fighters started in the morning called for a maximum effort. We put open fires under the aircraft and let them burn all night, disregarding all safety regulations. We forgot about safety because we had to get moving in the morning."[1]

The young ace had confirmed about thirty-six victories at this time. Daily encounters were steadily increasing his score until 28 November 1941, when he got careless. At dusk he was involved in a dogfight, whose aftermath will haunt him all his days.

"It was already virtually dark when I tangled with several Russian fighters. I shot one of them down, and as he went plunging earthward in flames, I watched his fiery path to final impact. He landed with a mighty burst of flame. Watching this spectacular crash not only dis-

[1] A captured Russian pilot gave the squadron a cold-weather hint: mix gasoline in the oil at engine shutdown. The gas evaporated quickly next morning as the engine warmed up.

tracted me from combat with the other Russians but also temporarily blinded me with its brilliance.

"Another Russian got on my tail. He riddled my engine and I went down. I decided to try a belly landing, but in the darkness did not realize my landing speed was too high. Hitting the ground with a crash in open countryside, I *bounced*. The impact point was just short of a little valley.

"Hurtling into the air, I had to dive again immediately as the aircraft was at stalling speed. All I could do was dive head on into the far wall of this valley. Petrified, I watched aghast as the valley wall rushed up at me out of the gloom. My head slammed into the instrument panel, and that was all I knew."

German soldiers pulled the shattered Rall out of the wreckage and sent him back to a field hospital. When he regained consciousness, he couldn't move his legs and was in constant pain. One leg felt dead, the other hypersensitive. The field hospital had only rudimentary facilities and no X-ray. The stricken young pilot was accordingly moved to the rear areas.

Finishing up eventually in a properly equipped hospital in Bucharest, he was soon X-rayed and diagnosed. The morale-breaking facts were passed on to Rall. His back was broken in three places, and he was lucky to be alive. The medical verdict: "No more flying." As a combat pilot, he was finished.

The doctors clapped him in a body cast and kept him in the Bucharest hospital until after Christmas of 1941. He was then transferred to the University Hospital in Vienna, because the critical complexity of his case required the attention of a neurologist professor. At this hospital some good fortune came to ameliorate the bad. He met his future wife, Hertha, a pretty blonde who was a doctor there.

For nine tedious months Rall struggled with his afflictions and with the sentence of "No more flying" ringing in his mind. Aided by a potent will and the resilience of youth, he gradually regained motility. Once he began moving about under his own power, his thoughts turned to the possibility of flying again.

A visit from a pilot friend who was commanding a nearby fighter school gave him the opportunity and the hope he needed. He persuaded his friend to let him try flying again with an old biplane. He needed to refamiliarize himself with flying to find out if his skills had been impaired. There was also the psychological problem. He had to convince himself that he still had what it took.

Rall flew the old kite. Soon he felt as though he had never left flying. Keenly competitive as an ace, he had heard reports of the strings of kills run up by his squadron mates and other JG-52 aces. He had to get out of the hospital and back to the front.

He took advantage of the ignorance of Luftwaffe regulations prevailing in the Army-run hospital to have himself reassigned to JG-52. His testy insistence on returning to his unit cut through red tape and in August he was on his way back to Tagaenrog and more combat. He was a long way down on the scoring ladder—forty, fifty, and sixty kills behind some of his contemporaries.

He went after the Russians with a fiercely aggressive spirit, determined to regain his lost eminence. By November 1942, three months after he came back to his wing, he was credited with 101 victories. This was an average of two kills every three days for three solid months. He was back in the race.

His 101st victory secured him the award of the Oak Leaves, just seven and a half weeks after he had been awarded his Knight's Cross on 3 September 1942. He took part in the massive battles on the southern sector of the Eastern Front, pausing only to dash back and marry his physician sweetheart. He followed the Army all the way down to the Caucasus, back up to Stalingrad, and all the way back with the retreat.

The battles in the Kuban and around Novorossisk are burned into his memory. In the Kuban peninsula area he encountered the first Spitfires flown on the Russian Front. A Russian Guards squadron in the area was equipped with the British machines, quite a change from the American Airacobras most frequently seen in the air. Rall feels that the quality of these aircraft, which was superior to contemporary Russian types, was of significant assistance to the Soviet Air Force. His views on the lend-lease effort are based on his experience as a combat pilot:

"The quality of the lend-lease aircraft was important, but pilot quality was important too. The machine can only respond to a man, when all is said and done. In my experience, the Royal Air Force pilot was the most aggressive and capable fighter pilot during the Second World War. This is nothing against the Americans, because they came in late and in such large numbers that we don't have an accurate comparison.

"We were totally outnumbered when the Americans engaged, whereas at the time of the Battle of Britain the fight was more even and you could compare. The British were extremely good. But not the Russians, not at the ordinary level. The Russians, however, had special Red Banner Guards units where experts were concentrated.

"These Guards pilots were more like the British, real fighter types— not flying masses like the others. They fought the fighter battle and they were good. So the value of lend-lease aircraft depended on who got the aircraft on the Russian side."

The victor in 275 air fights was himself a victory eight times between 1939 and 1945. He made seven forced landings and had to bail out once. He bellied his aircraft in on the Russian Front in all attitudes and conditions. Crippled gear, dead engine, engine on fire, partially severed fuselage, and damaged controls were all in the game for Rall. His belly landings were as varied as they were spectacular. He walked away from all of them except the crash in which he broke his back.

His closest escape was on 12 May 1944, when he was commanding II/JG-11 on the Western Front. This was a special high-altitude fighter unit intended to engage the Allied fighter escort while German heavy fighters tackled the bombers. Rall ran up a series of kills with this unit before being shot down by a P-47 near Berlin.

A Yankee bullet sliced off Rall's left thumb. He had to bail out, clasping the spurting stump as he came floating down in desperate agony. He thumped down in a field, exhausted and covered in blood. Shaking himself free of his parachute, he looked up to see an angry German farmer advancing on him with a pitchfork. Rall stood up.

"I am German," he said.

The farmer kept coming at him, his face contorted with rage.

"*I am German!*" roared Rall, trying to stem the flow of flood from his thumb stump. Still the farmer advanced, obviously intent on impaling him with the pitchfork.

Having survived five years of war in the air, Rall wasn't about to see it all end with a German pitchfork in his chest. Cursing the farmer in perfect German, he lumbered off across the plowed field, drenched in his own blood, angry, exhausted, and desperate.

Finally the farmer lowered his fork, realizing that he was not being tricked by a German-speaking Englander or Ami. The grateful Rall was then able to make his way to a telephone and thence to a hospital. In the hospital, he got something worse than the wound.

In the operating room he sustained a diphtheria infection of his thumb. This kept him hospitalized from 12 May 1944 until November the same year. The wound healed raggedly and the flesh was disturbed in the healing process as a result of the infection. He flirted again with paralysis for a long time due to the diphtheria.

In November he was released from hospital and reported to Galland's staff. He took over a school for squadron leaders, which had an opera-

EASTERN FRONT TRIO: Dieter Hrabak, esteemed *Kommodore* of JG-52 is flanked by Guenther Rall (left) and Major Helmut Bennemann on the Eastern Front late in 1942. Bennemann had 92 victories and commanded I Gruppe of Hrabak's highly efficient JG-52. (*Rall Collection*)

tional as well as a training mission. Operating out of Koenigsberg-Neumark, he commanded this unit until the Russians moved in early in 1945. In March 1945 he was made *Kommodore* of JG-300, flying the long-nose FW-190s. This unit was known as the Ram Fighters (*Rammjaegers*) and he ended the war as its C.O.

Among his unforgettable experiences of aerial combat, Rall cites his mid-air collision with a Soviet fighter in 1943:

"This was just at the time when the FW-190 came in on the Russian Front, and I had not actually seen one before. The Russians were using German formations in that sector a lot, flying in *Rotte* and *Schwarm* formations much of the time. The aircraft I spotted below me looked very much like the FW-190 photos and silhouettes I had seen, so I wanted to make sure before shooting them down.

"I couldn't see the color and insignia on the other aircraft, only the silhouette. So I chased him at high speed, pulled up, and at that moment saw the aircraft against the ground instead of against the sun. The Red Star was glaring back at me from his fuselage. I couldn't turn away, because otherwise he would have just turned too, and shot me down like a duck.

"I turned back from the left and down, pulled the trigger, and there was an ear-splitting, terrifying crash. Collision! I bounced on this Russian from above. I cut his wing with my propeller, and he cut my fuselage with his propeller. He got the worst of it, because my propeller went through his wing like a ripsaw. Losing his wing, he went into a spin from which he had no hope of recovery. I was able to belly in before my fuselage gave way, but I will never forget the sound and impact of that mid-air collision."

Guenther Rall is a man of vivid memory. He states that he can still see in his mind's eye almost every kill he ever made, and this is obvious from the graphic descriptions he gives of his aerial battles. He *never* exaggerates, but simply tells with the intensity of a man who is actually able to relive these events exactly what happened. His explanation for this remarkable power of recall is straightforward:

"In my case, and I cannot speak for others in this regard, these combats are simply burned into my memory like movie films. When you enter aerial combat, you have absolutely nothing else on your mind. Every iota of your consciousness is concentrated on that particular action in which you are fighting for your existence. You just never concentrate with such intensity on anything else in life, and the vividity of the memory is in proportion to the degree of concentration.

"I am not able to separate the victories in my mind numerically. I cannot tell you about a certain kill and say, 'This was number twenty or thirty-eight.' But in each action I can tell you exactly what my position was, where the sun was, and the relative movements of myself and the enemy aircraft with which I fought."

One such memory he recounts is his pursuit of a Soviet fighter down in the Caucasus area:

"I knew I had him. We were hurtling along together, with me on his tail. He could not escape. Both aircraft were just at the same speed, and at deck level. He tried to make a shallow left turn, which gave me my opportunity. I squeezed the trigger. Blam! I hit him with the first few shots and he went in immediately, kicking up a tremendous shower of sand. Nothing remained of him but a bunch of scattered debris. When he hit, he disintegrated."

Rall has been somewhat underestimated in Luftwaffe history as a marksman. His views on shooting are different from those of Erich Hartmann, who disclaims any prowess as a long-range or deflection shooter. Rall was undoubtedly one of the four best shots in the Luftwaffe, and like Erich Rudorffer and Joachim Marseille, a deflection shot of uncanny skill. The 220-victory ace Heinz Baer, second only to Marseille in downing Western-flown aircraft, considered Rall the greatest angle-off gunner in the Luftwaffe.

Rall himself attributes his shooting prowess more to hard work than anything else:

"I had no *system* of shooting as such. It is definitely more in the feeling side of things that these skills develop. I was at the front five and a half years, and you just get a *feeling* for the right amount of lead.

"Fritz Obleser[2] was many times my witness in various kills. He flew with me often. I used to say to him: 'Look at me, and I will show you how to do it.' He was surprised and exultant, as well as incredulous, that you could kill an aircraft from such positions as are possible to one who has the feel for deflection shooting.

"Sometimes Obleser would be literally shouting with surprise at some of these kills. I couldn't always turn around directly on their tails. In some cases, an attempt to do so would have put them on my tail and allowed them to kill me. Sometimes, I would put the nose up and with that *feeling* for the lead which I have described, press the triggers at the moment my intuition and experience told me was right. Boom! The other aircraft flies right into that hail of bullets and shells.

"So I say that I had no system, and do not consider myself a genius fighter pilot. I had kills from the farthest to the shortest range—even down to a mid-air collision—and I say emphatically that it was hard work and experience that gave me my success."

Rall flew approximately eight hundred missions in the 1939–45 period, entering aerial combat about six hundred times. A talented pilot and marksman exposed with this frequency to aerial combat, and able to survive, should emerge with a handsome victory tally. In October 1943 he ran up to forty kills. He had numerous days of multiple kills. His determination to prevail in the scoring race, in spite of his nine-month removal from combat with a broken back, led him to prodigious efforts to stay in front of his wingmates.

---

[2] Oberleutnant Friedrich "Fritz" Obleser became one of the outstanding aces of JG-52, with 120 kills in World War II, including nine U.S. aircraft. He is now a Colonel in the new German Air Force.

Hartmann recalls how Rall took an exceedingly modest part even in the straitened social life of his Group. He went to bed early, and was up early hunting the enemy. Rall is undeniably more highly strung than either Hartmann or Barkhorn, and is probably endowed with a keener sense of rivalry and competition. His transfer to the Western Front put an end to his big scoring days, and his long hospitalization after the loss of his thumb saw him lose out to the eternally busy Hartmann in the scoring.

One of Rall's most memorable encounters was with an Airacobra, French-flown, on the Russian Front:

"My adjutant was flying with me and I spotted the enemy aircraft below us. I initiated the first attack out of the sun, and they didn't see me. I had this Airacobra in my reticle, and suddenly he turned just a little bit to the left. It was a very slight left turn. The full side of his aircraft was exposed.

"I pulled lead and pressed the triggers. There was a blinding sheet of fire in the air as the fuel burned right in the tanks. He didn't explode. It was just the fuel that burned. This gigantic sheet of flame was at least one hundred meters long, and I had no option but to rush right into it at high speed.

"At that time the ailerons on the Me-109 were fabric, and when I came out on the other side of that fantastic fireball there was no fabric on the ailerons any more—just the metal structure remained. The paint on my aircraft was blistered off as though a blowtorch had been dusted over it from nose to tail.

"This Airacobra was about four thousand meters high, and he went down like a brick. He crashed upside down, flat on his back, and just lay there.[3] A wisp of smoke curling up was all that remained of what had been a formidable fighter plane only moments before. That aircraft completely burned out in the air. I will never forget this encounter."

Nor will the third-ranking ace forget an encounter with a P-2 at long range:

"I spotted him, chased him, and he saw me. He was damned fast, and he dived. I couldn't close him. Finally in a gentle left turn I pulled what I thought was the right amount of lead. I knew I was really 'reaching' because he was somewhere near the limit of my bullets' trajectory.

"I fired. At his wing root I immediately saw the explosions peppering him in a fiery shower. His wing came off and he spun in. With his high speed he was at the limit of his aircraft's structural strength. The slight extra impact of my bullets caused his wing to shear, and he spun to the ground in seconds."

Rall flew all the main German fighter types of the Second World War, including the long-nosed FW-190 and the Me-262 jet. He also flew captured Allied machines, including the P-51, P-47, P-38, and several Marks of the Spitfire. The British thoroughbred was his favorite

---

[3] P-39 and P-63 Bell "Airacobra" and Bell "King Cobra" were noted for their flat spin characteristics.

Allied aircraft. His preference remained unshakably for the Me-109 among the German fighters:

"I always felt confident flying the Me-109, even down to the armament. In the FW-190 you had four guns, and much more hitting power, against the three guns of the Me-109. Nevertheless I did not like the outboard guns on the FW-190 because the high G-forces caused jamming and mechanical troubles. I preferred three guns in the center of the aircraft, right along the longitudinal axis. This meant you had to aim very carefully, but when you did, our excellent ammunition got the job done. It had high explosive power, and once you hit an enemy aircraft that was 'good night.'"

Rall's comments on the advantages of having guns close to the center line of the aircraft are borne out by American experience. The Lockheed P-38 had its guns concentrated in the nose of the aircraft, while the P-51 Mustang and P-47 Thunderbolt had wing-mounted guns. The P-38 guns were less susceptible to jamming due to G-forces than those on the P-51 and P-47.[4]

The Germans were encouraged by their fighter leaders to fly the numerous captured, reconditioned, and black-crossed Allied fighters that were available. Rall was especially eager to try them out, and during his period in command of the squadron leaders' school he flew as a "British" or "American" pilot against his students. In mock aerial combat the squadron leaders were able to gain valuable insight into the fighting qualities of enemy aircraft and to learn how to exploit their weaknesses.

At war's end, Major Guenther Rall was *Kommodore* of JG-300 operating from a base near Salzburg. The fighting power of the unit was minimal because of lack of facilities and gasoline. When the Americans were reported rolling down the Autobahn, Rall decided it was time to call it a war. He disbanded JG-300.

German units everywhere were similarly disintegrating. Once proud and disciplined formations melted into loose mobs of fugitive ex-servicemen trudging across country in an effort to reach their homes and families. Rall joined the great trek.

Picked up after a few days, he was sent back to Salzburg as a POW because he had no proper papers. A transfer to Heilbronn near Heidelberg followed, and he found himself interned in a vast POW "camp." Hundreds of German ex-servicemen were confined behind a fence. At night they lay out in the open air. There was neither food nor facilities.

The Camp Commandant appeared one morning and ordered all Luftwaffe officers to stand in line. Then he began calling out names. "Barkhorn!" "Krupinski!" "Rall!" The names were familiar to many of the listening prisoners. At first, Rall thought it was a call for highly

---

[4] Most fighters today carry a single 20mm cannon, the M-39, a single-barrel 1500 rounds-per-minute gun, or the Gatling type gun M-61, a six-barrel 4000/6000 rounds-per-minute gun. Malfunction of the single gun, in this concept, pulls the teeth of the fighter plane in close combat!

GUNS CONCENTRATED IN THE NOSE: The Lockheed P-38 mounted its guns in the nose of the twin-engined fighter. *(Bodie Archives)*

LUFTWAFFE LIKED THE P-38 "LIGHTNING": This photo dramatically illustrates why the German fighter pilots liked to fight against the P-38. The twin-engine nacelles created large "blind spots" where the P-38 pilot could not see and the Luftwaffe took advantage of this deficiency. Germans claim they liked to give new pilots their first victory by letting them have first crack at a P-38.　　　　*(USAAF)*

decorated pilots, and he was apprehensive. He had won the Swords, Germany's second highest award, on 13 September 1943. He knew Barkhorn had won the same decoration on 2 March 1944, and that Krupinski had been awarded the Oak Leaves the same day as Barkhorn had won the Swords.

Decorations were far from the Allied mind. The late enemy was segregating all the pilots who had flown the Me-262 from their comrades-in-arms. After they picked out Rall, he was questioned at Heilbronn.

"How would you like to go to America?" he was asked.

To this first surprising question Rall could only answer in the affirmative. He says of this period:

"There was a difference in attitude toward us at this time. We were against the Russians first of all, because we knew them. We were in favor of the Western powers and we would do anything to keep the Russians out. We already had endured the experience in the eastern areas of Germany with the raping of women and similar excesses. This was why, when they asked me to go to America to help build a jet force, I was eager.

"I saw it as a mission that made sense. Of course, today the psychological attitude is perhaps hard to understand, on our side, but going back to those days leaves no doubt in my mind that we did right."

He was also asked if he would fly a mission against Japan. He feels this was no more than probing by his interrogator, but the question was asked. When the Americans were through with their German prisoners, the collection of aces was sent to England. They were given fifteen minutes to collect their belongings and report to the camp gate. There were eight of them.

"After about a half hour's drive, the driver stopped. He opened the trunk and revealed a rare sight to us famished Germans. Corned beef, tomato juice, beer, and other delicacies we hadn't seen for years were laid before us. They were treating us well because they wanted to get something out of us, but we were happy the war was over and happy to enjoy decent food again."

Their destination was the British interrogation camp at Bovingdon, the famous Camp 7 where many former foes of the Battle of Britain met face to face for the first time. Galland, Barkhorn, Heinz Baer, Krupinski, and Rall were among the more notable of His Majesty's guests. Plied alternately with excellent food and questions about the Me-262, Rall was free with his answers and took handsome portions of the victuals in return.

"There was nothing to be secretive about. They had captured many Me-262s intact, and the Luftwaffe had ceased to exist."

A fatter Rall was taken back to the big POW camp at Cherbourg, where two hundred thousand Germans were in confinement. The feeding problems at this massive internment center were insuperable. Like a camel, Rall had to survive on the mezzanine hump he had built up at Bovingdon. He had dropped ten pounds when he was again taken to Britain. This time he went in the company of Hans-Ulrich Rudel, the fabulous Stuka pilot. They were flown in a British Beechcraft to Tangmere, the historic RAF fighter base in southern England.

Two weeks at Tangmere gave Rall a chance to regain the weight he had lost. He answered shoals of technical questions. One of his hosts was famed RAF ace Bob Stanford Tuck, with whom he is friends to this day. The interlude ended when Rall, who was a prisoner of the Americans, had to return to Cherbourg.

RELIVING THE GREAT DAYS: RAF ace Bob Stanford-Tuck (left) "flies" a model Spitfire while his old wartime adversary, Adolf Galland, evades him in a model Me-109. Galland and Stanford-Tuck are personal friends. The RAF ace spent most of the war in German P.O.W. confinement but was one of the English luminaries of the Battle of Britain. (*Toliver Collection*)

His belly had been going in and out like a concertina from the alternate stuffing and starvation. He was also beginning to feel the cumulative strain of nearly six years of war. He explained to the camp surgeon that he had been seriously wounded and paralyzed during the war, and wanted to go home to the care of his doctor wife. He was released. This simple solution to his problems came as a big surprise to Rall. "All I had to do was ask," he said.

Fortunately, he had moved his wife out of Vienna before the Russians came, and they were reunited in Bavaria to begin picking up the pieces. Something of the psychological burden Rall bore during the war—aside from his combat flying—can be adduced from what his wife endured while he was away fighting.

Hertha Rall lost four babies during the war. Three pregnancies were aborted as the result of bomb explosions. During the fourth pregnancy she was coming up from Vienna by train to join Guenther when the train was strafed by fighters. She had to get out of the train and run for her life. As a result, she lost the child. The emotional strain of such things would take its toll of the strongest man.

They began rebuilding their lives, starting, in Rall's phrase, "from absolute zero." They were a couple without children and moved to Recklingen near Tübingen, site of one of Germany's finest universities. Guenther Rall's goal was to enter the university and study medicine. The same ugly and frustrating problem arose which ace after ace was to confront in postwar Germany.

"You are a militarist, and you cannot study here!"

In this connection, Rall offers the following observation concerning

German military officers which is not generally known either in Western countries or in Germany itself:

"A regular officer was never allowed to join a political party in prewar Germany. It was absolutely prohibited to us. So we were actually the clean ones and they blamed *us*. We were just soldiers. This was a matter of internal German policy which was completely wrong. The arrangement forbidding us to join political parties went back to the old Weimar democracy. Some officers were *honorary* members of the National Socialist Party, but this had nothing to do with the regular joining and serving of the party, which was prohibited. I never was in a political party because I was a regular officer. I was not permitted to join, even if I had wished to do so."

Rall now went through the same kind of grim pillar-to-post ordeal that was the lot of many other German aces after the war. He wanted to work in the worst way—at anything—but always the "militarist" accusation was thrown at him. He once got a job in a textile mill. He was no sooner on the payroll than there was trouble with the union officials. "You are an ex-officer—no job for you," they said. And out into the cold The Third Man went again.

He moved to Stuttgart finally, and went to work for the giant Siemens organization. Many companies that were owned, managed, or inherited by German military officers became rallying points for other ex-military personnel victimized by Germany's unfair postwar policy toward soldiers. Siemens was run at this time by old soldiers from the First World War. They didn't believe that a soldier should be treated shabbily for doing his duty, and Rall found a home at last. He became a representative for Siemens in southern Germany and stayed with the firm until 1953.

Hertha Rall was the physician at a famous school in Salem/Baden and Guenther left Siemens to become administrator of the school and assistant to its headmaster, Prince George Wilhelm of Hanover. The former ace knew that Steinhoff and Hrabak were already at work in the Chancellor's office preparing the reactivation of the armed forces. He also knew that he would join the new German Air Force when the time came.

On 1 January 1956 he returned to his original profession. He retrained in the T-33 at Landsberg under American instructors. F-84 gunnery training at Luke AFB in Arizona followed. He was then assigned to the Inspector for Fighter-Bombers in 1958. Late that year General Kuhlman, the Inspector, asked Rall if he wanted to fly the F-104 Starfighter. His answer was an enthusiastic yes.

He returned to the United States in November 1958 and was checked out in the F-104. In March the following year, General Kammhuber ordered him to establish a Project Staff for the F-104, which he ran for the next five years with skill and distinction. He handled all the testing and introduction of the new weapons system into the German Air Force of today.

NUMBER THREE ACE TO 3-STAR GENERAL:
Generalleutnant Günther Rall was Chief
of the Luftwaffe (Inspekteur Der
Luftwaffe) in 1975, still actively piloting
the latest model jet fighters. *(Rall Collection)*

A six-month course at the NATO Defense College in Paris preceded his appointment as *Kommodore* of a fighter wing at Memmingen equipped with the F-104 and F-84. In April 1966 he became Inspector for Combat Flying Units with his HQ at Wahn Air Base near Cologne, the job he holds as this is written. He was promoted Major General in November 1967, and has many good years still before him.

The distinguished airman and ace was Chief of the GAF from Dec. 1970 to April 1974 and was the German Military Representative to NATO in Brussels until his retirement. He now represents jet-engine manufacturer MTU (Motoren-Turbinen-Union München GmbH).

The old days nevertheless seem very far away in the jet age, except when conversation with his contemporaries or the questions of an interested historian turn on the mental movie projector of Rall's amazing photographic memory. Then you can take a vicarious ride into the very vortex of aerial combat, side by side with one of the greatest aces of them all.

8

The Happy Falcon—
Wolfgang Falck

*"He looks like a falcon.
He is not big enough to be an eagle."*
THE AEROPLANE,
1 March 1940

THE biggest air battle since the First World War between the Germans and the British was fought on 18 December 1939 over the German Bight. Scrambled by early warning radar, Luftwaffe fighters made a classic interception of an RAF Wellington bomber force attacking Wilhelmshaven. There had been no prior encounters in strength between the RAF and the Luftwaffe.

The attack was a disaster for the British, and German propaganda fully exploited the Luftwaffe victory. By comparison with later air battles of the war it was a fairly pettifogging encounter, but in late 1939 it was major news. Three German officers were selected for the propaganda build-up. Films, broadcasts, and numerous illustrated newspaper and magazine stories were part of the exploitation.

The three new German heroes were Lieutenant Colonel Carl Schumacher, the Wing Commander, and the leaders of his two most successful squadrons—Johannes Steinhoff of the Me-109s, and Me-110 Destroyer leader Wolfgang Falck. As the story of the German victory was circulated and broadcast throughout Europe, the editorial staff of Britain's famed aviation periodical *The Aeroplane* encountered an old acquaintance. The editor of the magazine had met Falck several times before the war.

Observing dryly that German versions of the battle were perhaps a little inflated, the British editor nevertheless used kind words in introducing his readers to Wolfgang Falck—now an enemy pilot:

"He looks like a falcon. He is not big enough to be an eagle. But he has the aquiline features which artists and novelists love to ascribe to heroic birdmen. He speaks excellent English and is a charming companion."

COLONEL WOLFGANG FALCK was major personality in the Luftwaffe night fighter force, but fell from grace with his superior, General Kammhuber, and ended the war without a command. American intelligence personnel liked this amiable former enemy so much they forged new papers for him. He represents U. S. aerospace companies in Germany today. *(Falck Collection)*

This cogent description of Wolfgang Falck is as valid today as it was more than a quarter century ago. His plumage is now gray where once it was black, but he still looks like a falcon. His splendid and arresting nose dominates a face in which determination and kindness have learned to live without fighting a civil war.

Falck in the middle nineteen seventies is even more charming than the British editor found him before the war. His charm now bears the patina of maturity. He could rightly be called "The Man You Cannot Hate." He is affability personified, and his special gift is for making his visitor feel like the center of the universe.

Large American corporations know the value of this capacity to communicate in a magically personal way. Hence it is not surprising that Falck has been a consultant to North American Aviation, Inc. His aviation background includes formidable organizational and administrative achievements, together with his long history as a pilot. These formal qualifications are given an extra dimension through his gift of reaching people. His assignment gave all these attributes full rein.

He is the lowest-scoring Luftwaffe ace with whom we will deal in detail in this book. He is credited with only seven victories—all gained in the Me-110. In this respect, perhaps it is nominally true that he is "not big enough to be an eagle." But he is a far bigger bird in Luftwaffe history than many eagles with over a hundred victories. Like his contemporary, number two ace Gerd Barkhorn, Falck is still spoken of a quarter century after his glory days with affection and esteem by all who knew him.

The Falcon first got airborne in 1931, as a member of the 100,000-

man Reichswehr, the modest Army allowed Germany under the Versailles Treaty. The Army selected thirty of its brightest young men every year for training at the German Air Transport School under Keller. Falck's boss at Schleissheim, where he spent his training year, was Rittmeister Captain (Ret.) Boeller. The enthusiastic twenty-one-year-old Falck found the First World War ace, "Blue Max" holder, and last commander of the Richthofen Circus an inspiring figure.

In 1932 the Russo-German agreement which provided for German pilots to be trained in Russia was still in effect. From each class passing out from Schleissheim, ten of the thirty Army pilots and five of the ten Navy pilots were selected for fighter pilot training in Russia. No accurate information was given to the parents of these young fighter pilots as to the whereabouts of their sons.

Ostensibly they had joined the German-Russian Air Co., which flew an airline from Koenigsberg in East Prussia to Moscow. Actually they were stationed in Lipetsk at the HQ of a Russian fighter wing. Falck describes this wondrous arrangement, under which the future enemies assisted each other:

"It was something of a lash-up. Our staff was German, but all the mechanics, hangar workers, and maintenance people were Russians—Russian soldiers—since it was a military base of the Red Army. Part of the hangars were for the Russians and part for the Germans. We had a regular United Nations aircraft to fly, the Fokker P-13.

"It was a Dutch-designed aircraft, with a British Napier 'Lion' engine, flown by German pilots in Russia, and all the technical manuals were in Spanish. We had a hell of a time with those manuals. Germany was not allowed to have aircraft, and so the machines had been bought by a South American government, I don't know which one, and then sold and reshipped to Russia for German use. At least five nations were thus involved in the 'secret' training of German pilots in Russia."

When Falck returned to Germany he had to face a serious problem of adjustment. The fiction of a Reichswehr without planes or pilots was still being maintained. Fresh from fighter pilot training, it was a decidedly Unhappy Falcon who returned to the dull routine of peacetime infantry with its emphasis on "square-bashing." For eighteen months they had trained in the presence of heroic aces whom they were inspired to emulate. Now they were forbidden to tell their infantry comrades even that they were pilots.

The situation had unforeseen difficulties:

"When the time came to get out on the rifle range, those of us who had been to Russia simply ripped the bull's-eyes to shreds. Curious and cursing sergeants, their eyes bulging, demanded to know how in hell we could shoot like that. I invented a yarn about my father having been a big hunter."

This grind continued for two years. The only interruption was a six-week annual refresher course on the Arado 64 at Schleissheim. In 1934 Falck became a Lieutenant, and simultaneously was ordered to write a letter to the Minister of War asking to be retired. He was twenty-four. What seemed like the end of a quick military career was actually the beginning of a long one of completely different character. His resignation accepted, Falck became a *Kettenfuehrer* at the Fighter Pilots' School in Schleissheim.

Hitler had come to power. The new Luftwaffe was being expanded as rapidly as possible. Falck's first official flying job was as an instructor at the time when Trautloft, Luetzow, and other future luminaries of the Luftwaffe were being prepared for their careers. These men were born in the 1910-14 period and were professional squadron leaders at the outbreak of war. Soon thereafter they would become group commanders and then wing commanders.

When Hitler reoccupied the Rhineland, a new fighter group was established in Kitzingen and the instructors from Schleissheim joined this unit. Falck and his fellow instructors flew down to Frankfurt am Main in their Arado 65s, and the new group was the first Luftwaffe unit to be stationed there. The magnitude of Hitler's early gambles has been emphasized in numerous historical works. Falck adds this observation concerning German air power during this period:

"We were the *only* group at this time that had real machine guns and ammunition. The other groups had neither machine guns nor ammunition. Their aircraft were as harmless as moths. One French fighter wing would have been able to obliterate the whole German Air Force in those days."

The Happy Falcon was later transferred to the Richthofen Fighter Wing, where he commanded the 5th Squadron and later became adjutant to the Wing Commander. This was an assignment which any young fighter pilot would covet and not wish to change. Fate had a different rendezvous with Falck.

When the III *Gruppe* of the Richthofen Wing was established, Falck was given a squadron in the new formation. Then, shortly before the Second World War the entire III *Gruppe* was transferred to a Destroyer wing, ZG-76 (*Zerstörergeschwader*), and was switched to

Me-110 SQUADRON LEADER "MARIENKAFER STAFFEL": Wolfgang Falck was a *Staffel-kapitan* with ZG-76 in early days of WWII. Here he is at Jever before his glory days as founder and first *Kommodore* of NJG-1—the only captain to be a wing commander in the history of the Luftwaffe. (*Falck Collection*)

the Me-110—then a highly touted but untried bird.

Falck's squadron of Me-110s was the first German unit in the air in the Second World War, with all twelve twin-engined fighters airborne on 1 September 1939. He flew in the Polish campaign from Silesia, after which his unit was transferred to the German Bight and took part in the historic battle with RAF Wellingtons described earlier in this chapter. The battle made Wolfgang Falck one of the best-known squadron leaders in the Luftwaffe in 1939–40.

His fame soon began paying dividends. In February 1940 he received a phone call from General (later Field Marshal) "Smiling Albert" Kesselring, ordering him to Düsseldorf to take command of I/ZG-1. The Falcon was gaining altitude rapidly.

He led his *Gruppe* of Me-110s in the invasion of Denmark in 1940. Operating from a base at Aalborg in the far north of Denmark, the Happy Falcon now became the central fighter in a series of events which significantly influenced the course of the air war over Germany in later years. The inspiration for his historic contribution reached him in a strange place for a fighter pilot—lying face down in a ditch with clods of earth raining on him.

The RAF did everything in its then limited power to disrupt the German invasion of Denmark. Skimming over Falck's base in the first light of dawn, they dropped bombs on the hangars and took delight in spraying the bolting pilots with machine gun fire. A little-understood aspect of the Second World War in the air is that it began with virtually no comprehension of either the need for or the operational basis of night fighting. This was why the RAF was initially unmolested in its predawn sorties. No one thought they could be brought down at night.

A fighter pilot for eight years, leader of a *Gruppe* of powerful, heavily armed, twin-engined Destroyers, it was an Unhappy Falcon who raced neck and neck each morning with his pilots to see who would hit the slit trenches first. From this muddy and uncertain shelter, Falck and his fighter pilots stared incredulously as their Me-110s burned before their eyes. Livid with rage, Falck was determined to act.

A void clearly existed in Germany's aerial dispositions. The intolerable plight of the fighter pilots lying in ditches and being bombed was an irritating but minor aspect of a major problem. Falck tells the story of how he tackled this task:

"There we were, fighter pilots, sitting in ditches. God, how we hated it. We had a young radar officer with us, and he would toll off his predictions. 'The British are coming across the Bay. They will be here in ten minutes . . . eight minutes . . . three minutes . . .' and then all hell would break loose. I began putting two and two together.

"In this period, radar was very new to us—something that is easily forgotten now that it is so commonplace. The proper methods of using this instrument had not yet been developed. My reasoning was that if we knew where the bombers were, and when they were due to arrive, then there must be a possibility of intercepting these raiders. Anything was better than sitting in a ditch waiting for a bomb on my head.

"My view was that there must be a way to take off before they came, and then after the raid to fly out to sea with them in the darkness and fly with them until daylight. Then we could shoot them down. I worked out a system for this, after conferences with the searchlight commander and the radar man.

"We set up a specially coded map, and I tried it first with three crews. We had to find out if it was possible to fly at night with the Me-110. In retrospect, this now seems perhaps incredible, but it demonstrates how little we knew in those days and how ill prepared we were for what was to come."

As late as the spring of 1940 there was no German night fighter force, and experiments had to be conducted to see if the Me-110 could be operated at night without excessive losses. This indicates how much development was telescoped into the next two or three years, by which time the Germans were sometimes clawing down between fifty and a hundred Allied bombers at night through fighter action.

Falck's experimental unit had stellar personnel. There was Falck himself; Werner Streib (sixty-five night kills and one day kill during the war); Guenther "Fips" Radusch (sixty-four night kills); and Sergeant Thiel, a pilot who was later killed by German flak. Streib and Radusch were both experienced pilots, "Fips" Radusch having flown He-112 fighters in the Spanish Civil War, where he was credited with one kill.[1]

Streib's career as a night fighter ace will be dealt with extensively in Chapter Ten. In 1940 at Aalborg, it is ironic that Streib was, in Falck's words, "our leading pessimist on the possibilities of night fighting." Streib became a great ace and pioneer night fighter. He is often called the "Father of Night Fighting," an appellation more appropriate to Falck.

The elite pioneer unit began training. The pilots were familiarized with the schedule and procedures set up with the radar and searchlights. But the RAF was determined not to leave the Happy Falcon in peace as he prepared to clip the night bombers' wings.

"During this period the RAF attacked us again, rather late at night. We became so angry just sitting on the ground taking it that I said to my guys, 'Let's take off and get those Englishmen!' We dashed for our aircraft, and without radio, helmets, or parachutes we hurled ourselves into the air. We didn't even wait to fasten our seat belts. We broke every rule in the book in our mad rush to get airborne and shoot down a bomber.

"After takeoff, everyone was on his own. There was no radio link between us. After some time I saw a British bomber and tried to attack him, but he was pretty far from me, about four hundred meters. He spotted me and we exchanged fire. Then he dropped down into a heavy mist just above the North Sea. I lost him.

"Streib found a bomber too, only to lose him in the mist the same

Colonel Radusch, 73-victory ace, has retired from the new German Air Force.

way as I. Radusch was the star of the morning. He not only found another bomber, but came back with a lot of bullet holes in his aircraft. Only Sergeant Thiel failed to make contact.

"This was the proof we needed that it was possible to intercept and down these night raiders. With good radar and good communications, it *must* be possible. A sobering element in the operation was the sight of the airfield as we returned after dawn. The runway was pocked with bomb craters. Any one of those craters would have demolished an Me-110 had we dropped a wheel in it during our mad scramble."

Flushed with success, Falck sat down and wrote a comprehensive report on his experiences and findings. He laid out his theories of night interception so that a child could follow them. He claims today that it was one of the few reports from a fighter pilot that was ever actually read in the German Air Ministry during the war. He got instant action.

Ernst Udet visited Falck personally and discussed the report. Then came Colonel General Erhard Milch (later Field Marshal Milch) and General Albert Kesselring. For a time, there was more brass around Falck than could be found in the trombone section of the Berlin Symphony Orchestra. Elaborating these theories for his visitors helped him develop new angles and details. High-level interest in night fighting was hot, but then came the Battle of France, which saw all else shoved aside.

Falck took part in the French struggle with ZG-1. With the campaign successfully concluded, his *Gruppe* was battling with the RAF from a base at Le Havre when he received an urgent phone call from Kesselring.

"Falck," said Kesselring, "you are to fly back *today* with your group to Düsseldorf. You will begin forming the night fighters immediately to defend the area by night."

"But *Herr General*, we have taken heavy casualties and need time to train replacements and get new aircraft."

"I am sorry, Falck. You must fly back *today* and start work on the night fighter program."

Returning with the whole group, minus Olt. Lutz' squadron, to Düsseldorf to get the ball rolling, Falck confronted a situation requiring a diplomat rather than a soldier. A searchlight regiment under a Lieutenant Colonel was stationed in the city. This unit had been cooperating with an experimental Me-109 squadron in night fighting. They had many losses and no kills.

The commander of the Me-109 squadron was a Major of obstructionist tendencies, and since Falck was not only a Captain but also a *Gruppenkommandeur* the situation was delicate. Falck was trying to organize the ragged setup when he was ordered to The Hague on 26 June 1940. Reichsmarschall Goering himself wanted to meet the perceptive young leader with the night fighting ideas.

His conference at The Hague was an experience Falck is unlikely to forget:

"In the anteroom I met the radar officer from Jagdgeschwader Schumacher at Jever, 1st Lt. Teske, whom I had not seen for a long time. Then I was called into a big room, overpowering not only in its dimensions, but also in the personalities it contained. There was the resplendent Goering, Ernst Udet, Albert Kesselring, Chief of Personnel General Kastner, and General Bruno Loerzer, Goering's onetime mentor and personal friend.

"I was the little Captain, come to tell my story to these big men. True to form, Goering took the floor. Swaggering up and down, he gave his version of the situation. 'Germany will soon have a big victory. The only problem is the RAF at night. Now, there's only a *few* of them and they don't make any *real* trouble, but it is the only danger. We have to make some arrangements. We are going to have a new organization in the Luftwaffe—the night fighters—to counteract this night raiding. You, Falck! You've had some experience and you wrote this report. I'm making you Wing Commander of *Nachtjagdgeschwader* 1 (NJG-1). Congratulations!'

"He shook hands and told me to fly back to Düsseldorf and get busy. He didn't promote me, so it was the first time in the history of the Luftwaffe that a Captain was a Wing Commander. I was flabbergasted.

"My Me-110 Group was to be I/NJG-1. The Me-109 Group of the uncooperative Major would be II/NJG-1. I began explaining the problem of myself and the Major when Goering cut in: 'Fly back and tell that Major he is fired. Tell him to go home and await orders there. Pick out a new officer to command that Me-109 Group. You also need a good radar man and a good flak man. You have your pick of officers in the Luftwaffe.'

"This was close to *carte blanche*, so I immediately said that I would like my original radar man from Jever. I didn't know Goering. He ordered the officer brought in, and said to him: 'You are to be *my* personal specialist in radar. Falck, you can look for another man.' That was the way The Fat One worked."

Falck fired the Major back in Düsseldorf and promoted Macky Steinhoff to command II/NJG-1. The Lieutenant Colonel commanding the flak proved difficult, but Falck gently pointed out that he was now *Kommodore* of a wing. "Since we cannot give each other orders, I suggest we cooperate," he said. The flak man would have none of it. He angrily impugned the bravery of the night fighter pilots. Falck reacted by arranging for the flak officer to fly in an Me-110 the following night.

"I want you to see how it is, Colonel, up there in the dark, with your own flak firing at you and British gunners shooting multiple machine guns at you. Please go ahead and have this experience."

The Colonel declined, but thereafter was the soul of cooperation.

Soon afterward two squadrons of aircraft were sent to NJG-1 from a bomber wing. They were Do-17s. This was to be Falck's new Intruder Group for night fighter operations over British bases. NJG-1's insignia showed a falcon riding a lightning bolt striking a map of Britain. More and larger units were added until NJG-1 had a substantially larger establishment than any normal fighter wing.

As the wing burgeoned and its victories against the night raiders mounted, organizational changes were necessary. Kesselring was soon on the phone again to Falck.

"This night fighter thing is getting bigger and bigger. Colonel Josef Kammhuber of the General Staff will be appointed Division Commander to coordinate searchlights, radar, and air operations."

Within a few days, the energetic Kammhuber arrived at Falck's base:

"I did not know Kammhuber very well then. He came to my office and said, 'Please can you tell me about these operations from your viewpoint?' He told me to stay seated and was kindness itself. In a few days all that changed of course, but we were as close as twins for the next three years. Kammhuber was outstanding, capable, and realistic, and I admired him."

Major innovations in the night fighter organization and operations were introduced by the Kammhuber-Falck team in the ensuing years. Cooperation of searchlights, flak, radar, and fighter units was brought to a high level of efficiency. Some of these measures will be detailed in the next chapter, "The Night Fighters' War." Falck was nominally a Wing Commander, whose normal establishment would be three groups of fighters. He soon found himself commanding *eight* groups

DEFENSE COMMAND POST: Colonel Wolfgang Falck, center, studies plot with 1st Lieutenant Walther Wever at Berlin-Wannsee Defense Command Post. 1st Lieutenant Wever was son of first Luftwaffe Chief of Staff and was killed in the Me-262 jet on 10 April 1945. Wever is believed to have had over 40 victories. Falck was C.O. of *Luftflotte Reich* in night fighter operations. Officer on right is Major General Nielsen. (*Falck Collection*)

strung out from Norway to Brest.

He was in effect a Division Commander, although he never rose above the rank of Colonel, and his official night fighter command never extended beyond the gigantic NJG-1. Kammhuber became a General and set up his HQ in Utrecht in The Netherlands. As Kammhuber's chief deputy for three years, Falck shared all the serious problems of 1940–43 with his Chief. The very qualities of initiative and vision in Falck which had launched the night fighters eventually led to the dissolution of the partnership. The two men were not always able to agree on the massive problems arising in night fighter operations.

Falck's position was not unlike that of Galland. He wanted to concentrate his fighters for efficiency, economy, and operational success. Kammhuber's organizational genius went in the direction of an expanded organization. Their differences eventually led to a stony meeting in Schleissheim.

"Take a vacation," Falck quotes Kammhuber. "I have no job for you in my command. Go home and you will get your next orders from the Ministry."

Thus ended one of the great command and organizational teams in the history of the Luftwaffe. The Allies undoubtedly gained from its dissolution.

For three years and five days the Happy Falcon had been *Kommodore* of NJG-1. During this period Germany's greatest night fighter aces had been under his command. They ran the gamut from pioneers Werner Streib and "Fips" Radusch to Hans-Joachim Jabs (28 night victories), Helmut Lent (102 night kills), Heinz-Wolfgang Schnaufer (121 night victories), and Heinrich Prince zu Sayn-Wittgenstein (83 night victories). We will meet all these successful pilots in Chapter Ten, "Knights of the Night."

Following his dismissal from Kammhuber's staff, Falck was given the responsibility for the day and night fighter defense of the Reich, based in Berlin. He was there until the abortive bomb plot against Hitler in July 1944. Thoroughly fed up, Falck then went to see his old comrade Adolf Galland.

"Adolf, I want you to give me a job—a piloting job if possible—but not at home."

Sympathetic to Falck's situation, and able to understand his plight because of his own position, Galland cast about for a suitable post for his friend.

"I could make you Fighter Leader in the Balkans, with your HQ near Belgrade. Is that far enough away for you?"

Falck jumped at the offer. At this stage of the game, though, his luck was running poorly. He arrived in Belgrade the day Rumania switched sides in the war. Bulgaria followed suit five days later.

"I had only one fighter group in my kingdom and one radar regiment. Soon afterward, even the cohesion of these units was lost. Reports poured in that the Russians and Titoists were coming. I was a king without a kingdom. I followed the example of Germany in shortening the lines, and shortened mine to Vienna."

He was withdrawn from Vienna to Potsdam to become Chief of Staff of the Training Command, although by this time training activity had become largely academic. On 1 March 1945 he was given an assignment commanding fighters in the Rhineland.

"There was a catch to this job, as I soon found out. I just couldn't find my staff or HQ in the Rhineland. I don't know to this day what happened to them. So I drove on through southern Germany in the final hours of the war, and eventually became a POW of the Americans on 3 May 1945 in Bavaria."

As a Colonel of the Luftwaffe General Staff, Falck was a marked man. The intention of the Allies at that time appeared to be that all German generals and General Staff officers be given lifetime imprisonment at hard labor. Falck was free in barely a month.

His pervasive charm quickly turned his erstwhile foes into friends. They became more than friends. An American Military Police Captain and a Lieutenant of the U.S. Intelligence Corps—who must remain nameless—took the Happy Falcon under their wings. They not only made stamps for his personal documents, but also forged all the necessary signatures. Then they sent Falck home in their own car. One of the American officers lives today in New York, still a close friend of the caged falcon he freed.

The ex-Colonel who had commanded thousands of officers and men for a period of years took to farm laboring. He was at hard labor without being in Allied custody. He moved to northern Germany and became associated with an engineer trying to build a simple and economical car for farmers. While working on this project he got a telegram from a friend in Bielefeld who said there was a big job waiting for him in the industrial city. There was no Mercedes limousine waiting now to take ex-Colonel Falck to his appointment.

"I got on my bicycle and rode like hell to Bielefeld. It was the *British Army* that wanted me. They were looking for a former German officer as Chief of Staff for the 47th Royal Engineers Materiel Depot."

He reported for an interview with the C.O. of the British outfit. The Englishman came right to the point.

"We want a German staff type to boss our German workers and tradesmen. You'll do."

"It's impossible. I was a Colonel with the Knight's Cross to the Iron Cross and a member of the General Staff. The Allies will imprison me."

The Britisher ignored Falck's objection.

"When can you start?" he said.

"I can start today, but I am sure you will not like me."

"Why in hell not?"

"Because I am a German officer."

"Yes, we know that. That is exactly why we want to hire you."

"In some quarters I am regarded as a war criminal."

"Don't be a bloody fool. We need someone we can trust."

"But I have been decorated with the Knight's Cross."

"Yes, we know that too. That proves to us that you're OK. That's exactly the kind of man we need."

Falck took the job. He became Civil Officer of 47 Section Stores, Royal Engineers, in the service of his erstwhile enemy. His postwar civil career, which really began with this job, led eventually to his present job with North American Aviation, Inc., as a consultant in Bonn.

Falck's seven confirmed kills were all gained in the Me-110. His first three victories were against Polish aircraft and he then downed three Blenheims and one Wellington. He entered combat many times over the English Channel with Spitfires and Hurricanes, although he did not actually participate in the Battle of Britain.

"Flying against Spitfires and Hurricanes in the Me-110 was one of the most unpleasant experiences of my life," he says today. On at least one occasion, however, his attempted interception of a Spitfire had a pleasant ending. He was flying in his twin-engined fighter from Hamburg to Deelen in Holland and back when ground control radioed him the position of a lone Spitfire near him.

"I spotted the Spitfire, but he was too far from me and too fast, so I couldn't close in. Then, a little later, when I was coming in for a landing, I had started to let down from about five thousand feet when I saw this Spitfire *landing at our airfield*. The British pilot's oxygen had failed. In his daze he had seen only an airdrome below. When he revived, he was most unhappy. It was a cheap kill for our unit, and I was happier to meet him in our officers' club than in the air."

The English pilot traded tales with his Luftwaffe captors much as was the custom in the First World War. When the time came for him to be sent back to HQ at Frankfurt, Falck was equal to the occasion. He rewarded the Englishman for his kind remarks about the Me-110 by sending him to Frankfurt in the rear seat of one of the twin-engined fighters. That night, the RAF pilot telephoned his late host from Frankfurt to thank him for the ride and his hospitality.

This was not the only time in Falck's career where an ounce of human feeling neutralized a ton of hatred. He once had a downed RAF Flight Lieutenant as a lunch guest. The Englishman wore a massive bandage on his head. Seated at Falck's right hand, he was withdrawn and obviously apprehensive.

"He didn't dare to eat his soup," Falck recalls with a smile. "He was afraid it was poisoned. So I explained to him that we were all soldiers together, and that we were all under discipline in our Air Force as he was in his. I offered to change soup with him as assurance against poisoning."

The RAF man finally succumbed to the Falck charm, ate his soup, warmed up to the young Germans around him and eventually took off his huge bandage, revealing a small cut on his forehead. After lunch,

CHIVALROUS FALCON: Colonel Wolfgang Falck, fourth from right, treated five crewmen from downed RAF bomber to lunch at his Wing HQ in Arnhem. Falck enjoyed chivalrous meetings with his foes. Full story of this encounter is told in text. Young RAF pilot with large bandage on right eye initially feared Falck would poison him, but quickly warmed up and removed massive bandage to reveal small scratch. (*Falck Collection*)

he and Falck took a stroll through a beautiful little garden which Falck maintained on the base, and the two former enemies admired its lushness together.

That night, the RAF pounded the German base and unloaded a 250-pounder squarely in the Happy Falcon's idyllic park. At breakfast, the German commander chided his RAF guest.

"It's a shame that your people want to bomb my park while you're here. Barracks you can bomb, OK. Planes you can bomb, OK. Even homes if you like. But not my park."

During Falck's ditch-diving days at Aalborg he had another British Flight Lieutenant as an involuntary guest. The Germans viewed him with considerable curiosity as one wielding the power to send them bolting into slit trenches. This particular Englishman was a high-spirited type and was more concerned about a broken date in London than in being shot down. He got along famously with Falck. At lunch he confided his plight to his captor.

"It's a fair bastard being stuck here, Captain. I had an absolutely wonderful girl dated tonight. Six o'clock at Trafalgar Square station."

"I'm sorry for you," said Falck gallantly, "but I am happy you are my guest, and happier still that you are still alive."

With that, the Germans took up their glasses and drank the Englishman's health, welcoming him to Denmark. After a few minutes, the Englishman tried another approach.

"Captain Falck, can you fly to London in the Me-110?"

"Sure, easily."

"Well, you fly to London and meet my girl. You're a nice man and she would like you too."

"JUST THE MAN WE WANT . . .": Colonel Wolfgang Falck had the Knight's Cross, 7 aerial victories and a long war behind him in high command in 1945. He feared that the Allies would imprison him as a staff officer in accordance with propagandist threats in wartime. The British, however, told him he was "just exactly the kind of man we want" and put him to work bossing German technicians and tradesmen at the 47th Royal Engineers Materiel Depot in Bielefeld. *(Falck Collection)*

Falck is fundamentally a humanist, a man who is the reverse in all respects of the typical "German officer" depicted in Hollywood films. The celluloid German is a caricature. Falck is as real as a stubbed toe. To say he loved his enemies would be excessive, but he neither hated nor even disliked his foes.

He was always ready with a handshake for a downed enemy. Kindly and honorable treatment for a captured enemy pilot was a natural course of action for him, even in a war in which almost all the decencies of civilized conduct were inundated by hate propaganda. Falck and many German aces like him did not have to rise above the corrosive falsehoods of propaganda. Descent to that level, from the high standards of soldierly conduct which were innately theirs by both training and heritage, was something in which they did not indulge. Chivalry was more than an old-fashioned word to them.

The Happy Falcon is a frequent visitor to the United States these days, and is one of America's warmest admirers. His first visits caused him an embarrassment which he now enjoys relating as a joke on himself.

"At social gatherings, I would often in the custom of American affairs, move about alone and introduce myself as 'Wolf,' which is the normal abbreviation of my name in Germany. I got some remarkable reactions from American ladies at cocktail parties until one of my associates told me the implication of 'Wolf' in America."

Following the war, Falck's services have been very much in demand. He worked as an apprentice in a chemical-pharmaceutical company in Bielefeld and passed the examination. Then he became a salesman for the "Bielefelder Spielkarten GmbH" and worked his way up to become manager and finally director. In 1961, North American Aviation, Inc. of Los Angeles hired him as their German representative but after six years with them he was hired by McDonnell Douglas Corp in the same capacity. He is still with MDC but is a busy man in other endeavors too. He is the President of the German Fighter Pilots Asso., the Vice President of the German Aero Club, and a member of

HAPPY FALCON HAPPILY MARRIED: Wolfgang Falck has graduated from wartime night fighting in the Me-110 to peacetime sport flying in light aircraft. Here he is with his wife in Germany about to take off on a business trip. Falck is frequent visitor to the U. S. *(Falck Collection)*

the Godesberger Sport Flying Club, the "Alten Adler" Flying Club of Munich and the Flying Club of St. Johann of Tirol/Austria. In his late sixties, Falck is tall, lean and straight, with the physical stamp of a professional officer. He says of his present place in the world:

"If someone had told me in the ruin of 1945 that I would in twenty years be with an American aerospace and research company, I would simply have said, 'Poor man, you are stark, raving mad.'"

One of his friendly competitors in securing defense business in Germany is Adolf Galland, who pays the Happy Falcon this tribute:

"Wolfgang Falck was not only one of 'The First' who flew in 1939, but also one of the greatest in terms of pioneering and innovations to the new art of night fighting. He was one of our best men."

9

The Night Fighters' War

"Night fighting? It will never *come to that!"*
GOERING,
1939

THE young German pilot eased the stick forward and sent his twin-engined Me-110 plummeting into the shadows between the stabbing fingers of the German searchlights. From the sprawling Ruhr below came a hail of antiaircraft fire, aimed not at the Me-110 but at its quarry, a Whitley bomber of the RAF. Flak bursts banged and puffed around the German fighter, but the eagle-eyed pilot was oblivious to everything except the enemy bomber. The Whitley droned onward, a full load of bombs in its belly destined for the industrial heartland of Germany below.

The fighter rapidly overhauled the bomber. Squinting through the gloom, the German pilot pulled lead on his adversary and pressed his triggers. The 20mm cannons barked, the explosions hammering through the slender airframe, the muzzle flashes blazing in the blackness and partially blinding the pilot. The young German cursed quietly. His attack had gone wide. The Whitley went sailing on toward its target, but the fighter pilot was not to be denied.

Flinching as the searchlights bathed his aircraft sporadically in blue-white brilliance, he banked around for another attack. This time his aim was true. A stream of cannon shells thundered into the bomb-laden belly of the Whitley. Flaming fuel cascaded from the stricken bomber. A convulsive blast rent the air, and the remains of the Whitley went cartwheeling down in blazing shreds.

Oberleutnant Werner Streib of the Luftwaffe had scored the first kill by a night fighter over Germany. The date: 20 July 1940.

In the next five years Streib sent another sixty-five Allied aircraft

NIGHT FIGHTER AND DAY FIGHTER: The first to score a kill over Germany at night (20 July 1940) Werner Streib, 66 victory ace of NJG-1, poses with the ace who shot the most opponents down, Erich Hartmann (352 kills). Occasion for this photo was Streib's retirement from the Luftwaffe in 1966. *(Hartmann Collection)*

to join the thousands of RAF bombers downed by German night fighters. His first-to-last career as a night fighter pilot and leader made a solid contribution to what was in some respects the most successful element of German air power—night fighting. The Germans scored the greatest fighter victory of the war at night. They downed 107 RAF bombers[1] during the British attack on Nuremberg on the night of 30/31 March 1944. Such massive victories were rare, however, and revealed little of the years-long battle of the night fighters against a stubborn and technically ingenious foe.

Night fighting received less attention in prewar years than any other phase of aerial warfare development. This was true not only in Germany, but also in the Allied nations. This omission was to handicap both Germany and Britain in defending themselves against night bombing from the air. Night fighting techniques were largely developed from 1940 onward, and the full significance of the night fighter force was not appreciated by the German High Command until it was almost too late.

Night fighters were resisted politically and psychologically in Germany, and got far less than their fair share of Germany's amazingly advanced aerial technology. This situation had its roots in the experiences of the First World War, on which air power doctrine was largely based in the period between the wars. The lessons of the first war were in a certain sense misapplied, inasmuch as bombardment gained the ascendancy over pursuit in the high councils of the Allied nations as well as in Germany. Fighter aviation was regarded as a secondary aspect of air power in most prewar doctrine, and this was reflected in the dominant role assigned the bomber in development, design, and production.

In the United States, this resulted in the USAAF entering the Second World War without a fighter aircraft capable of meeting either the German Me-109 or the Japanese Zero on equal terms. Therefore

[1] The RAF estimated its losses at ninety-four bombers in this action, but RAF statistics show only those aircraft which failed to return. An additional thirteen bombers were damaged to the point of salvage.

it should be borne in mind, as German military myopia is examined, that Germany's war planners were not the only men who failed to see the new dimension of air power accurately.[2] Some of Germany's derelictions have already been outlined in Chapter One. The history of night fighter development reveals many more. The men who flew fighters at night had to bear the burden of these errors.

Just as the fighter aspect was the minor aspect of German air power, so was the night fighter the minor aspect of fighter power—so minor that it barely existed prior to the war itself. In 1939 the Luftwaffe had one squadron of Me-109 fighters set aside for night fighting experiments. This so-called "Moonlight Squadron" is in retrospect one of the strangest anomalies of the war.

General Eisenhower has said that "All hindsight is 20-20 vision," but even allowing for this it now seems incredible that so little effort was invested in the night fighter. Bomber designers and bomber advocates were in no doubt that these aircraft would be used by day *and* *night*. Night bombers made an impact even in the First World War, the German Gotha raids on Britain being a case in point. In contending with a night bomber force—a weapon which all the major nations intended to use and which they expected their future enemies to use against them—there was a conceptual and technological vacuum.

Fighter aviation's most ardent advocates seemed at a loss to fill this void. Between the wars, exercises in night fighting served only to re-emphasize the dependence of profitable night fighter attack on individual pilot ability, a factor already evident in the First World War. Seeking and finding the enemy bomber at night, and shooting it down, reduced itself to ineluctable *human* factors which resisted concretion into doctrine and formal presentation in training manuals.

A high-level conviction existed in Germany that the very rarity of such outstanding individual ability at night fighting minimized the hazards to a night bomber force. Night fighters were regarded as an acceptable risk. This conviction was reinforced and sustained by the continuing and complete dependence of the night fighters on weather conditions. Accordingly, even the "Moonlight Squadron" was disbanded early in 1940, and Germany stood naked before the coming nocturnal storm.

The initiative of Wolfgang Falck in tackling the night fighter problem in the spring of 1940 has already been outlined. From the first sorties he organized with radar direction, night fighting soon began to find its way. With Falck's leadership, a special diet and youthful enthusiasm, Werner Streib and his fellow experimenters also found that night fighting skill could be developed.

A notable discovery in the early period was the marked improvement

[2] America's famed Air Force General H. H. "Hap" Arnold had said in the early thirties, "Fighters will be ineffective in wartime." In 1934 he again concluded that it was doubtful whether single-engined pursuit planes would even be flying in the next war. But late in 1939 Arnold wrote, "It has been demonstrated recently beyond a doubt that the best antiaircraft defense is pursuit aviation."

of visibility from fifteen thousand feet and above. Streib quickly developed his latent talent for night action, and he later scored two kills in three nights over the Ruhr, the first of which has already been described. The punch and counterpunch drama of the night air war over Germany thus began with pilots like Streib, Radusch, and Helmut Lent using essentially First World War tactics against the invaders.

Visual contact, blind luck, and truly superior piloting and shooting skill remained the essentials of success against the Wellingtons, Whitleys, Hampdens, and Blenheims of the RAF in those days. The success of the pioneer night fighters was such that a general reappraisal of night fighting soon followed.

By the end of September 1940 the Luftwaffe High Command began viewing the long-term threat of the RAF bombers with some concern. The invasion of Britain had been set aside. There was the definite possibility that Britain would now rally and recover, and the continued RAF night bomber raids presaged the direction and mode of Britain's main thrust against the Reich. These events occurred while a vital technical revolution was unfolding.

Airborne radar was now technically feasible. Here was an area in which night fighting techniques could be significantly advanced. The Telefunken organization was awarded a development contract for airborne radar for the night fighters. As to aircraft, the march of events resulted in some re-evaluations of the machines that were available and suitable for night fighting.

The disastrous combat advent of the Me-110 in its designed role required that the twin-engined heavy fighter be otherwise employed than in escorting bombers to England. Night fighting proved to be the answer. In the absence of Spitfire opposition, the Me-110 demonstrated its fair share of virtues. The machine had considerable endurance, adequate hitting power and performance, and the additional crew member became an asset as operator of the complex airborne radar gear.

In practical night combat, the Germans also soon found that it was not essential to employ a fast fighter in the night interceptor role. The fast (285 mph) Ju-88 bomber had sufficient speed to bring off night interceptions, plus the advantages of great range and payload. The Ju-88 could carry heavier armament, more ammunition, more electronic equipment, and the additional crew to operate the radar. The Ju-88 was accordingly pressed into service as a night fighter. This was a radical departure from its original design as a dive bomber, but the aircraft served throughout the war as the mount of some of the Luftwaffe's leading night aces.

The Dorner Do-17 bomber with a speed of 236 mph was also used as a night fighter and also as an intruder. No effort was made to design and develop a high-performance night fighter specifically for the role. This was generally in line with the disastrous 1940–41 period in German aircraft production.

Ernst Heinkel's privately designed He-219, a 1940 effort intended to meet the Luftwaffe's economy-inspired desire for multipurpose aircraft, turned out fortuitously to be Germany's finest night fighter. More will be said later concerning this machine, which, like the Me-262 jet, did not appear in sufficient numbers early enough to be decisive.

The belated recognition of the night bomber threat in mid-1940 led to a certain rallying of Germany's human as well as its technical resources. As recounted in the previous chapter, these moves brought to the fore Colonel (later General) Josef Kammhuber as General of the Night Fighters. Destined to become one of the leading figures in the history of German air power, Kammhuber served four years in the First World War after volunteering in 1914. Born in Bavaria in 1896, he was *Kommodore* of a bomber wing in 1939, and during the Battle of France was shot down at the ripe old age of forty-four.

Kammhuber was thus at the peak of his youthful powers when charged with the organization of Germany's night defenses in July 1940. Short in stature, Kammhuber was long on energy, ability, and drive. He set up the defense system later known as the "Kammhuber Line," extending from the island of Sylt to the mouth of the Scheldt River.

The system began as a fifteen-mile-deep strip of searchlights in front of the flak batteries, with the night fighters stationed in air standby areas. The airborne defenders could thus pounce on the bombers when the invaders were caught by the searchlights and before the flak opened fire. The system was refined and elaborated in accordance with practical experience and technical advances.

Radar strips were placed in front of the light strips when the Wurzburg-Riese radar unit became available after October 1940. The thirty-kilometer range of these new radars permitted night fighter operations on a "dark night" basis ahead of the light strips.

The "Himmelbett" system (literally, the Heavenly Bed) was then developed to maintain pressure on the raiders for as long as possible. Colonel Wolfgang Falck describes a typical "Himmelbett" system as follows:

"Sketch   shows the construction of a Himmelbett system in which on principle all equipment was installed in the center.

1. 1 *Beacon* which served the night fighter as orientation point, and to which he was electronically "tied."
2. 1 *Freya Radar* with a 60–100-km range, which detects the approaching enemy aircraft and reports it to the
3. *Wurzburg-Riese "A."* The Wurzburg-Riese units have a range of about 30 km. The "A" unit takes over the target and transmits the data according to direction, distance, and altitude to the Command Post S.
4. *The Wurzburg-Riese "B"* constantly guides the night fighter and reports his data also to the Command Post S.
5. At the *Command Post* the data are projected by a red (target) and

blue (night fighter) light spot reflector from underneath on the

6. *Seeburg-Tisch.* This table consists of a glass plate on which the whole area is drawn like a map, and from which the fighter controller guides the night fighter to the enemy bomber until the night fighter can take over the target either visually or with his aircraft radar.

"Later on, two or three night fighters were used in one Himmelbett system. These aircraft were 'stacked' at various altitudes and guided in succession towards various targets."

Adjoining Himmelbett systems were made to overlap, and the command posts connected by telephone. A target which was not shot down in one "Heavenly Bed" could thus be transferred to the next without difficulty. A number of such command posts were combined to form a night fighter division, and in the divisional command post the entire area situation was projected on vast glass walls. Galland among others has written of the fascination exerted upon ambitious Gauleiters and city officials by the wondrous divisional displays. They were widely coveted as a status symbol by Party officials.

RAF bombers had to pass through a series of such areas both approaching and leaving their targets. The Germans sought to inflict maximum damage—both physical and psychological—by maintaining virtually continuous night fighter or flak pressure on the bombers. At least, this was the goal of the defenders.

In practice the system did not completely fulfill its purpose, even when supplemented with additional combined night fighter oper-

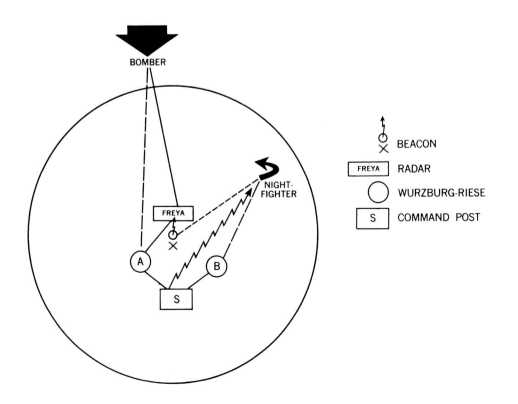

ations areas along strategic routes, e.g., Britain to Berlin. Far wider zones were required for the perpetual harassment of the bombers which the system attempted. Only a limited number of night fighters could be directed in any given area, and this limited the kills that could be inflicted on the invading forces. The system was doomed to eclipse as soon as the RAF could increase the size of its bomber force, since German night fighters could only rarely shoot down enough attackers to make the loss rate prohibitive.

Kammhuber's vigorous expansion of the night fighter force, as well as the organization of the defenses, was limited by equipment shortages. In addition, he had to battle high-level incompetence, and the demands of the Eastern Front from mid-1941 onward were insatiable. Nevertheless, Kammhuber turned Falck's bold beginning to good account. By December 1942 there were six night fighter wings defending the Reich.

General Kammhuber must be credited with outstanding achievements, working as he did with limited resources in a field where virtually every step broke new ground and where there was no doctrine or experience from the past on which to draw. His support of the long-range intruder operations against RAF bases in Britain exemplified his vision. Such operations, if built up from their early success as Kammhuber wished, could have done much to abort the early thousand-bomber raids, and perhaps even have dislocated such operations.

Like other night fighter operations Kammhuber proposed and espoused, intruder strikes against British bases were killed politically. Hitler could see no merit in hurting the RAF if the damage was done where the German civilians could not see it. Like most rational men of ability in high command in Germany, Kammhuber was destined to run afoul of the political leadership. His forced "resignation" in 1943, and subsequent banishment to an obscure command in Norway, was a severe loss to Germany.

The RAF was able to drop approximately thirty-five thousand tons of bombs on Germany during 1941. Impressive by prewar and Battle of Britain standards, this figure nevertheless concealed the grim outlines of a crisis. Bomber Command had suffered severe losses at the hands of the German night fighters. The situation in Britain was serious.

Within the British defense establishment Bomber Command was at this time virtually fighting for its life as a major instrument of Allied strategy. Had the German High Command grasped the signal importance of strangling the night bomber offensive at its birth, the history of the war might well have been different.

The Germans may see now how close they came in 1941 to aborting the major instrumentality of their country's ruin. Not only were Germany's night fighter pilots wreaking havoc, but Bomber Command had operational problems distinctly its own. The night navigation of the bomber crews was disastrously poor. Deprived of many advantages of classical air navigation through inclement weather and the corruption of radio aids, the valiant British crews could do little more than grope their way to the general vicinity of their targets.

Forced up above oxygen height, without oxygen, to avoid flak and searchlights; flying in regions of heavy icing without effective de-icing equipment; riding loads of explosives through the air in highly flammable aircraft without self-sealing fuel tanks; flying in perpetual fear of night fighter attack—theirs was a desperately courageous effort. These harassed crews were far removed in skill, confidence, and equipment from those who came in later years, and their impact on the enemy was minimal.

Photo reconnaissance of targets purportedly attacked by these bomber crews showed all too frequently that they were lucky to come within several miles of their targets. Because the power of the later night offensive has left a deeper historical mark, there is a tendency to skip over these earlier years when the damage done by the night bomber force was not of sufficient magnitude to matter. To the end of 1941, this was certainly true.

German industry had not been paralyzed. Not even one seriously damaging blow had been struck at Germany by the night bombers. On the contrary, Germany was pushing the Royal Navy to its limits in the Atlantic, driving the British Army to the brink of defeat in North Africa, and seemingly overwhelming even the Soviet colossus. The demands from all fronts for bombing aircraft to offset the real threats to Allied power got a better hearing in high British councils than in Bomber Command. The RAF was obviously not achieving much with its ragged night offensive against the Reich.

To sustain the development of Bomber Command against the many rival calls for bombing aircraft, Air Chief Marshal Sir Arthur Harris mounted the first thousand-bomber raid. He had to prove that Germany could be hurt by night. By using scratch crews and ransacking the British Isles for aircraft, Harris brought off the Cologne raid in May 1942. This strike had dramatic consequences in both Britain and Germany.

The German defense was saturated. The inherent weakness of the night fighter system was revealed by the inconsequential losses the Germans inflicted. On a bright moonlight night they were able to score only thirty-six kills out of a force of a thousand bombers. Furthermore, the bomber hordes flying to Cologne had shown with awful clarity that great numbers of aircraft would disrupt the night fighter system. This experience portended the later abandonment by the RAF of its traditional approach and departure in formation—waves of bombers—in favor of the stream tactic.

In spite of numerous shortcomings, the German night fighters up to the end of 1941 had fought the RAF to a draw. The impact of bombing on German industry had been held within tolerable limits. Civilian morale was not a problem. The decision of the previous autumn to proceed with airborne radar development had begun to yield practical hardware, and Telefunken had prototype versions of its Lichtenstein B.C. 409 mc radar available in the summer of 1941.

The radar sets promised to strengthen the interception capability of the night fighters. The pilots had depended up to this time on visual contact, even after they were directed to the incoming bombers by the radar controller on the ground. The basic night fighting tactic was to stay above fifteen thousand feet in air standby areas, taking advantage of the superior night visibility thus afforded, and leaving enemy aircraft at lower altitudes mainly to the flak.

All interceptions and downings prior to the advent of the Lichtenstein B.C. radar had depended ultimately on visual contact. With airborne radar, visual contact became necessary only in the final phases when closing in to fire. The Lichtenstein B.C. received top priority and in the early spring of 1942, NJG-1 in Holland blooded the first operational versions of the new radar units. The new-fangled contraption evoked a mixed reception from the pilots.

A veritable forest of antennae appeared on the noses of the Ju-88s selected for the first installations. Helmut Lent, who eventually scored 102 night kills as well as eight day victories, was among the aces of NJG-1 to view this development with alarm and disapproval. The Ju-88 could ill afford the 25-mph loss of speed which the antenna installation imposed on the aircraft. The degradation of performance left the Ju-88 with a very narrow speed margin over the new RAF Lancasters, which were making their presence felt over Germany in increasing numbers.

The Lancaster's performance was also a surprise to the Germans. The RAF's classical evasive maneuver against night fighters, the corkscrew, was brought to a new level of effectiveness with the Lancaster. Rapidly changing speed, altitude, and direction the Lancasters gave their own gunners a field day, and the astonishingly maneuverable bombers could throw off an inexperienced German night fighter pilot.

As theory moved into practical warfare, another unwelcome factor required attention. Operation of the Lichtenstein B.C. was naturally deemed the function of the radio operator, who also served as rear gunner in the Ju-88. The radar set's display included three cathode-ray tubes which gave horizontal location, vertical location, and distance of the enemy aircraft. Juggling with the equipment and passing data to the pilot demanded the radio operator's intense concentration on the screens. After fifteen minutes of staring at the glowing phosphors the radio operator lost his night vision. He could not function efficiently as a rear gunner at night, and the night fighter thus lost some of its combat strength as the price of interception.

A radar operator added to the crew strictly for the interception task remedied this problem. The radio operator–rear gunner was left in his original role. Working out such "bugs" took time, during which the apathy of some NJG-1 aces deepened. Captain Ludwig Becker turned the tide in the summer of 1942 by scoring the first radar-directed kill.

NIGHT-FIGHTER ACE LUDWIG BECKER: NJG-1 night fighter pilot Captain Ludwig Becker scored the first night kill for the Luftwaffe using radar for directions onto the target, summer of 1942. He went on to score 46 night victories. *(Nowarra)*

The young squadron leader sent confidence in and enthusiasm for the new equipment soaring.

The two-mile range of the Lichtenstein B.C. gave the night fighters new eyes. Determined to try to prevent expansion of the Cologne-type mass raids, the night fighter pilots fell on the RAF savagely. British countermeasures attested to the success of the German airborne radar. Jamming techniques were developed by the British, and in the summer of 1943 the RAF began sending radar-equipped Beaufighters as escorts. Led by the redoubtable British ace Bob Braham, the Beaus further harassed the German night fighters.

Mosquito night fighters followed. The German Ju-88s, Me-110s, and Do-17s were no match for the radar-equipped Mosquitos. The fast, maneuverable and heavily armed Mosquitos homed on the Lichtenstein units carried in the German fighters. German scientists countered with "Naxos," a warning device which gave a progressive aural alarm at the approach of a hunting Mosquito.

Successive versions of the Lichtenstein overcame British jamming, and allowed the German night fighter force to inflict losses on the RAF far exceeding its own. These seesaw battles of technical ingenuity, sustained in the air by the courage and resourcefulness of the pilots, saw the Germans peg level with their foes until the summer of 1943. The balance changed on the night of 24/25 July 1943, at the beginning of the Hamburg fire raids.

Eight hundred RAF heavies attacked Hamburg with devastating

effect. From the time German radar detected the invaders, it was evident that the night war was taking a dramatic new turn. The British used the so-called Laminetta method of disrupting German radar. Tinfoil cut to the wavelength of German radar was dropped from the bombers. Because of their reflectivity and dimensions, the tinfoil strips returned echoes to the German radar receivers out of all proportion to their actual size. The light weight of the strips increased the effect, since the foil fell only slowly and was often carried far aloft in updrafts.

The thousands of massive radar echoes created chaos in the German ground stations. Radar screens now displayed only huge blurs. All possibility of intelligent night fighter direction evaporated, and the airborne radars in the German fighters were similarly corrupted. With their electronic eyes put out, the Germans watched in horror as the RAF made a shambles of Hamburg in a series of night raids. By day, the USAAF heavies maintained the pressure.

"Window" or "chaff," as the British called their tinfoil strips, was a tactical triumph. The strips veiled an even more ominous tactical breakthrough. The bomber stream had been born. RAF bombers had previously approached their German targets in formation, usually in visual contact with each other. This traditional tactic had given the Germans a chance to contend with their foes.

The RAF heavies now came in on narrow fronts, wave upon wave, but in no definite formation and only rarely in visual contact. The stream of bombers, dropping tinfoil as it came, ripped a breach in the defense with which the German night fighters were powerless to deal. Germany's nocturnal umbrella had been torn to shreds.

This paralyzing tactical blow, with the indescribable horror of the ensuing fire storms which swept through Hamburg, called for immediate countermeasures from the German radar experts. Until such countertactics could be devised, an awesome gap had opened in the German night defense. The nocturnal Martian drama had reached its nadir.

A bold and dynamic young figure now leaped upon the stage, and he was to dominate the scene in the ensuing months. Major Hajo Herrmann,[3] not yet thirty and a veteran bomber pilot, was an independent-minded and perceptive officer with a flair and a feeling for the novel. Anguished by the nocturnal destruction of German cities, he was convinced that a void existed in night fighter operations.

He reasoned that it was now impossible to prevent the RAF, with its new H2S navigational aid, from locating its metropolitan targets. This hard, irreversible fact meant that German cities would continue to burn at night. Herrmann's idea was to turn this tragedy into a tactical asset, and make it work against the British.

Instead of persevering with blackout regulations and measures which were now useless, Herrmann proposed that German cities be fully illuminated. As an officer on the Luftwaffe Operations Staff at

---

[3] Nine aerial victories and winner of the Swords.

Wildpark Werder, Herrmann had many times seen how the masses of heavy bombers broke through the night fighter defense. No fighters operated above the cities, the aerial defense of which was left to search-lights and flak.

From the ground Herrmann had seen how the bombers were held in searchlight beams for minutes at a time. He knew that if he were aloft in a fighter he could shoot down those bombers. He would not need radar or complex ground control because he could see his quarry in the searchlights. A flak-free zone in which the fighters could attack the bombers was the only modification needed to the existing setup.

Herrmann's proposal was therefore to light up the cities like day, bring in all possible searchlights and turn the air above metropolitan centers into illuminated arenas in which his fighters could assault the invaders. His direct line of thought extended to the fighter types. He recommended the use of fast, single-engined Me-109s and FW-190s. There would be no ground control and no radar.

These fighters would tear into the bombers with the basic attributes of the fighter pilot—good eyesight, determined piloting, accurate shooting. The young ex-bomber pilot was convinced his plan had a place in the German defense. The void it would fill was obvious to any-one who could watch the bombers circling unmolested above the cities. He never had any ideas of substituting his tactic for the existing night fighter system. Herrmann saw it as a supplement, not a substitute.

His proposal introduced an anachronistic element into the now complex business of night fighting. Successful night fighter operations had become dependent on a vast plexus of radar and communications, without which the night fighter pilot was blind, lost, and ineffectual. To use such simple, direct methods as Herrmann proposed was to short-

WILD BOAR: When the RAF corrupted German radar in 1943 with the use of "window," colonel Hajo Herrmann ad-vocated night attacks on the bombers by single-engined fighters attacking the RAF heavies by the light of German searchlights. Called "Wild Boar" tactics, they shook the RAF with some heavy losses when first introduced. *(Jagerblatt)*

circuit all that had been so arduously built up since 1940. Already there was an "Establishment" in the night fighters, and Herrmann's radical return to 1940 encountered its stout resistance.

The reaction of night fighting commanders and technical experts ranged from reasoned written criticism to personal criticism of Herrmann. Opponents pointed out that he was a bomber pilot, not a fighter pilot. His practical experience of night fighting was limited to being shot at by night fighters over London.

Herrmann had developed his tactical acumen the hard way. He had flown over three hundred missions as a bomber pilot under widely varying conditions. The Battle of Britain, the struggle for Malta, and the brutal war in the Arctic against Allied convoys were all part of his experience. The Knight's Cross at his throat attested to his qualities and skill.

Graying at the temples at twenty-nine, mature beyond his years, and utterly determined, Herrmann proved a compelling advocate for his innovation. An ardent supporter was Major Werner Baumbach, the Luftwaffe's leading bomber pilot. The two men secured an audience with Goering on 27 June 1943, and Herrmann won over the Reichsmarschall with a masterful presentation.

Favorably disposed to strong, dynamic personalities, Goering was convinced that Herrmann's proposal had merit. He authorized an experimental commando. The ex-bomber pilot quickly rounded up ten FW-190s and Me-109s and the pilots to fly them.

Equipped with 85-gallon belly tanks mounted externally, the single-engined machines would be able to stay aloft at least two hours. Extra fuel endurance was essential if they were to reach distant cities under attack and still be able to fight at full throttle against the bombers. They would only have a limited time in which to press home their attack, and to run out of fuel at the critical moment would be a disaster.

Ready for a baptism of fire on the night of 3/4 July 1943, Herrmann led his commando into the air when bombers were reported on their way to the Ruhr. He had set up a flak-free zone over the Ruhr area. From sixty-five hundred meters upward Herrmann's pilots could operate without being shot down by the friendly gunners below. But something had already gone wrong with the plan.

The bomber stream was not going for the Ruhr. Cologne was the target. Herrmann cursed. The flak gunners around Cologne did not even know his commando existed. They would blaze away at everything that moved above them. Too late. In the distance Herrmann could already see the bombers coming. The night fighters were attacking them in the regular night fighter areas. Blazing trails streamed downward as stricken bombers hurtled earthward. The RAF was breaking through the defenses again, even though they were losing bombers. Herrmann knew then that he would hurl his commando on the bombers, flak or no flak.

He shuddered inwardly as he saw several more bombers explode and plunge earthward in the distance. They were the enemy, but it was a hell of a death. The British crews would be operating at the peak of nervous energy. As a bomber pilot, he knew the strain they would be under, wondering if tonight they were going to "buy it" or get back home. Herrmann would add to the strain with his unexpected fighter attack.

"Christmas trees" and multicolored markers arced and floated through the sky, popping, glowing, glaring luridly. Star shells and flares burst with eye-searing brilliancy, and below in the distance Herrmann spotted the even rows of orange flashes as the bomb loads thundered into the ancient city. The raid was nearing its climax.

The probing, blue-white searchlight beams found the bombers and locked them in their brilliant grasp. A murderous hail of flak, peppering the sky above the city, stirred London memories in the onrushing Herrmann. Engines screaming wide open, the commando slashed among the bombers. The tactic was every man for himself, rip at any bomber in range, tear them down.

They were like wild boars, scenting their enemies and ripping through the underbrush at full pelt for the kill. Herrmann's unit took its name from the fearless forest juggernaut—the Wild Boar. Above Cologne on that first fiery night they gave meaning to the name.

Herrmann hurled his nimble FW-190 at a light-drenched Lancaster. Closing in from the port quarter he came up so quickly on the slower bomber that his own aircraft was bathed in unearthly brilliance. Turbulence from the British machine and the ceaseless, nerve-fraying jolts of close flak bursts threw the German fighter around like a leaf.

Steadying his aircraft, Herrmann could see the helmeted British pilot squinting downward from the port side of the Lancaster. He was taking in the lurid scene below, oblivious to his own imminent doom. Bomber crews had become accustomed to the relative sanctuary over the cities, with the flak their only foe. Sanctuary ended for the RAF as Herrmann triggered the FW-190's four cannons.

The withering blast thundered into the Lancaster's belly. The bomber staggered convulsively, then flared alight from nose to tail. Plunging earthward the raider added its mortal glare to the sea of light above the city. Sucking the stick back, Herrmann went climbing out of the hellish flak.

Gaining altitude he could see other bombers falling in flames. Darting here and there were the diminutive silhouettes of the single-engined German fighters—dwarfed by the British giants. Tracers laced the sky as Herrmann's pilots tore into their foes. He could see they were scoring heavily. His primitive mode of attack was a success.

Herrmann headed for home base and awaited the return of his commando. Nine of the ten fighters made it back safely, among them a thirty-two-year-old former transport pilot named Friedrich-Karl Mueller, who never expected to fly a fighter during the war. He typified the kind of men Herrmann had picked for his Wild Boar commando.

"Nose" Mueller was a former Lufthansa commercial pilot in peacetime who had found his way first into the bomber force and then into the
air transport force. Herrmann's bomber piloting experience had taught
him the value of solid training, expecially for the demanding business of
night flying. To avoid a prohibitive accident rate in his unit, Herrmann
had "The Nose" transferred to his commando as blind-flying instructor.

The thin-featured Mueller had a prominent proboscis, a gaunt
resemblance to movie actor Wallace Beery, and a superlative gift for
Herrmann's free-swinging brand of night fighting. In spite of his age,
which made him an "old man" fighter pilot, "The Nose" became the
top-scoring single-engined night fighter ace of the war. He clobbered
thirty bombers in fifty-two combat missions, twenty-three of his victims
going down in Wild Boar attacks. These handsome accomplishments
won Mueller the Knight's Cross and he ended the war as a Major in
command of a group in NJG-11.

The first strike of the Wild Boar commando brought down twelve
heavy bombers. An elated Goering ordered Herrmann to form a complete new wing of Wild Boar fighters, to be designated JG-300. The
Wild Boar's progenitor would be the wing's *Kommodore*. When the
Hamburg fire raids began less than a month later, Major Hajo Herrmann was much more than the *Kommodore* of a half-formed fighter
wing. He was the man of the hour.

The shattering effect of the Hamburg fire raids on Goering has been
graphically described in Adolf Galland's book *The First and the Last*.
The blustering Reichsmarschall was undermined by the holocaust
that swept through the city. He was also unnerved by the nullification
of the German radar defenses.

Goering made a desperate phone call to Herrmann, then fully
occupied in building JG-300 at Bonn-Hangelar.

"Germany has only you to depend on now," said the despairing
Goering. And he ordered Herrmann into the fray with the few aircraft
then available.

The Wild Boars tore into the RAF during the remainder of the fire
raids, but there were only twelve of the new-style fighters and they
could not turn the tide of the battle. They were facing seven hundred
RAF heavies. Herrmann's men fought hard and brought down many
bombers, but their kills were simply not numerous enough to matter.

In a smashing vindication of Herrmann's original concept, *all*
German night fighters, with or without radar, were ordered to operate
as Wild Boars for the duration of the emergency. Until the German
experts found the technical counter to "window," the entire night
fighter force would be following Hajo Herrmann's tactical lead. There
was no other way to fill the gap.

On the night of 24/25 August 1943, the RAF attacked Berlin in force
with another Hamburg-style catastrophe in mind. Under ideal Wild
Boar conditions Herrmann's units downed fifty-six invaders. With
excellent visibility and a flak-free zone above 4500 meters, massed

searchlights and savage determination, the Wild Boars made the RAF suffer. Again on 1 September 1943, forty-seven British heavies were downed over Berlin. Three nights later, twenty-six more went down. Similar numbers were heavily damaged. The Wild Boar was making its presence felt.

These casualties caused consternation and dismay in RAF Bomber Command. Every prior indication was that Germany's night fighters had been brought to their knees through the corruption of their radar. By discarding radar temporarily and hurling in the Wild Boar, the Germans countered the RAF effort to wipe out Berlin.

Herrmann was ordered to build JG-300 into a full division of three Wild Boar wings. But as the winter closed in, things became harder for the Germans. Bad weather worked against the Wild Boar technique. Nevertheless the night fighters were able to inflict better than 5 percent losses on the RAF in sixteen major raids.

The toll taken of the bombers was not easily achieved. With their radar aids the British no longer needed to make visual sightings of their targets. The clouds became a merciful veil between the British bombers and the Wild Boars. As a counter tactic, Herrmann arranged for the searchlights to turn their beams on the cloud base. His fighter pilots could then look down from above and see the bombers silhouetted like cut-outs on frosted glass.

Herrmann's men faced two foes—the RAF and the weather. The weather proved the more formidable enemy. Aces of the flying skill of "Nose" Mueller were rare. He could find his way down to base through a low cloud ceiling, but pilots without his experience and training began crashing in bad weather with alarming frequency.

As the winter wore on, the situation became worse. After a nerve-clanking battle with the bombers, many Wild Boar pilots were not equal to finding their way home in bad weather. More and more often the less experienced had to take to their parachutes to survive. Their fighters were left to crash without ever receiving a hit.

Just as the Wild Boar spent its force, the German radar experts restored dark night locational ability to the night fighters. The Lichtenstein SN2 airborne radar countered RAF "window." On 16 March 1944 the 30th Fighter Division was ordered disbanded. A few units continued on, but the night of the Wild Boar was over.

Hajo Herrmann had risen to Colonel and Inspector of Aerial Defense, and was awarded in succession the Oak Leaves and Swords to his Knight's Cross. Scarcely three dozen fighter pilots won the Swords between 1939 and 1945. Herrmann also became an ace by personally downing nine RAF heavy bombers. His rise had been meteoric.

With the passing of the Wild Boar, Herrmann no longer was the focal point of the German night defense. He commanded the 9th *Fliegerdivision*; and the *Rammkommando Elbe*, in which armored FW-190s were used to ram B-17s, was another innovation of his as daring as was the Wild Boar.

1942 AMERICAN AIRCRAFT: Clockwise from top left are the North American Aviatin B-25 "Mitchell," the Consolidated B-24 "Liberator," the Boeing B-17 "Fortress," the Bell P-39 "Airacobra," and the Curtis P-40 "Tomahawk." *(USAAF)*

Hajo Herrmann's war ended with a stroke of bad luck. In an effort to rescue a comrade forced down behind the Russian lines, he fell into the clutches of the Soviets. He was incarcerated in Russia for eleven years. When he returned to Germany in 1955, he was one of the last of the prominent German fighter aces and leaders to be released.

Rarely has any airman had such a dramatic rendezvous with destiny as that which befell Hajo Herrmann. Without the counter tactic which his prescience, combat instinct, and common sense brought to fulfillment—in spite of the opposition of his own side—"Bomber" Harris of the RAF might well have knocked Germany out of the war by the spring of 1944.

Herrmann stirred tactical thinking. When the Wild Boar petered out, new tactics were in the making to deal with the bomber stream. Colonel Viktor von Lossberg, also a bomber pilot and a thoughtful tactician, urged that infiltration of the British bomber stream be adopted as the primary counter tactic to the stream itself. Von Lossberg envisioned the night fighters joining the British bombers in the stream on both the approach and the departure flights. Each fighter could conduct its own individual pursuit operations once in the stream.

This tactic was responsible for the greatest fighter victory of the war —day or night, German or Allied—when the Germans claimed 107 kills during the Nuremberg raid of 30/31 March 1944. The British estimated their losses at ninety-four heavies, but thirteen additional bombers were damaged to the point of salvage even though they made it back to Britain.

Another triumph of the infiltration tactic was Operation Gisela on the night of 4/5 March 1944. The Germans downed seventy-five heavy bombers over Chemnitz. If such tolls of the invaders could have been exacted on a steady basis, the RAF would have found it difficult to sustain the night bombing. The occasional brilliant achievement could not compensate for the telling steadiness with which the RAF drove home its attacks week in and week out.

By October 1944 the Allied radar experts had virtually neutralized German airborne radar. The German night fighter force went into steady decline thenceforth until the end of the war. Individually brilliant feats continued, but the night fighters were overwhelmed by the numerical and technical weight of the enemy, and their most valorous efforts counted for nothing in the ultimate outcome.

German night fighter operations on the Eastern Front were much more limited than in the West, and did not involve the sophisticated techniques and organization demanded for fighting the RAF. In the early stages of the Eastern Front struggle, night operations were confined to occasional combat by JG-54 pilots during bright summer nights in the northern sector. Under these conditions, night fighting techniques were hardly necessary.

As the war burned on, the Russians began nettling the German High Command with nocturnal nuisance raids. The extensive dropping of guerrilla troops behind the German lines at night also became a source of concern. The Army asked Luftwaffe Chief of Staff General Johannes Jeschonnek to initiate countermeasures. Galland in turn was charged with making the forces available.

The sheer crudity of the Russian night operations posed serious problems. The Russians used old wood-and-canvas aircraft which flew at 50–100 mph—usually at treetop height. Their interception and destruction was a hazardous task for the German night fighter pilots. The incredulous Germans soon found that the Russians were dropping their partisans without parachutes directly into snowdrifts, trusting that they would survive this rough arrival behind the lines in condition to harass the enemy. Many partisans were killed in these crude drops.

Important partisans fared better. They were sometimes dropped in large, straw-stuffed sacks or in packing cases filled with straw. Modern energy-absorption experts could probably explain why the Russians were able to walk away from such unceremonious landings, but walk away they did. They were often observed by German pilots standing erect in the wreckage of a shattered packing case, signaling that they were whole, or else running wildly for cover in anticipation of strafing.

Guerrillas were frequently carried in open nacelles under the wings of Russian aircraft. After a chilling subzero ride, they would have to hurl themselves to earth at the proper moment, usually without a parachute, to face an enemy who would show them no mercy. Reliable estimates set German Army losses due to partisan warfare in excess of three hundred thousand men killed—testimony to the efficacy of the primitive.

The partisan operations exemplified the primitiveness of the Eastern Front in general, of which more is said in Chapters Eleven and Twelve. The Germans were able to make only limited use of radar under such conditions; their night operations became mainly confined to "bright night" operations with searchlights. Only one night fighter wing was active in the East, as opposed to six wings facing the RAF in the West.

NJG-6 on the Eastern Front developed one of the war's most ingenious and tactical instruments, the "Dark Night Train." These railroad-borne night fighter bases increased the striking power of NJG-6 through mobility. Each Dark Night Train consisted of perhaps eighteen railroad cars, completely self-contained and able to shift its operational site at short notice. A night fighter base could thus be set up anywhere the railroad went.

The first six cars, called the "Fast Train," could move in thirty minutes from any given site. Eight additional closed cars were coupled to the Fast Train, together with three to five open freight wagons. The entire train could be made ready to move in two hours or less. Each train housed and supported a squadron.

In the first car the Germans set up their combat information center and radar control. The car was soundproofed, connected by telephone with the rest of the train and to Army units via radio. The squadron leader was accommodated in the first car, where he had complete administrative facilities.

The second car had five compartments designed to house three pilots each. The flyers slept on bunks with spring mattresses. With folding tables, stools, drapes, and rugs they were among the most comfortable Germans in Russia. At the end of the second car was a washroom with six washbowls, mirrors, and running water supplied from a 900-gallon tank.

The squadron NCOs were accommodated in the third car, sleeping six to a compartment. The following two cars were set up in dormitory fashion for up to thirty men. A supervising sergeant enjoyed the luxury of a small compartment to himself.

A dining car with long tables and compact stowage for all dishes and utensils was hooked on next to the second dormitory car. One end of the dining car was reserved as a recreation area. Easy chairs, books, radio, and games were supplied, and the recreation area could be curtained off from the dining area if necessary.

A galley car was next to the dining car. Complete cooking and storage facilities for foodstuffs were provided. Additional storage for clothing, ammunition, dry foodstuffs, and other stores was available in additional closed carriages. A complete machine shop was included.

Livestock was kept in another closed car, out of the weather. A power car with heavy-duty generator to supply the total power requirements of the Dark Night Train was the last closed carriage. Freight wagons were used for heavy-duty items such as oil, gasoline, and water for the aircraft, spare parts and engines, motorcycles and occasionally the C.O.'s Volkswagen.

The night fighter train thus provided unusual flexibility. Rapid relocation of the squadron's base depended only on the existence of railroad tracks and a landing strip. The trains also acquired personality. They reflected the tastes of the squadron leader. Some trains emphasized hardware, others sought to ameliorate the privations of the

Russian Front. Captain Hendrick van Hermskerck became famous for his night train arrangements, which included a bar called "The Blue Grotto."

Against this broad background of strategic thrust and tactical parry, overlaid by a seesawing of technical fortunes, the Luftwaffe's night fighter aces emerge as truly outstanding individuals. In a sense, they were the lone wolves of the air war, flying independently where qualities of individualism and initiative were paramount. Their vigor and skill were the most consistent positive factors on the German side of the night war. The time has come to explore the careers of a number of German knights of the night in detail.

10

Knights of the Night

> *"Pauka! Pauka!"*
> VICTORY CRY OF THE NIGHT FIGHTER PILOTS

I N scoring the first of the Luftwaffe's many thousands of night kills, Werner Streib in 1940 founded his own personal legend. Because of his brilliant pioneering work, and also because he was older than most of the early night fighter pilots, he became known as "The Father of Night Fighting." The title is also an accolade from his contemporaries to an outstanding pilot, leader, and personality who left his mark in the history of the Second World War.

Streib belongs to that unique corps of professionals, including Steinhoff, Barkhorn, Hrabak, Rall, Trautloft, and a handful of others, who were trained in the prewar Luftwaffe as young officers, became aces, and later served in high rank in the new German Air Force. Brigadier General Streib, still very much alive after five years of aerial combat, retired in 1966 and lives now in Munich.

Born in 1911 in Pforzheim/Baden, Werner Streib was twice almost swallowed into the world of commerce. He served a three-year banking apprenticeship in the early nineteen thirties before joining the German Army as an infantryman. After the war he became a successful food packager in Germany, but on both occasions the Air Force eventually claimed him.

When Streib joined the Army in 1934 it was his last look at civilian life for eleven years. Like Werner Moelders, Walter Oesau, and Wolfgang Falck—the latter eventually became his C.O.—Streib effected a transfer from the Army to the emergent Luftwaffe. Beginning as an observer in one of the old-style reconnaissance units, he later applied for pilot training. By 1937 he was flying with the Richthofen Wing at Juterborg-Damm.

STREIB'S FINAL OPERATION: Lt. General Werner Streib retired finally from military service with the new German Air Force in 1966. Saying farewell at his retirement party is Ursula "Usch" Hartmann, wife of Germany's ace of aces, Erich Hartmann. With Wolf Falck in Denmark in early days of WWII, Streib pioneered basic night fighting tactics and techniques. He scored Germany's first official night fighter victory, added 64 more and a single day victory in WWII. Streib ended war as Inspector of the Night Fighters and won the Swords to his Knight's Cross. *(Hartmann Collection)*

When war broke out, First Lieutenant Streib was a twenty-eight-year-old professional serving in Falck's Destroyer squadron. His service with this unit opened the way for all that he later accomplished. Falck's 1940 night fighting experiments revealed Streib's aptitude for the night fighting art, even if he began as the experimental unit's leading pessimist regarding night combat.

His first kill was a daylight victory over a Blenheim bomber of the RAF. His other sixty-five kills were all at night, beginning with the downing of a Whitley on 20 July 1940. Streib's early successes paved the way for a serious night fighting effort, and he became a foundation member of NJG-1. By October 1940 he was a Captain and *Gruppen-kommandeur* of I/NJG-1. When his unit moved to Venlo in Holland, astride the Britain-Ruhr bomber track, he found opportunities aplenty for increasing his victory tally.

Streib had twenty-six confirmed kills by the end of May 1941, and by June 1943 was a Major credited with fifty night victories. By mid-1943 he thus had more victories by night than the top British ace of the war gained by day—Group Captain "Johnny" Johnson, with thirty-eight kills. Streib also outscored by night the top-scoring American ace of the war—Major Richard I. Bong with forty daylight victories in the Pacific Theater of Operations.

While Streib's victory total seems large by Allied standards, it is appropriate to examine his scoring record in detail. He bagged his tenth kill on 14 October 1940. He needed until May 1941 to reach twenty-six victories. He took seven and a half months, operating from the world's most active night fighter station, to increase his score from ten to twenty-six—an average of approximately two confirmed kills per month. The victories thus came hard and slowly during this embryo night fighting period.

An additional year of operational flying, involving scores of nocturnal sorties, was required before Streib added twenty-four additional victories to reach the half-century mark. A more convincing case for the conservatism of German scoring and confirmation procedures would be hard to find. Comparative evaluations of scoring between the Luftwaffe and the Allied air forces invariably exclude the far larger number of missions flown by the Germans. Kills by the night fighter pilots on both sides were among the hardest-earned victories of all.

HEINKEL-219 NIGHT FIGHTER: On the night of 11/12 June 1943, Werner Streib flew the first interceptions and combat with this new plane designed to match the performance of the RAF's Mosquito. Streib shot down five Lancaster bombers in 30 minutes that memorable night but when he landed at Venlo the bomber crashed just off the runway, the crew unhurt but the fighter totaled! *(Caler Collection)*

Streib's fame spread through the Luftwaffe after he won his early victories over the Ruhr. As he added luster to his reputation he was regarded as a night fighting expert. His expertise led to significant contacts with Ernst Heinkel during the development of the He-219 into an operational aircraft.

Since the He-219 was the same kind of lost opportunity to the night fighters as the Me-262 jet was to the day fighter pilots, it is not amiss to briefly review its history. Heinkel conceived the design as an all-purpose aircraft. His purpose was to meet the almost obsessive devotion of the Luftwaffe High Command to aircraft meeting multiple operational requirements—with the emphasis on dive-bombing capability.

The He-219 resembled the De Havilland Mosquito of the RAF in at least one important respect. The British "wooden wonder" was also a private venture, and would probably never have seen the light of day save for the enterprise and faith of Sir Geoffrey De Havilland. The British pioneer so believed in his creation that he financed the prototype from the De Havilland Company's own resources in the face of adamant RAF opposition to the design.

Just as the He-219 was conceived for application to anything from dive-bombing to reconnaissance, by way of long-range bomber, night fighter, and torpedo bomber for the German Navy, so did the Mosquito turn up in a bewildering array of operational roles. Originally conceived as a fast, unarmed bomber, the Mosquito served as practically everything except that.

The opposition from RAF brass to the Mosquito design was paralleled by German Technical Office resistance to the He-219. Aware of the numerous shortcomings of their aircraft, the German night fighter pilots agitated for a well-designed night fighter. By the winter of 1941–42 the He-219 was finally given attention as one of the few designs on hand suited to the task.

The RAF disrupted Heinkel's scheduling by bombing the factory at Rostock-Marienhe, and much preliminary design work went up in flames. Despite this setback the energetic Germans had a prototype in the air by the end of November 1942. The performance and potential of the new night fighter were sensational. A formidable weapon had been forged for the night war.

Field Marshal Milch dampened enthusiasm by remaining an advocate of the converted Ju-88 for night fighting. Continuing with Ju-88 conversions imposed minimum strain on the German aircraft industry, and Milch found it hard to justify the introduction of a completely new aircraft. To dramatize the overall superiority of the He-219, Streib flew a prototype against Colonel Viktor von Lossberg in a Ju-88S in mock night combat.

Streib emerged the clear victor in these exhausting encounters. The relative merits of the two machines were tested over a wide range of night fighting conditions and the He-219 was decisively superior. Milch caved in and an order for three hundred He-219s went to Heinkel.

Streib was still *Gruppenkommandeur* of I/NJG-1 in June 1943 when the first production He-219s were delivered in Venlo. Ground crews made the long-awaited new aircraft ready with feverish enthusiasm. They had talked of little else but the He-219 for months. When Streib sped down the runway on the night of 11 June 1943 for the operational debut of the new night fighter, Heinkel factory technicians and NJG-1 ground crews felt that a new era was beginning. They were right.

With Unteroffizier Fischer behind him manning the radar, Streib brought off a brilliant penetration of an RAF bomber formation

ANTENNAS APLENTY: Nose section of this He-219V-16 night fighter bristles with radar antennas essential to night interception. Heinkel machine was only German aircraft of the war designed specifically as a night fighter. Germans used specially fitted Me-110's and Ju-88's for most night operations. Conceived as a multi-purpose aircraft, He-219 proved to be the best night fighter of WWII. (*Nowarra Collection*)

heading for Berlin. The lively fighter could fly rings around the British heavies, which were Lancasters. The fire power of the He-219 was fantastic.

Four 30mm cannon in a ventral tray and two 20mm cannon in the wing roots provided forward-firing armament capable of demolishing the heaviest bomber. A short burst properly placed would be sufficient. For a half hour the tense Streib jinked his spirited fighter around in the bomber stream. Listening to Fischer's directional instructions he closed in time after time and, picking up the bombers visually, blasted away with his battery of six cannons.

All the cannons were located behind the pilot. There was no night blindness from the muzzle flashes. Streib's massive volleys of cannon shells found their mark time after time. Bomber after bomber exploded or burst into flames and went plunging to earth, its ten tons of bombs a pyre for its ten crewmen.

When the sweating Streib pulled clear of the Lancaster formation a half hour after the interception he had yelled, *"Pauka! Pauka!"* five times. And five times his victories had been confirmed by ground observers alerted by the night ace's victory cries. The victorious fighter was undamaged save for an impenetrable greasy film on the windshield. Leaking oil from the Merlins of the Lancasters had been blown against Streib's aircraft by the bomber slipstreams.

The nimble machine had been able to avoid the best shots of dozens of RAF gunners. Streib had been able to press home his attack and score his kills in minimum time, reducing his exposure to enemy fire. Everything was perfect—until he started his approach to the airfield at Venlo.

He could not get his flaps to depress. The greasy windshield made the situation even more hairy. Barreling in at over 100 mph in the dark, Streib "bent" the brand-new He-219 in a spectacular crash. He ended the operation Hollywood-style when the cockpit section completely separated from the rest of the aircraft. Strapped in this enclosure, Streib and Fischer went skidding along the runway after a brief involuntary flight, coming to rest on the grass minus their aircraft. They emerged from the enclosure bewildered, triumphant, and unhurt.

Word of the five downed bombers had already been flashed to Venlo. The climax to the He-219's baptism of fire was less than glorious, but there was no doubt that in the air the new fighter was all that had been promised. Despite the convincing advent of the machine, Milch continued to resist full-scale production of the night fighter. He was able to impose his will on affairs until he was finally removed from his post. Production genius Albert Speer gave the He-219 top priority in early 1944, but by then it was too late to be decisive in the critical night battles.

The He-219 was the only German fighter aside from the Me-262 which was consistently able to take the measure of the British Mosquito. Ten days after its operational advent with NJG-1, the new Heinkel had shot down six Mosquito intruders and twenty-five heavy bombers. With its heavy firing power, fantastic maneuverability, and 419 mph maximum speed the He-219 was undoubtedly the weapon needed to redress the balance in the night war. Less than three hundred were produced before the surrender, and only half that number saw combat.

Streib became *Kommodore* of NJG-1 on 1 July 1943, and he continued as one of the He-219's ardent advocates. In March 1944 he became Inspector of the Night Fighters, in which post he ended the war with sixty-six aerial victories and a high standing among the fraternity of aces. He had fought a long war.

After the war, ace night fighter pilots had neither commercial nor military value in Germany, and Streib re-entered the business world— this time as a food packager. He married in Munich in 1947 and led a businessman's life until March 1956. He then rejoined the German Air Force as C.O. of the Flight Training School at Landsberg. He served ten more years in the Air Force, rose to Brigadier General, and retired in 1966.

NJG-1 was the schooling ground for many leading night fighter aces,

RARE PAIR: Colonel Helmut Lent (left) had 102 night fighting victories and 8 day victories in WWII. Second from left is Heinz-Wolfgang Schnaufer, the greatest night fighter pilot of all time with 121 night kills. Schnaufer ended the war as a Major and survived. Lent was killed in a landing accident in 1944. Schnaufer's crew stands on the right in this rare photograph of the two night fighting Diamonds winners. (*Nowarra Collection*)

including the night fighter "ace of aces" Major Heinz-Wolfgang Schnaufer. His 121 night victories do not rank him anywhere near the top numerically among all the aces, but in terms of real achievement he is unsurpassed among the fighter aces of the Second World War.

Schnaufer did not score his first victory until 2 June 1942, but by the end of the war he had amassed his 121 kills in 164 combat missions. He more than doubled, at night, the day victory tally of the top-scoring Allied ace of the war, Colonel Ivan Kojedub of the Red Air Force.

Schnaufer and "Bubi" Hartmann were the two most successful aces of the war in their respective spheres. They were also two of the youngest, since both were born in Württemberg in 1922 within two months of each other. As with Hartmann, youth was undeniably a key element in Schnaufer's success, since night fighting took a heavy toll of any pilot's nerves and stamina.

To the nerve-wracking problem of finding the enemy in the dark was added the ever-present threat of the aggressive British air gunners. They manned multiple batteries of machine guns and stood a good chance of spotting the night fighter before they were spotted themselves. Their job was to see the night fighter and let him have it as quickly as possible.

The gunners in the bombers also knew that they were fighting for their lives. They shot down hundreds of German night fighters during the war. Survivors of the night war on the German side retain a healthy respect for the air gunners of the RAF.

To the threat of vigilant gunners was added the risk of "friendly" flak from the ground. German night fighter pilots were shot down by their own side on many occasions. Others fell victim to RAF night fighters escorting the bombers. These haunting dangers made the night fighter pilot's task one of the most demanding of the war.

The British knew better than anyone the hazards faced by a night fighter pilot in defending the Reich. They knew from first hand that it took guts and courage to fly night after night among the bomber streams. As Germany's top night fighter ace, Heinz-Wolfgang Schnaufer enjoyed wartime fame in Britain exceeded only by that of Galland and Moelders.

The British bomber pilots were probably Schnaufer's greatest admirers. His name and tales of his wild assaults on the Lancasters and Halifaxes were discussed in many an RAF mess. He was spoken of as a living personality, much as Immelmann, Boelcke, and Richthofen were discussed by their British foes during the First World War. This distinction was accorded few German pilots of the 1939–45 war because little was known about them on the Allied side. Censorship and propaganda—the terrible twins with which both sides dehumanized the conflict—were responsible.

The British nicknamed Schnaufer "The Night Ghost of St. Trond," after St. Trond in Belgium, Schnaufer's operational base. On 16 February 1945 the British actually broadcast a birthday greeting to the young ace from a military radio station in Calais. It was a throwback to the chivalry of earlier days when the British could say "Happy Birthday" to the twenty-three-year-old nemesis of Bomber Command.

The RAF admired him, but also feared him. Fame and accolades awaited the British intruder pilot who could bring back Schnaufer's scalp. Squadrons were sent to nail him. None did, and he survived the war to pass into both legend and history as one of the unforgettable airmen of the conflict.

Strikingly handsome, Heinz-Wolfgang Schnaufer's arresting appearance was the outer manifestation of his strong personality and powerful will. Dark-haired and olive-complexioned, slender and young, he was endowed with the qualities of intelligence and character that produce successful men in all walks of life.

He was apprenticed to his deadly night fighting trade in 1939 after a model high-school career. He volunteered for officer's training in the Luftwaffe, and underwent a full-length, peacetime-type pilot's training in spite of the war. After passing through regular Fighter School and then Destroyer School he elected to become a night fighter pilot.

His first C.O. was Captain Helmut Lent, of II/NJG-1. Already an ace and a distinguished leader, Lent was to be Schnaufer's rival in the night fighter scoring race until his death in October 1944. Lent and Schnaufer were the only two night fighter pilots in the Luftwaffe to win the coveted Diamonds.

There was no finer leader in the night fighter force than Lent, and Schnaufer thus began his rise under the best possible circumstances. He had a sound training, and a good unit in which to win his first victory. Schnaufer was two weeks short of his twentieth birthday when he scored his first kill on 2 June 1942. By August the following year he had twenty-one victories and was in command of No. 12 Squadron of NJG-1.

The aggressive young ace began to ring up strings of multiple kills at night. The Propaganda Ministry in Berlin began to feature his name more and more often in its broadcasts to Britain. The Schnaufer legend was taking form, etched with fiery clarity in Germany's night skies.

He paid little heed to fog or adverse weather conditions. Supremely confident of his piloting skill, he could lead his crew anywhere with him. He was the greatest of the "lone wolf" fighter pilots, banished now from the daylight skies, who could function only at night. But even the lone wolves of the night war were dependent on their crews in a way no daytime fighter pilot ever knew.

On most of his flights Schnaufer was accompanied by Fritz Rumpelhardt as radio operator, and Wilhelm Gaensler as gunner. The three men became a deadly combination in the Me-110. Teamwork developed from a blend of hard experience and intuition turned the twin-engined fighter into a death-dealing wraith in the night skies—a lethal ghost with a flaming touch.

The heart, brain, and inspiration of the combination was Schnaufer. His aggressive spirit could not be quenched while there were enemy bombers in the air. He would violate orders to get at his foes.

Schnaufer's squadron was grounded 16 December 1943 because of dense fog. No enemy bombers had been reported anyway. He sat disconsolately in the squadron communications hut as the dull evening passed away. Suddenly an electrifying report rasped over the radio.

"Enemy bombers crossing the North Sea!"

"They're coming," said Schnaufer. His face glowed with excitement.

"Take off! Take off!" He shot the order over his shoulder as he went

FLAK VICTIM: Captain Rudolf Sigmund of NJG-3 had scored 26 night victories in eighteen months with the night fighter arm when he was downed by German flak over Kassel. He died on 3 October 1943, with 28 victories total and the Knight's Cross. *(Nowarra Collection)*

plunging out into the night to his own machine.

Schnaufer nursed his heavy-laden Me-110 through a desperate takeoff, unable to see fifty feet in front of him. Climbing at full throttle, the fighter suddenly burst through the murk and an elated Schnaufer spoke to his crew on the intercom. "See boys, it's clear as crystal up here . . ."

Schnaufer's words trailed off. His catlike vision picked up a fleeting shadow against the firmament above him. A careful look convinced him that he had broken through the cloud at the right moment. The lone aircraft was a British bomber, far ahead of the bombers just reported crossing the North Sea when he took off. That meant only one thing. The aircraft above him was a Pathfinder, loaded with flares, incendiaries, and marker-pyrotechnics called "Christmas trees." The Lancaster also carried something even more important.

The most unwelcome man in Germany was the British bomber force commander, nicknamed "The Master of Ceremonies." After marking the target with flares, Christmas trees, and other pyrotechnic devices, the Master of Ceremonies orbited the target and directed the bombing. A Master of Ceremonies was undoubtedly in the bomber ahead of Schnaufer.

The young ace knew that if he could down the Pathfinder he would disrupt the bombing strike. All experience had proved that if the Master of Ceremonies could be shot down the bombing raid would be greatly diminished in impact and accuracy. The Night Ghost moved in on the Lancaster, determined to make sure of this kill.

Schnaufer had already found in the night war that closing in to point-blank range was the key to killing enemy bombers. His experience and methods thus paralleled those of Hartmann, the top day fighter ace, on the Russian Front. Closing in was more difficult and deadly at night. If the British gunners spotted a night fighter close astern they got a point-blank shot at their attacker. But this time, Schnaufer ignored the risks and went all the way.

At fifty yards range the Me-110's windshield was filled by the bulk of the speeding giant. Schnaufer pressed his gun buttons. The hammering roar of the cannons shook the fighter and the tracer lit up the Lancaster's fuselage on its short journey to its target. A livid, eye-blanching flash and a deafening roar flooded Schnaufer's senses. And the Lancaster was gone.

Showers of burning pieces, a fluttering wing in flames, and a vividly erratic pattern of pyrotechnic blazes lit up the night sky. Fragments of ignited Christmas trees floated down in fiery but harmless splendor. They would mark nothing but the crash of the invader.

The brilliant spectacle held Schnaufer and his crew transfixed. As the flames diminished, Schnaufer snapped back to alert. The night sky was no place to take time out. He spotted a second Lancaster, steering the same course as the first. Here was an audience for Schnaufer's "Jazz Music"—four 20mm cannons mounted to fire upward and forward from the fuselage behind the pilot's head. A blast of accurate fire from the Jazz Music installation was sufficient to down the biggest RAF heavy.

Schnaufer swept under the Lancaster and pressed the button for

BITER BITTEN: Captain Hans-Heinz Augenstein was redoubtable night fighter ace with 46 aerial victories and the Knight's Cross. He met an unusual fate when he was shot down by an RAF long range night fighter near Muenster. (*Nowarra Collection*)

Jazz Music. Four fiery lances stabbed upward, plunging into the belly of the British bomber. Flames belched from the stricken Lancaster, which wobbled and started into a dive. The British tail gunner spotted Schnaufer and began firing. He was still hosing tracer at the Me-110 when the Lancaster was finally engulfed in flames. Kill number two for the Night Ghost.

Traffic was getting heavy. Schnaufer banked around, his eyes piercing the gloom. Another four-engined shadow! He eased under the Lancaster and pressed the Jazz Music button again. The lethal chorus blasted deafeningly behind him. The shells went whizzing into the long fuselage above. Schnaufer did a quick double-take. The British machine flew on, not even changing course or showing any sign of damage.

The Night Ghost eased up directly behind his quarry and triggered his forward-firing cannons. A flicker of flame licked back from the bomber's tail. A hit this time. Then in one consuming blast the Lancaster disintegrated. Caught in the fireball, Schnaufer felt its heat like a whiff of hell.

His wings seemed to catch fire momentarily. The fighter dropped like a stone, with Schnaufer fighting for control. He lost fifteen hundred feet of altitude before the Me-110 responded fully. Drenched in sweat the Night Ghost decided to call it a night. He had been operating at the summit of his powers for a long time. He was clanked and ready to head for the barn. Then came the quiet, matter-of-fact report of gunner Willi Gaensler on the intercom.

"Lancaster, six o'clock high."

The sweating Schnaufer pulled around and made a firing pass at the bomber. He cursed as he saw his tracer go wide. Maybe this was one Lancaster too many, he thought to himself. A hail of bullets from the bomber's rear turret stormed around the Me-110. Then the Lancaster went into the RAF's special evasive maneuver, the corkscrew.

The big British machine whirled and dived and climbed. Schnaufer found himself admiring the guts of the enemy pilot as well as the flying qualities of the heavy bomber. But the Night Ghost had stayed with Lancasters in corkscrews before. For Schnaufer, it was a question of waiting for the right moment.

As the bomber reached the top of one of its corkscrews, the Night Ghost had arrived at the right point in time and space—thirty meters behind and slightly below his quarry. As the British bomber hung at the top of its corkscrew, the Night Ghost's guns roared again. The broadside riddled the Lancaster's fuel tanks and the bomber went plunging down in flames.

In less than an hour Schnaufer had scored four kills—including the Master of Ceremonies. He could well be pleased with his achievement, which he was able not only to repeat, but also to exceed on some occasions. He once aborted a big RAF strike against Stuttgart by shooting down the Master of Ceremonies, but he nearly lost his own aircraft and life in the process.

The British rear gunner saw him coming and threw out a lightning bomb—a massive charge of flash powder used to blind night fighter pilots closing in for the kill. Deprived of his night vision, the Night Ghost was a sitting duck for the British gunner, who promptly riddled Schnaufer's fighter. Before the young German could pull away, the British gunner's fire had carried away his radio and his radar antennae.

Getting his night vision back, Schnaufer went into the attack again, without any radar help this time. He blew up the stubborn Master of Ceremonies in a point-blank attack, but blazing debris set his port engine on fire. Struggling back to base on one engine, Schnaufer watched his gunner cut down another Lancaster with some sharp-shooting. The four-hundred-bomber force, deprived of its Master of Ceremonies, unloaded its lethal cargo in the woods near Renningen instead of on residential Stuttgart.

Such operations became a steady routine for Germany's greatest night ace. He probably saved more civilian lives than any other single German fighter pilot. When he knew that a big raid was afoot, he was like a man possessed until he had aborted it by downing the Master of Ceremonies or had taken a toll of the raiders with his guns.

His best scores were on 25 May 1944, when he took only fourteen minutes to down five Lancasters, and 21 February 1945, when in the predawn hours he shot down two Lancasters, following up that same evening with seven more Lancasters before midnight. Not many fighter pilots in broad daylight have scored nine confirmed kills in a day in two missions.

On 16 October 1944, Heinz-Wolfgang Schnaufer was awarded the Diamonds, Germany's highest wartime decoration. He ended the war as a Major in command of NJG-4. The British were particularly eager to question him after the surrender. He was taken to Britain with other leading aces for interrogation. The British also took along his Me-110.

With 121 victory bars painted on its tail, the historic machine was exhibited in London's Hyde Park. For weeks on end British males from septuagenarians to small boys came to stare at the aircraft and incredulously count the victory bars. They still count the victory bars, and they still whistle with amazement, for the tailplane is on display at the Imperial War Museum in London—a permanent memento of the German pilot who was Bomber Command's most effective and most respected foe.

He who studies the lives and fortunes of fighter pilots is likely to emerge a fatalist. Heinz-Wolfgang Schnaufer certainly provides air history buffs with a strong nudge in that direction. Having survived countless nocturnal battles with the heavy bombers, having evaded the superior Mosquito fighters sent to knock him down, having avoided his own flak and all the perils of the night war—including innumerable

PIGGY PET: Captain Hermann Greiner of NJG-1 pulls away from affectionate lickings of piglet used as a mascot by the night fighters of his unit. Greiner's war career included 50 aerial victories, 46 of these being at night. He won the Knight's Cross and ended the war as a *Gruppenkommandeur* in Heinz-Wolfgang Schnaufer's NJG-1. *(Nowarra Collection)*

landings and takeoffs at night in inclement weather—he returned from Britain to civil life in 1946. He entered the family business. He was only twenty-four. Life could still hold plenty.

Four years later on the Biarritz–Bordeaux highway Schnaufer was tooling along in his Mercedes Cabriolet when a truck lumbered onto the highway from a side road. The Night Ghost stamped on his brakes, swerving to avoid the truck. The sickening, metallic thump of colliding vehicles echoed across the intersection. The Mercedes overturned, hurling Schnaufer into a ditch where an avalanche of heavy steel oxygen bottles from the truck thundered down on top of him.

He lingered in a French hospital for two days. On 15 July 1950 Germany's greatest hero of the night war died in France. No one at the hospital knew that the fabled Night Ghost of St. Trond had departed this life. He was just an unfortunate young German whose luck had run out. For three years, hundreds of highly skilled men with efficient weapons had wanted to kill him and had set out to kill him. That which eluded the Royal Air Force was accomplished by a French truck driver with bad brakes.

Schnaufer's closest rival among the night aces was his erstwhile C.O., Helmut Lent, the only other night fighter ace in the world to score more than one hundred night victories. Lent is credited with 102 night victories and eight additional day kills. He was the first night fighter ace to win the Diamonds.

Born in 1918, Helmut Lent was the son of a Protestant minister. His family background and home training, combined in young Lent with a fine education and superior intelligence, produced the highest type of German youth. He was a deeply religious man, but not a proselytizer. His comrades had to choose their own way in life as an act of free will, but in times of stress Lent's depth of character and strong religious conviction were an inspiration to his men. He had many of the character traits of Werner Moelders.

A tall and slender man, Lent's culture and learning were expressed in a remarkably sensitive face. He could conceivably have followed his father as a minister, had gliders and then the Luftwaffe not attracted him in 1937. He was trained as a fighter pilot and later as a Destroyer pilot. Posted to Wolfgang Falck's squadron in ZG-76 in 1939, he proved himself in this unit to be not only a leader, but an exceptional pilot and marksman.

"NIGHT GHOST": Heinz Wolfgang Schnaufer was the deadliest night fighter pilot of all time, with 121 confirmed victories at night in WWII. Schnaufer won the Diamonds to his Knight's Cross, and ended the war as *Kommodore* of NJG-4. Schnaufer commanded also a crack crew, of whom the most prominent members were radio operator Fritz Rumpelhardt and gunner Wilhelm Gaensler. The "Night Ghost" died in a car accident in 1950. (*Nowarra Collection*)

In the heavy Me-110, Lent scored one of the first kills of the war on 2 September 1939. He was a member of Falck's successful squadron in the celebrated Battle of the German Bight, in which he downed two Wellingtons. He added another five kills in Norway to complete his tally of eight day victories. Lent was a Destroyer ace as well as a night fighter ace, and eight victories in the Me-110 in 1940 was a considerable achievement.

Lent became a squadron leader in NJG-1 when Falck was ordered to build NJG-1 around his own group. The sensitive Lent reached an impasse shortly afterward, when his failure to score night kills upset him psychologically. Wolfgang Falck recounts this little-known aspect of Lent's career:

"After we converted to night fighting, Lent's pilots were getting kills, but he as the squadron leader was not scoring. He became so angry that he actually lost his nerve. In spite of the difference in ages[1] and positions, we had a very fine personal relationship because he came from the same part of Germany where my family lived. In addi-

[1] Falck was eight years older than Lent—an "old man" as fighter pilots are reckoned.

NIGHT STALKER: 44 aerial victories at night won 1st Lieutenant Paul Gildner the Oak Leaves to his Knight's Cross. Like many successful night fighters he started with the Me-110 Destroyer units, scoring 4 aerial victories in daylight in the early days of the war. A tactical innovator, he flew continuously at night until he lost his life in a night crash in February 1943 in Holland. (*Nowarra Collection*)

tion, we were both sons of Protestant ministers. I liked him, understood him, and liked to fly with him. Because of this relationship, he came to me when his pilots were scoring at night and he was not.

"'I cannot carry on in this position under these circumstances,' he said. 'I want to be transferred to the day fighters again.'

"His case was not unlike that of Steinhoff, who also did not want to be a night fighter.

"'Stay here another month,' I said. 'If you are not successful I will see what I can do about having you transferred. But if you are successful, as I know you will be, you will stay here with NJG-1.'

"In that four weeks he was indeed successful, and rose later to Group Commander and Wing Commander. He was one of our greatest aces."

Lent was among the most persistent of the night fighter pilots. He entered aerial combat over three hundred times during his four and a half years of night fighting. He had thirty kills by the end of August 1941 and the British radio monitors who listened to and sometimes recorded German operational communications already knew him as one of the enemy's best. By January 1943 he was Germany's top-scoring night ace, with fifty kills—most of them four-engined heavy bombers.

Multiple kills were frequent in his career, and like Schnaufer, he always tried to single out and shoot down the Master of Ceremonies after the British introduced this tactic. He would infiltrate the bomber stream as the British force approached the target, exhaust his ammunition, then land to refuel and rearm. He would take off again immediately and re-infiltrate the stream of departing bombers, often chasing them far out over the North Sea, downing them as he went.

These fighter attacks on the bombers were far from one-sided. As has been emphasized, the British gunners could and did shoot back. RAF night fighters, first Beaufighters and later Mosquitos, added greatly to the hazards. Lent almost lost his life to a British night fighter.

Chasing a departing force of Halifaxes over the Zuider Zee, Lent came up astern of one of the bombers, triggered his cannons and blew up the British machine with a hit in the fuel tanks. The blazing aircraft on its way down silhouetted another Halifax. Lent swarmed to the attack, and again there was a shattering mid-air explosion as the bomber disintegrated.

A third Halifax, hit in the tail, plunged down trailing a fiery plume. The now-sweating Lent searched the inky heavens around him for another victim. He sensed rather than saw a fleeting shadow to starboard. There was a thunderous roar in his aircraft, livid flashing below and around him, and a searing pain in his shoulder. He was hit!

Black smoke and the stench of burning rubber swirled into the cockpit and the ace lost consciousness. The fighter plunged down out of control, the shouts of Walter Kubisch, Lent's radio operator, ringing emptily in the intercom. For a few anguishing seconds the fighter rushed wildly earthward. Then Lent, regaining consciousness, grasped the controls. Stifling a groan of pain as the strain of straightening out the fighter stabbed through his wounded shoulder, he got the riddled bird under control.

The sieved fighter landed at its base soon afterward, and a grateful Lent clambered down to receive medical attention. An English Mosquito escorting the bomber stream had almost ended his career. Twice more he was wounded in eerie night battles with the bombers, but on each occasion gave far more than he got.

By 1944 the twenty-six-year-old Lent had risen to Colonel, and was *Kommodore* of NJG-3. His incorruptible character, dauntless spirit, and combat achievements attracted the attention of both Hitler and Goering. Like Galland, Lent was accustomed to speaking his mind when asked questions by Goering and others. His experience, success, technical knowledge, self-respect, and obvious capacity for leadership marked him for larger things. Falck and Kammhuber had both left the night fighters, and leaders in this specialized field were at a premium.

LT. COLONEL HANS-JOACHIM JABS started out as a Destroyer pilot against France and England, and then converted to night fighting when the Germans switched the Me-110 to less vulnerable employment than combat against RAF fighters. An outstanding leader, Jabs ended the war in command of NJG-1 and with the Oak Leaves to his Knight's Cross. 50 aerial victories in WWII. Jabs survived the war, and is now a vice president of the German Fighter Pilots Association. *(Nowarra Collection)*

In the fall of 1944 it was rumored that Lent was to become General of the Night Fighters.

About this time he was anxious to visit his old friend and fellow night ace Hans-Joachim Jabs, *Kommodore* of NJG-1,[2] then stationed at Paderborn. He took off in daylight on what was no more than a routine flight. With him were three men: First Lieutenant Herman Kloss, Second Lieutenant Walter Kubisch, his radio operator, and Second Lieutenant Werner Kark, the latter a war correspondent. The flight ended in tragedy.

As Lent came in to land, his fighter grazed a high-tension wire, knocking out one engine. The aircraft quickly lost altitude, with Lent fighting for control. The machine plunged into the ground, killing Kloss and Kark outright and mortally injuring Lent and Kubisch. Kubisch had been Lent's radio operator since the 1939 Polish campaign, and he died the next day. Doctors fought hard for Lent's life for two days, but the night ace who so resembled Werner Moelders in life went to the same kind of airman's death—a flying accident in which not a shot was fired.

Unconquered by his enemies, Lent was to the last day of his life an inspiring individual. His contemporaries say that no small element in his drive to prevail over the bombers was the revulsion he felt at the human tragedy of aerial assaults on civilians. He was deeply touched by the carpet-bombing deaths of old men, women, and children. His reaction was that of a religious man:

"War is a horror, but if it has to be, then it should be fought in fairness, with honor and chivalry to preserve something human among the horror. Attacks on women and children, air mines and phosphor dropping on our peaceful population in cities and small towns—all that is unbelievably foul."

Decent men and women in all nations shared Lent's revulsion at the way in which all bonds between human beings were severed during the war. Propaganda would have had the world believe that German soldiers never felt and spoke as did Lent. This propagandist distortion of the truth ill served the healing of the war's wounds.

Lent's squadron leader, Group Commander, and Wing Commander at various times, Wolfgang Falck summarizes the young ace in these terms:

"Helmut Lent had the education, background, and bearing of a man who can carry responsibility. And more importantly, he realized the responsibility of leadership. He was a great young man."

Schnaufer and Lent, the two top-scoring night aces, both came to night fighting via the Destroyer route. Numerous other leading night fighters, including Werner Streib, Guenther Radusch, Hans-Joachim Jabs, Prince Egmont of Lippe-Wessenfeld, and Manfred Meurer began their careers in the Me-110 as day fighter pilots. The third-ranking night fighter ace of Germany and the world, Major Prince

[2] Jabs—fifty victories.

65 NIGHT KILLS: Captain Manfred Meurer switched from flak gunner on the ground to night fighter pilot in the air, and ran up a staggering talley of 65 night victories between March 1942 and January 1944. He won the Oak Leaves to his Knight's Cross for his aerial bravery and achievements. Meurer's career and life ended when his He-219 night fighter collided with a four-engined Allied bomber at night over Magdeburg, bringing both aircraft to earth in flames. (*Toliver Collection*)

Heinrich of Sayn-Wittgenstein, differed from most of his successful contemporaries by beginning his flying career as a bomber pilot in 1939.

Danish-born Wittgenstein was an intense, somewhat austere young man who disciplined himself to the highest standards of conduct and demanded the same standards from others around him. The central pillar of his personality was individualism, which inevitably led him to fighter piloting as opposed to the less individualistic bomber pilot's role.

In 1939 he was a twenty-three-year-old bomber Captain and took part in the Battle of Britain. After more than 150 missions as a bomber pilot, he requested and was granted a transfer to the night fighters in August 1941. He had been flying the Ju-88 as a bomber pilot, and this fast bomber was in extensive use as a night fighter by 1941. He became the top-scoring Ju-88 pilot of the war.

The young Wittgenstein revealed in both his appearance and his attitudes that his aristocratic heritage was not something from the dead past, but a living reality of which he was the bearer and embodiment. Deep, abiding patriotism, neither centered on nor anchored to ephemeral political regimes, was the foundation of his character. Service as an officer in the armed forces was his family tradition and his youthful goal. Little else in life meant anything to him but service to his nation.

Slimly built, with a slender face and high forehead, his bearing was that of a confident, well-educated man of good family. He was ambitious, intelligent, and forthright, but he was as out of place in a bomber squadron as Hitler at a Churchill dinner party. Flying in formation and dropping bombs—and being shot at by heavily armed fighters—was not a way of life in which Wittgenstein could find satisfaction or take pride. Furthermore, he did not fit in on a personal basis with his squadron mates. He was too highly strung, too intense, too much of a fighter to be at home.

Had he been born in 1890 instead of 1916, he would have found the lone-wolf air fighting of the First World War's early years an exciting fulfillment. In the Second World War, only the night fighters offered the fighter pilot similar opportunities to be independent and self-reliant—free of the shackles of aerial teamwork without which the day fighter pilot could not survive.

After his transfer to night fighting he rose rapidly to squadron leader, then to Group Commander and Wing Commander. He was an exacting taskmaster. He never ceased finding fault with the operational organization of the Luftwaffe, the condition of his own aircraft, or himself. He was a compulsively courageous fighter, and this was at once his strength and his weakness.

Again we are indebted to Colonel Wolfgang Falck for the following contemporary observations of the Prince at the height of his career:

"Wittgenstein was a most capable pilot and extremely ambitious, as well as an individualist. He was definitely *not* the type to be the leader of a unit. He was not a teacher, educator, or instructor. But he was an outstanding personality, a magnificent fighter, and a great operational pilot.

"He had an astonishing sixth sense—an intuition that permitted him to see and even to feel where other aircraft were. It was like a personal radar system. He was also an excellent air-to-air shot.

"During the time that he was under my command, I was ordered one night to Berlin to the Ministry. So was Wittgenstein, unbeknown to me. He was to receive the Knight's Cross the following morning from Goering. By an amazing coincidence we got the same train, the same sleeping car, and the same compartment.

"I was happy to discuss problems with him free from distractions and interruptions and I was determined to make the most of our lucky encounter. I was keen to know his opinion on several operational problems. He was very nervous, with fidgeting hands and an obvious air of anxiety about him. He was anxious because the other night aces might be successful while he was 'sitting in a train doing nothing'—as he put it.

"He was at this time in rivalry with Streib or Lent, I forget which, and they were within a kill or two of each other. It made him nervous to think he was giving his rival a scoring chance while he went to get his Knight's Cross. I also had a devil of a time getting him to go on vacation for the same reason."

This firsthand account of Wittgenstein's dedication to his career buttresses some of the almost legendary accounts of his perfectionism and driving will. His ground crews and his air crews found that their best was barely good enough for the Prince. From himself he demanded consistent success, consistent improvement, and a degree of discipline bordering on the inhuman.

In late 1942 he was sent to Russia by Falck to help devise tactics countering Soviet night air operations. The Prince took command of one of the first Dark Night Trains, described in the previous chapter, and rang up a solid twenty-nine kills in Russia. When Falck visited him during a tour of Russian Front night fighter bases, Wittgenstein was again anxiety personified:

STELLAR INVESTITURE: Leading personalities of the Luftwaffe fighter force at an investiture were, from left, Major Prince Sayn zu Wittgenstein (a night fighter ace with 83 victories), Major Hartmann Grasser (103 aerial victories and onetime adjutant to Werner Moelders), Captain Walter Nowotny (258 aerial victories and one of Germany's finest young leaders), and Major Guenther Rall, third ranking ace of Germany and the world with 275 aerial victories. *(Grasser Collection)*

"I saw personally that in one night he made three kills in fifteen minutes. That was not enough for him. It excited his deepest anxieties that on the Western Front they were scoring more kills than he in the East. He was downright envious. It was not always easy for us to co-operate with him as a subordinate because of this tremendous ambition."

Wittgenstein's two best scoring nights were both on the Western Front. In July 1943 he had his best night, with seven confirmed kills—a formidable achievement. On the night of 1 January 1944 he downed six RAF heavies. He continued to score well and by May 1944 took a narrow lead over Lent in the scoring.

On 21 May 1944 he tackled another big RAF formation near Schoenhausen and scored five kills. The fifth kill went in as a brilliant flamer, and in the glare of the dying bomber a Mosquito night fighter got his black Ju-88 boresighted. A sharp burst from the British fighter's heavy armament sent Prince Heinrich of Sayn-Wittgenstein to Valhalla.

His operational career as a night fighter covered a little over two and a half years, as compared with four and a half years for Lent and over three years for Schnaufer. In devotion to duty, he left a personal record unsurpassed in the Luftwaffe. In a phase of history dominated by individuals, he is best remembered for his individualism, and if the Prince is not remembered with great love by his contemporaries, at least he won their unstinting respect.

The night of 21 May 1944 was a victory for the RAF bombers over the night fighters—their relentless antagonists. The Prince was not the only night ace shot down. Captain Manfred Meurer also died, in a mid-air collision with an RAF heavy near Magdeburg. Meurer was a brilliant pilot and a rising star in the night fighter force.

Meurer had sixty-five night kills at the time of his death, although his night fighting career started in the spring of 1942. A slow starter like some of the top day aces, ex-flak gunner Meurer had a scant ten victories in his first year as a night fighter. Between February 1943 and his final operation fourteen months later, he ran up forty-five night victories.

He was *Gruppenkommandeur* of I/NJG-1, which was equipped with the He-219. He was flying the coveted fighter when he collided with his four-engined foe. The team of Meurer and his long-time radio operator, Master Sergeant Gerhard Scheibe, was a serious loss to the Luftwaffe. The two warriors were just hitting their stride in the He-219. Meurer had won the Oak Leaves and Scheibe was the first radio operator in the night fighters to win the Knight's Cross. Such teams were impossible to replace in mid-1944, and in spite of RAF losses that same night, 21 May 1944 was a victory for the RAF bombers. The two dead night fighter aces between them had accounted for three wings of Bomber Command aircraft.

The Germans kept excellent statistics and records of the careers of their fighter pilots, but numerical standings have little to do with the status an ace enjoys among his contemporaries. Leadership, personality, and character frequently result in a far higher ranking for a fighter ace than his kill tally alone might justify. Such a man is Lieutenant Colonel Hans-Joachim Jabs.

He is credited with twenty-two day and twenty-eight night victories, gained in the full span of the war from 1939 to 1945. He is one of the few German aces to emerge repeatedly victorious from battles with RAF Spitfires and Hurricanes while flying the Me-110. This feat is generally regarded among the German pilots as the ultimate achievement—downing Spitfires while flying a much inferior aircraft. Twenty-one of Jabs' fifty kills were fighters, including twelve Spitfires and four Hurricanes.

Born in Lübeck in 1917, Jabs joined the Luftwaffe in December 1936 and passed out as a pilot almost two years later. He was originally trained as an Me-109 pilot. In March 1940 he was transferred to ZG-76, flying the Me-110. Some of the Luftwaffe's best young pilots were taken from the Me-109s at this time, and in the Me-110 many did not survive the Battle of Britain. Jabs did.

Americans are inclined to think of the German pilots as being somewhat stolid in their approach to decorating their aircraft. The reverse is true. The Germans were imaginative and original with their insignia and personal escutcheons, and made lavish use of Disney-style characters as well. Long before the Flying Tigers had become a household word in the United States with wildly painted tiger mouths on their aircraft, the German pilots of II/ZG-76 in which Jabs served were

ZERSTORER (FIGHTER-DESTROYER) AND NIGHT FIGHTER THE MESSERSCHMITT 110: Göring said that the Me-110 and the pilots who flew it would be like Hannibal's calvary protecting the elephants as they escorted the German bombers on attacks against Great Britain. Shown here is a Me-110 from the Haifisch Gruppe, with the sharks teeth painted on the nose. It was this photo that caused Erik Shilling to suggest the design used on the American Volunteer Group (AVG) P-40s in China and Burma. (*USAF Photo*)

already using such a device.

The distinctively painted noses of the Me-110s caused the unit to become known as the "Shark Group" (*Haifisch Gruppe*). The group developed an extremely potent morale, and this spirit was quickly reflected in a string of kills scored in the Battle of France. Jabs contributed four fighters of the French Air Army and two RAF Spitfires. By the time the British had been turned out of France, Jabs was an ace.

The really "hairy" phase of his career followed—the close escort of Luftwaffe bombers raiding Britain in 1940. Jabs not only survived the Battle of Britain, but downed eight Spitfires and four Hurricanes by the battle climax on 15 September 1940. He was one of the most successful Destroyer aces in the Luftwaffe.

Retrained for night fighting in September 1941, Jabs joined NJG-3 in the defense of Hamburg. His day fighting days were not over, however, since he was one of thirty Destroyer pilots chosen to help protect *Scharnhorst, Gneisenau,* and *Prinz Eugen* in "Operation Thunderbolt," described in Chapter Two.

Scoring opportunities like those of the 1939–40 campaigns did not come his way for the next two years, and by the end of June 1942 Jabs had added only one more kill, bringing his score to twenty. In November 1942 he was transferred to Werner Streib's IV/NJG-1, operating from Leeuwarden in Holland. Jabs' fortunes now took an upturn.

The new Me-110 variants with NJG-1 were radar-equipped, and boasted the upward-firing Jazz Music cannons and 30mm forward-firing cannons. Jabs began scoring steadily again, and by January 1944 had forty-five kills to his credit. When Streib moved up to *Kommodore* of NJG-1, replacing Falck, Jabs took over IV/NJG-1. When Streib was later promoted to Inspector of the Night Fighters, Jabs succeeded him as *Kommodore* of NJG-1.

As a Wing Commander Jabs still flew combat frequently, and on one occasion again met up with his traditional daylight antagonists, the Spitfires. On 29 April 1944 he was preparing to land at the Arnhem base of his wing when eight of the British fighters bounced him. They were the 400-mph Mark IX variants, and their aggressive attack had Jabs thinking they were seeking revenge for 1940.

He hauled his Me-110 clear of their first firing pass. As the Spits went barreling by, Jabs was already thinking and acting like a top-notch aerial fighter. A fearlessly aggressive response has turned the tide of many an air battle in favor of a lone fighter set upon by numerous enemies.

He turned into their next pass and let fly with his long-range cannons. A fiery blast shook the heavens as a Spitfire disintegrated. A shower of blazing wreckage sent the others scattering. Before the rattled British pilots could collect their wits, Jabs went diving balls out for the field at Arnhem.

The British leader rallied his formation and came screaming after the escaping young *Kommodore*. Again Jabs chose the right moment for aggressive action. Turning into them again with his big cannons hammering he caught one of his pursuers with a withering hail of heavy shells. The Spitfire plunged down in flames, but this time there was no explosion or distracting debris.

Jabs felt his fighter trembling and sagging under numerous hits. Fleetingly he thought of his crew as cannon shells and bullets chewed up the Me-110's wings and went thudding, banging, and pinging into all parts of his machine. His stomach churned furiously as he waited for the searing pain of bullet wounds or the blackness that would engulf him if a cannon shot him in the back or the head.

With throttles firewalled and smoke and coolant belching from both engines, Jabs held the fighter's nose down and grimly plunged toward his base. He could see it now. There was still a chance. But the hellish hail of projectiles kept coming.

"As soon as we stop rolling, jump out and run like hell," he told his crew on the intercom. The field was coming up fast to meet the fleeing fighter.

Holding out till the last possible moment, Jabs lowered his landing gear, praying it would function. He heard it thump into place. Thank God! Then another prayer that the tires weren't shot to shreds. Lurching down on the turf, the Me-110 miraculously held together. Jabs could see grass through the huge shell holes in the wings. Easing her to a stop as three Spitfires overshot on a firing pass, Jabs knew he had only moments to save his life. Out! Out!

The ace and his crew bolted across the grass as the deadly roar of three Merlin engines crescendoed behind them. Two dozen guns blasted the smoking Me-110 into scrap as the breathless Jabs threw himself under cover. He had downed his last Spitfire.

Jabs ended the war as a Lieutenant Colonel in command of NJG-1, downing two Lancasters on 21 February 1945 for his final kills of the conflict. Five and a half years in the Me-110 made it a long war for the dark-haired ace. He made a new life for himself in postwar Germany as a businessman and city councilman in Reinfeld in Schleswig-Holstein. The wife he married in 1940 bore him two sons, and he lives quietly today in Lüdenscheid in Westphalia, the war a long way away.

The limitations of this book preclude coverage of many colorful careers and special contributions to the night fighter effort made by a host of aces and ace-leaders. Major Prince Egmont of Lippe-Weissenfeld, known sometimes as "The Other Prince" in the Luftwaffe, had fifty-one night kills in a first-to-last career that could easily fill a book by itself. Colonel Guenther Radusch, with sixty-five kills in a career dating from the Spanish Civil War, is one of the major personalities of the night fighter arm. Major Wilhelm Herget, another 1939–45 veteran, with fifty-seven night kills and fifteen day kills, wound up his war flying the Me-262 with Galland. Lieutenant Colonel Herbert Luetje,[3] last *Kommodore* of NJG-6, with fifty-three kills in a five-year career, was one of the top night fighting experts.

All these officers and others won the Oak Leaves and survived the war, yet space limitations preclude anything more than an outline mention of their contributions. Similarly, not even the briefest outline of night fighter aces and their special war dares fail to emphasize the contribution made to night fighting success by the crews.

Without the skill, patience, and devotion of the radar-radio operators there would be many fewer night fighter aces in the history of the Luftwaffe. They would rarely have been able to find anything to shoot at. Without the vigilance and good shooting of the night fighter gunners there would today be many fewer living night aces. The ace night fighter pilot relied heavily on his crew, a relationship freely acknowledged by surviving aces.

Despite a superlative human element pursuing its tasks with sacrificial devotion, the German night fighters lost the technical battle. The ensuing battle of attrition soon became a foregone conclusion.

---

[3] Luetje died in 1967.

The night aces suffered the same fate as their daytime counterparts—they were overwhelmed by a blizzard of machines.

Fighting with consummate bravery, and driven by the constant compulsion to save the lives of noncombatants subject to nightly slaughter, the German night fighters were a determined corps of soldiers. Defending their country was to them something more than a recruiter's catch phrase or more of Goebbels' empty polemic. They were both feared and respected by their foes, and they almost defeated Bomber Command. Had the insight and strategic grasp of their highest leadership equaled their qualities and skill as soldiers, they might even have defeated Bomber Command.

At war's end, Major Heinz-Wolfgang Schnaufer issued his last order to NJG-4. With this document the night ace of aces said all that was left to be said of the grueling struggle from which he and his men had emerged with honor but without victory:

Command Post, May 8, 1945

TO MY FAITHFUL NJG-4

Men of my Wing:

The enemy has entered our land; our proud planes have been handed over to them; Germany is occupied and has unconditionally surrendered.

Comrades, this disheartening fact is bringing tears to our eyes. The future lies dark and mysterious before us and will probably bring us grief and sorrow. One thing, though, will live within us forever—the tradition of our wing and our achievements. This tradition will help us and strengthen us when we are humiliated and it will help us stand proudly and look at the future with clear and open eyes.

Once more I would like to recall to your memory the development of our glorious wing—so dreaded by the enemy. Exactly three years ago on 1 May 1942 the wing was established to protect southern Germany from night attacks. Mainz-Finthen, Laupheim, Jauvincourt, and Laon-Athies were our points of support until in 1943 Florennes, St. Dizier, and Coulommiers were added.

We did not prove our development with empty names. There—where night after night our planes rose to the sky—the land of southern Germany and France is marked by numerous scars caused by the impact of destroyed and burning bombers.

579 bombers,

that is three complete bomber divisions, have been destroyed in bitter battles and under the most difficult conditions by NJG-4.

Successful night fighter operations in all kinds of conditions on Avranches, on Mynnvegen, on long columns of trucks and railroad cars in the hinterland have cost the enemy tremendous losses. Therefore the names "Wildvogel" and "Wisbel" to us have a good sound. Distance flights over England were one of the last strikes of our wing. The destruction of pontoon bridges near Wesel meant a glorious ending to a hard battle.

Comrades, all these successes could be realized only because of your intrepid attitude, your assiduity, and your faith in Germany.

At times the hard blows from our adversaries made it seem as if our unit also would be crushed under their rolling mill of war. But we always stood up again and returned their blows until last. This unequal battle caused us great sacrifices—102 crews, including 400 officers and noncommissioned officers, did not return. Fifty officers, noncommissioned officers, and crew died in the performance of their duty—some during ground attacks. They have given everything for Germany and our wing, and have the right—from this moment on—to demand of us that we remain decent, respectable, and upright German men.

With a feeling of sadness, but also with a feeling of pride, I bid farewell to my wing and thank you for your confidence in me, which you showed in times of crisis.

When again, in a different Germany, you must labor hard, then you my men of NJG-4 will feel that you have done everything within human power to win this war for Germany.

Long live our beloved Fatherland!

> Signed: Schnaufer
> *Kommodore*, NJG-4

Thus it ended, and the victory cry of *"Pauka! Pauka!"* would ring through the night no more.

11

Air War in the East

*"The Eastern Front of World War II has many
lessons for the West of today, but they are seldom studied."*
LIEUTENANT GENERAL JOHANNES STEINHOFF

FORMER fighter ace Herman Goering was the only member of
Hitler's entourage or the high command of the Wehrmacht to raise
strong objections to Hitler's plan to invade Russia. He confronted the
Fuehrer with these objections face to face and in no uncertain terms.
Goering historically has many black marks against him, but his stand
against the invasion of Russia is to his credit, although he did not crown
his objections with his resignation as would a man of character.

Had Hitler listened to Goering, there would undoubtedly have been
a second round to the Battle of Britain. North Africa may well have
fallen to Rommel and the history of this century been altered, but the
Fuehrer was in no mood to listen to any opposing voice. The assault on
Russia was the fulfillment of all his neurotic dreams. When he decided
that the time had come, nothing could dissuade him from his life-and-
death attempt to demolish the Bolshevist colossus. To Goering's urgent
protest that the Luftwaffe was exhausted and needed time to rebuild
and refit, Hitler was impervious.

"I've made up my mind," said Hitler to Goering, and the die was
cast.

The German Army advanced into Russia behind an aerial battering
ram of bombers, fighters, and ground-attack units which smashed the
equipment of the Soviet Air Force with incredible rapidity. Luftwaffe
fighters played a dominant role in the invasion. They shot down with
practiced precision the Soviet machines that rose to the challenge, and
destroyed hundreds of Russian aircraft on the ground. The history of
aerial warfare has no comparable example of such total aerial conquest
of one major nation by another.

The German Army was thus able to move forward with lightning speed, once more making full use of tactical air power without hindrance from enemy aircraft. The emphasis was again on close support within the tactical air power monopoly. Minus its air arm, the Red Army had to retreat to survive. The only hope for the Russian commanders was that the momentum of the German *Blitzkrieg* would be dissipated on the endless steppes. The Russians fought for time.

Spectacular as these initial triumphs of German arms were, they could not conceal or indefinitely postpone the reappearance of the same gaping void in German air power which had cost the Luftwaffe the Battle of Britain. The German air armory still had no strategic bomber. Nevertheless, the Germans were recklessly attacking a country whose sheer physical size could devour the German Army. Everything depended upon a lightning victory.

Hitler's war plans envisaged a Russian campaign of six to eight weeks' duration. Moscow would be in German hands in two months, according to the Fuehrer's estimates. The remainder of the country would then succumb to the loss of the master power center. Fighting without reserves as he had since 1939, Hitler sent his legions to the very gates of Moscow before an early, sudden, and savage winter froze the German Army rigid.

Engaged in total war at full strength from the first day of the Polish invasion, the Luftwaffe had suffered heavily in the Battle of Britain. When Germany invaded Russia, not even the fighter losses of the Battle of Britain had been made up, in either pilots or aircraft. Yet it was this exhausted Luftwaffe which paved the way for the German advance to Moscow. Like the Army, the Luftwaffe had not winterized its equipment and its personnel had no winter clothing. The Luftwaffe soon found the winter a worse enemy than the Russians.

Hundreds of thousands of Soviet soldiers had gone into the bag as prisoners of war during the advance to Moscow. Staggering masses of war materiel were captured. The Red Air Force was eliminated as a factor in the first months of the war, yet despite these reverses the Russians made a comeback. They were able eventually to overpower the Germans in the field and to outnumber them in the air fifty to one. Lack of a four-engined strategic bomber in the Luftwaffe was the hinge on which this reversal of German fortunes turned.

Russian soldiers and technicians escaped to tne east in thousands, but they did not go empty-handed. They uprooted and took with them entire armament factories, which were re-established beyond the reach of the short-winded Luftwaffe bombers. These factories were immediately put back into production with the feverish energy human beings manifest when they are fighting for their lives. Before long, the Russian armament industry was performing prodigies of production, not only with aircraft, but also with tanks,[1] artillery, and motor vehicles. No German bombers came to disrupt this production.

[1] Soviet tank production, 1941–45:   150,000 units.
   German tank production, 1941–45:   25,000 units.

While German soldiers were literally freezing to death in the winter of 1941–42, the embattled Russians were working furiously to restore their war-making capacity. Locked in the frozen embrace of the winter, the Germans were mercilessly harassed by Red Army units trained and equipped to fight under these conditions. The winter was the worst enemy, and today in Germany its marks may be seen on many middle-aged German men who are minus fingers, thumbs, and ears.

The Germans were able to resume the initiative in the spring of 1942, but the winter paralysis of the invaders had given the Russians a decisive respite. Hitler's dream of conquest became a nightmare of progressively more horrible dimensions. The fighter pilots in particular could observe the Soviet comeback.

CONFIRMED KILL: There's no doubt about this Luftwaffe kill, a two-seater IL-2 ground attack aircraft which crashed north of Jassy, Rumania on 12 August 1944 after encountering German fighters. IL-2 Stormoviks were hard to down because of heavy armor plate and low altitude at which they flew. Luftwaffe pilots tried to hit them in the oil cooler under the fuselage. *(Nowarra Collection)*

Beyond the reach of German bombers, the Russian aircraft plants were working around the clock, seven days a week. No such effort was put forth in Germany at this time. In 1941, Russia produced 7500 fighter aircraft while the Germans, whose homeland and industry were both essentially intact, produced only 2292 fighters.[2] This formidable Russian production was supplemented by the first five hundred lend-lease aircraft sent from the United States and Great Britain.

That the Russians were allowed to recover in this way will long remain one of military history's enigmas. Very few strategic attacks were made by the Luftwaffe in 1941. Only Moscow received any systematic attention. From 21 July 1941 to 5 April 1942 the Luftwaffe launched seventy-six daytime and eleven night raids against Moscow. These attacks were essentially nuisance raids. Nothing was done to halt

[2] German High Command Report, 1945.

the flood of fighter production.

Russia's fighter production and the lend-lease supplement were available for Eastern Front operations exclusively. The Germans had to spread their slender production between the Eastern Front, the Channel Front, North Africa, and the Mediterranean. Fighters were playing a decisive role in all these German efforts. In addition the Germans were being forced to build up their night fighter force, which further drew on their fighter production. The battle of materiel had thus decisively tipped against the Luftwaffe by the spring of 1942. More was to come.

By October 1944 the Russian aircraft industry had produced 97,000 combat aircraft! The Soviet plane builders accomplished near-miracles of production, and the oft-heard contention that the Red Air Force was sustained solely by lend-lease aircraft is at variance with the facts. Even without lend-lease aid, the Russians completely outstripped the Germans in aircraft production.

Loose talk about lend-lease aircraft aid persists to this day. Americans often seem blind even to the more recent lessons of Sputnik, and continue to deprecate Soviet war-making potential. Lend-lease has even led to the smug assumption of indirect credit for Russian victories by some Americans. A preferable attitude is to seek and learn the lessons of the Russo-German conflict, as General Steinhoff so often urged during his American stay. Certainly it is a wiser course than to assume superiority as did the Germans in 1941.

From the inception of lend-lease to 1 October 1944, the Soviet Union received from the Western Allies some 14,700 aircraft—roughly equivalent to one sixth of Russia's own production. Some 8734 of these aircraft were from the United States, and 6015 came from Britain.

Of these aircraft, 8200 were fighters. The bulk of the fighters were Curtiss P-40s, Bell P-39 Airacobras, Bell P-63 Kingcobras, Hurricanes, Spitfires, and small quantities of P-51 Mustangs and P-47 Thunderbolts. The vast majority of these fighters were inferior to the Me-109 and FW-190 against which they were pitted. An objective evaluation of the Allied fighters sent to Russia permits no other conclusion than that the Soviet Air Force was sent the types least desired by the USAAF and RAF—with a few Spitfires and Mustangs thrown in as a gesture.

The Russians were glad to get these aircraft, especially in 1941–42. They quickly found that the Curtiss P-40 was inferior in dive and climb to the Me-109, and as a consequence Russian pilots were chary about accepting aerial combat in this machine. They used the P-40 extensively for ground-attack work, for which they also favored the P-39 and P-63. The Russians already had a better fighter than either the P-40 or the Hurricane—the two most numerous lend-lease types in 1941-42—in their own MIG-3.

The idea has taken root since the war that the Red Air Force could not have functioned without lend-lease aircraft. This is clearly untrue, and the views of Germany's fighter aces vary widely as to the value of

DEAD DUCK: Luftwaffe fighter pilots shot away a lot of this Tupolev SB-2's structure before the Russian aircraft plowed into a meadow on the German side of the front. (*Nowarra Collection*)

these British and American machines to the Soviet air effort. There is also an emotional tendency in America to confuse the quality and magnitude of the aid with the valor and devotion of the merchant seamen who carried it on the Arctic convoys—unsurpassed feats in the war's catalog of heroic deeds.

Ace of aces Erich Hartmann (352 victories) described the impact of lend-lease aircraft to the authors in these terms:

"The Airacobra and the Kingcobra were valuable to the Russians in my opinion not because of their flying performance, which was inferior both to Russian-designed fighters and to the Me-109. They were markedly superior, however, in weapons and the weapons system. They had a big edge over contemporary Russian aircraft in this respect. The gunsight on Russian fighters at this time was often only a circle on the windshield. I mean a *hand-painted* circle on the windshield.

"Then came the Airacobra, Kingcobra, Tomahawk, and Hurricane, and all had gunsights of modern Western design. From this time on, the Russians began to shoot the same way we did. In the earlier days, incredible as it may seem, there was no reason to feel fear if the Russian fighter was behind you. With their hand-painted 'gunsights' they couldn't pull lead properly or hit you—other than by luck. But after the lend-lease aircraft came in and the Russians got on to the gunsights, it was very different—especially from longer distances."

Major Hartmann Grasser (103 victories) states that after their early reverses the Russians steadily improved in all departments, as their experience widened and their tactical know-how expanded. Grasser says that after front-line experience filtered down to the training levels in the Red Air Force their combat ability markedly increased, and Grasser leaves no doubt that the continuous appearance of British- and American-built aircraft on the Russian Front was disquieting to the Luftwaffe, even if not a menace.

Guenther Rall (275 kills) confesses to a mild shock when he first encountered Spitfires in the Crimea. His view is that pilot quality

TOUGHEST RUSSIAN BIRD: The Soviet IL-2 "Stormovik" dive-bomber was considered to be the most rugged Russian aircraft of the war by the German pilots who flew against them. Heavily-armored IL-2 could absorb incredible quantities of machine gun and cannon fire and still keep flying. Bright burst in this photograph is probably a 20mm cannon shell hitting the Russian machine. *(Toliver Collection)*

rather than the origin of the machine told the tale in air battles. His experience in this connection is related in Chapter Seven.

Lend-lease aircraft were important and valuable to the Russians, but it is hard to make a case for their being decisive in the Eastern Front air war. A more signal role in the sustenance of the Soviet air effort was played by the high-octane aviation gasoline which the Russians received from the United States under lend-lease. The Soviet output of this commodity was woefully deficient, and this Allied contribution filled a critical gap in the Russian war economy.

Additional comments from a German source on the quality of Soviet aircraft are offered by Dr. Ing. Karl-Heinz Steinicke:

"In a pamphlet on warplanes, published in 1943 with the collaboration of the German Ministry of the Air Force, we read that the maximum speed of the Russian plane with the best performance at the time, the MIG-3, was only 570 km/hr. In a noteworthy foreword, Field Marshal Milch had recommended the pamphlet warmly.

"On the other hand, we can say today that the data given in this pamphlet were erroneous not only concerning the speed, but also regarding the engine and the shape of the aircraft type. Apparently these errors were made deliberately to belittle the quality of the enemy's planes. It is an old German fault to indulge in conceit. At the time, however, this underestimate of our enemy's weapons was responsible for the defeat we must still bear today.

"German military intelligence was unable to make available to the combat elements, before the Russian campaign began, adequate information on the type and performance of the Soviet aircraft. When the advance began in June 1941, we hardly knew much more about Russia's planes than we did at the time of the Spanish Civil War. As a result, we were as much surprised as the antitank gunners were by the ninety-ton tanks and the T-34, as well as by the large numbers in which everything Russian seemed to appear.

TOP SCORING ALLIED ACE, WWII: Major-General Ivan N. Koshedub of the Red Air Force was the top-scoring Allied ace of WWII with 62 aerial victories over the Luftwaffe. He is said to be first Russian pilot to shoot down an Me-262 jet, in February 1945. Postwar career of Koshedub is said to have included leading MiG fighters from North Korean bases during Korean conflict. Three times awarded Hero of Soviet Union decoration. *(Chalif Collection)*

"We were also surprised when, after the first missions, the Pe-2 entered the picture, the IL-2, MIG, LAGG, and so on. In July and August 1941, during the first aerial combats over Kiev, elegant low-wing monoplanes with straight engines appeared next to the Rata. A few of them had been seen over Lemberg during the first few days, but this didn't cause much of a surprise because they were held to be our own.

"The reaction, of course, was devastating, but only because of poor intelligence work."

Dr. Steinicke adds the following assessment of Soviet aircraft and their pilots, based on British and American technical data and combined with German experience and reports:

"The best-known and most successful Soviet pilots of the war were Ivan Kojedub[3] and Alexander Pokryshin. While Kojedub flew a La-5 and a La-7 to obtain his sixty-two downings, Pokryshin downed his fifty-nine planes flying mostly the Airacobra. These figures are noteworthy inasmuch as Russian pilots, in the first years of the war, were ordered to operate as far as possible over Russian territory only. In any case, they are almost 100 percent higher than the downing figures of the most successful American (forty), Briton (thirty-eight), and Frenchman (thirty-three).

[3] Major General Kojedub (sometimes spelled Kozhedub) is reported to have commanded an air division in North Korea which was equipped with MIG-15 jets. It is possible that he added to his victory record there, but it is also reported that his unit was given such a mauling by the Americans that he was recalled to the USSR.

"A comparison of the German and Russian fighter planes most used in 1942 is as follows:

	Me-109 F4	MIG-3
Engine performance	DB601 1300 hp 12 cyl. in-line	AM-35A 1350 hp 12 cyl. in-line
Armament	1 2cm gun 150 rounds. 2 machine guns 17- 7.9mm, each 500 rounds	1 12.7mm machine cannon 300 rounds. 2 machine guns, 7.62mm, each 375 rounds
Flying weight	2650 kg	3300 kg
Range	710 km at 500 km/hr at 5000 m.	820 km at 550 km/hr at 5000 m.
Sources	Kens-Novarra	William Green, England

"Noteworthy especially in this comparison is the range of the MIG-3. In spite of a greater speed the MIG-3 could fly 110 km farther than the worthy Me-109F-4. Many times, this inferior range was a handicap to a German pilot, because it made a premature return flight necessary. A pursuing German pilot had to break off aerial combat. Now it is understandable, too, why Russian combat airfields were located much farther behind the front than the German combat airfields. The latter were so close to the front near Kursk in 1942, during the march on Voronezh, that they were fired on by medium-caliber Russian artillery.

"It is also astonishing that the absolute maximum speed of the MIG-3 was higher than that of the Me-109F-3. Since the Russian MIG-3 was more maneuverable than the Me-109, it is really remarkable in retrospect that the German fighter pilots were so successful on the Russian Front. There were, of course, Soviet fighter planes that were not as efficient. Nevertheless the Russians had an excellent radial engine by the beginning of 1943, the fourteen cylinder Shvetsov M-82 FN with 1640 hp. This engine was quite the equal of our BMW 801, and was built into the La-5 among other aircraft. The La-5 had two 20mm cannons located in the center of the aircraft above the engine and firing through the propeller disc."

Soviet aircraft losses were in proportion to Soviet aircraft production, and both were massive. The most conservative estimates of Soviet wartime aircraft losses, including figures from Soviet sources, set the minimum at 70,000 aircraft, but 77,000 to 80,000 is a more likely figure. The combined war losses of the USAAF and RAF were by contrast around 40,000 aircraft—approximately 40–50 percent of Russian losses. The air war on the Eastern Front was undeniably the biggest air war of all.

When the staggering numerical size of the Red Air Force is realized, the large victory totals of the German aces on the Eastern Front are seen in a different light. At peak strength, the Luftwaffe was never able to rally more than six hundred day fighters on the Russian Front, and fought most of the war with five hundred fighters or less. The Luftwaffe fighter force sent against the huge Russian air arm was smaller than the glorious "Few" in Spitfires and Hurricanes with whom the RAF began the Battle of Britain.

In the 1940 confrontation, the RAF fighters were defending primarily southern England, a well-defined and relatively small area. The Luftwaffe fighters in Russia were strung out from the Arctic Ocean to the Black Sea. They confronted an implacable enemy who, once recovered from his early reverses, hurled hordes of planes into the air in a savage battle of attrition. As a result, the Luftwaffe fighter pilots on the Eastern Front had more targets closer to their bases, and flew more often and for longer tours of duty than any other fighter pilots in history. No wonder their scores were high.

In the Western nations, Russian Front victory totals credited to the Germans have been generally deprecated. The huge tallies of kills are usually dismissed as a result of aerial combat with a low-caliber enemy. While this assessment may be true of the first six months of the Russo-German war, thereafter it became less and less valid. German aces fought under such widely varying conditions in Russia, shouldered so

BATTLING THE WEATHER: On the Eastern Front, the WWII Luftwaffe frequently found the weather to be a more formidable opponent than the Russian armed forces. Here JG-52 ground crews manhandle an Me-109 through mud created by spring rains and melting snow. *(Krupinski Collection)*

many different burdens, and fought so hard and long that to regard their lot as "easy" violates both the facts and good sense.[4]

The authors have found that generalities about the low caliber of Russian fighter pilots are subject to dramatic exceptions in the experience of all the German aces they have interviewed. Insufficient allowance is made in assessing Soviet pilots for the steady improvement after the 1941 debacle. This recovery was such that on some occasions even the best of Germany's aces were lucky to get a draw. Major Gerd Barkhorn's experience with a Russian "honcho" in Chapter Six is a classic example, and this book will present additional instances in the next chapter.

Fighter production was not the only aspect of air power in which the Russians eclipsed the Germans. The Soviet Union planned and prepared long before the war to create a massive pool of trained pilots. The Germans by contrast built their Luftwaffe around a peacetime-trained prewar elite, with no adequate provision for expanding pilot training facilities to meet war demands.

This vital element of air power was approached by the Russians with realistic and farsighted planning. Germany began the war with one fighter pilot training school. Russian prewar preparations enabled them to produce fighter pilots as fast as they produced aircraft. The strangest aspect of this contrast between the air power concepts of the two nations is that the Germans had access to intimate knowledge of Russian thinking and practical air power development. The Germans never used this knowledge.

The Russians owed the Germans a substantial debt in the birth and development of the Soviet Air Force. German technical aid to Russia began with the establishment of a Junkers branch factory at Fili, near Moscow, in 1923. The Russians proved quickly that once they were shown how to execute a given manufacturing process, they could repeat it with speed and precision. Furthermore, they revealed a sharp talent for simplification of complex designs and processes. They were still intent on simplification when they took captured German rocket scientists to Russia after the war, gave them everything they needed and told them to "simplify" the V-2 system.

German accounts of these early years in Russia leave no doubt of the Soviet capacity to eventually stand alone in aircraft production. In 1927 the Russians took over the Junkers factory and continued with their own manufacture of the Ju-22 all-metal, high-wing, single-seat fighter and Jumo engines. The K-30 three-engined bomber was produced by the Russians in this same plant.

Founded in 1923, the Red Air Force boasted one thousand aircraft in one hundred squadrons by 1928. Colonel Wolfgang Falck has recounted in Chapter Eight his experience at the Russo-German

---

[4] Lieutenant Katia Budanova, Russian aviatrix, flew sixty-six combat sorties during the Stalingrad battles of 1942 and was credited with eleven aerial victories. She was wingwoman to Lieutenant Lilya Litvak, the top woman ace of the world with thirteen victories. No! Combat in the air is never easy.

aviation training school at Lipetsk, 150 miles south of Moscow. Set up in 1924 to secretly train German air force pilots, the shared base provided the Russians with many advantages.

The eager Russians were able to study German training methods, tactics, organization, and procedures developed in the German Air Service of the First World War, and subsequently refined in the postwar years. The Germans in turn became familiar with Soviet problems and thinking. The base continued in operation until 1931, so the Russians had adequate opportunity to gain insight into German air doctrine.

The burgeoning Red Air Force outstripped the development of its supporting organization, communications, and tactical knowledge in the nineteen twenties. By the early thirties when the Lipetsk arrangement was terminated, the Red Air Force was a large and cumbersome aggregation of relatively obsolescent aircraft.

When Russia committed Red Air Force units to the Loyalist side in the Spanish Civil War, these deficiencies of command and control were fundamental weaknesses in Soviet air power, according to Colonel Hans-Henning von Beust, later Bomber Group Commander on the Southern Sector of the Eastern Front. Russian pilots in Spain were fiercely aggressive, but they lacked the supporting organization and training to make their fighting spirit effective, in von Beust's view. Aware of their deficiencies, the Russians struggled to close the gap, but they still exhibited the same weaknesses after the German invasion, according to this experienced officer.

When Hitler seized power in 1933, the Red Air Force had fifteen hundred first-line aircraft and Russia's annual production had reached two thousand machines. Rock-hard realist Josef Stalin said in that same year, "What the Soviet Union needs for the protection of its economic development and the pursuit of its foreign policies is an air force ready for action at all times." His goal was to have *one hundred thousand trained pilots* available.

As Head of State and supreme ruler of Russia, Stalin did not have to argue his wishes through a reluctant Congress or worry about the cost

FOCKE-WULFS READY TO GO: FW-190F-8 with engine running is ready for takeoff. These planes belong to Kommodore Trautloft's JG-54 on the Eastern Front. (*Toliver Collection*)

of his ambitious program. A flying association called OSSOAVIAKIM was established under military jurisdiction. Functioning as a civil flying club, OSSOAVIAKIM gave thousands of youths paratroop, glider, and flying training.

The arrangement resembled the promotion of gliding in Germany under the Weimar Republic and later under Hitler, but it was driven forward with far greater energy and with close government supervision. Much later, in 1938, Hitler demanded a fivefold expansion of the Luftwaffe. This was his response to the challenge of British aerial rearmament, and was intended to maintain a solid numerical advantage for the Luftwaffe.

Hitler thus saw further and more clearly than the Luftwaffe General Staff, which did not have the drive, imagination, or will—let alone the resources—to implement the Fuehrer's directive. The fivefold expansion was progressively watered down and innumerable barriers to its fulfillment arose. In a few short years, the German fighter pilots were to suffer the consequences of their high command's failure to increase aircraft and pilot strength as Hitler demanded.

Russia's pilot training scheme meanwhile proceeded full blast throughout the thirties. Graduates of OSSOAVIAKIM were entitled to join the Red Air Force for further training. This follow-on course lasted three years, and by the end of 1940 the goal of one hundred thousand trained pilots had almost been reached. Military pilot training extended two years beyond this, the graduates being sent to fighter pilot schools for six to nine months of advanced training.

Behind the pilot training scheme stood its reason for existence—the Soviet aircraft industry. Improved out of sight since the first days of the Junkers plant at Fili, the industry was booming with activity. The Germans were given a full and frank look at these developments, and what they saw should have been sufficient to cool the ambition of any would-be conqueror.

In April 1941, Lieutenant Colonel Heinrich Aschenbrenner (later Generalleutnant), the German Air Attaché in Moscow, arranged for some Luftwaffe engineers to tour the Soviet aircraft industry. This was *after* the Battle of Britain, when the Russians already suspected that Germany would turn its attention eastward. The astonished Germans found some of the factories they visited employing thirty thousand laborers per shift, three shifts per day. At the end of this inspection, famed MIG fighter designer Artem Mikoyan, brother of Anastas Mikoyan, told the Germans the purpose of the tour.

"We have now shown you all we have and all we can do," he said. "We shall destroy anyone who attacks us."

This formidable warning went unheeded.

Russia's two-pronged drive for air power—production and training—paid off when the Soviet Union needed it most. The invasion debacle would automatically have eliminated from the war any less well-prepared country. Russian aircraft production, already more than twice that of Germany in 1941,[5] rose to two thousand planes per month in the spring of 1942. There were pilots available to man these machines, and thus the Red Air Force rebounded from its defeat.

The same situation in reverse was the ultimate undoing of the Luftwaffe fighter force. When Udet committed suicide in 1941, German fighter production was at a trickle, in spite of the simultaneous engagement on several fronts of Luftwaffe fighters. Udet's successor was the hard-driving Erhard Milch, Goering's deputy. Milch went to Johannes Jeschonnek, Chief of the Luftwaffe General Staff, and offered to boost fighter production to one thousand aircraft a month. This seemed to Milch the most obvious step to take in view of the Luftwaffe's heavy and growing commitment of fighters.

Jeschonnek turned down this offer. "Three hundred and sixty fighters a month is sufficient. I have only three hundred and seventy crews to man them," was his laconic response. He was disinterested in training expansion or any kind of build-up that would not be of immediate use. He was a body-and-soul backer of Hitler's gamble to conquer Russia, and he knew that Germany had to win quickly with what was available or lose everything.

In the mighty gamble of the Russian invasion, everything thus turned on one roll of the dice. The stakes were victory in eight weeks, or national doom. When Russia did not succumb, the years of neglect and dereliction in the general constitution of German air power, in training,

RUSSIA'S MOST FAMOUS ACE: Colonel Alexander I. "Sacha" Pokryshkin became the most famous Russian ace of World War II with 59 aerial victories over the Luftwaffe. As a tactician and fighter aviation advocate he stood above all other Soviet flyers of the war. Pokryshkin commanded Guards Fighter Regiments against leading German fighter formations. German aces who flew on all fronts in WWII classify such Russian units as equal to the world's best in skill and fighting ability. Pokryshkin later became a Russian general. *(Chalif Collection)*

---

[5] German aircraft production, all types of aircraft:

1940—16,665	1943—28,420
1941—13,378	1944—44,738
1942—17,987	

Figures include new aircraft, conversions, and repaired aircraft returned to operations.

production, and development created a succession of desperate problems. The fighter pilots on the Eastern Front reaped most of the wild harvest.

The invasion of Russia had many incredible aspects besides those pertaining to air power and particularly fighter power, which have been described. Stalin knew that a German attack was imminent. Certain critical movements of air units from the Balkans to the Russian frontier were brought to his personal attention by Churchill. Yet the Germans took the Russians completely by surprise.

The situation was akin to the Pearl Harbor fiasco, where even radar warnings of the approaching Japanese invaders were ignored or misinterpreted. The Luftwaffe found Soviet airfields packed with aircraft—lined up in some cases in parade formation. Sticks of bombs and low-level strafing runs demolished whole squadrons in minutes. Airfield after airfield was reduced to smoking shambles.

According to Generalleutnant Hermann Plocher, the 1st Air Fleet on the Northern Sector of the Eastern Front between 22 June and 13 July 1941 destroyed 1211 Russian aircraft on the ground and 487 in aerial combat. Reports of the Southern and Central Sectors for the same period are not available, but tallies are available for the period 22–28 June 1941. These records show losses of 700 Soviet aircraft in the Northern Sector, 1570 in the Central Sector, and approximately 1360 in the Southern Sector. This total of 3360 aircraft destroyed in a week checked with reports of Russian POWs interrogated early in July 1941.

The Germans maintained this pressure through the ensuing weeks and obtained outright air supremacy in the Central and Northern Sectors and a solid air superiority in the Southern Sector. Defending their homeland, the Russian fighter pilots of these early days were real tigers. When attacking German bases or formations, however, they showed a basic lack of aggressiveness.

Colonel Hans-Henning von Beust says of this period:

"How can one expect real enthusiasm in combat from airmen with aircraft, weapons, and other equipment so hopelessly inferior; who themselves were so vastly inferior in techniques, tactics, and training to their opponents, and who were aware of the terrific reverses the Soviet Union had just suffered."

That the Russians could spring back from such reverses is a tribute to the doggedness of the Russian fighting man.

A valuable German prize of the early period was Colonel Vanyushin, Commander of the Russian 20th Air Army. He provided his interrogators with a view of the assault from the "other side of the hill." Vanyushin attributed the German success of 22–28 June 1941 to the following factors:

1. Clever timing of the attack.[6]

---

[6] There is no evidence that the timing of the German attack was anything other than a stroke of luck for the Germans.

2. Critical weakness of Soviet air units because of a re-equipment program then in progress.
3. Re-equipment was being carried out at forward airfields.
4. Proximity of Soviet air units to the border.
5. Masses of aircraft sent into action by the Luftwaffe.
6. The generally poor condition of Russian airfields.
7. Russian negligence in many areas.
8. Failure of Soviet Command.

In the vernacular, this means that the Russians were caught with their pants down, as were the Americans at Pearl Harbor. Only a few of the highly skilled and experienced fighters and fighter-bombers were needed to take out an entire air base. Russian POWs interrogated by the Germans could not understand why there had not been hundreds of mid-air collisions between the German planes. The invading aircraft seemed to swarm around their bases like clouds of giant locusts.

The Germans in truth went into this major air war practically blind. Third-ranking German ace Guenther Rall (275 victories) said when interrogated after the war that German estimates of Russian fighter forces were extremely vague. The Luftwaffe pilots had no precise knowledge of the types of aircraft they could expect to encounter. The normal data available to combat pilots—such as aircraft performance, armament, and silhouettes of the enemy machines—were lacking. The Germans relied mainly on the quality of their own weapons and pilots to win victory in a lightning war.

The air war in the East began with the destruction by the Luftwaffe of the *equipment* of the Red Air Force. Russian productive capacity and pilot reserves remained untouched. Nor did the thousands of ground-destroyed Russian aircraft lose their crews. The formidable productive power of the Soviet aircraft industry—which had been adequately demonstrated to German air leaders and engineers—was allowed to uncoil without hindrance from the Luftwaffe.

SOVIET HERO FIGHTER ACE: Ivan Kozedub, three times Hero of the Soviet Union, ace with 62 victories according to most authorities, was leading ace of the Soviet Union in WWII. Kozedub (varied spellings of his name are Kojedub, Kozhedub, and others) supposedly led an Air Division in the Korean War but all attempts by the authors to confirm this and other facts about Soviet fighter aces even as late as 1976 have met with little success. (*Novosti Press-Moscow*)

The over-emphasis on close support in the Luftwaffe led to the gross misemployment of German bombers in Russia. After the early battles, not even a small percentage of the bomber force was detailed to smash the Soviet railway network behind the front, assail factories, or otherwise strike at Soviet nerve centers. Bombers were used instead like artillery, dropping their loads right in front of the advancing troops.

General Adolf Galland, whose career began as a close-support specialist and advocate, expressed his view on tactical air power in Russia to the authors in these terms:

"The Luftwaffe was not used as an Air Force, but as advanced artillery. This is not the right way to use bombers, dropping bombs on the enemy's front line. That is the task of artillery. The Air Force should attack where the enemy's nerves come together. The reason for this misuse of the bombers was that the Army was impressed by immediate, visual success in support of its operations. The bombers should have been attacking airfields, railroads, and bridges behind the lines. But you cannot see immediate results from this. The effects come later, perhaps in days or weeks, and this was not satisfactory to the German Army.

"The Luftwaffe taught the Army to use aviation in direct support, which is right in certain circumstances, but it was *not* taught as a universal principle. The Luftwaffe was frittered away in continued close-support operations. This approach produced experts like von Richthofen. He was a man who said, 'I am concentrating all my wings in this area from 1100 to 1300.' Then the Army had no choice. They were forced to advance and occupy the zone attacked by close support. So very often in Russia *the Luftwaffe and not the Army* started an offensive in a given area.

"Often Hitler gave the orders to Goering or to Jeschonnek, and they would pass the orders to von Richthofen or another commander of his type to move the Army ahead. The Army commanders would often object, saying in effect, 'We do not have sufficient forces, or artillery, or transport.' When this got back to Hitler he would simply say to the Luftwaffe, 'Move the Army ahead.'"

By absorbing the bombers in the close support of the Army, the Germans diverted this striking force from attacks on Soviet industry, transportation, and communications. As a consequence, the total production of Soviet industry had to be destroyed *after* it reached the front. This was the origin of the blizzard of Soviet aircraft of all types with which the German fighter pilots had to contend. In battling this immense flood of machines they amassed scores which by all prior standards of aerial warfare were enormous.

These Eastern Front scores, among which one hundred downings was relatively commonplace, were possible for the following main reasons:

1. Most Soviet aircraft, including most lend-lease aircraft, were technically inferior to the Me-109, Germany's main fighter on

the Russian Front.

2. The Germans operated from airfields within a few miles of the front line. They could take off and engage in combat within a few minutes.

3. The Eastern Front German pilots flew more missions involving aerial combat than German, American, or British pilots on any other front

4. The Germans were tactically superior until at least the middle of 1943, and psychologically were superior until the end.

5. Soviet tactical air power presented them with thousands of targets in the immediate front-line environs, not only fighters, but dive bombers, fighter-bombers, medium bombers, and assorted support aircraft.

6. Most Soviet fighter pilots were inferior to most British and American fighter pilots. The Soviet pilots of other than fighter aircraft did not stand much chance against an experienced Me-109 pilot.

7. German Army units on the ground frequently observed aerial combat and were able to provide kill confirmations in numerous instances.

The majority of German fighter pilots who fought on both fronts give a clear edge to the Royal Air Force pilot over all others. The Americans rank next, and then the Russians. This generality is usually subject to individual exceptions. There are some German aces of vast

NUMBER TWO RUSSIAN ACE: Guards Colonel Alexander Pokryskin, 59-victory ace. Gutty far beyond normal, this Soviet fighter pilot was a Soviet Hero many times over. (*Novosti Press- Moscow*)

experience who ran into Russian pilots that they considered better than the pilots of the Western powers.

When the Russians began concentrating their hot pilots in the elite Red Guards squadrons, the Germans facing them had their work cut out. As Guenther Rall expressed it, "They were the real fighter types—individualists—not the dull masses of the ordinary squadrons." These Red Guards units had a feisty morale and would often tune their radio transmissions to German wavelengths, challenging the Luftwaffe's best aces to come up and fight.

Russian aces like Kojedub, Pokryskin, and Rechkalov were second to none as tacticians, and they outscored the best British and American aces handily. The standard Western concept of the Russian fighter pilot as a brutish clod sent up to provide target practice for the high-scoring German aces is an oversimplification. The Red Air Force had many crude pilots, but it also produced some who were extremely sharp.

Even some of the crude ones were not lacking in guts. Numerous German aces are positive that on occasion their Russian opponent tried to ram them—hardly an act of cowardice. Russian pilots generally tended toward caution and reluctance rather than toughness and stamina, to crudeness rather than combat efficiency, abysmal hatred in battle instead of fairness and chivalry. But no German pilot could ever be sure that he was not going to run into the fight of his life over the Russian Front.

Dozens of German aces were shot down and killed in Russia, the most notable being Oberleutnant Otto Kittel (267 victories) and Oberleutnant Anton Hafner (204 victories). Such luminaries as Erich Hartmann (352 kills), Gerhard Barkhorn (301 kills), Guenther Rall (275 victories), Heinz Baer (220 victories), Anton Hackl (192 kills), and Erich Rudorffer (222 kills) were all shot down or forced down at one time or another by Russian fighters. They survived forced landings and parachute jumps to fight again.

These facts illustrate that while it is easy to say, "It was easy," on the Russian Front, hard experience taught the Germans that it was easy nowhere if you ran into the wrong man. The notion that fighter piloting was a picnic for the Eastern Front German aces has enjoyed long and wide currency. The facts should lay it to rest at last. An appropriate factual refutation is found in the combat career and scoring record of a prominent Eastern Front ace, Captain Joachim Brendel.

Captain Brendel is virtually unknown outside Germany as an ace, but he is credited with 189 aerial victories. Since he began his combat career at the time of the invasion of Russia, and fought nowhere else, many aspects of his war record are typical of Eastern Front aces. He flew 950 missions, including 162 in direct support of Army units, engaging in aerial combat on about 400 of these missions. He won the Oak Leaves to his Knight's Cross on 14 January 1945.

Mr. Hans Ring, the documentation expert of the German Fighter

MOTHER RUSSIA: Airmen from JG-52 bicycle into a typical Russian village located in the Crimea. Hundreds of similar villages dotted the Russian Front and changed hands several times during the war. *(Krupinski Collection)*

Pilots' Association, and one of the foremost authorities on the German aces of the Second World War, kindly assisted the authors in developing this short history of Captain Joachim Brendel.

Brendel started slowly. On his fourth mission he caught up with a fleeing twin-engined attack bomber, a DB-3, and after firing nearly all his ammunition set the bomber on fire and saw it crash to the ground. This victory was on 29 June 1941. Usually combat pilots improve greatly and score many kills after they get their first victory behind them, but the reverse was true with Brendel.

He went into a shell. He flew steadily as a wingman, but missed many opportunities to add to his tally. Some 116 missions later, on 31 March 1942, Brendel scored his second kill. Considering the level of air activity over the Russian Front he was an exceedingly slow starter. By 12 December 1942 he had ten victories. He had been flying combat for eighteen months with the busy JG-51.

Brendel was disappointed with himself. The mounting kill tallies of his fellow pilots depressed him further. But New Year 1943 brought a sharp change for the better, as he mastered his inner difficulties and found his shooting eye. By 24 February 1943 he had twenty victories.

By 5 May 1943 he had thirty victories, by 10 June he had forty, and on his 412th mission on 9 July 1943 he scored his fiftieth kill. Four months later, on 22 November 1943, he flew his 551st mission and had doubled his score. He stood at the magic one hundred milestone.

He needed eleven more months to get his next fifty victories. He scored his 150th kill on his 792nd mission, 16 October 1944. Brendel reached his final tally on 25 April 1945—189 victories in 950 missions.

As a further illustration of the level of activity engaged in by this typical Eastern Front ace, the following tabulation shows ten days of combat in his career, from 5 July 1943 to 14 July 1943, with the types and numbers of aircraft which he engaged in combat during this time.

He scored twenty victories in this ten-day period.

Date	Mission	Types and Numbers of Enemy A/C Engaged
5 July 1943	400	6 Lagg-3
,,	401	8 IL-2, 2 MIG-3
,,	402	4 MIG-3, 2 IL-2
,,	403	4 La-5
6 July 1943	404	15 Boston DB-7, 15 MIG-3
,,	405	2 La-5
,,	406	4 Lagg-3
7 July 1943	407	6 MIG-3, 8 Bostons
,,	408	9 IL-2
8 July 1943	409	30 IL-2, 15 various fighters
,,	410	8 MIG-3, 4 Bostons
9 July 1943	411	12 IL-2, 6 Lagg-3
,,	412	6 Lagg-3
10 July 1943	413	15 MIG-3
,,	414	6 Lagg-3
11 July 1943	415	14 MIG-3
12 July 1943	416	20 IL-2, 15 La-5
,,	417	8 La-5
,,	418	15 Lagg-3, 2 IL-2
13 July 1943	419	10 fighters, 8 IL-2
,,	420	1 IL-2, 3 Lagg-3
,,	421	4 La-5
14 July 1943	422	6 IL-2, 4 Lagg-3
,,	423	2 Lagg-3

From this tabulation it may be seen that Brendel was exceedingly busy during this ten-day period. From these encounters he was able to confirm only twenty victories, as has been pointed out.

Joachim Brendel's 189 kills included 88 Ilyushin-2 (IL-2) aircraft, the rugged "Stormovik" dive bomber. German aces who flew on the Russian Front agree that it was the most difficult Soviet aircraft to bring down, almost impervious even to cannon fire. Brendel also downed twenty-five Yak-9 fighters. He was shot down once himself by Russian flak, was shot down once by a Yak-9 and made a forced landing, and was rammed once by another Yak-9 and had to parachute.

Clearly it was a long, hard war for Joachim Brendel, even though he was one of the most successful German aces on the Russian Front. Historically significant is the incredulity with which the large victory totals were greeted even by the German command during the early days of the Eastern Front battles. They were well aware how long it had taken the gifted "Daddy" Moelders to top von Richthofen's First World War record of eighty victories. As a consequence, Luftwaffe wing and group commanders were constantly accused of *padding the claims of aircraft shot down*. Even the German High Command did not believe the front-line pilots. Goering's wild assertions to this effect were a feature of the "Kommodore's Revolt" in Berlin in January 1945.

The commanders in the field at wing and group level reacted to these indignities by initiating voluminous record-keeping, passing these responsibilities down to the individual pilots, operations officers, and debriefing Intelligence officers. Through this strict and demanding procedure, the commanders expected better reports, as well as a sharpened awareness on the part of the fighting pilots. The plan worked.

The pilots were required to keep track of their geographical position at all times,[7] note the number and types of aircraft in the enemy gaggle, log the exact minute (clock time) of a kill, and observe other actions in the air at the same time. Besides being able to confirm a fellow pilot's kill, the would-be ace had to strive for tactical advantage over the enemy he was engaging, so he was kept busy. Their diligence has at least made the historian's task easier.

Conditions on the Eastern Front from Leningrad to the Black Sea were physically taxing. The Russians in retreat took everything of utility with them, and flattened or burned whatever they could not carry. The fighting pilots of the Luftwaffe lived under cruel physical hardship, sleeping in dugouts with tents over them and often living this way for months on end. To live in a building of any kind, or a wooden hut, was a luxury.

Shifts in the front and the highly mobile warfare that frequently broke up the static patterns sometimes brought their airfields under Russian artillery fire. The most elementary comforts of civilized life were lacking, and the grind of constant aerial fighting never ceased. No one who was there found it easy.

In the Far North, conditions were even worse. Here JG-5, the Polar Sea Wing, plied its fighter trade to help throttle the Arctic shipping convoys. JG-5 is probably the least-known German fighter wing of the war, but it made an admirable record under conditions of indescribable personal hardship for its personnel. JG-5 produced a number of outstanding aces, including Theo Weissenberger, Walter Schuck, and Heinrich Ehrler—all of whom scored over two hundred victories during the war. We will meet these three aces later, since they all eventually flew the Me-262 in the final defense of the Reich.

On the Eastern Front the German fighter pilots were actors in a gigantic drama. Their stage extended from the Polar Sea to the Black Sea. The drama evoked stellar performances from many of these participants, and it is time to move in for a close-up of some of them.

---

[7] Landing in Russian territory usually proved fatal.

EARLY Me-(Bf-109s): Three early-model Me-109s stand ready alert on August 10th, 1939. *(Dölling)*

LONG-NOSE FOCKE-WULF 190s: These long-nosed late model FW-190s were assigned to NJG-1 in early 1945 and were part of Professor Tank's latest effort in fighters. *(Dölling)*

VERY IMPORTANT VISITOR: Adolf Galland flew to the far north to visit JG-5. Dölling took this picture shortly after Galland landed his Me-109. *(Dölling)*

GALLAND IN FINLANDIA: Another shot of Galland dressed in his white winter flying suit with fur collar, taken just after landing for a visit with JG-5. *(Dölling)*

JACOB NORZ—117 VICTORIES: Leutnant Norz, known by the nickname of "Jockel," shot down 12 Soviet aircraft on June 27th, 1944. KIA 16 September 1944. This photo taken at time of his 28th victory, 8 June 1943. *(Dölling)*

RUDI LINZ—JG-5—70 VICTORIES: The wastelands of frozen northern Norway and Finland (Petsamo is a hundred miles northwest of Murmansk, Russia) was a hell of a place to be fighting a war. Linz lost his life there after 70 victories, on 9 February 1945. *(Dölling)*

CHALK UP ANOTHER ONE!: Crew Chief of an ace marks another victory on the rudder of a fighter in Finland. JG-5. *(Dölling)*

PLAYBOYS OF THE AIR??: Fighter pilots will launch a party at the slightest suggestion. These JG-5 pilots in upper Finland thought the number 100 a good excuse. (l. to r.) Jakob Norz (profile); Berger; unknown; Heinrich Bartels; Hermann Segatz; Josef Kunz; Rudi Müller. *(Dölling)*

STATION-MASTER OF TANGMERE: Wing Commander Douglas Bader is shown in these two photographs during a visit to JG-26, the unit credited with shooting him down. In left photo he is being questioned by Hauptmann Horst Barth (back to camera). In the picture at the right, Bader enters auto to begin his journey which took him to Oberursel for interrogations, thence to Colditz Castle where he was interned for the duration of the war. *(Galland Collection)*

REICHSMARSCHALL GORING AND GRAF: Göring and Hermann Graf, then the most successful Luftwaffe fighter pilot, meet to talk tactics. The Reichsmarschall knew dogfighting tactics from WWI and tried to get the WWII fighters to adopt the same turning battles with the best man winning. Speed robbed modern fighters of maneuverability but Hermann Göring did not seem to comprehend this. *(Obermaier Collection)*

WAR HEROES: Ace Hermann Graf and ace Egon Mayer meet school children as part of the Luftwaffe's campaign to draw recruits into the Air Force. Mayer was the first pilot to pass 100 victory mark in the Western Front. He was killed in air combat on March 2, 1944 after his 102nd victory. Hermann Graf shot down 200 enemy aircraft in 13 months and was the first to reach the 200 kill mark, which he did on October 2, 1942. *(Obermaier Collection)*

HELMUT LIPFERT: 203 victories, Lipfert flew 700 missions and was shot down often but never injured. He was Kommandeur of 1 Gruppe of JG-53 the last days of the war. *(Obermaier)*

12

Aces of the Eastern Front

"Find the enemy and shoot him down, anything else is nonsense."
BARON MANFRED VON RICHTHOFEN,
1917

MAJOR WILHELM BATZ grew up between the wars with the Red Baron as his ideal of a fighter pilot. He began his military career in the prewar Luftwaffe, but never scored a victory until 11 March 1943. Fifteen months later, Batz had only fifteen kills—a long way short of von Richthofen's eighty-victory record of the First World War. Nevertheless, Willi Batz had 237 confirmed victories to his credit by war's end, wore the Oak Leaves and Swords at his throat, and had written one of the most phenomenal scoring records in the history of aerial combat. He almost trebled von Richthofen's score.

The saga of Willi Batz started in earnest when he entered the infant Luftwaffe in 1935 as a peacetime career officer. He was eager to be a fighter pilot. During his training it was found that he had the aptitudes and skills fitting him for the unspectacular task of instructing future pilots. He was kept at the instructing grind from 1937 to 1942, at which time his pleas for transfer to a combat unit coincided with a shortage of trained officers on the Eastern Front.

In their previous work *Fighter Aces*[1] the authors outlined the importance to a successful fighter pilot of air-to-air shooting ability. This arcane skill in many cases made aces out of mediocre pilots. Many accomplished pilots minus shooting ability never became aces. There was nothing mediocre about the piloting of Willi Batz. He was one of the most highly skilled pilots in the Luftwaffe, with over five thousand hours to his credit as an instructor. Flying an airplane was as natural to him as walking. His main difficulty was finding his shooting eye—a task that almost drove him to distraction.

---

[1] *Fighter Aces* by Colonel Raymond F. Toliver and Trevor J. Constable. The Macmillan Company, New York, 1965.

STURM, BARKHORN, BATZ and FONNEKOLD: These four aces of JG-52 had destroyed *831* aircraft in aerial combat but when the Soviets could put up 60 more for every one shot down, the dent was small. Sturm had 157 kills, Barkhorn 301, Batz scored 237 and Fönnekold 136. They made major contributions to JG-52s record of over 10,000 aerial kills in WWII. *(Batz Collection)*

Posted to JG-52 in December 1942, he served first as Steinhoff's adjutant. He shared quarters with his doughty C.O. Batz alleges that Steinhoff's snoring would awaken the dead, and invariably he would be blasted into reluctant wakefulness in the predawn hours. On one occasion the awakened Willi took Steinhoff's Knight's Cross and draped it around his sleeping C.O.'s head. "For distinguished snoring" said the small placard.

Steinhoff took the ribbing in good part, but he had a counter tactic.

"If it is foggy in the morning," he told his adjutant, "let me sleep an additional hour."

Willi Batz the polished pilot went on mission after mission. "I shot hundreds of thousands of holes in the air while aiming at enemy aircraft," he says of this period. After four months of wild gunnery and almost ceaseless operational flying, Batz had still to make his first kill. Exasperated and disgusted with himself, he asked for a transfer to the bombers.

His request was declined, and on 11 March 1943 he finally scored his first victory. When he was made a squadron leader in May 1943, he was probably the only squadron leader on the Eastern Front who was not an ace—a rare distinction in the Luftwaffe fighter command. He had no trouble facing the facts:

"I got the promotion not because I was a good fighter, but because I had seniority. I was twenty-seven years old—too old for a fighter pilot. Most of them then were twenty-one or thereabouts, and I was an old man among them. I was a good adjutant but a bad fighter, and my C.O. told me that point-blank. I agreed with him."

By June 1943 he was a squadron leader with one kill. He managed another that month, but by June 1944 still had only fifteen victories. His morale for aerial combat was at a low ebb. The confidence essential

TUTORED ERICH HARTMANN: 1st Lieutenant Josef "Jupp" Zwernemann was one of the battle-wise aces of JG-52 who tutored Erich Hartmann when he arrived raw at the Eastern Front. Zwernemann had 126 victories and the Oak Leaves to his Knight's Cross. Hartmann called him a "muscles and head flyer"—one who combined a vigorous fighting style with full use of the intellect. He died on the Western Front in combat with a P-51 Mustang of the USAAF. (*Hartmann Collection*)

to success was lacking. In eighteen months of combat on the busiest front of the war, one of the Luftwaffe's most highly skilled pilots had scored less than one kill per month. In the USAAF this was called "buck fever." Batz had it bad. "I was a mass of inferiority complexes," is the way he summarizes his plight.

A pause ensued which influenced the future career of Willi Batz decisively. Falling sick in February, he was grounded for two weeks. He was able to watch some of the aerial fighting from the ground, without himself facing the daily grind of operations. The experience renewed his perspective.

Returning to operations, he found he could not do a thing wrong. Throughout the summer of 1944 he was steadily downing three or four enemy aircraft a day, as the war diary of JG-52 reveals. He ran up some staggering bags of daily kills, including fifteen on 30 May 1944 on seven separate missions, and sixteen on one day in August 1944 in Rumania. Willi Batz ran up a phenomenal 222 kills between March 1944 and the end of the war a year later. This year is probably a record. The authors have not been able to discover a better combat performance.

Batz took over command of III/JG-52 from Guenther Rall in May 1944, and was thus operating in very fast company. Erich Hartmann, Fritz Obleser, and Walter Wolfrum were among the young, fast-scoring pilots in the group at this time. Competition in scoring was keen, and stimulated every pilot to give of his best.

He remained in command of III/JG-52 until January 1945, when he was transferred to II/JG-52 in Hungary. This proved a fortunate change. At the end of the war he was able to extricate his group from Hungary via Austria and return to Germany, thus eluding the Russian confinement which befell the other two groups and the wing staff.

The Russians made at least one determined attempt to nail Willi Batz, at the time when he was cutting a swath through their formations. German pilots used code names on the Russian Front instead of their own names, and Batz had the name "Rabitsky" for a long period. He tells the story:

"I was supposed to change this name every month or so for security reasons, but I thought Rabitsky was a good name and I decided to keep it. The Russians soon knew that Rabitsky was me, and that I was shooting down dozens of their aircraft. This was how Ivanov, the Russian

MOELDERS AND KESSELRING 1941: As one of the Luftwaffe's greatest tactical minds, as well as a brilliant combat pilot, Werner Moelders was responsible for many of the innovations that produced the excellence of the fighter arm. In July 1941, in Russia, Moelders explains a point in the application of tactical air power to General, later Field Marshal Albert Kesselring. Moelders pioneered Forward Air Controller technique in Russia, using Storch aircraft. (*Toliver Collection*)

ace, was able to set a trap for me.

"I was flying at about six thousand meters when out of the sun four Russian fighters came hurtling down. I made a sharp half roll away—a reverse. As I leveled off, another eight Russian fighters tried to jump me from a lower altitude. It was a tactic Ivanov favored.[2]

"I had to make another half roll to the underside, and then gave my aircraft everything it had in a dive to get away. The highest speed on my aircraft's indicator was 740 kilometers per hour (590 mph). The needle was right over on the pin, the engine howling and screaming, the whole aircraft vibrating.

"I had no other chance to escape. Ivanov was in the first bunch of fighters at seven thousand meters when I was at six thousand. When I leveled off from the half roll away from Ivanov, the second formation was ready to jump me. The idea was that a pilot evading the first bounce would then think himself secure, drop his guard and relax long enough for that second bounce to succeed.

"I will never forget this encounter. My aircraft afterward was a total loss. The wings and fuselage had started to separate."

A forced landing behind the Russian lines was the worst fate that could befall a German fighter pilot on the Eastern Front outside of being killed in action.[3] If his captors shot him on sight, he could consider himself fortunate. There were things worse than death awaiting a fighter pilot landing in Russian territory under general circumstances.

[2] The Russians had employed a form of the Double Attack System, which has only recently, with reluctance, found favor in the USAF.

This prospect struck more terror into the German pilots than their adversaries in the air. One young German pilot, twenty-year-old Second Lieutenant Hans Strelow, reportedly shot himself with his pistol after being forced down in Russian territory 22 May 1942. He was a squadron leader with sixty-eight kills on the Russian Front and wore the Oak Leaves. The highly decorated officer was especially liable to Russian reprisals.

Willi Batz came close enough to a forced landing in Russian territory for it to be one of his unforgettable experiences:

"Together with Gerd Barkhorn, I was sent on visual reconnaissance behind the lines. We were looking for Russian fighter bases behind the front. The distance to the Russian bases from the center of the front was 200 to 250 kilometers. We were at maximum distance behind the front, about 250 kilometers, and flying at six thousand meters *when my engine quit.* All the horrors of Soviet capture and confinement rushed into my mind. My feelings were of stark terror as my aircraft went down in a flat glide.

"At about two thousand meters I looked down and saw that my electric gasoline pump was off. I hit the switch. After about five seconds the engine burst into life. And to me it was *life!* At low level I went all out for my home base. I have never known such a feeling of relief."[4]

EARLY STARTER: One of the Luftwaffe's outstanding aces in the struggle against the RAF in the first years of the war was Hans "Assi" Hahn, who ended the war as a Major. Hahn flew for 3 years against the RAF on the Channel front starting in 1939. He downed 68 RAF aircraft, 62 of them single-engined fighters, and most of them Hurricanes and Spitfires. He served later on the Russian front, ran his aerial victories up to 108 and finished up in Russian prison camps for seven years. He was released in 1950 to return to civilian life. *(Hahn Collection)*

In the Crimea, he had another experience rivaling the first:

"Somewhere on the Black Sea was a Russian ship that the German command wanted located and destroyed. Bombers and photo recce

---

[3] It is said that Soviet Lieutenant Vladimir D. Lavrinekov (thirty victories) shot down an Me-109 which crash-landed in a field. The German pilot ran to a nearby ditch to hide. The Soviet Lieutenant landed his aircraft beside the Me-109, ran over to the ditch, choked the German to death, then took off again.

[4] Numerous American pilots can recount a similar moment of truth. At long last, however, aircraft designers have developed a fuel system that does not require changing tanks.

planes had failed to find the vessel, so in the last extremity it was necessary to send fighters out over the sea to try and locate the ship. Nobody, but nobody, liked to fly over the sea with the Me-109 or any other single-engined aircraft.

"I asked my squadron if they would like to take the mission, but they all declined. So I flew the mission myself with a young wingman. We got about one minute beyond sight of land when to my dismay my oil pressure went up and gas pressure dropped too low. Back to the land? It was a desperate feeling, because nobody wants to go down in the drink. I decided that I would fly five minutes more before turning back.

"I made a good decision. Within that five minutes we spotted the Russian ship. We strafed it and exhausted our ammunition, and the ship fired back. Ammo gone, we went racing back to the land, exultant at having located the missing vessel. I soon sobered up.

"'You have a black streak on your undercarriage,' came the voice of my wingman on the R/T.

"The Russian ship had shot out my oil cooler, and my oil was leaking out. Now I really had oil pressure problems. The flight back to base was nerve-wracking, and climaxed by a crash landing."

Like most German aces on the Russian Front, Batz made his share of forced landings. Four times battle damage resulted in forced landings, and on two other occasions he cracked up landing under special circumstances.

"On one occasion, at the beginning of my service in Russia, every pilot had to fly around the field three times while the ground crews examined his aircraft visually for dangerous battle damage or wrecked undercarriage. I got the OK once like this, and then my gear just crumpled when I set her down."

His second washout will be of interest to students of Me-109 history:

"In Austria near the end of the war we were operating from a base that had a bitumen runway. Such luxury! For years we had been operating from grass strips near the front. The unaccustomed experience of using the bitumen strip played havoc with our group. Out of forty-two aircraft, thirty-nine cracked up on landing due to the sensitivity of the Me-109 to its brakes and the strange feel and response of a solid runway. Only the first three aircraft landed safely. The strip caused us more damage than the Red Air Force."

Willi Batz flew 445 combat missions in scoring his 237 victories. He thus averaged one kill for every two sorties flown—a formidable achievement. He was the 145th German soldier to win the second-highest award of honor, the Swords. He won the Knight's Cross on 6 April 1944, the Oak Leaves on 26 July 1944, and the Swords in April 1945.

He was wounded three times. An IL-2 once sprayed his aircraft from dead ahead with machine gun fire, shattering his instrument panel and filling his eyes with finely powdered glass. His goggles were up on his forehead at the time. On another occasion he was lightly wounded in the leg, and a flak burst near his fighter drove a shower of splinters into

GREAT LEADERS: Field Marshal Albert Kesselring, who later appeared as a major German leader in the aerial struggles in the Mediterranean, walks and talks in Russia with Colonel Werner Moelders, master tactician and first combat pilot in history to score 100 aerial victories. Moelders died in plane crash, but Kesselring survived the war. *(Toliver Collection)*

his face, at least one of which reposes to this day near the curve of his jawbone.

As Colonel Batz he is an officer of the new German Air Force. He is stationed at Wahn and lives near Hanover. A distinguished-looking man a shade under six feet in height, he has a pink complexion and a large, straight nose. His penetrating blue eyes are unmistakably those of a fighter pilot, but they no longer have the stern cast of war days. They twinkle with good humor and crown an engaging smile.

Willi Batz has the bearing, dignity, and courteous, correct character that have long been the hallmark of the professional German soldier. He is extremely intelligent, as befits one of the quickest and deadliest fighter pilots of all. His slender, well-manicured hands gesture constantly as he talks, and they move with the smooth physical coordination developed in thirty years and thousands of hours of piloting.

He is the fourth-ranked living fighter pilot of Germany[5] and the world. He reserves his greatest enthusiasm for the advice he gives to young fighter pilots or to young would-be fighter pilots. "Fly with the *head* and not with the muscles. That is the way to long life for a fighter pilot. The fighter pilot who is all muscle and no head will never live long enough for a pension."

The doctrine of "fly with the head and not with the muscles" was the central element in the command success of a famed Eastern Front ace and leader, Colonel Dietrich Hrabak, *Kommodore* of JG-52. Hrabak is credited with 125 victories, all but eighteen of them scored on the Eastern Front. His standing with his contemporaries far exceeds his standing on the ace list. Indeed, his name is likely to come up in any conversation with German fighter pilots, and invariably he enjoys their highest esteem. He ranks forty-fourth in the list of the world's fighter aces.

[5] Fourth-ranking ace is Lieutenant Otto Kittel, 267 kills. He was followed by Major Walter Nowotny, 258 kills, and Major Theo Weissenberger, 238 kills. Batz follows with 237 victories, but all the aces listed between him and Rall are dead.

JG-52 ACE: Lt. Peter Duettmann typifies large number of high-scoring aces in JG-52 who remain almost unknown outside Germany. As the most successful fighter wing in history, JG-52 had more than thirty aces in its ranks with over 100 victories. Duettman's 152 victories won for him the Knight's Cross to his Iron Cross. (*Nowarra Collection*)

Born in 1914 in a small village near Leipzig, "Dieter" Hrabak as a young boy was enthralled by the feats of the pioneer aviators of the time. The ocean conquerors like Lindbergh were his heroes. He was educated in the Humanities and after graduation from Gymnasium entered the German Navy in 1934.

Quartered in the next room to him was another cadet, named Johannes Steinhoff. Today in Building 14 at the German Defense Ministry in Bonn, Steinhoff occupies an office just down the hall from Hrabak. Professionally and personally they have been close for more than three decades.

Like Steinhoff, Hrabak underwent the standard naval officer's training before transferring to the Luftwaffe for pilot training in November 1935. He confesses to having cracked up or "bent" a number of aircraft during training, including a Focke-Wulf trainer, a Heinkel 51, and an Me-109D. He describes himself in this period as being "a ground loop specialist."

Qualifying as a pilot in 1936, he was assigned to a fighter group in Bernburg. This unit's Technical Officer was Adolf Galland, and the two future leaders made each other's acquaintance at this time. When the group was split into two cadres as the nuclei of two new groups Hrabak went with the unit assigned to Bad Eibling. Here his squadron leader was another of the Luftwaffe's outstanding personalities, Hannes Trautloft, whom we will meet in due course.

Hrabak took over command in January 1939 of a squadron in the so-called Vienna Fighter Group. Consisting almost entirely of Austrian pilots and mechanics, the unit moved to Upper Silesia shortly before the Polish invasion, and then took part in that action.

Hrabak was shot down in his very first fight over Poland on 1 September 1939. He was one of the first German fighter pilots to be downed in the Second World War. He had to wait by his crashed aircraft until Army units picked him up. He was forced down six times

GENERALFELDMARSCHALL AND KOMMODORE: Generalfeldmarschall Wolfram von Richthofen confers with Major Dietrich Hrabak, Kommodore of Jagdgeschwader 52 on the Soviet Front on May 18th, 1943. The occasion was to mark and honor JG-52s 5000th aerial victory. Center background is Richthofen's adjutant and aide. *(Hrabak Collection)*

more during the war, but never lost a drop of blood or had to resort to his parachute.

With the Battle of France, Hrabak moved down through Luxembourg to Abbeville as a squadron leader in the independent No. 76 Fighter Group. This unit then moved south to Orléans flying in support of the Army. He scored his first kill 13 May 1940 near Sedan, and it was an action that also provided some education:

"We had to protect our troops moving over the Meuse and we had many bridges to watch. Then suddenly this Potez 63 recce aircraft appeared. I was leading a four-ship *Schwarm*. We went down immediately and tackled the Frenchman.

"I started shooting. I could see that I got some quick hits because the left engine began smoking. The French machine quickly made a belly

ARTISTIC ACE: Lieutenant Edmund "Paule" Rossman was a man of artistic temperament who developed elegant and self-preservational style of attack that kept him alive through 640 missions and 93 victories. Rossman never believed in instantly assaulting a sighted enemy aircraft, but weighed entire situation before attacking to maintain high chance of success. Awarded the Knight's Cross he was one of Erich Hartmann's combat tutors, and passed into Russian confinement on 9 July 1943 when he landed "Dawn Patrol" style to rescue a squadron mate downed behind Russian lines. *(Hartmann Collection)*

landing near some German infantry units. There was no trouble confirming this kill.

"We wanted to see this Potez burn. So we waited until the crew got away from the wreck and then we shot at it again and again, making pass after pass and shooting off all our ammunition—just to see a dead aircraft burn. Ammunition exhausted, I gathered my pilots and climbed away ready to head for my base at Trier on the Moselle River.

"Suddenly we were jumped by nine Curtiss P-36 fighters, American machines bought by the French. We couldn't do anything but run like hell. This was good experience for me. I learned never again to do such a silly thing as firing off all my ammunition at a worthless target. I was learning to use my head."

Hrabak flew in the Battle of Britain and had eighteen kills to his credit at the time he left the Western Front in the spring of 1941. He was a foundation member of JG-54 *Grunherz*, the "Green Heart" wing, which was formed from No. 76 Fighter Group and two additional groups with Hannes Trautloft as its *Kommodore*. The wing was later to win immortal fame on the Eastern Front.

Twice over England Hrabak's aircraft suffered engine hits and he was lucky to stagger back to France in one piece. He maintains a stout regard for the Spitfire, and ranks the Royal Air Force fighter pilot easily first among his foes. After leaving the Channel Front he flew in support of the German Army in the invasion of Greece and was then

THE KEYS TO SUCCESS: Colonel Dietrich Hrabak (left) as Kommodore of JG-52 had under his command the most successful fighter wing of all time. With 125 victories himself, Hrabak appears here with four of the Luftwaffe's outstanding fighter pilots—Erich Hartmann (352 victories), Lt. Karl Gratz (138 victories), Lt. Friederich Obleser (127 victories) and Major Wilhelm Batz (237 victories). (*Hartmann Collection*)

posted to East Prussia to prepare his group for the invasion of Russia. He stayed with JG-54 until October 1942, when he was promoted to *Kommodore* of JG-52 on the Southern Sector of the Russian Front.

His erstwhile fellow cadet in the German Navy, Steinhoff, was now one of his group commanders. JG-52 wrote a memorable record on the Eastern Front, and its top pilots included at various times Steinhoff, Gerd Barkhorn, Erich Hartmann, Guenther Rall, Walter Krupinski, Hermann Graf, Willi Batz, Helmut Lipfert, Adolf Borchers, and Fritz Obleser among others—all aces with at least one hundred and mostly more than two hundred victories.

Hrabak was a dominant influence on JG-52, and his determined advocacy of "fly with the head and not with the muscles" saved the lives and shaped the careers of many of the successful aces who served with the wing. Hrabak had an axiom which he never failed to impress on young pilots: "If you come back from an operation with a kill but without your wingman, you lost your battle." Erich Hartmann, all-time top ace and student of Hrabak, learned this lesson well and never lost a wingman during his career.

Hrabak flew the full 1939-45 span. His 125 victories were gained in over eight hundred missions. His most indelible war memory, however, is not of any of his own combats.

"My own aerial battles never made the impression on me that I received from one stupendous event—Stalingrad. The circumstances after Stalingrad were so terrible as to be indescribable. The plight of my dying, starving countrymen in the snow, and my complete inability to

DIETRICH HRABAK-KOMMODORE JG-52: April 1943 in Russia, 125 victory ace Hrabak confers with his crewchief concerning estimated time in commission of his Me-109. Hrabak considered the fighter crewchiefs the "Iron Men" of the Luftwaffe and had the greatest respect for them. *(Hrabak Collection)*

KATSCHMAREK AND KOMMODORE: Kommodore Hrabak, right, discusses combat tactics with his *Katschmarek* (wingman) Sergeant Wilmanns, in April 1943 on the Russian Front. Hrabak was a firm believer that without the eyes, devoted vigilance and guns of the wingmen, there would be far fewer living aces. *(Hrabak Collection)*

do anything to help is a memory I will carry to my grave. Flying over these scenes of desperate tragedy was a soul-searing experience that is burned into my memory."

In lighter vein, he tells the story of the Russian IL-2 "Stormovik" he encountered. The aircraft won fame as the most durable Russian machine in the air. The Soviet bird could really soak up punishment, as Hrabak now recounts:

"I was flying with one of my formations and a *Schwarm* of four Me-109s set upon a solitary IL-2. One by one the fighters emptied their guns into the Russian machine at point-blank range. The IL-2 continued to fly on, unfazed by the storm of bullets and shells. I was astonished.

"'What's going on down there?' I asked on the R/T.

"Back came the classic answer: '*Herr Oberst*, you cannot bite a porcupine in the ass.'

"I never saw any aircraft that could absorb battle damage and still fly as did the IL-2."

Dieter Hrabak today is an intelligent, courtly, and charming man with a superb command of the English language. He is modest about himself to the point of reticence. Shortish and bald, with graying sideburns, he still has the piercing eyes of an ace who could spot his foes far away in the air. Like his friend and present C.O. Macky Steinhoff, Hrabak has not only a sense of humor, but the even rarer capacity to laugh at himself—to see the humor in his own failings and errors.

After the war in which he rose to Colonel, Hrabak wanted to be an architect like his father. He had the courage at thirty-two to begin serving a bricklaying apprenticeship as a prelude to a formal education in architecture. He applied for enrollment at Tübingen University.

"You are a militarist," he was told. "There will be no education for you." He dropped architecture and went into the commercial world with a machinery firm, rising to sales manager. He pursued this until staff work was begun in Chancellor Adenauer's office on the new German Air Force.

He was among the first German pilots to take refresher training on jet fighters in America in 1955. Since that time he has visited the United States frequently. He is an admirer of America and its people, with an understanding of the world which would have been hard to find in a military man of thirty years ago.

Dietrich A. Hrabak retired from the new Luftwaffe in the gradeneralmajor on 1 October 1976. His last position was Kommando Luftflotte which could be compared to Commander of Tactical Air Command (TAC) in the USAF.

Hrabak's numerous admirers among ex-aces include Erich Hartmann, who first flew combat in JG-52 during Hrabak's tenure. Hartmann tells a story about his old *Kommodore* which exemplifies the loyal feeling Hrabak evoked in his pilots:

"Everybody knows that the Oak Leaves were a decoration for which it was necessary to get a special number of kills. Hrabak would get it

HITLER HONORS WAR HEROES: 25 November 1943 at the "Wolf's Schanze" at Lötzen in East Prussia, Hitler conferred decorations on JG-52 Kommodore Hrabak, left, Schlactgeschwader SG-2 Kommodore Hans-Ulrich Rudel and Oberfeldwebel Erwin Hentschel, also of SG-2. *(Hrabak Collection)*

when he had 125 victories, which was the requirement on the Russian Front at that time.[6] All of us in the wing knew this. He had about 120 kills at the time. So all the old tigers in the wing got together and arranged to fly with him on the next couple of missions.

"Hrabak knew nothing about this, of course. When we heard from Wing HQ that Hrabak was flying with the 8th Squadron, only the old-timers went up. We flew with him and made absolutely sure his back was kept free while he got those kills.

"This was the finest tribute that we could pay a leader. If the leader was bad, the old tigers would say, 'Let him go . . . maybe this time he won't come back.' With Hrabak we were honored to go up and *make sure* he came back."

There are only a few Luftwaffe leaders who emerge from in-depth questioning of their contemporaries without any negative views being expressed. Dieter Hrabak earned that distinction in a force that had more than its share of able and courageous ace-leaders. He is one of the Luftwaffe's rare birds.

Hrabak's squadron leader in 1936 and Wing Commander in the Battle of Britain was Hannes Trautloft, and like Hrabak he enjoys more historical fame as a fighter leader than as an ace. Trautloft became a Lieutenant General in the new German Air Force, one of the few professionals from the old prewar Luftwaffe to serve throughout the war and return to high rank in the *Bundesluftwaffe*.

Trautloft is a towering moose of a man, a sharp contrast to the wiry,

---

[6] Hrabak was the 337th winner of the Oak Leaves, awarded 25 November 1943. On the Western Front at this time, 125 *points* were needed for the decoration. See Chapter One.

57 AERIAL VICTORIES: Big, handsome Hannes Trautloft was a man who saw the light side of life and loved every minute of it. He lived it to the hilt as Kommodore of JG-51. He was an outstanding fighter leader. *(Obermaier Collection)*

GENERALMAJOR HRABAK: The erstwhile Kommodore of JG-52 retired from the Luftwaffe 1 October 1966 in the rank of Major General. Prior to retiring Hrabak was General Kampfverbände der Luftwaffe which means he was Commanding General of the Luftwaffe's Tactical Air Command. *(Hrabak Collection)*

medium-sized men who make up most of acedom's numbers. He is outgoing, friendly and frank, with a deep and almost reverent feeling for history and the historic. Credited with fifty-seven confirmed aerial victories, he began his combat career in the Spanish Civil War, in which he downed four enemy aircraft. He won forty-five victories on the Eastern Front and the remainder against Britain and France.

Trautloft's stature among old Luftwaffe birds is not only a physical thing. His special place is as a tutor. The extremely short development time of the Luftwaffe before the war started made the presence of gifted teachers like Trautloft all the more important at group and wing level. He shared some of the qualities of both Galland and Moelders.

Like Moelders, he could teach his young pilots to fight in the air and stay alive to fight again. And like Galland, he was strong and frank enough to resist the wastage of the fighter arm. He was idolized by his pilots, and ostracized by the high command because of his directness.

The twenty-eight-year-old Trautloft was appointed *Kommodore* of JG-54 when the wing was formed for the Battle of Britain. He set the stamp of his leadership and personality on the "Green Heart" wing. Historically, JG-54 and Trautloft are inseparable, and it was his tutelage that developed some of Germany's greatest aces.

The quality of JG-54 can be judged from a small selection of its stellar personnel. Some of the top men were First Lieutenant Otto Kittel (267 kills), Lieutenant Colonel Hans Philipp (206 kills), Major Walter Nowotny (258 kills), Major Erich Rudorffer (222 kills), and Captain Emil Lang (173 victories). We will meet all these pilots in this book.

The authors are indebted to General Trautloft for providing the following pen portrait of First Lieutenant Kittel, fourth-ranked fighter ace of Germany and the world:

"Otto Kittel was one of the quiet ones, yet still one of the greatest German fighter aces. With 267 aerial victories he belongs historically with Hartmann, Barkhorn, and Rall.

"Born in 1917 in Komotau, Otto Kittel joined No. 2 Squadron of JG-54 in the fall of 1941. Small in stature, he was a quiet, serious soldier. He spoke slowly, with hesitation. In his temperament, he was in no way what the public imagines the fighter pilot type to be. Shooting down an aircraft seemed to be an unsolvable puzzle to the young pilot, and his successes were long in coming.

"Once placed in the company of Hans Philipp, Walter Nowotny, Hans Goetz, Franz Eckerle, and other talented fighters of No. 1 Group, his fighter knowledge filled in rapidly. Once hesitant, he became comet-like, climbing steeply. He never looked back.

"On 23 February 1943, Sergeant Otto Kittel sent the four-thousandth opponent of the Green Heart wing burning to the ground. At the same time he booked his thirty-ninth kill. On 26 October 1943 as

9 VICTORIES IN 1 DAY: Captain Joachim Kirschner was one of the Luftwaffe's brilliant young pilots who ran up 188 aerial victories in two years. On 5 July 1943 he downed 9 Russian aircraft. Awarded the Oak Leaves, he was only 23 years old when Communist partisans shot him after he parachuted from combat with Spitfires over Croatia. One of German's least-known big scorers. (*Obermaier Collection*)

KITTLE—4th RANKED ACE: Slow-starting Otto Kittel found it hard to bring in his shooting eye as a fighter pilot, but when it arrived, he made a meteoric rise to become top-scoring pilot of the ever-busy JG-54 in Russia. He had a total of 267 victories when hit by flak and killed on 14 February 1945. *(Boehm Collection)*

Master Sergeant Kittel he became the twenty-eighth pilot of JG-54 to be awarded the Knight's Cross.

"A proud series of victories now began, made all the more remarkable by the difficult circumstances at the front. The Russian Air Force was becoming ever stronger, and the retreating German armies increasingly called for Luftwaffe help. By April 1944, Kittel had 150 kills and for heroism in the face of the enemy was promoted to Second Lieutenant and made squadron leader.

"In the hard battles in the 'Kurland' the name Otto Kittel became a byword even in the forward trenches of the infantry. It was in Kurland that he also met his fate. He had been promoted by this time to First Lieutenant, and decorated successively with the Oak Leaves and Swords to his Knight's Cross. He was hit by flak and died on 14 February 1945. With 267 victories he was the most successful pilot of JG-54.

"Even with his great successes, Otto Kittel remained till his death a quiet, unselfish man. That is why we loved and honored him."

General Trautloft also contributes the following sketch of another leading ace of JG-54—Lieutenant Colonel Hans Philipp:

"Hans Philipp was born on 17 March 1917, the son of a physician. He came to JG-54 after the Polish campaign, in which he scored his first victory. He subsequently flew in the Battle of Britain, in Russia, and in the defense of Germany.

"On 12 March 1942 after his eighty-sixth victory, he was honored as the eighth officer of the German armed forces to be awarded the Swords to his Oak Leaves. Just over a year later, on his twenty-sixth birthday, he shot down two enemy aircraft and was at that time the most successful German fighter pilot, with 203 victories.

"Hans Philipp was a sensitive type of fighter pilot. His real and deepest *forte* was the hunt, paired with cunning, the burning desire to outthink and outfight his foe. For that reason he liked the fighter-to-fighter battle. Against mass bomber formations he said it was like 'running against a barn door,' where one did not need to fly.

"His flying world was thus the dogfight, the unique dance of the experts, the fencing of masterly foil-handlers whose deadly certain thrusts are as lightning quick as they are coldly calculated and trained beforehand. He took full part in all the joys of life, and for that reason he knew his way around Lille as well as Riga. Transferred to the defense of Germany as *Kommodore* of JG-1 on 1 April 1943, he wrote me a long letter from Holland four days before his death.

"I shall reproduce a few lines of this letter because I believe that in this way I shall not only characterize this talented fighter pilot, but also recall a memory of a time which for us fighter pilots was especially hard:

"'. . . sometimes it would be quite plausible for me, as the Old Man could still stand behind. For I know now that God knows I was not turned loose too late [he means his appointment as Wing Commander of JG-1]. Perhaps you really can't grasp in the whole, Colonel, how one has to drive oneself here [defense of Germany in Holland]. For once, one lives comfortably, there are enough girls, everything is here, and on the other side the fight in the air is especially difficult. Difficult not only because the enemy is superior in numbers, and the Boeings well armed, but because one had just left the deep chairs of the ready rooms and the music-impregnated atmosphere of the quarters.

"'To fight against twenty Russians that want to have a bite of one, or also against Spitfires, is a joy. And one doesn't know that life is not certain. But the curve into seventy Fortresses lets all the sins of one's life pass before one's eyes. And when one has convinced oneself, it is still more painful to force to it every pilot in the wing, down to the last young newcomer.'"

Hans Philipp was killed in action near Nordhorn on 8 October 1943 in combat with Thunderbolts escorting a bomber force.

Leading such men as Kittel, Philipp, Nowotny, and others was a moving experience for Trautloft. He is remembered for putting his wing first and himself second. Commanding JG-54 was probably the high point of his military career, although in July 1943 he was appointed to Galland's staff as Inspector of Day Fighters, West. This was a higher post than *Kommodore* of a wing, but it was not a satisfying assignment.

DOGFIGHTER: Lt. Colonel Hans Philipp drew his first combat blood in Poland, with virtually uninterrupted aerial warfare following until his death four years later in combat with U.S. Thunderbolts. Philipp is credited with 206 aerial victories. His love for the aerial fencing match that was the dogfight, led him to describe attacks on Allied bombers as "like running against a barn door." He won the Swords to his Knight's Cross. (*Boehm Collection*)

With Galland, Trautloft sought in vain to bring home the realities of the air war to Goering and the high command. He ended the war as C.O. of the 4th Division Aviation School, a training command. He flew 560 missions, is credited with 57 aerial victories, and won the Knight's Cross. His place in history is secure.

The Eastern Front provided an ex-blacksmith's apprentice named Hermann Graf with opportunities to employ and perfect his talents as a fighter pilot. He started in 1939 as a sergeant pilot with JG-51, and by 1945 had risen to Colonel and *Kommodore* of JG-52 on the Russian Front. With 212 victories to his credit he was one of only nine German airmen to win the coveted Diamonds. During the war, he was the most heavily publicized ace in Germany. Since the war, he has become the most controversial of all Germany's air heroes, particularly within the fighter pilot fraternity.

Hermann Graf came up the hard way. Born in 1912, his opportunities as a youth in Germany between the wars were limited. His parents could not afford a secondary school education for him, and he thus had no chance to acquire this essential preliminary to a professional officer's career. Circumstances forced him into a more mundane sphere.

He was apprenticed in the family tradition to a blacksmith at Engen, where he was born. Graf formally became a blacksmith by serving out his time, but dropped the trade on completion of his apprenticeship. He preferred a clerical post in the Engen municipal offices. He remained in this job until the outbreak of war, at which time he was almost twenty-seven years old.

An air-minded young man, he was a long-time member of the Air Sport Association of Baden. He had taken up gliding as early as 1933, and by 1936 had also qualified as a pilot of powered aircraft. A member of the Luftwaffe reserve of pilots, he was called up immediately after the outbreak of war and given the rank of Flight Sergeant.

Some accounts of Graf's life assert that he joined the National Socialist Party after Hitler's seizure of power, but there is no firm evidence of this. That he became a favorite of the National Socialist propagandists later in the war is, however, beyond question. His selection as a typical National Socialist hero and the tremendous volume of publicity circulated about during the war were probably the most unfortunate things that ever happened to him.

Graf flew against the Western Allies during the campaign in the Low Countries, and also in Greece and Crete. He did not confirm a victory until 4 August 1941, which made him one of the slow starters. His running-in period came to an end on the Eastern Front.

A little more than thirteen months after his first victory Hermann Graf was credited with 172 kills and had won the Diamonds. This phenomenal scoring run was climaxed on 2 October 1942 when he became the first ace ever to confirm two hundred aerial victories. Dr. Goebbels' propaganda engine was already running wild on Hermann Graf.

He was depicted as a shining example of National Socialist youth. His humble blacksmith's beginning and meteoric rise from Flight Sergeant to Major in three years were heavily emphasized. He was sent on a lecture tour of Germany and Austria, and as a footballer of some skill he was duly present and introduced to adoring crowds at soccer matches. His picture and accounts of his aerial battles appeared in newspapers and magazines.

This amounted to an assault on Graf's character structure. His position was akin to that of numerous young people from small towns

NATIONAL HERO WITH BEAR CUB MASCOT: Colonel Hermann Graf was favorite of Dr. Goebbel's propagandists during WWII, mainly because of his humble beginnings as a blacksmith's son and subsequent meteoric success as a fighter ace. Graf flew from 1939 to 1945, and rose in that time from sergeant-pilot to Colonel. He was one of only nine fighter pilots to win the Diamonds and ended the war in command of JG-52 in Czechoslovakia. Graf was Erich Hartmann's C.O. at that time, and both violated General Seidemann's orders to fly out and surrender to the British. Graf and Hartmann stayed with their men and their families, and were imprisoned in Russia as a consequence. Graf had 212 aerial victories in WWII. (*Haussmann Collection*)

and with limited backgrounds who "hit it big" in Hollywood. They all too often find that the glamour treatment is more vicious than valuable.

Graf carried his new-won fame well. To his men during the war he was a good leader, and in the words of Erich Hartmann, "a hell of a fighter." Cool-headed in combat and considerate to his subordinates, he had a good feeling for new pilots and the need to help them find themselves. Because he was considerably older than most of the men he flew with, as well as a national hero, he enjoyed a rare status which, in fairness to him, it must be said he never sought.

He was Colonel Hermann Graf with 212 victories, leading JG-52 when the war ended. He had flown over eight hundred missions, and in addition to his 202 kills against the Red Air Force proved his mettle by clawing down ten American heavies on the Western Front. He was turned over to the Russians after capture by U.S. forces, and the process by which his heroic image was blurred was thereby set in train.

Graf was now stripped of his heroic aura. The glory, glamour, and excitement of war days were gone. The dehumanized, depraved existence of a Soviet prisoner was now his lot in life. The men who had made him a hero were either dead or about to be hanged. Hermann Graf's world, built up by desperate combat on his part and by propagandists who followed his every move on the other, simply crumbled into nothing.

Erich Hartmann was a *Gruppenkommandeur* in JG-52 under Hermann Graf, and later was a fellow prisoner in Russia. His comments on the fallen idol have merit:

"I liked Hermann Graf. He was a very good fighter pilot. He kept flying after he got the Diamonds, and I admired him for this. Others stopped flying when they got the Diamonds. Afterward in the prison camp, everybody had his standpoint. Graf's standpoint was that we had lost the war, all regulations were finished, and that we could live only on the Russian or the American side. He was realistic. 'We have to begin a new thinking,' he said. 'I am on the Russian side, and therefore I would like to live with the Russians.' It was up to Graf to decide this for himself.

"There was no brainwashing, nothing like that. It was his own decision, and therefore we separated. That was the difference between us. He put it down in writing. 'I am happy now to be a Russian prisoner. I know that all I have done before is wrong, and I have now only one wish. That is to fly with the Russian Air Force. I will be happy if I get the rank of Lieutenant Colonel.' The Russians simply put him in another

SIXTH TO REACH 100: 1st Lieutenant Max-Hellmuth Ostermann started as an Me-110 pilot and had 9 kills before he went to the Russian Front, flying the Me-109. He was awarded the Swords to his Knight's Cross, but lost his life when jumped by nine Soviet fighters deep in Russian territory. *(Obermaier Collection)*

camp, that's all, and let him write about what he knew."

Despite his preference to live under the Russians, Graf was not released until 1950. Hartmann bears him no ill will, and Gerd Barkhorn, once asked if Graf was married now to a wealthy woman, responded typically with "I hope so." A few years ago, however, Graf was ostracized from the German fighter pilot fraternity for bending in the Soviet direction, an action largely due to German ace Assi Hahn's book *I Tell the Truth*, dealing with his Russian prison experiences. Hartmann regards Hahn's book as apocryphal.

Ten years under the Soviet yoke also taught Hartmann some tolerance. He found that every man had his breaking point. Years later, it has been easy for some fighter pilots who were not prisoners of the Russians to maintain an unrelenting attitude on these matters, which would seem unfair to Graf.

Former Major Hartmann Grasser was also imprisoned with Graf. As we shall see when we meet Grasser more fully in due course, he exemplifies the professional German officer. In Russia at the time, he bitterly opposed Graf's action in succumbing to the Russians. Today at fifty-two, Grasser views life in a different way:

"I was hard during my prison time in Russia. I criticized another if he left the straight line. But now I have more experience of life and a sight more tolerance. I have a better understanding for human weakness. That is why I am not hard against Hermann Graf as some others are.

"I have told others of my views, because *nobody* ignorant of the atmosphere of Russian confinement can judge a man's action under

HARTMANN'S PROTEGE: Ace of aces Erich Hartmann broke in this young pilot, Hans-Joachim Birkner, when he first came to the front from training school. Birkner served as Hartmann's wingman, learned his lessons well and scored his first kill flying on "Bubi's" wing on 1 November 1943. By July 1944 Birkner had 98 confirmed victories and the Knight's Cross. A brilliant future was predicted for him, but he was killed in a takeoff accident 14 December 1944. He had 117 victories. *(Toliver Collection)*

these conditions. I do not think it was right that Graf was pushed out of the Fighter Pilots' Association. It would be better and more human to give him another chance."

Grasser sums up the case of Hermann Graf in these terms:

"He was a good shot and a good fighter, but he was not a man of the caliber of Moelders, Galland, or Maltzahn. You cannot compare them. Graf is a nice man, a brave man, and a man of ambition, but he did not have the same education, character, and intellectual capacity as the others. It is important to distinguish between mistakes and defects of character. Because of his background, I think Graf failed to see through the way he was used by Dr. Goebbels. And in Russia he was a young man not so well fortified against every attack on his character and integrity. I think now is the time to forgive and forget in the case of Hermann Graf."

The authors have dealt at some length with the controversial rather than the combat aspects of Graf's career, because he is the *only* winner of the Diamonds or the Swords among the aces to fall from grace since the war. One of the purposes of this book is to help heal old wounds and recognize bravery wherever it appears. Hermann Graf was a brave man, and he has written his own autobiography in a book entitled "200 Luftsiege in 13 Monaten" which is worthwhile reading.

In the ancient Rhine city of Cologne, a graying, slender, slightly stooped businessman in his early fifties mingles unobtrusively with his fellows in the commercial world. He owns a factory near Cologne which presses metal parts for industry. He has a charming wife, two sons of university age, and a fast, red Porsche that is the only link with his exciting past. When he slides behind the wheel of his quick car the years seem annihilated. His smoothly coordinated movements recall the fighter piloting skill that brought him 103 aerial victories.

Major Hartmann Grasser is today a determined civilian. Perhaps more than any other German ace the authors have met, Grasser exemplifies the professional German officer. He is an archetype for his breed. Tenacious, deadly, and determined as a fighter, upright and decent as a soldier, chivalrous and sportsmanlike as an ace, he was doomed to disillusionment in the postwar world. His American captors conveyed him to Soviet confinement.

After three years in Russian prisons, a clerical error in the MWD office at Moskva Camp 27 resulted in his release. He returned home resolved never again to serve as a German officer, lest another defeat see him treated again "as a bandit" by his late enemies. With the kindred experience of POWs in Korea and now Viet Nam, Americans are better situated today to see the merit in Grasser's views. His background lends them added strength.

Hartmann Grasser was born in Graz, Austria, on 23 August 1914. After a typical boyhood spent in the aftermath of the First World War, he began his pre-military training in 1934. He attended the Athletic Academy, the Naval School at Neustadt (where he earned his pilot's

COLORFUL CAREER: Hartmann Grasser ended WWII with 103 victories, but unfortunate enough to fall into clutches of Russians, he was illegally imprisoned in the Soviet Union until 1949. He thereafter instructed civil pilots in India, and military pilots in Syria before returning to Germany to become a manufacturer. (*Grasser Collection*)

certificate), and the Glider School at Rositten. This two-year period was climaxed by six months at the Aviation School at Johannistal.

After two years as a *Fahnenjunker* at the School of Aerial Warfare, he passed his officer's examination in 1938 and was promoted Second Lieutenant. He was a fully qualified pilot, with the benefit of a thorough and exacting peacetime training. Later it helped to save his neck. He was flying the Me-110 at the outbreak of war, and was a good enough pilot to become an ace in the heavy fighter, surviving Me-110 service in the Battle of Britain.

Transferred in February 1941 to JG-51, he became adjutant to Colonel Werner Moelders, in whose company as a pilot in the JG-51 Staff Flight he made two hundred sorties against Britain. In Moelders he saw the embodiment of everything that a young German officer might hope to become. "Daddy's" surpassing character thereafter became Grasser's ultimate standard of manly conduct and bearing.

Fairness in battle to men like Grasser was an integral part of their military outlook, as well as of their moral makeup. Grasser winces visibly even today when he speaks of the revulsion he felt in Poland at having to undertake strafing missions on the roads. Why? "Because the enemy on the roads had no fair chance to fight back." The outlook of these German officers on such matters contrasts vividly with the actions of the "Hollywood Germans" in hundreds of sadistic war films originally intended to inflame hatred of the Germans, but ultimately destined to help retard the orderly restoration of civilized life to postwar Europe.

Grasser went to Russia with Moelders, and in September 1941 was given command of II/JG-51. He saw the fall and rise of Soviet air power at first hand:

"In the beginning, it was the low quality of the Russian planes which cost them losses. But after two years they improved their planes so much and so improved their experience that the whole aerial situation altered. The Russians then could get more advantage, because their planes were better and more numerous, their pilots were better and their training was vastly improved."

Grasser commanded II/JG-51 when this formation was detached from the wing and sent to North Africa to assist JG-27 and JG-77 in the desert and Malta struggles. He ran up his kill tally to 103 by August

UNFORGETTABLE MOMENT: Major Hartmann Grasser reaches from the cockpit of his Me-109 to shake delighted hands of his squadron mates after scoring his 100th aerial victory. Grasser ended war with 103 aerial victories won on all fronts, and the Oak Leaves to his Knight's Cross. (*Grasser Collection*)

1943, after which he was transferred to the staff of the 4th Fighter Division as Fighter Commandant Paris.

His North African experience exposed him to what lay ahead for Germany:

"It was like a blizzard of aircraft. In Africa we were outnumbered twenty to one, so it was impossible to get any real success. To get out with your neck, to get home in one piece—*that was success*. At first, the Americans lacked experience. Then we had a chance to surprise them and compensate for their numerical superiority with our experience and tactics. But with time, they got experience, and we were thereafter unable to do anything."

Withdrawn from Mediterranean operations to the defense of the Reich, Grasser served as Fighter Commandant Paris, then as a *Gruppen-kommandeur* with JG-1 *Oesau*. His operational career as a fighter pilot now covered almost five years and seven hundred missions. He was a Major with the Oak Leaves to his Knight's Cross, but he was at the end of his physical and mental resources.

Trautloft as Inspector of Day Fighters arranged for Grasser's transfer to Galland's staff. He was charged with the recovery of the fighter forces, a training and organizational job aimed at building up reserves. His hard labors here were wasted when Hitler heard about the reserves. The Fuehrer hurled the hard-won reserves first into the invasion battle and then into the ground-support role in the Ardennes.

Major Hartmann Grasser was *Kommodore* of JG-210 at the surrender. He had fought a long, hard war. His 103 kills included French, British, American, and Russian aircraft. He had fought in Poland, Norway, the Battle of Britain, Russia, North Africa, and the Central Mediterranean, and finally in the defense of the Reich.

As a professional soldier and officer, he expected fair treatment from

16 BIG ONES: Lt. Johann Pichler (right) takes a moment to relax beside his Me-109 in Russia. In a 1940-44 career he clawed down 16 four-engined bombers, passed into Russian captivity when the hospital in which he was recovering from wounds passed into Russian hands. Pichler had 75 victories in WWII and won the Knight's Cross. (*J. Crandall Collection*)

his late opponents. He received something less. He was delivered to the Soviet authorities under the agreement between Roosevelt and Stalin, and passed into Russian confinement. This was the nadir of his experiences with his fellow men in war and peace. His comments have pointed significance for the American nation today, when young Americans are being exposed to the same kind of soulless incarceration:

"For a prisoner of war, so-called, in Russia, and especially a highly decorated German officer it was very difficult. There wasn't any possibility of compromise. You either became an abject slave of the Russians or you were lost. And that was a question of character. Americans now have the same situation with their prisoners in Viet Nam, and in China during the Korean War. Prior to Korea, this kind of thing had not touched the American nation, but now they can gather their own experience with these problems.[7]

"Spending part of your life under these conditions is incredibly difficult. We were without any human atmosphere. They did everything possible to break your will. There is much talk today in the world about rights—civil rights, human rights, national rights. In Russia we lived without *any* rights, with no possibility to defend our rights. The Red Cross and other civilized institutions for prisoners of war were not present in Russia. We were *lost*.

"The harsh and inhuman conditions under which we lived are indescribable. And all the pilots were so young—too young for such ordeals and assaults on their character and integrity. *No one who has not experienced this atmosphere is fitted to judge the actions of anyone who has.*"

When he returned from Russia, Grasser's view on military service had fundamentally changed. He resolved that he would never again

[7] For a firsthand account of an American ace in North Korean hands, see *Honest John* by Walker M. Mahurin, G. P. Putnam's Sons, New York, 1962.

BADLY BENT: This IL-2 Stormovik ground attack aircraft is beyond all aid after being shot down on the Russian Front in 1942. IL-2 was difficult to down because of heavy armor plating, low altitude at which it flew, and ability to absorb astounding amounts of fire from machine guns and 20mm cannons. *(Nowarra Collection)*

wear a German officer's uniform. In 1949 he went to India to train civil pilots in Allahabad and New Delhi, and the following year became an advisor to the Syrian Air Force in the Ministry of Defense in Damascus. This was the end of his flying career.

Returning home resolute against further military service, he started a factory pressing steel parts for industry. When Colonel Guenther "Henri" Maltzahn was sounding out officers for the new German Air Force shortly before his death in 1953, he approached Grasser and offered him command of a wing. The former POW stuck to his guns. He turned down his old comrade and has remained a businessman ever since.

The onetime fighter ace works hard, takes joy in his family, and has a broad view of the world and its problems. He is more perceptive than most of his old Luftwaffe contemporaries and expresses his views fearlessly and frankly. His life is that of a settled family man, and is indistinguishable from that of hundreds of British and American pilots against whom he flew in wartime.

Major Hartmann Grasser confines his flying these days to the commercial airlines, when, as he puts it, "I take my rotten bones to Italy once a year." He is a throwback to the medieval knight, a fair and chivalrous foe of the kind that once lent a certain magnificence to war. But as Churchill so aptly expressed it: "War was once cruel and magnificent; now war is cruel and squalid." Warriors of Grasser's breed have no place in a world where millions may well be obliterated with one blow, and the process called "war."

One of the bravest men in the Luftwaffe by the common agreement of all the aces who knew him, including Hartmann Grasser, was Captain Emil "Bully" Lang. A barrel-chested, bulldog-faced fighter of unsurpassed daring and dash, Lang made his name on the Eastern Front with JG-54 in 1942–43. When he was killed in aerial combat with Thunderbolts on 3 September 1944, he was credited with 173 kills, twenty-five of them against the Western Allies.

"GRAF PUNSKI" A LUFTWAFFE LEGEND: For sheer dash and verve, few pilots could equal Walter Krupinski, nicknamed "Graf Punski" because of his style of living on the ground when not fighting in the air. "Graf Punski" would have aides scour the countryside and other unit messes for food, liquor and ladies, but he never let down for a moment on the job. His 197 victories include 20 victories on the Western Front, and he flew more than 1100 missions between January 1941 and the end of the war, which found him in Galland's JV-44—the Squadron of Experts. *(Krupinski Collection)*

Lang was really an old man as fighter pilots go. He was thirty-three when he joined JG-54 in 1942—a ripe old age at which to begin a combat career. A veteran Lufthansa pilot, "Bully" Lang knew his flying, and in one three-week period piled up an almost incredible seventy-two kills. This stellar achievement included the world all-time record of eighteen kills in one day. No one who saw him hurling himself on Russian formations will ever forget the sight.

Near St. Trond on 3 September 1944, he was engaged in a wild battle with USAAF Thunderbolts. At seven hundred feet one of his enemies scored a hit in Lang's hydraulic system. His undercarriage dropped, diminishing the speed and maneuverability of his fighter. He was then quickly shot down and killed.

Lang had 173 confirmed kills in 403 missions and won the Oak Leaves to his Knight's Cross. When German pilots are asked to discuss the relative bravery of their contemporaries, "Bully" Lang's name is invariably mentioned. In this sense, he won a measure of immortality in his brief and violent combat career.

Slender, angular Helmut Lipfert of Lippelsdorf/Thueringen is one of the Knights of the Air who led a truly charmed life, if charmed is being shot down fifteen times without being injured. But fly and fly again he did and when the war ended his trophy belt carried 203 notches. The authors are grateful to Captain Lipfert for the following account of his 128th victory scored 4 June 1944 while Boeing Fortresses and Consolidated Liberators were attacking targets in Rumania. At that time Lipfert was leading number II *Gruppe* of JG-52.

Today there were no clouds in the sky. How sad! The technical personnel busied itself polishing the already polished planes and were glad there would be something to shoot down. The gentlemen from

HUNGARIANS WITH THE LUFTWAFFE: Hungarian pilots were attached to JG-52 in 1944 to aid in the struggle against Russia. From left, the officers here are Captain Pottjondy (Hungarian 102nd Brigade), Lt. Erich Hartmann of JG-52 with 352 kills, Captain Gerhard Barkhorn of JG-52 with 301 kills, Major Kovacs of the Hungarian Forces, Captain Helmut Lipfert of JG-52 with 203 kills and Captain Heinz Sturm of JG-52 with 82 kills. *(Hartmann Collection)*

the headquarters, too, were represented and showed happy faces. Only the pilots were silent and not to be seen. Three hundred four-engined planes were reported to be on the way—that was food for thought for us. Perhaps some of us hoped, too, that they would change course and not come to us at all. But they wouldn't do us this favor. We had to take off.

I assigned the pilots. The ones whose names I called obviously were anything but pleased. Then the eight men stood before me and looked at me. I had not yet said that I would fly with them, although that was self-evident for me. When I saw the depressed faces, I knew immediately that they were wondering whether I would fly too, or stay home. I found out how right I was when I said, then: "I am coming along too, of course."

Their faces took on a brighter expression. We took off and landed for a short tanking stop in Zilistea, taking off again immediately. I had conceived a plan of operations. Under no circumstances did I want to "hack away" again at a lone flyer. I had found out that such lone planes were mostly so-called antiaircraft cruisers which, instead of the bombs, had better protection than the other four-engined planes. (These were YB-41 specially armored Fortresses.) They were used as decoys. We were guided well from the ground and were the first of the fighter planes to sight the enemy. As my plane rose, I saw three big formations of approximately forty planes each fly by above me at a high altitude. Their covering fighters swarmed around at great heights which I estimated at 13,000 meters. The planes up there swarmed about and glittered in such a way that I didn't even want to look up. Gradually, in good order, we got closer to the big silvery birds. The three formations flew as follows: The first one to the right above, the second one in the

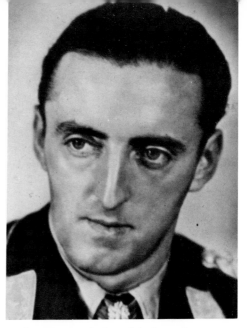

CONTROVERSIAL PERSONALITY: Colonel Hermann Graf rose from sergeant pilot to Colonel in command of JG-52 during WWII. He won the four highest German decorations in eight months, and in one blistering 17 day period in Russia downed 47 Red planes. In Soviet jails after WWII, the onetime Diamonds winner and national hero compromised himself and fell from grace within the fighter pilot fraternity. His war record as a fighter pilot remains among the most brilliant. (*Obermaier Collection*)

middle, about three hundred meters lower, and the third at the same height as the first. Probably the two formations above were to cover the lower formation with their weapons. A hundred and twenty planes with ten weapons, at least, in each—that might provide quite a bit of fireworks, not to mention all the fighters that could get us from behind.

"Don't despair, my little band!" This expression was really suited to the situation.

In closed formation, we overtook the bottom formation. I had decided to conduct the first attack from the front. Far in front of the four-engined planes I then said:

"Attention! We will turn back in a moment and attack from the front. Everybody keep going without firing until I start. Everybody turn! Close ranks, get close and stay together! Anyone who flies alone is bound to be shot down."

As a matter of fact, my pilots carried out an aerial exercise which under different circumstances would have been a joy to behold. I flew ahead, because I was the commander and could not stay behind. The wings lagged behind a bit. Nine brave pilots, nine little Me-109s against such a great number of enemies.

The Americans now seemed to have noticed what was in store for them. Perhaps they hadn't thought that we wanted to attack, because they began to change their course—which would have forced us to start the attack anew—rather belatedly. Now this change of course came too late—we were already too close for them to succeed with this maneuver. The big birds were now coming toward us at a tremendous speed. We were flying at approximately 450 km/hr, the Americans 350–380 km/hr. We were approaching each other at a speed of at least 750 km. The formation that was flying above opened fire from the front above. The string of pearls of the tracer fire sparkled around us.

"Don't fire yet, don't fire yet," I shouted twice. Then the moment came. "Give them all you have and get real close." That was the last time I shouted.

Then all hell broke loose. I crouched down in my cockpit and fired. What happened around me I didn't see. I aimed directly at a bomber coming toward me and had no other thought but that he had to come down.

Tatters were flying from my four-engine bomber, explosions flashed outward from it again and again and then I had to pull away, otherwise I would have sped into him. I swept very closely above the enemy formation and immediately behind it pressed downward. The first thing I looked for were the enemy fighters. They were out of sight completely.

Next to me, almost at the same altitude, six Me-109s were still flying. A few had gotten off course a little. I brought them together again and immediately began to turn again. We wanted to attack once more, from behind. We turned around. The question came over the radio: "Where has the enemy been contacted?"

Well, if our comrades didn't see this demonstration, there's no use— or was it that they simply didn't want to go after the "fat ones"? So I didn't even answer but concentrated entirely on the approaching re- newed attack. In the meantime, we were pretty well back in formation and were gradually approaching the four-engined planes. They opened fire again. We ducked and crouched down in our planes as much as possible. Then our guns spoke, too. Seven of us came near, fired like the devil, sped through the formation, and were reduced to three by the time we got out of the formation again.

When we were sufficiently ahead of the formation we turned around once more. This time the bombers frustrated our concerted attack by turning away from their direction of flight. All we could still do was to fire at the last ones laterally from the front. During this attack, I hit one of the bombers quite well. When we had passed the formation, I counted my brood. Only two of us were left. Flying faithfully next to me was my dear Kaczmarek, the young commissioned officer Tamen.

I was not inclined to speed into the "fat ones" once more. I ordered Tamen to come close and together we went after a victim of the first attacks. Behind the stream of bombers, at least eight big bombers were wavering along singly. They all left a heavy smoke trail. So now together we went after one of these smelly, smoking planes. When I made my first attack the bomber still put up a considerable defense. I shot his left engine in flames. Tamen followed me. He fired quite well, too. Then, after looking out for the enemy fighters, I adjusted my flight to that of the bomber and fired into its fat fuselage until it literally burst apart. This happened so quickly that not a single crew member bailed out.

A little farther ahead, a second injured Liberator was struggling along. We attacked it without regard to its defensive fire. Each of us made two attacks. The plane was already afire and then Tamen ran out of ammunition. The Liberator reared and curved to the last and fired around wildly, but it was all to no avail. I kept behind it and did not relent until it too exploded. Two men bailed out first.

German fighter planes were now attaching themselves to all the smoking bombers that had been cut off from the formation. Even though we had chalked up only two victories that day—one was credited to Tamen and one to me—my group had done the preparatory work for all the other downings. A total of nine planes was shot down.

Tamen and I landed together in Buzeau. We got out of our planes and congratulated each other on the victories—and on having survived. We had good reason, because we were the only two who had come home unscathed, and without a single hit. Five of our comrades had been shot down. Two pilots were killed instantly, one was machine-gunned by the Mustangs while landing in his parachute. Lieutenant Ewald bailed out of his burning plane at the last moment and suffered very serious burns so that his recovery was doubtful for a long time. Another pilot was also able to save himself by bailing out. Two planes were forced by enemy fire to make emergency landings and one Me-109 had landed on an enemy field. That was a disastrous outcome.

Helmut Lipfert, today a quiet and unobtrusive schoolteacher in West Germany, is seldom seen by his cohorts of World War II. Perhaps he prefers to forget the war years as well as the subsequent postwar years, which have not been easy for this dynamic gladiator of 1943 and 1944. Lipfert flew his first combat mission on 16 December 1942, scored his first combat victory, a La-5, on 30 January 1943. Two years and two months later he flew his seven-hundredth combat mission and scored his 203rd victory. One hundred of these had been chalked up in just over eleven months, the other 103 took him slightly over fourteen months. He was a consistent professional fighter pilot, handsome, dashing, and glamorous, but he often withdrew into long periods of serious contemplation. He is the world's thirteenth-ranked fighter ace. Lipfert wrote his own very interesting book "Das Tagebuch Des Hauptmann Lipfert", Motorbuch-Verlag 1973 Stuttgart. He lists all of his 203 victories.

Volumes could be written about the German aces of the Eastern Front. This glimpse of their achievements must represent also the deeds and fighting records of dozens of men the authors are unable to mention. This sampling nevertheless gives a fair cross section of the men who battled above the Steppes.

To the objective historian there can be no doubt that fighter piloting on the Eastern Front was not easy, as has often been represented in some quarters. In most respects, it was the hardest front of all for the German aces—bleak, uncompromising, vast, constant, and grueling. Many who fought there had to suffer years of illegal confinement, which no one has yet described as easy.

As Erich Hartmann once said, "Thirty of us against three hundred to six hundred Russian airplanes at a time? Does that sound easy?"

Before we leave the Eastern Front it might be well to tell a story about a Luftwaffe pilot whose career was typical of so many who flew against the Soviets. Hans-Joachim Kroschinski lived through the war, an ace with 76 aerial victories, but he lost his sight and a leg in com-

THIRTY VERSUS SIX HUNDRED? WHAT ARE THE ODDS?: The Blond Knight of Germany who fought with his head and not with his muscles knew that dogfighting was not the answer against such odds so he religiously stuck to the "hit-and-run" tactic. A competitor first-class, Hartmann had to master the tendency to try to turn with the enemy pilots. *(Toliver Collection)*

bat. But it is best to let him tell about it, as he did in a letter to author Toliver:

"Now you wish to hear my story, Ray. In general, I don't talk too much about it but will do it only because of you.

"I became a soldier after volunteering for the Air Force. My training began in NeuKuhren, a city in my home state of East Prussia. It was June of 1941 when I was assigned to fighters for training and in June of 1942, as a Corporal, I was assigned to JG 54 on the Eastern Front. I was in the 2nd Squadron and we moved to Gatschina just after my arrival. In the squadron were Otto Kittel (without a victory at this time but he eventually scored 267), Herbert Brönnle (57), Seppel Wöhnert (86) and other excellent fighter pilots. Fritz Tegtmeier (146) was my element leader.

"On my second mission, I had my first victory, a MIG-1. Our mission that day was to fly into the area around Leningrad, south of Lake

76-VICTORY ACE PAID HEAVY PRICE: Leutnant Hans-Joachim Kroschinski, shown here with his wife Elli, scored 76 victories, most of them on the Eastern Front, but his last sortie cost him both eyes and his right leg. Regardless, he still leads a productive life with the assistance of his helpful and efficient wife. *(Kroschinski)*

Ladoga and along the Wolchow River to Lake Ilmen. I was happy to have my first kill. By Christmas I had 5 victories and had received the Iron Cross 2nd Class, and the Front Flight Clasp in silver. Also I was promoted to Sergeant.

"During the heavy fighting in the winter of 1943, I had shot down 14 airplanes and was awarded the Iron Cross 1st Class but I did not like the transfer to Rechlin that came at that time. Rechlin was an Air Force testing base and was testing the new 21 cm. rocket launchers and rockets and a new parachute bomb. Both new weapons showed great potential for use against concentrated bomber formations. Both weapons were not bad but they could have been very successful had they been used in larger numbers against the enemy. I was happy to be sent back to JG 54 at the front early in May. Since January, JG 54 had been converted to the FW-190 A2 instead of our old Me-109 G4s. Despite the fact that the FW-190 was more powerful and better suited to the average pilot, I preferred the Me-109 which had never failed me. It must have been an unspoken link of trust between plane and pilot.

"Walter Nowotny (258 victories) was in the 3rd Squadron next to us and I knew him very well. By this time we transferred from the northern to the southern part of the front and our station was Bolrudka, north of Poltava, and we were in action around Charkow. I was now a Rotte leader and had 25 victories.

"After a short time we moved to the area around Orel. It was early in July and I was shot down myself for the first time. After an alarm takeoff, I overlooked an La-5 while I was climbing and I got hit good and had to bale out of my burning fighter. It was near Karatschew where I hit the ground. I was lucky to land on the German side of the lines with minor burns on my face and a lacerated chin.

"In September I was ordered to the IV Gruppe where I was flying Me-109s again. Rudi Sinner (39) awarded me the German Cross in Gold. But in the middle of November, I was reassigned again back to my old squadron which was now stationed at Orscha, at the middle sector of the front. Our combat zone was around Witebsk. I was promoted to Sergeant Major on Christmas Day.

"In January of 1944, our Gruppe moved again to the northern sector, near Wesenberg in Esthonia, near the Lake Peipus. It was a terrible airbase. We started and landed on a 40 meter wooden strip with tall snow barriers on both sides of the runway. The front was quiet at that time, though. At the end of March, I was disappointed to be ordered to a Reserve Fighter Group at Liegnitz. For the next six months I had to train young pilots to be fighter pilots before they went to the front. At this time I had 46 victories to my credit.

"We did see some combat near Liegnitz as I got to fly several sorties against enemy four-engine bombers. Some of the young pilot-trainees who were about to graduate, got to fly on these missions too. The day after Easter I shot down a Fortress II. During that mission, five of the

TRAUTLOFT'S BIRD: Hannes Trautloft was the redoubtable Kommodore of JG-54 on the Eastern Front, and this is one of the Me-109's flown during that time by him. With 57 aerial victories, Trautloft survived the war, served with the Bundesluftwaffe. (*Trautloft Collection*)

young pilots had to bale out and when they were hanging in their parachutes they were attacked by Mustangs and three were shot dead. On another mission up to Upper Silesia, near the city of Hindenburg-Gleiwitz, I shot down a Liberator.

"In August, the E-Gruppe moved to Sagan Kupper, and at the end of September I was ordered back to my original Gruppe, but to the 3rd Squadron instead of the 2nd this time. My destination was Kurland, which was cut off by the Russian Army.

"In the city of Insterburg, only 28 Kilometers from my hometown of Gumbinnen in East Prussia, we had an alarm takeoff. I was flying a new FW-190 and over Gumbinnen I intercepted a YAK-9 and shot it down. I felt very good about that victory.

"A few days later I moved again to Kurland and landed at Scrunda where my old group, I/JG-54 was stationed. We had suffered much attrition and had only two fighter groups left in the battle of Kurland. The I and II/JG-54 Gruppes were using bases at Cirava, Libau and Windau.

"On the other side, the Soviets had an estimated 6000 aircraft available and we were lucky if we could bring 40 to 50 fighter planes up to combat them. By the time the peninsula Sworbe had to be evacuated we took off from Windau to protect our Navy (the Prince Eugen and some destroyers). Then in December we moved to Frauenburg in Lithuania and now we were located at the southeastern sector of Kurland. My score now was 71 enemy planes downed.

"Then I got myself into deep trouble on December 21st. The third Battle of Kurland had begun that day and around 0830AM there was an alarm takeoff against a Pe-2 bomber formation. I led a flight and at about 5500 meters I sighted the Russians. They were flying in three 4-ship formations and I set up and attacked the plane on the right outside of the trail formation, shooting him down on the first pass. Then I shot down 4 more.

"When my fifth victim was falling, I hit his propellor-wash and my plane bucked around in the turbulence, turning me broadside to another Pe-2 just ahead of me. In that split second, the Russian tail gunner fired and hit my fighter, causing it to catch afire instantly. I tried to get out but my canopy jammed, probably having been hit by one of the enemy bullets. Desperately I heaved on it and when it broke loose I was thrown out of the airplane too.

"I fell for a long time before opening my parachute because it was so cold. When I did pull the ripcord and the chute checked my fall, I noticed that my right felt boot was gone and blood was streaming from my ankle. A bullet had smashed it.

"Adding to my bad luck, I landed in a tree top and dislocated my right shoulder, making it painfully difficult for me to get down from high in the tree. When I did get down I fell totally exhausted in the snow. Though it was very near the front lines, I had some luck because some German soldiers came to my rescue and carried me to a bunker where I was given first-aid. For the next four weeks I was moved from place to place before arriving at the Air Force Veteran Hospital three miles east of Malente where I finally got proper medical treatment. On Christmas Day of 1944 I was promoted to Lieutenant and was decorated with the Knights Cross (Ritterkreuz). For me, the war was over, I had 2nd and 3rd degree burns all over my face, was blind and had my right lower leg amputated. After I was released from the hospital, I stayed in the town of Malente. My parents and my grandfather were refugees from East Prussia and we lived there in two small rooms. The first years, until 1950, were very hard on us because there was not enough work and too many refugees in Schleswig-Holstein.

"I had enough time to think about the non-sense of war and when I was at my lowest ebb in life I discovered that music gave me new hope and inspiration. Bach, Beethoven, Brahms, Schubert and Mozart are my favorites.

"Sooner or later, the old comrades who survived the war and imprisonment, got together and we formed the German Fighter Pilots Association. I met my wife "Elli" on a train after a reunion of the fighter pilots at Geisenheim in October 1961. We were married in August of 1962.

"You ask about my impressions of some of the JG-54 pilots. Trautloft made a very good impression on me. By that time he was already a good leader and remarkable organizer. He was like a father to everyone in the squadron, a good advisor with a ready helping hand.

"Otto Kittel was a good friend of mine. We were in the 2nd Squadron together, in the First Group, under the leadership of Hans Philipp (206 victories). Kittel was a quiet, reserved and earnest person. It was annoying to him that he had trouble getting his shooting eye and it took him two years before he became perfect. From that moment on, no one could stop him and every mission he flew was successful with two or three victories.

EN ROUTE TO THE EAGLE'S NEST: Four Luftwaffe aces feel no pain as they inhale the mountain air before ascending to Hitler's Eagle's Nest at Obersalzberg to be decorated by the Fuehrer. In their prime on 4 April 1944 are from left Walter Krupinski (198 kills), Gerhard Barkhorn (301 kills), Joseph Wiese (133 kills) and Erich Hartmann (352 victories). They had been on all night drinking bout on the train to Hitler's fortress in the sky. *(Hartmann Collection)*

"Hanschen Philipp was a talented but slightly frivolous fighter pilot with lots of luck. Walter Nowotny was a good comrade and excellent troop leader. He was an aggressive fighter pilot, sharp-minded and a good athlete like most fighter pilots are. When it came to parties and drinking he could hold his own, too."

On the Western Front, things were different in many ways, and we move on to meet some of the German aces who made their names against the Anglo-American aerial offensive.

13

Aces of the Western Front

"The Luftwaffe did not ask for quarter, and we flew hard against them until the morning of VE-Day."
GROUP CAPTAIN J. E. JOHNSON,
top-scoring ace of the RAF[1]

HEAVILY engaged from the outset of the Second World War until the surrender, the Luftwaffe fighter force in the West enjoyed only a few months of unalloyed success. Triumphant early conquests ended in the skies above Dunkirk when the RAF fought the Luftwaffe to a bitter draw. Unlike the Eastern Front, there was to be no letup or pause in the West. The Royal Air Force was never smashed as was the Red Air Force in 1941, and in due course the USAAF added its strength to the attacks on Germany.

In the West the Germans had to battle with well-trained and determined foes mounted on top-quality aircraft. Superior radar and unexcelled communications heightened the striking power of the RAF. The Battle of Britain cost the Luftwaffe some of its finest pilots, irreplaceable, peacetime-trained professionals. The Russian invasion required the transfer East of every available air unit, leaving the protection of the West Wall to two fighter wings, JG-2 *Richthofen* and JG-26 *Schlageter*. The numerical balance was thus tipped to the Allies in mid-1941 for the duration of the conflict.

American air power weighted the scales irretrievably against the Germans. The daylight bombing offensive further added to the physical and tactical burdens of the German fighters on the Western Front. While in the East numerous instances occurred of balky Russian pilots, in the West the RAF and USAAF went looking for the Luftwaffe, challenging the Germans without surcease.

Because of their aggressive spirit, numerical superiority, seasoned training, excellent machines, and superior communications, the Western Allies posed a sterner threat to the Luftwaffe fighters than was

[1] Quoted from *Wing Leader* by Group Captain J. E. "Johnny" Johnson, D.S.O., D.F.C., RAF. Published by Chatto and Windus, Ltd., London, 1956.

466 AERIAL VICTORIES: Werner Schröer (114) and Erich Hartmann (352) ogle the entertainment during a light moment in February 1945. Two months later Schröer was awarded the Swords decoration. He was one of the very few to score 100 victories over the Americans and British. *(Schröer Collection)*

found on the Eastern Front. The German response produced some of the most successful and skilled aces in the history of aerial warfare. Never lacking in targets and flying after the Battle of Britain period over or near their own terrain, these German aces were able to survive repeated downings by the Allies. Compelled to fight for years with only the briefest respites, they accumulated scores two to three times as large as the best of the Western Allies.

JG-26 spawned such formidable aces as Adolf Galland (104 Western victories), Joachim Muencheberg (102 Western kills plus 33 in Russia), and Josef "Pips" Priller (101 Western kills). JG-2 *Richthofen* produced

CAPTAIN FREDERICK C. LIBBY (c) of Sterling, Colorado seen leaving Buckingham Palace after receiving Britain's Military Cross from King George V on December 13, 1916. Man on the right is Captain Stephen Price, Libby's pilot when the latter scored 10 aerial kills as an observer. Former Colorado cowboy Libby later became an RFC fighter pilot and shot down a further 14 German aircraft for a lifetime score of 24 aerial victories. *(Imperial War Museum)*

many aces in the tradition of the Red Baron, including Kurt Buehligen (112 Western victories), Egon Mayer (102 Western victories), and Josef "Sepp" Wurmheller (93 Western kills plus 9 in Russia).

Functioning on both the Western Front and in North Africa, JG-27 produced the immortal Hans-Joachim Marseille, whose 158 victories against the RAF tops the Western Front scoreboard for the Germans. JG-27 was also the home of the redoubtable Werner Schroer, whose 114 kills (including 12 in the East) were scored in 197 missions. Gustav Roedel was another JG-27 ace, with 97 victories against the Western Allies as well as a solitary kill on the Eastern Front.

Before these young warriors rose to fame, German fighter pilots of another generation wrote a final glorious chapter to careers which began in the First World War. The Germans who became aces in both world wars, and there were at least two such pilots, accomplished a feat unequaled by the pilots of any other nation. Incredible as it may seem, German aces who had flown successfully in the primitive fighters of the first conflict, actually entered combat again in the Me-109 in the Second World War. They shot down British and French pilots young enough to be their sons. This martial paradox deserves to be recorded.

The most famous German ace involved was Major General Theo Osterkamp. Thirty-two victories in the First World War as the leader of Naval Fighter Squadron No. 2 in France had already secured his place in history. He emerged from the first war wearing the Pour le Mérite, the coveted "Blue Max." Between the wars he remained closely connected with aviation, first in racing, and later in the new Luftwaffe as C.O. of the Fighter Pilot School.

With a high, round forehead and sharp features, the slender, lithe Osterkamp was an inspiring figure to his students. Intelligent and a gentleman to his fingertips, he epitomized the first generation of German fighter aces. His students affectionately called him "Uncle Theo" (Onkel Theo), a nickname he retained until his death on January 2nd, 1975, at the age of 83.

He began his First World War career as an aerial gunner, much as did Captain Frederick Libby, the Colorado cowboy who was the first American to down five enemy aircraft in aerial combat.[2] Strangely enough, the two men were air gunners on opposite sides of the line at the same time, and, like Libby, Osterkamp qualified as a pilot in the early spring of 1917.

Osterkamp's First World War victims included French, British, and American aircraft. His twenty-fifth and twenty-sixth kills were two Spads of an American unit which collided when he bounced them. The next day the Americans got their revenge, bouncing Osterkamp and shooting him down. He was back in the air that same evening and downed a French Breguet for his twenty-seventh victory.

[2] Captain Frederick Libby, M.C., R.F.C., scored ten kills as a gunner, fourteen as a pilot. His twenty-four downings were all airplanes, the largest tally of airplanes downed by any American in World War I. See Fighter Aces by the authors for the story of his career.

ACE OF TWO WARS—25 YEARS APART: Generalleutnant Theo Osterkamp scored 32 victories in WWI and 6 more in WWII before he was grounded by his headquarters. Osterkamp died in 1975 at the age of 83. *(Galland Collection)*

After the war he joined the Iron Division, and fought against the Russian Bolsheviks in Finland, Estonia, and Lithuania, flying the Junkers D-1. He managed the German team for the Challenge de Tourisme Internationale air race in 1933, and later formally joined the new Luftwaffe.

In late 1939 Osterkamp formed JG-51, the wing which was later to bear the name of Werner Moelders. He flew on operations against both France and England with JG-51 until the end of July 1940. On 15 April 1940 he celebrated his forty-eighth birthday. When he retired from combat he had confirmed six additional kills against the British and French, and he was awarded the Knight's Cross in August 1940. He ceased operational flying on Hitler's orders.

A father figure and comrade to men like Galland and Moelders, he served with distinction as commander of the fighter division which included JG-26 and JG-51 on the Channel. After the war he went into business and for some years had his offices with Adolf Galland in Bonn. Galland says that Uncle Theo was too trusting to make a fortune in business, but in 1966 Osterkamp retired comfortably to Baden. Once the father image of the fighter aces, he became the great-grandfather figure, since most of his Second World War pilots were grandfathers themselves. He was a popular figure at gatherings of the German fighter pilot fraternity.

Harry von Buelow-Bothkamp led the Boelcke Fighter Squadron in the First World War and was credited with six kills. At the outbreak of the Second World War he was *Gruppenkommandeur* of II/JG-77. Five years younger than Osterkamp, he was nevertheless far past the age for modern fighter piloting.

At forty-two von Buelow tangled successfully with British and French youngsters. He was promoted to *Kommodore* of JG-2 in the spring of 1940 and flew in the Battle of Britain. He ran up eighteen victories in the Second World War before ending his combat days. Like Osterkamp he moved up to higher commands where he did well, and he was also awarded the Knight's Cross.

Dr. Erich Mix didn't quite make ace in the First World War, so he finished the job in the second conflict. When the war broke out in 1939 he was a forty-one-year-old *Gruppenkommandeur* in JG-2, with three First World War victories to his credit. He ran up thirteen kills against the French Air Army and RAF before quitting combat. He served later as *Kommodore* of JG-1 and eventually became Fighter Leader (*Jafü*) Bretagne.

Other First World War pilots who flew combat in the second conflict include Major General Werner Junck (five victories World War I), Major General Karl-August von Schoenebeck (eight victories World War I), and Major General Joachim-Friedrich Hueth. The latter officer lost a leg as a fighter pilot in the first war, and led the Me-110s of ZG-76 in 1940, for which distinguished service he was awarded the Knight's Cross. He was the officer alleged to have had a pistol handy when Douglas Bader sat in one of the Me-109s of JG-26.[3]

The most eminent ace of the First World War to fly combat in the second war was Major General Eduard Ritter von Schleich, who won fame as the "Black Knight" with thirty-five victories in the earlier conflict. He also won the "Blue Max" and later led formations of the Condor Legion in Spain. Active in the organization of flying for German youth in the thirties, he became *Kommodore* of JG-132 after his return from Spain. This unit was subsequently redesignated JG-26 *Schlageter*.

Eduard von Schleich flew with his wing until the end of 1939. The authors have not been able to verify if he confirmed any additional victories, but he did fly fighter combat in the Second World War at the seemingly incredible age of fifty-one. In both Korean and Viet Nam wars, the US had several aces in the 49-51 year bracket.

One of von Schleich's admirers is Adolf Galland, who says of him: "He was a gentleman of the old school, perhaps too much so for the grim business at hand. His subordinates liked and respected him, not only as a First World War ace, but also for the determination and diligence with which he sought to keep pace with the new era." Schleich served with distinction in various commands throughout the war after leaving JG-26. He died in 1947.

One of the most brilliant young aces of the Battle of Britain was Major Helmut Wick, *Kommodore* of JG-2 at the time of his death on 28 November 1940. Credited with fifty-six victories against the British and French, he was leading both Galland (fifty-two) and Moelders (fifty-four) when he was killed—a testimony to his fighting skill. He is but little known in Allied countries today.

Born in 1915, Wick was a young Second Lieutenant with JG-53 on the outbreak of war. Fourteen months later, aged only twenty-five and already a Major with forty victories, he succeeded Harry von Buelow as *Kommodore* of JG-2 *Richthofen*. His clear, penetrating blue eyes were the key to his amazing aerial marksmanship, and an unfor-

---

[3] Actually, Hueth was unarmed.

DOWN IN THE SEA: Major Helmut Wick had 56 victories over the RAF when he met his end in aerial combat over the English Channel. He parachuted but was never seen again. As *Kommodore* of JG-2 he was forthright, upright and strong in his views. *(Bender Collection)*

gettable physical aspect of a forthright, aggressive personality.

Wick was not only aggressive, he was impetuous. That helped him in the air, but sometimes got him into trouble on the ground. He was no respecter of rank when provoked, and he would let fly with his tongue and gold braid be damned. The Commander of Air Fleet No. 3, Field Marshal Hugo Sperrle, once ran afoul of Wick.

On completing his inspection of Wick's squadron, Sperrle turned to the young ace and complained about the general untidiness of the ground personnel. A typical General's comment, it could easily have been passed off with an assurance or two. Wick exploded.

"*Herr Feldmarschall*, we are fighting the British every day, all day. These men have to work like hell to refuel, rearm, and repair our aircraft so we can fight the RAF. Don't you think that's more important than getting a damned haircut?"

Sperrle's monocle popped from his eye. He was wrong and he knew it. He said no more.

Wick's philosophy was that of a fighting man. He summed it up in these terms:

"As long as I can shoot down the enemy, adding to the honor of the Richthofen Wing and the success of the Fatherland, I am a happy man. I want to fight and die fighting, taking with me as many of the enemy as possible."

He took fifty-six foes with him before his own fighter was shot from under him south of the Isle of Wight on 28 November 1940. His squadron mates saw their young *Kommodore* hit the silk and drift downward into the English Channel, over whose somber waters he had claimed so many of his victims. Helmut Wick was never seen again. During his absence on this last operational flight an extremely strong grounding order had been sent to JG-2's base, ordering Wick not to fly again. The order was too late.

Wick's successor as *Kommodore* of JG-2 was tall, thin Wilhelm Balthasar, whose combat experience dated from the Spanish Civil War. He was a Spanish War ace with seven kills, and ran up an additional

REICHSMARSCHALL HERMANN GOERING, sporting the Great Cross of the Iron Cross at his throat, looks approvingly at the tail of Adolf Galland's Me-109 in France. 94 victories are marked on the machine. Goering took over command of Richthofen Circus on the Western Front in WWI after the death of the Red Baron. Although the progenitor of the Luftwaffe, Goering lacked any comprehensive understanding of the development of air power, often fought with Galland over decisions when latter had accurate perception and understanding of air power on broad basis. (*Galland Collection*)

twenty-three victories in the Battle of France. He won a reputation as a leader and was a fitting successor to Wick.

Balthasar was an exceptional instructor of young pilots, and knew how to phase men into the grim business of aerial warfare. His diligence in this regard once caused him to flirt with disaster, in an incident which is not without its humor.

During the French campaign, Adolf Galland was flying an Me-109 which was camouflaged experimentally with new light yellow colors and patterns. Flying at three thousand feet, he heard a voice on the R/T which he recognized at once as Balthasar, talking to the three other pilots in his *Schwarm*.

"You see that English Spitfire below us at about three thousand feet at three o'clock in the yellow camouflage? I am going to bounce him. Watch carefully and I will show you how to shoot down an enemy."

Galland looked around and could see the friendly *Schwarm* far above him, peeling off for the bounce.

"Wilhelm!" said Galland on the R/T. "Please don't shoot me down, it's me, Adolf! Watch and I will waggle my wings."

To Galland's relief there was no firing as Balthasar flew down alongside him and beamed across at the future General of the Fighters. The two men later joked many times about the "near kill" over France.

Balthasar's personal roots were in the tradition of chivalry. One of his deepest interests in wartime was talking to downed RAF fighter pilots. As in the custom of the First World War, he would have them brought to his mess for *Schnaps*, a meal, and an exchange of views before handing them over to POW authorities.

The conversation was usually confined to mutual criticism and admiration of each other's planes and tactics. On one occasion, however, Balthasar had an interview which went beyond this—"one step beyond," so to speak. A young British pilot asserted in Balthasar's mess at the end of June 1941 that Ernst Udet had committed suicide by shooting himself in the head with a pistol. This amazing statement was made nearly five months before Udet's self-destruction by this very means.

The young Englishman took a lot of convincing that he was talking rubbish. His German hosts were at pains to assure him Udet was alive and well. Four months later, it was the Germans' turn to be incredulous, and pilots who were present marveled at the English pilot's precognition. By that time too, Balthasar was dead.

MOELDERS PROTEGE: Captain Hermann-Friedrich Joppien downed 25 RAF aircraft in the Battle of Britain in JG-51 *Moelders* under watchful eye of the immortal "Daddy." By the spring of 1941 he had downed 42 British planes. He went to Russia with Moelders and JG-51, lost his life when his aircraft mysteriously fell from the air. Joppien had 70 victories and the Oak Leaves. Moelders once reprimanded him for strafing a civilian train. *(Nowarra Collection)*

The second fighter pilot to win the Knight's Cross, Balthasar subsequently received the Oak Leaves. He had forty victories in the West to add to his seven Spanish War kills when he tangled with RAF fighters near Aire on 3 July 1941. His machine was hit, and a wing sheared off during combat, sending him crashing to the ground.

Balthasar's pilots found the First World War grave of the ace's father. They buried Wilhelm Balthasar in the next plot with a similar headstone. They lie side by side today in Flanders far beyond the borders of the Fatherland in whose service they both lost their lives.

Black-haired, dark-complexioned Gerhard Schoepfel is an executive of Air Lloyd at Cologne-Bonn Airport today, and he looks at least ten years younger than his sixty-four years. In 1940 he was one of the most successful German aces of the Battle of Britain, and he succeeded Adolf Galland as *Kommodore* of JG-26. Schoepfel is heavier now, and doesn't move quite as fast as he did in his glory days, but the flashing quality of the ace is still to be seen in his piercing dark eyes, quick comprehension, and blunt, direct response to questions.

Gerd Schoepfel entered the Luftwaffe in 1935 as a twenty-three-year-old ex-infantryman. Like most of the German pilots who were successful early in the war, he benefited from a detailed peacetime training. He was a squadron leader in JG-26 on the outbreak of war, and bagged his first victory near Dunkirk during the evacuation of the British Army. In a high-altitude battle he brought down a Spitfire.

By the climax of the Battle of Britain in mid-September 1940, Schoepfel was credited with twenty kills and wore the Knight's Cross. He flew on dozens of operations over England with Galland, who came to JG-26 as *Gruppenkommandeur* of III/JG-26 in 1940. When Galland was promoted *Kommodore*, Schoepfel took over III/JG-26.

LT. COL EGON MAYER (Left) was first German pilot to bring down 100 aircraft on the Western Front, winning the Swords to his Knight's Cross. He holds up log book here while Captain Eckart-Wilhelm von Bonin (37 night victories 2 day victories) looks on. Mayer was killed shortly afterwards in combat with USAAF Thunderbolts, his 102 victories for the war including 25 four-engined bombers. *(Nowarra Collection)*

He flew seven hundred missions between 1939 and 1945, but was shot down only once, late in the war, during the defense of the Reich. He had to bail out and, landing heavily, he dislocated his shoulder. He has a permanent memento of this occasion, since his left arm is shorter than his right, and he demonstrates the difference with a smile.

Schoepfel was wounded lightly a number of times, and once in a way that makes him laugh even today. He was leading his *Schwarm* against Spitfires when a burst of machine gun fire hit his aircraft. The bullets plowed into the back of his instrument panel, and an adjusting stud from one of the instruments was propelled right into Schoepfel's mouth.

He tells a story of 1940 chivalry in the downing of an American RAF pilot named Clarke, over France:

"Clarke was an American who was an RAF volunteer. He had blazing red hair. Strangely enough, the young sergeant pilot in my squadron who brought Clarke down in France also had a shock of red hair. After Clarke belly-landed and jumped out, the young German sergeant flew over the wreck, just as Clarke pulled off his helmet. He was astounded to see his late adversary with a shock of red hair like his own.

IN RICHTHOFEN'S STEPS: Major Siegfried Schnell shot down 87 Western-flown aircraft in his total of 93 victories attained before his death on 25 February 1944 on the Russian Front. Schell was one of the leading aces of JG-2 on the Channel Front during the Battle of Britain. He rose from sergeant-pilot to Major with the Oak Leaves to his Knight's Cross. (*Nowarra Collection*)

He told me about it, and that evening we brought Clarke to our base and the two redheads met on the ground."

Schoepfel was present when the captured Douglas Bader was brought to the HQ of III/JG-26 as a visitor. Galland has related in his book how guarded Bader was about divulging information, even though it was not the province of the German fighter pilots to get such information. Nor did they attempt to obtain it. Much later, Schoepfel went to the Interrogation Camp at Oberursel where Bader was professionally questioned, and asked for the information obtained from the English ace. The Germans got nothing out of Bader—his file was a blank save for name, rank, and serial number.

Schoepfel served successively as Fighter Operations Officer in southern Italy, as Fighter Leader Norway, *Kommodore* of JG-4, and Fighter Leader Hungary. In the closing days of the war he was *Kommodore* of JG-6 in northern Czechoslovakia, with forty confirmed Western kills to his credit. On General Seidemann's staff at war's end, he fell

RUGGED FOE: Colonel Walter Oesau began his career with the Condor Legion in Spain, where he shot down 8 aircraft. "Gulle" Oesau was an aggressive and capable fighter pilot who rose to command both JG-2 and JG-1 before his death in aerial combat on 11 May 1944. He won the Swords to his Knight's Cross on 16 July 1941 and was credited with 125 aerial victories. General Steinhoff calls him "the toughest fighter pilot in the Luftwaffe." (*Obermaier Collection*)

into the clutches of the Russians and languished in Soviet prisons for four and a half years.

Schoepfel gets a kick out of telling the story to American visitors of four U.S. airmen who were prisoners of war at the JG-6 airfield near Prague, just prior to the German withdrawal:

"The Russians were breaking through everywhere, and we knew their arrival at the airfield was probably only a matter of hours. I said to the prisoners, 'We will leave you here for your Russian Allies to pick up.'

"'No thanks,' said their spokesman. 'We'd rather leave with *you*.'"

After his release from Russian confinement, Schoepfel worked as a chauffeur for a while for a former member of his wing. Then he got into business as a merchant, and in the early nineteen sixties returned to the aviation field. He lives now in Bensberg, his family is grown, and he exemplifies the solid German citizen of today.

The old days are never far away for Gerd Schoepfel, and they are unlikely to be as long as he remains with Air Lloyd. His office is located on one side of the hangar where Adolf Galland's Beechcraft Bonanza is parked. The black-maned Galland, so little changed in appearance since war days, is a frequent visitor. As Schoepfel's old C.O. warms up his aircraft there is always the echo of yesteryear to jog the memories of the two German eagles who flew together a quarter century ago.

Sometimes the past can come eerily close to rebirth for both of them. Galland and Schoepfel acted as technical advisers for an epic film about the Battle of Britain made in the United Kingdom. Nowadays when they fly to England they don't have to worry about the flak, and their British friends are waiting for them with cognac instead of cannons.

One of the few pilots to beat Schoepfel to twenty victories on the Western Front was Walter Oesau, a rugged ex-artilleryman who had cut his combat teeth in the Spanish Civil War. Former Condor Legion ace Oesau had eight kills on the outbreak of the Second World War, and by 18 August 1940 had registered a further twenty victories over the British and French with JG-51 *Moelders*. He entered the war as a squadron leader, and by August 1940 was in command of II/JG-51.

Oesau was a shortish, stocky man who exuded physical toughness and stamina. "Macky" Steinhoff calls him the "toughest fighter pilot in the Luftwaffe." The late distinguished German historian Hans-Otto Boehm termed him "one of the great tutors" of his young contemporaries, in the same sense as Moelders, Luetzow, Trautloft, Ihlefeld, and others. Galland calls him "one of the greatest fighter pilots produced by Germany in the Second World War. He was tough-minded as well as a brilliant aerial fighter."

In three hundred missions, "Gulle" Oesau scored 117 kills in the Second World War, forty-four of them on the Eastern Front. His seventy-three victories against the Western Allies are a remarkable achievement considering the time at which they were scored. He had forty kills by February 1941, flying against the best of the RAF.

He moved to the Russian Front in June 1941, and ran up forty-four kills against the Red Air Force before returning to further combat in the West as *Kommodore* of JG-2 *Richthofen*. On 26 October 1941 he became the third Luftwaffe fighter ace to reach one hundred kills. Only Moelders and Luetzow reached the century mark ahead of him, Luetzow beating him by a scant two days.

As Colonel Oesau he became *Kommodore* of JG-1 *Oesau* in October 1943. The wing was given his name as a tribute to his leadership and achievements. The grind from 1939 to 1943 had taken a serious toll even of this flint-hard fighting man. Major Hartmann Grasser, who was one of Oesau's group commanders in JG-1, was with the dauntless ace when he was shot down:

"Oesau was at this time at the end of his physical and intellectual powers. German fighter pilots and leaders like him had to fight throughout the war without any rest, and I think that was one of the greatest mistakes of our leadership.

ARTILLERYMAN TURNED ACE: Colonel Walter Oesau was a onetime artilleryman who switched to fighter piloting in the 1930's. "Gulle" Oesau cut his combat teeth as a fighter pilot in Spain with the Condor Legion, where he scored 8 confirmed victories. As a Battle of Britain participant, Oesau had scored 20 more victories against the RAF before the September 1940 climax of the BOB. Tough-minded Oesau was greatly admired as fighter pilot and commander by such luminaries as Galland and Steinhoff, and had 117 victories at the time of his death in combat near Aachen against Mustangs and Lightnings protecting B-17 formations. Walter Oesau won the Swords to his Knight's Cross, which he defends here against the playful assault of a feline friend. *(Haussmann Collection)*

"I was with Oesau in this final fight when he was brought down near Aachen. He tried to tackle the escort fighters for a formation of Boeings. He was followed down by two Mustangs and by Lightnings, too. Outnumbered, he could do nothing, and neither could we. In this way, we lost most of our best men."[4]

The man who so narrowly preceded Oesau as the second German ace to reach one hundred aerial victories was Colonel Guenther Luetzow. Bearer of a distinguished military name and family tradition, he was born to lead in the fashion of his forebears. Like Oesau and Balthasar, he was an ace from the Spanish Civil War, where he gained five victories. To these he added a further 103 kills in the world conflict, all but eighteen of them on the Eastern Front.

Although most of Luetzow's victories were against the Red Air Force, his main historical association is with the Western Front. He made an immortal mark as a leader. Historically it may be said that one of the practical tests of a Luftwaffe fighter leader's character and integrity was his ability to excite Goering's antagonism. In this respect, Guenther Luetzow had no equal.

As a man of breeding and character, Luetzow stood in vivid contrast to the squalid, self-indulgent Goering. No small element in their mutual dislike stemmed from Goering's instinctive feeling of inferiority to a man who embodied everything honorable, correct, and decent about the professional German soldier. Luetzow met all life's challenges head-on and unflinchingly, and was thus the reverse of the Reichsmarschall, who insulated himself with the comforts of Karinhall against the sights and sounds of national ruin.

[4] The morning following Oesau's death in the air, General Galland telephoned to adjutant Hartmann Grasser to order Oesau transferred immediately from the battle front to Galland's staff, unaware the brilliant ace had been killed.

SPOKESMAN FOR THE REVOLTING KOMMODORES: 108 victories, including 5 in Spain, Günther Lützow (left) was the second fighter pilot to score 100 aerial victories. Lützow, shown here talking to Hannes Trautloft, was a real gentleman with a great sense of humor. He died while flying an Me-262 jet on April 24th, 1944. (*Neumann Collection*)

Born in Kiel in 1912, Luetzow was descended from the old Prussian family of the same name which contributed so much to martial tradition. The warriors of Fehrbellin and Rossbach were among his ancestors, and at the other extreme in his lineage stood men of the cloth. Luetzow's education was initially directed more toward theology than military life, and his academic training was in a Protestant cloister school.

The events of his time led him inevitably to military life in spite of his religious education. The early experience nevertheless fortified his naturally strong character, and he became a leader of exceptional quality, respected and admired throughout the Luftwaffe. His rapid rise to one hundred victories in aerial combat by October 1941 enhanced his reputation and assured him of his place among the immortals of German air history.

Luetzow's character and courage, intelligence and debating abilities were such that he was chosen as the spokesman for the fighter arm at the now-famous "Wing Commanders' Conference" with Goering in Berlin in January 1945. Galland had already been dismissed as General of the Fighter Arm, and Luetzow raised this matter immediately, together with Goering's abuse and mistrust of the fighter pilots, in his presentation of the wing commanders' grievances. Goering had asked for a summary of their grievances, and Luetzow was just the man to lay them on the line.

Goering blew up. Angrily terminating the conference, the livid Reichsmarschall flung out of the room shouting his intention to have Luetzow court-martialed. The gallant Luetzow was not actually

"GULLE": Combat experience as a fighter ace in Spain (8 victories with the Condor Legion) gave Walter "Gulle" Oesau a flying start into WWII. In the Battle of Britain he was one of the luminaries of JG-51 and of the Luftwaffe effort against the RAF. Rapidly promoted as a tough-minded and dependable leader, he rose to Colonel in command of JG-2 before his death in combat on 11 May 1944. His lifetime victories total 125, and include 10 4-engined heavy bombers. (*Nowarra Collection*)

subjected to this indignity, but he was banished to Italy to take over as Fighter Leader from Colonel Eduard Neumann, his long-time friend.

The authors are grateful to Edu Neumann for the following reminiscence of this Italian interlude:

CHIVALROUS FOE: Major Georg-Peter Eder lived by the ancient code of chivalry during a violent 1940-45 combat career in total war. Eder had a superstition about the number 13, emblazoned it boldly on all his aircraft, and became known to the Allies as "Lucky 13"—a pilot who did not slaughter defeated foes in the air. Eder also clawed down 36 heavy bombers, and flew 150 missions in the Me-262 jet. He was one of the elite pilots assigned to Walter Nowotny's *Kommando* to develop new tactics suited to the Me-262. Eder ended WWII with the Oak Leaves and 78 confirmed victories. *(Wolf von Schweinitz)*

"He was a tall, haughty-looking man—a real gentleman with a fine sense of humor. He was the typical and well-educated Prussian.[5] When the Italians heard that a Prussian would succeed me, they were terrified. But later, after he left Italy, they cried at the depth of their loss.

"We were not allowed any contact with each other, because Goering was afraid we would conspire. I had been ordered to Germany, but without a special mission. When I went to say goodbye to the Italians, Luetzow had to leave the Verona staff, and I had to take a detoured route to Verona so we could not meet each other. But I telephoned him and said: 'This is the Reichsmarschall speaking.' Luetzow answered, 'Ha! Ha! Anybody can say that.' We had a funny conversation in double-talk, not knowing that Goering's organization had tapped the radio but not the phones.

"Some months later, before the end of the war, I relieved him at Verona because he insisted on going with Galland in JV-44."

After a distinguished war career as combat pilot, Inspector of the Day Fighters, Division Commander, and Fighter Leader Italy, Colonel Guenther Luetzow decided he wanted to end the war with Galland in JV-44, the "Squadron of Experts." At least he could help prove the decisive superiority of the Me-262 in combat and soldier again with an honorable fighter's self-respect. A typical decision for Luetzow, it led to his death.

He scored two additional kills in the jet fighter, and then went missing 24 April 1945 near Donauwoerth. There was only one Me-262 claimed by a fighter pilot that day. USAAF Major Ralph F. Johnson, address unknown, now deceased, claimed a kill over a jet. However, it is more likely that Guenther Luetzow lost his life attacking the hordes of B-17s and B-24s roaming over Europe that day.

Luetzow won the Knight's Cross on 18 September 1940, the Oak Leaves on 20 July 1941, and the Swords on 11 October 1941 as the fourth fighter pilot so honored. He failed to survive the war by less than

[5] As opposed to the caricature of the Prussian so well known in Western countries generally and then enjoying currency in Italy.

two weeks. General Adolf Galland, with whom the ace ended his career, pays his late friend "Franzl" Luetzow this historic tribute:

"Guenther Luetzow was in my opinion the outstanding leader in the Luftwaffe. I place him above all others."

As this book has shown, numerous German aces with relatively low scores have nevertheless succeeded in etching themselves firmly in the history of combat flying. A Western Front ace with "only" seventy-eight confirmed victories, Major Georg-Peter Eder won his immortal niche as the most chivalrous ace in the Luftwaffe. With wartime propaganda in the past, together with the deliberate distortion of German character it induced, Georg Eder's conduct as a combat pilot may now be seen as in the highest tradition of arms. He never willingly or wantonly killed a foe in more than four years of combat flying.

Georg-Peter Eder is today a vigorous, ebullient Frankfurt merchant in his middle fifties. He is about five feet seven inches tall, and weighs around 185, a stocky, sturdy man who is friendly, effervescent, and talkative. Eder is obviously a fighter pilot to anyone familiar with the breed. More than thirty years have passed since he flew a fighter, but his quickness in conversation, alertness, and dynamism mark him as a war eagle, and he bears a facial resemblance to that noble bird.

Born in Frankfurt 8 March 1921, Eder had a typical German high school education before entering the Luftwaffe as a *Fahnenjunker* in October 1938. On 1 April 1939 he was sent to the flying school at Berlin-Gatow, and a year later won his wings and assignment to Fighter School No. 1 at Werneuchen. He was on his way.

The eager nineteen-year-old pilot was assigned to his first operational unit on 1 September 1940—No. 1 Squadron in I/JG-51 *Moelders*. He flew in the Battle of Britain but failed to score any victories. In June 1941 he went to the Russian Front with JG-51 and scored his first two kills on 22 June 1941, the day of the invasion. He had been an operational pilot for almost ten months before conquering his buck fever, in spite of an unhurried peacetime training and the guidance of JG-51's experienced veterans. He soon made up for his slow start.

Eder ran up a string of ten confirmed kills on the Russian Front in the next month, and took part in numerous close-support sorties. On 24 July 1941 he was shot down and badly wounded. This experience was to come his way with malefic frequency until the end of the war. *He was shot down seventeen times and wounded fourteen times between July 1941 and the surrender in 1945.* His body is laced with wound scars. Each time he recovered and returned to the shambles.

His first wound put him in hospital for ninety days. He was then assigned to the Fighter School at Zerbst as a squadron leader. He soon tired of this, and was assigned to No. 7 Squadron in II/JG-2 in February 1942. He took command of No. 12 Squadron the following month. Richthofen Wing aces like Kurt Buehligen and Egon Mayer, Josef "Sepp" Wurmheller and Hans "Assi" Hahn were fast company for any young fighter pilot.

Eder held his own in JG-2 until February 1944, and in this period he won renown in the Luftwaffe as an expert in the lethal art of tackling the American heavies. He is credited with downing at least thirty-six four-engined bombers. With Lieutenant Colonel Egon Mayer, *Kommodore* of JG-2, Eder is also credited with developing the head-on attack technique which brought them both considerable success against the four-engined bombers.

The volume of defensive fire from a formation of B-17s or B-24s was weakest in the forward hemisphere from the bombers. The Germans soon discovered this weakness. Eder and Mayer set about its exploitation with a tactic that took a cast-iron stomach and nerves of steel. They tried diving head-on into the bomber stream, continuing straight on through the line of bombers, firing as they went.

The rapid closure rate gave the American bomber gunners minimum firing time. Tail and side gunners could not shoot at the German fighters for fear of spraying their own formation with fire. Many eager American bomber gunners actually did shoot down their own aircraft when attempting to take German fighters under fire in these attacks.

Eder did not emerge from these encounters unscathed. He was shot down repeatedly by the Americans, and wounded almost every time. On at least nine occasions the Americans hit Eder's aircraft so badly that the handsome, happy, eagle-faced airman from Frankfurt had to take to his parachute—often wounded to boot. On other occasions he had to nurse his riddled and soggy aircraft in to a crash landing, again while wounded in several instances.

Eder became famous on the other side of the English Channel not for his daring assaults on the bombers, but for his chivalry in individual combat. Strangely enough, the RAF and USAAF pilots whom Eder spared in combat never knew his name, but they had his number. Eder was not propaganda material and he was not known by name to his foes as were Galland, Moelders, Graf, Nowotny, and a few others. His enemies knew him only as "Lucky No. 13."

GIANT KILLER: Major Georg-Peter Eder made a specialty of attacking American daylight bombers over Europe—considered a form of suicide in the Luftwaffe. Here he uses a model of a B-17 Fortress to refine the tactics that allowed him to shoot down 36 of the 4-motored bombers in daylight. He preferred to attack from the head-on position, so that rapid closure rate gave American gunners minimum firing time with maximum chance of missing. He was nevertheless shot down at least nine times by the USAAF heavies. In his 1940-45 war career, Eder shot down 78 Allied aircraft and won the Oak Leaves. He was shot down 17 times and wounded 14 times and ranks amongst the bravest fighter pilots of all time. (*Eder Collection*)

One of Eder's quirks was to consider number thirteen as lucky—counter to mystical beliefs on the subject. He made a point of painting thirteen on every fighter he flew, and he became known by this odd trademark. Former RAF pilot Mike Gladych, an expatriate Pole who is now living in the United States, is one of the Allied pilots who met Eder in the air. He owes his life to the German ace's chivalry.

Gladych detailed his aerial encounters with Eder in a magazine article a few years ago,[6] relating how the German ace crippled his Spitfire over Lille in 1943. One burst would have put "paid" to Gladych's account, but instead Eder rocked his wings and flew alongside his victim. He waved. He would not kill a beaten man.

The two pilots met each other again. This time Eder shot up Gladych's P-47 and was forcing the Polish pilot to land at Vechta. He could easily have killed his RAF foe. Capturing a complete enemy aircraft with pilot was the kind of achievement that meant more to Eder than blasting a helpless opponent. But Gladych cleverly tricked Eder so that the

FORTUNATE JG-26 PILOT: This JG-26 "Schlageter" pilot, with foot on the wing, was lucky to have a nice smooth pasture to belly his Me-109 in. (*Toliver Collection*)

German ace flew into his own flak while the Polish pilot made his escape unscathed.

The chivalrous German paid dearly this time for his honor in battle. The friendly flak riddled his FW-190 and he was wounded. He spent five weeks in hospital recovering. After the war, Gladych and Eder met by chance in Frankfurt, unaware that they had fought each other in the air until they started comparing notes. When it turned out that they had been adversaries, Eder's first act was to congratulate the Polish pilot on his ingenious escape.

Eder could have been a more handsome scorer had he been less merciful. He spared many lives and his foes knew him initially as "No. 13." As more and more of his Anglo-American enemies realized how fortunate they had been to meet Eder instead of another pilot, they began referring to him in mess talks as "Lucky 13." He continued

[6] *Real* Magazine, New York, April-May 1960.

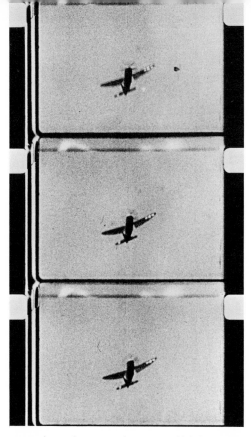

GERMAN COMBAT FILM SEQUENCE: Shown are three frames of gun camera film from an FW-190 attacking an American P-47 Thunderbolt. Note bullet strikes on wing root of the P-47 which blazed and crashed near Mönchengladbach. *(Toliver Collection)*

carrying the number on all his aircraft, and became one of the legends of the air war.

Eder flew with JG-1 *Oesau* from March 1943 until September 1944, rising to *Gruppenkommandeur* and taking part in the invasion front battles with this unit. He then served briefly with JG-26, replacing Emil "Bully" Lang as commander of II/JG-26 after Lang's death in combat, which has been previously described. In October 1944, Galland chose Eder to join the select group of eagles in *Kommando Nowotny*, flying the Me-262 out of Lechfeld and Achmer. Their task was to develop new tactics for the jet by actual trial in combat.

From this time until the end of the war he flew the Me-262 on approximately 150 missions. He claimed twenty-four kills in the jet, but most were never confirmed in the waning days of the war. Victory confirmations sometimes trailed actual claims by as much as six months, and in the final chaotic months of the war numerous claims were never confirmed despite complete fulfillment of all conditions save final official confirmation. A large number of Luftwaffe pilots have many more kills on this account than their official tallies indicate, but the authors have yet to meet a single ace who made anything of it. In the words of Gerd Barkhorn: "Give them to the poor people."

Eder confirmed twelve kills in the Me-262, one of them a P-38 which he rammed. In the Battle of the Bulge he flew the jet against the Brussels–Evere airdrome. About forty P-47s were parked in a line and Eder's rocket and cannon strafing attack destroyed most of them.

"Lucky 13's" luck ran out with the end of hostilities, and he found himself in the clutches of some enemies to whom chivalry was an obsolete code of conduct. A POW at Regensburg after the war, he was taken to England, and there treated rather less generously than he had treated his British foes in the air.

In the POW camp at Derby, coincidentally designated Camp 13, Eder was considered a special prisoner because of his experience with the Me-262. Camp 13 was unlucky for Lucky 13. He was interrogated at great length, and kept in a brilliantly lit room. A British military policeman once knocked him out with a gun butt when he refused to answer questions.

After two weeks in this room, his nerves broke down and he was committed for treatment as a manic-depressive. He was injected daily by attending physicians, and after a further ten days the British doctors decided he was not responding to treatment. "Send this idiot back to Germany," said the physician in charge.

He was shipped to Calais the following day, and thence via Lille to Bad Kreuznach. Malnourished and gaunt, he had eaten nothing for more than a week, and was a shadow of his former husky self. The 180-pound eagle had shrunk to a 98-pound weakling under the care of his late enemies.

He responded to proper treatment and was eventually returned to the exchange camp at Regensburg. On 6 March 1946 he was released and returned to his home in Frankfurt. For Georg-Peter Eder it had been a long war with a sour ending, from which he of all German pilots should have been spared.

His military achievements do not set him in the front rank of Germany's aces. Had he exploited every chance that his skills as a pilot opened to him, he might well have passed into history as a top-scoring ace. He chose to exercise mercy as an act of free will, and on that account has become a far bigger man. He brought new luster to the dimming traditions of chivalry, which hold that a real hero tempers his martial skills with mercy, and no one can ever take this distinction from Georg-Peter Eder.

GROUND LOOP: Here's an Me-109 the Allies didn't have to shoot down after being ground-looped by its pilot. Narrow landing gear made the German fighter difficult to handle on takeoff and on the landing roll. Hundreds of Me-109's were destroyed by ground loops, *(Toliver Collection)*

Lieutenant Colonel Egon Mayer was Eder's commanding officer in JG-2 when the two pilots had the tactical problems of battling the bombers. Like Eder, Mayer became known to his foes through a trademark. He was known to the RAF as "The Man With the White Scarf." His enemies respected his ability, even if they did not know his name. He was the first German ace of the war to achieve one hundred aerial victories on the Channel Front.

Born in August 1917, a few months after Baron Manfred von Richthofen died in combat on the Western Front, Egon Mayer was destined to serve from 1939 until his death in the wing named for Richthofen, JG-2. He rose to *Kommodore* of this elite formation. He was a glider enthusiast as a young boy, using horses from his parents' farm to drag sailplanes into the air at Ballenberg glider field.

After a regular peacetime training in the Luftwaffe he joined JG-2 in December 1939, and never left this unit for the remainder of his career. Slender, sensitive-looking Mayer started slowly, and was a long time finding consistent success as an aerial fighter. He needed twenty months on operations to score his first twenty kills, and along the way he was shot down four times by the RAF—including a subsequent one-hour dunking in the English Channel on one occasion.

Mayer took another year getting his next thirty kills, and his fiftieth victory came on 19 September 1942. All these victories except a handful won in France were against the RAF, which meant they were hard-won against rugged foes. In addition to being shot down four times as previously described, he frequently returned to base to force-land his damaged fighter.

95 EAST—95 WEST: Major Anton Hackl won the Swords to his Knight's Cross in WWII, for 190 aerial victories, equally divided between the Russian and Western fronts. Major Hackl flew with JG-11, JG-26 and JG-300. (*Boehm Collection*)

Resourceful under pressure, he once saved his own life by crash-landing his riddled fighter against the steep slope of a quarry. In another desperate set of circumstances he was forced to use his parachute from 250 feet, but survived. When daylight bomber attacks became the major problem for German fighters, he worked out the head-on diving assault, and with Eder led his pilots to prove it out in battle.

Mayer once downed three B-17s in nineteen minutes. He accomplished this feat 6 September 1943 as *Kommodore* of JG-2. The grinding battle with the American heavies and their fighter escort, the problems of trying to keep new pilots alive long enough for them to learn to look after themselves, and the remorseless criticism of the Luftwaffe High Command all took their toll of this officer.

On 5 February 1944 Mayer achieved a notable distinction. He became the first ace to win one hundred victories on the Channel Front, but he was on borrowed time. Less than a month later, on 2 March 1944, he led one of his groups against an American daylight raid. The heavies were escorted by a massive formation of P-47s which over-

4 APRIL 1944 AT OBERSALZBURG: Receiving medals from Der Führer, Hitler are, left to right: Major Kurt Bühligen, JG-2 (112 victories) Major Hans-Joachim Jabs, Kommodore NJG-1, (50 victories, 28 at night) Major Bernhard Jope, KG-40, Major Hansgeorg Bätcher, KG-100   *(Nowarra Collection)*

powered Mayer and shot him down. He was only twenty-six, and was interred at the cemetery of Beaumont le Reger.

Mayer is credited with downing at least twenty-five four-engined bombers among his 102 victories. To hurl oneself repeatedly on the death-dealing, seemingly impregnable bomber streams took sustained high courage. Mayer's feats were formally acknowledged by the Reich with the award of the Oak Leaves and Swords to his Knight's Cross.

The Allied pilots who knew him then as "The Man With the White Scarf" acknowledged him as a hard but fair foe. The German pilots he led would follow him to Hell itself—which attacking the American bomber formations closely approximated. Modest, fair, and concerned for those who served under his command he was one of the Luftwaffe's gentlemen.

Like Egon Mayer, Kurt Buehligen spent most of his war career with JG-2, and all of his 112 kills were scored against the Western Allies. Little known to his late foes and publicized but little in wartime, Buehligen wrote one of the superior fighting records of the war. Only Hans-Joachim Marseille and Heinz Baer shot down more Western-flown aircraft.

Buehligen came up the hard way. His aviation career began three years before the war as an aircraft mechanic. A burning desire to fly, ability to back his ambition, and personal forcefulness qualified him for fighter pilot training. Eventually he rose to Lieutenant Colonel and was the last *Kommodore* of JG-2 *Richthofen* before the surrender.

As a sergeant pilot he scored his first victory in the Battle of Britain, and during the final North African crisis in Tunisia he scored forty kills against the Western Allies between December 1942 and March 1943. At this time the RAF and USAAF enjoyed a numerical superiority over the remnants of the Luftwaffe in North Africa which eventually reached twenty to one. That Buehligen could repeatedly prevail in aerial combat under such conditions is adequate measure of his fighting skill.

His 112 kills also include twenty-four four-engined heavy bombers—almost equaling Egon Mayer's tally. He flew more than seven hundred missions, was himself a victory for Allied pilots on three occasions. His military career had an unpleasant anticlimax when he was incarcerated by the Russians from 1945 to 1950. Aggressive and indomitable as a fighter pilot, he proved to be one of the "strong men" under the rigors of Soviet jails, considered by all who endured it to be the acid test of character. Kurt Buehligen won the Swords, and he ranks near the top in the subtler awards of status and respect accorded him in the fighter pilot fraternity.

A fighter pilot who was not physically strong as well as mentally tough had little chance of survival under Second World War conditions. Only in the waning months of the struggle were hydraulic controls being designed into aircraft. Prior to that time, physical strength and vitality were essential for sustained combat at speeds in the 300–400 mph range. *Size* meant little. Colonel Josef "Pips" Priller proved that in a 1939–45 fighting career that brought him 101 confirmed kills against the Western Allies.

Pips Priller was only five feet four inches tall, and weighed about 150 pounds, but he was one of the most dynamic ace-leaders in the Luftwaffe. With black, slicked-back hair, uninhibited wit and quick, penetrating intelligence he stood out in any gathering of pilots. His

OUTSTANDING LEADER AND ACE: Colonel Josef Priller (center) was nicknamed "Pips" because of his short stature (5 ft. 4 in.) but he was long on combat ability and leadership. Here he confers with his wingman (left) during early service with JG-26, which he later rose to command. Priller was credited with 101 kills against Western-flown aircraft in 1939-45 career on the Western Front. (*Eder Collection*)

happy temperament and perennially smiling face pervaded his environment with buoyancy and optimism—no small factor in his success as a leader.

As the war rolled into its fifth year, Goering seldom laughed or smiled any more. But the quick wit and humor of Pips Priller could bring a happy grin to the face even of the unhappy Reichsmarschall. Priller was one of the few in the latter days of the war who could stand eyeball to eyeball with the forceful Goering and smilingly tell him why Germany was losing the war. Priller could get away with something others wouldn't dare attempt.

Pips got into the war in October 1939 as a squadron leader in Theo Osterkamp's newly formed JG-51. He flew with this unit through the French campaign and until after the climax of the Battle of Britain. He learned much from "Daddy" Moelders in these hard days, but on 20 November 1940 he began his long association with JG-26 *Schlageter*—the famed "Abbeville Boys."

He flew consistently against the RAF and USAAF until the end of January 1945, scoring steadily all the while. His victory tally of 101 aircraft includes at least eleven four-engined bombers. He became *Kommodore* of JG-26 on 11 January 1943, and held this rugged command until 27 January 1945, at which time he became Inspector of Day Fighters West.

The hot pilots who passed through JG-26 during the war included some of Germany's best. A typical selection would include Adolf Galland (104 victories), and his brother, Major Wilhelm "Wutz" Galland (55 Western kills); Captain Emil "Bully" Lang (173 kills, including 25 on the Western Front), and Major Walter "Count Punski" Krupinski (197 victories, including 20 in the West); Major Joachim Muencheberg (102 victories in the West and North Africa plus 33 in Russia), and Major Anton Hackl (192 kills, including 87 on

BLEAK DAYS—1945: The weather wasn't the only bad news in January 1945 when Colonel Josef "Pips" Priller (center) met Major Walter Krupinski at Plantlünne. The Battle of the Bulge was in progress and ended in failure for the German Army. Accompanying Priller is Major Franz Goetz, 63 victory ace from JG-26. Priller had 101 kills against the Western Allies, Krupinski a total of 197.

(Krupinski Collection)

the Western Front, 32 of them four-engined bombers).

All these high-scoring aces, and many others, served with Pips Priller in JG-26.

The top-scoring RAF ace, Group Captain J. E. "Johnny" Johnson, was skeptical about high German fighter pilot scores for a long time. However, in his book *Full Circle*, written as a sequel to his original work, *Wing Leader*, Johnson admits that it has been possible to document from RAF records almost all of Priller's claimed victories over RAF aircraft. This is further evidence of the rigorous criteria applied to kill claims by the Germans. Verification of the twenty-five-year-old downings of an enemy pilot from contemporary RAF records would be possible only if the information supplied from German sources was accurate.

On one wall of Priller's home in Augsburg there hangs a map of the Channel coast. Marked on this map by date, insignia, and place are all of Priller's 101 confirmed victories. Most of his kills were fighter aircraft.

Pips Priller ended the war with the Oak Leaves and Swords to his Knight's Cross, and with an immortal place in the hearts of his contemporaries. No man can attain the esteem Priller enjoyed with his comrades without exceptional personal qualities to complement his military achievements. His popularity remained undiminished through the years of peace.

A party-lover, Priller was able to indulge his generous nature through his marriage to one of the three daughters of the Rigele Breweries family, the lovely Johanna. The ace pilot who knew the art of the barrel roll began rolling out the barrels from the Rigele Brewery in Augsburg, which he managed after the war. He supplied the beer for gatherings of old German fighter pilots, and took large advertisements for his beer in the *Fighter News*, the regular publication of the German Fighter Pilots' Association, to help with printing expenses.

A social lion, his personality illuminated many uproarious gatherings of old comrades. When he died suddenly of a heart attack on 21 May 1961 at Augsburg he was five weeks short of his forty-sixth birthday. His family, friends, and old comrades were stunned. The fates which had preserved this striking individual through more than five years of combat flying had cut him off in the very prime of life. Pips is sadly missed by all who knew him. His postwar book, *A Fighter Wing Tells Its Story*, has not yet appeared in English. Priller was assisted with his book by the late distinguished historian Hans-Otto Boehm, and it provides Pips with a permanent memorial among all who flew or cared about those who flew.

One of the most colorful pilots in the Luftwaffe and one of its great guns in the Battle of Britain was Major Hans "Assi" Hahn, to whom there have already been frequent references in this book. He made his mark as one of the stars of JG-2 in the heyday of Wick, Balthasar, Oesau, and other redoubtable fighters. Assi Hahn joined JG-2 in 1939 as a well-trained and eager twenty-five-year-old First Lieutenant. When he was appointed to command II/JG-54 on 1 November 1942, and trans-

GREAT SHOT: Major Hans "Assi" Hahn was a fighter pilot who needed no "running in" but began scoring as soon as he went to the Front. Extremely successful against the RAF, his luck ran out in Russia with a forced landing behind the Red lines. Confined illegally by the Russians until 1950, his was the first familiar face seen in Germany by Erich Hartmann when the ace of aces returned to Germany in 1955. "Assi" Hahn had 108 confirmed victories and won the Oak Leaves to his Knight's Cross.   (Boehm Collection)

ferred to the Eastern Front, he had scored sixty-eight kills against the RAF.

Hahn is one of the rare fighter pilots who emerged with a kill in their first engagement. Brash Assi went one better. He downed two RAF Hurricanes in his first air battle on 14 May 1940 and both kills were confirmed. He had no "running in" period. He was good from the start.

Scoring steadily throughout the Battle of Britain, he had twenty victories by 24 September 1940 and was awarded the Knight's Cross. This put him in the front rank of German pilots at that time. A year later he had doubled his score, still engaged exclusively with the RAF, and was awarded the Oak Leaves. In the next fifteen months he added twenty-eight more British victims to his score. All but six of his sixty-eight RAF victories were single-engined aircraft, the majority of them Spitfires and Hurricanes.

On the Russian Front his luck continued to run well, and he downed forty Russian aircraft in only seven aerial battles. His best day was over Lake Ladoga on 6 January 1942, when he downed eight La-5 fighters. The luck which brought him through the Battle of Britain now ran out.

Forced down with engine trouble on 21 February 1943, Hahn had to land behind the Russian lines, which often meant death for German pilots. He spent seven years as a guest of the Soviet Government, and emerged from confinement in 1950 to take up life again as a businessman in West Germany.

Something of a *bon vivant*, Assi's enormous self-confidence let him recover quickly from his long confinement, and he lives the full life today. As mentioned earlier, he wrote a book about his prison experiences which he titled *I Tell the Truth*. Perhaps because of Assi's irrepressible personality, some of his fellow prisoners, including Erich Hartmann, find it hard to take his book seriously. In all fairness to Hahn, the authors feel that every person sees the world through different eyes, and that Assi is entitled to his opinions.

Assi Hahn is one of the Luftwaffe's leading "characters," as well as one of the top aces of the Western Front. Everyone has a funny yarn to tell about him, but the light side was not the only side to his personality. One hundred and eight aerial victories prove that.

MISSING IN ACTION: Lieutenant Gerhard Koeppen had amassed 85 victories by May 1942 and been awarded the Oak Leaves to his Knight's Cross. He went down in the Sea of Azov after a battle between JG-52 fighters and Russian Pe-2's. His actual fate is unknown. (*Nowarra Collection*)

Cast in a different mold was one of Galland's protégés, Major Joachim Muencheberg, not quite twenty-one on the outbreak of war, but from the beginning an obviously superior individual with the capacity for leadership and command. To these talents he added formidable skill as a fighter pilot, which brought him 133 victories. Some 102 of his downings were Western-flown aircraft.

Muencheberg was an early starter, and got his first kill in November 1939 while flying with JG-26 as a Second Lieutenant. By the middle of September 1940 he had twenty confirmed kills, a hefty tally in those days, and had already won the Knight's Cross. He flew briefly with JG-51 in Russia, scoring thirty-three victories on the Eastern Front in approximately eight weeks. He was then transferred to North Africa

FIFTH TO SCORE 100 VICTORIES: Colonel Herbert Ihlefeld, Kommodore of JG-103, JG-52, JG-1, JG-11, and JG-25 at various times in WWII, scored 130 victories which included 7 in Spain. (*Nowarra Collection*)

as *Kommodore* of JG-77 at the age of twenty-four.

Toward the end of the Tunisian campaign, he was lost almost by chance on 23 March 1943. He was surprised by American fighters, and in taking evasive action his Me-109 collided with parts of a US-flown Spitfire which disintegrated when he shot it down. He lost his life on his five-hundredth mission.

Major Hartmann Grasser was a contemporary and admirer of Muencheberg, and he contributes this assessment of the young leader's abilities:

"Joachim Muencheberg was a very fine man. I personally think he was as good a man as Steinhoff., with more experience and more quality. I emphasize this as a personal view with no disrespect for Steinhoff, whom I also regard highly. Muencheberg had the right point of view for the *center* of things—for the resolution of complex problems. It is true he was a very young man, but he was a highly intelligent individual, with a capacity to distinguish between the important and the not-so-important.

"He was well trained in the prewar Luftwaffe, and as a protégé of Galland had learned much in the interim. He was also very hard against himself. He was ambitious, but the ambition never disturbed the other qualities that made him an outstanding fighter and leader."

Joachim Muencheberg's 102 victories against the Western Allies were recorded by March 1943—an exceptional accomplishment. He received the Oak Leaves and Swords to his Knight's Cross[7] in recognition of his achievements, and had he lived and fought another year would almost certainly have joined the elite nine fighter pilots who received the Diamonds. The steady loss of such leaders was one of the Luftwaffe's heaviest burdens.

This book must leave unlimned the careers of numerous outstanding German aces on the Western Front. As in previous chapters, the aces whose biographies have been presented must stand as representative of many equally gallant, accomplished, and courageous pilots. Numerous German aces who fought in the West could sustain complete books with their individual adventures, but in the nature of the aftermath to the late conflict they will never claim the fame that might have been theirs.

In this category is Colonel Herbert Ihlefeld, who began his combat career as a sergeant pilot in Spain, where he won acedom with seven kills and later became one of the greatest tutors and wing commanders. He added 123 victories in the Second World War, 56 of them in the West, and he flew over a thousand missions.

In similar vein is the career of First Lieutenant Herbert Rollwage, whose 102 victories include 11 on the Russian Front and 91 against the Western Allies. Rollwage flew through most of the war as an NCO, and was the Luftwaffe's champion "giant killer." He not only downed more four-engined heavy bombers than any other ace, but he lived to tell about it. Forty-four of the four-engined heavies went down under his guns.

Colonel Gustav Roedel could easily fill a large book with his biography. He scored his first kill on the first day of the Polish invasion, and at the surrender had ninety-seven Western-flown aircraft to his credit. He also downed a solitary Russian. Roedel was one of the great first-to-last warriors.

The stories of these men and many others like them must remain for the moment untold. If a German ace made his reputation on the Western Front, in his own fraternity it was recognized he had made it the hard way. This status is accorded to Western Front aces to this day. Against the RAF and later, the USAAF, the victories came hard and slowly, as the German records of the air war unerringly reveal.

[7] Knight's Cross 14 September 1940; Oak Leaves 7 May 1941; Swords 11 September 1941.

980 COMBAT MISSIONS!: Oberst Gustav Rödel, JG-21, JG-27 and lastly Kommandeur of Jagddivision 2, came near flying 1000 combat missions. His 97 victories on the Western Front puts him near the top. He had 1 kill on the Eastern Front. *(Obemaier Collection)*

SUCCESSFUL BUSINESSMAN: Adolf Galland went to South America after the war, serving as consultant to the Argentine Air Force. He resisted all efforts to have him return to the new German Air Force, and was regarded by virtually everyone as German's best available leader. "Dolfo" chose to stay out, became a successful aerospace consultant and businessman and lives the good life. Galland maintains close touch with history and old comrades. Here he examines a collection of historic wartime photographs. *(Galland Collection)*

"WE MUST STRIKE AND RUN . . .": Werner Moelders uses his hands to demonstrate way for German fighters to avoid getting into turning battle with RAF Spitfires. British fighter could out-turn Me-109 and usually won such turning battles. When Galland and Moelders changed tactics to strike and pull away, German fighter losses dropped sharply. Two great leaders were friends and also rivals, with differing aims and ambitions, but on this occasion they showed they could work together to good effect. *(Obermaier Collection)*

DYNAMIC LEADER: Colonel Josef "Pips" Priller was an outstanding combat pilot and leader in the air, and one of Germany's greatest fighter commanders as *Kommodore* of JG-26 in final two years of WWII. He is one of the few German aces to score more than 100 victories against the Western powers, with the RAF able to confirm most of his kills over British aircraft since the war. Outgoing and humorous when not on business matters, Priller here makes his point with cigar in hand during a relaxed moment on the Western Front. 101 victories and the Swords to his Knights Cross. *(Toliver Collection)*

"DADDY" AND ADJUTANT: A Battle of Britain encounter is reviewed and relived by Hartmann Grasser (left), adjutant at this critical time to Werner Moelders who listens to him here. The two aces had just returned from a sortie over the south of England. In the background, armorers reload the guns on Moelders' Me-109. (*Grasser Collection*)

ONE OF SEVERAL BUT STILL THE ONLY ONE: The Luftwaffe fighter force had several Hans Hahn's in its ranks, but only one nicknamed "Assi"— elegantly clad here as one of JG-2's most formidable aces in the Battle of Britain. The jaunty "Assi" was less resplendantly clad during 7 years of Russian prisons. He had 108 confirmed victories including 68 on the Western Front, and was awarded the Oak Leaves. He was not released by the Russians until 1950. He wrote a book, "I Tell the Truth" about his experiences in Russian confinement. (*Hahn Collection*)

FORMIDABLE PAIR: Colonel Josef "Pips" Priller (left) drives home a point with 1st Lieutenant Adolf Glunz, a 71-victory ace under his command in JG-26. Photo was taken on Channel front after Glunz shot down 5 B-17's and a P-38 in two battles on 22 Feb. 1944. Glunz was typical of able but little-known fighter pilots who were backbone of German effort in the air. Glunz flew 574 missions, entered aerial combat 238 times but was never either wounded or shot down himself. 'Addi" Glunz was awarded the Oak Leaves to his Knight's Cross. (*Nowarra Collection*)

LEADER OF THE ABBEVILLE BOYS: Colonel Josef "Pips" Priller describing his 100th and 101st aerial victories. All Priller's victories were on the Channel Coast against RAF and USAAF competition. Priller died of a heart attack in mid-1961. *(Priller Collection)*

STEEP DIVE!!: Another shot of "Pips" Priller, Kommodore of JG-26 "Schlageter," describing the combat which resulted in his 100th aerial victory on the Western Front. The effervescent and ebullient Priller had a personality which endeared everyone who knew him. *(Obermaier Collection)*

FAST FRIENDS: A rare bird who avoids publicity is Colonel Eduard Neumann (right) seen here with Adolf Galland at a fighter pilots' gathering in the nineteen sixties. Edu Neumann is one of the great tutors and Kommodores of the Luftwaffe, most famous for his superb handling of JG-27 in North Africa. Galland and Neumann are close friends. *(Galland Collection)*

DEBRIEFING: Werner Moelders (right) and members of his *schwarm* from JG-51 during debriefing after fighter sweep over England. Photo was taken during Battle of Britain. *(Toliver Collection)*

A GOOD LAUGH: JG-26 pilots on standby in 1941 enjoy a joke while waiting the call to fly against the RAF. *(Eder Collection)*

"HE COULD TEACH YOU TO STAY ALIVE IN THE AIR . . .": Major Hartmann Grasser (right) considered it one of life's privileges to have known and flown with Werner Moelders as his leader and teacher in the air. Grasser stayed alive as Moelders had taught him and ended the war with 103 kills. *(Boehm Collection)*

GERMAN ACE—ENGLISH NAME: This Luftwaffe ace had 14 aerial victories and was in charge of the air defense of Ploesti during the USAAF's 1943 raids. His name is one of WWII's "believe it or nots"—Douglas Pitcairn. As Lt. Colonel Pitcairn, he served after WWII in the new German Air Force. *(Toliver Collection)*

"ABBEVILLE BOY": Major Karl Borris spent the entire war with JG-26 *Schlageter* battling the RAF and USAAF on the Western Front. Borris won the Knight's Cross and had 43 victories against the RAF and USAAF. He was in command of I/JG-26 at war's end. *(Nowarra Collection)*

SECOND PILOT TO HAVE 200 VICTORIES: Lt. Col. Hans Philipp was Kommodore of JG-1 on the Western Front and had 206 aerial victories to his credit when he was shot down and lost his life on October 8th 1943 in combat against 56th "Wolfpack" Group USAAF P-47s. *(Nowarra)*

CAUSE FOR CELEBRATION: When Werner Schröer landed at Wiesbaden Airport after his 100th aerial victory, in February 1944, his men met him with flowers and champagne. At the end of the war, Schröer was Kommodore of JG-3 "Udet." *(Schröer Collection)*

FIGHTER PILOTS worn out by excessive combat were sent to the *Jagdfliegerheim* in Bad Wiessee to recover. Erich Hartmann held his wedding celebration here. As soon as pilots were fit, however, Luftwaffe commanders returned them immediately to combat, keeping them flying until they were killed. (*Toliver Collection*)

MAJOR GEORG-PETER EDER relaxes with squadron mascot between attacks on the American daylight bomber streams. Indestructible Eder was wounded 12 times in winning his 78 aerial victories, and he managed to shoot down no less than 36 of the four-engined giants. He shot down many bombers in final days flying the Me-262, but couldn't confirm the victories due to the Me-262's high speed and tactical difficulties it created in staying with one's formation. (*Eder Collection*)

ONE BLENHEIM DOWN: A Bristol Blenheim ends its operational life on the Libyan desert after being downed by the Luftwaffe in 1941. (*Nowarra Collection*)

AXIS COHORTS: Japanese General O'Shima and entourage visited German night-fighter units during the course of his talks with Hitler and staff. Here he is escorted by Colonel Heinz Nacke who had 12 victories as a dive-bomber pilot prior to becoming a night fighter test pilot. (*Bender Collection*)

NOWOTNY'S WINGMAN: Lt. Karl "Quax" Schnörrer is seen here in historic snapshot taken on Eastern Front when he was Walter Nowotny's wingman in JG-54. Badly wounded in 1943, "Quax" later helped Nowotny test and develop combat tactics for the Me-262. Schnörrer won the Knight's Cross with 46 victories in 536 missions and his victories include 9 kills against 4-engined bombers while flying the Me-262. Shot down over Hamburg on 30 March 1945 in the Me-262, he lost his left leg. (*Nowarra Collection*)

BRIEFING IN RUSSIA: Colonel Herbert Ihlefeld, with 25 victories during the Battle of Britain, briefs his fighter pilots in Russia late in Fall of 1941. Ihlefeld had 7 kills in Spain before WWII and ended the war with a total of 130. (*Boehm Collection*)

LEOPOLD MUNSTER—95 VICTORIES: Known as "Poldi," Münster was awarded the Ritterkreuz on December 21st, 1942 and was soon thereafter promoted to officer rank of Leutnant. He lost his life in a mid-air collision with a B-17 Fortress near Hildesheim on May 8th 1944. *(Bender Collection)*

KOMMODORE OF JG-11: Major Jürgen Harder, from Swinemünde, had 64 aerial victories and was KIA on February 17, 1945. Harder had two brothers who were also fighter pilots and they too were killed in the war. *(Bender Collection)*

DISTINGUISHED SERGEANT PILOT: Sergeant Heinrich Bartels (right) was never commissioned although in a distinguished career with JG-5 and JG-27 he ran up 99 victories—including 42 Western-flown aircraft. Sergeant Bartels had been nominated for the Oak Leaves at the time of his death in aerial combat on 23 December 1944. *(Dölling Collection)*

94-VICTORY ACE, RUDOLF MULLER: Oberfeldwebel Rudi Müller from Frankfurt/Main, was one of the top aces in JG-5. Only the Russians know his fate, and they aren't telling, as he was captured and seen alive in a prison in Murmansk in 1947. "Bubi" Müller's picture was taken at Alakurtti, Finland. *(Obermaier Collection)*

FROZEN FIGHTER PILOT: Lt. Glockner of JG-5 *Eismeer*, which operated in the far north, gets a handshake on his return from a victorious operation before climbing stiffly out of his Me-109. JG-5 pilots are generally recognized to have had the worst harship of any Luftwaffe fighter units in WWII. *(Toliver Collection)*

FROZEN FINLAND: Oberfeldwebel Heinrich Bartels and Dölling pose after daybreak in the White Sea area. 28 Mar. 1943. *(Rasse—Dölling)*

TORRID TRIO IN THE NORTH: (l to r) Heinrich Ehrler (290 victories); Horst Carganico (60) and Rudolf Müller (101). (*Rasse—Dölling*)

FRANZ DÖRR—128 VICTORIES: Captain Dörr became Kommandeur of III/JG-5 in the North and on June 27th, 1944 shot down 12 Soviet aircraft in three sorties. (*Rasse—Dölling*)

WELL-TRAVELED AND 99 VICTORIES: Oberfeldwebel Heinrich Bartels from Linz/Donau got victories on the Channel Coast, in the far North with JG-5, and in the South with JG-27. He loved to dogfight and was known as one of the best of the "stick-and-rudder" pilots. KIA December 23, 1944 over Germany. (*Rasse—Dölling*)

MAKING UP FOR LOST TIME!: After 10 1/2 years in Soviet prisons, 352-victory ace Erich Hartmann wants to make up for the loss of all the happiness he missed in those trying years. His wife, Ursula Paetsch Hartmann is one of the loveliest and most charming of women, the perfect wife for the Blond Knight of Germany. This photo taken by the author 4 December 1967. (*Toliver*)

STEINHOFF AT HOME: 176-victory ace, Lt. Gen. Johannes "Macky" Steinhoff entertains author Toliver in his Wachtberg/Pech home in December 1967. New Luftwaffe was, at first, reluctant to take Steinhoff back into the service because his burns disfigured his face and, as he would become a general officer very soon, there were those who thought his face would be repulsive to the Americans and British. However, Steinhoff's dynamic personality and high intelligence won out and he soon became Inspektor of the Luftwaffe. (*Toliver*)

FAMOUS FIGHTER: This Me-109 on the ready pad in North Africa belongs to the Pick-As or "Ace of Spades" wing, JG-53. While Me-109 is more correctly designated the Bf-109, pilots who flew the machine in the Luftwaffe have always referred to their beloved mounts as the Me-109. (*Nowarra Collection*)

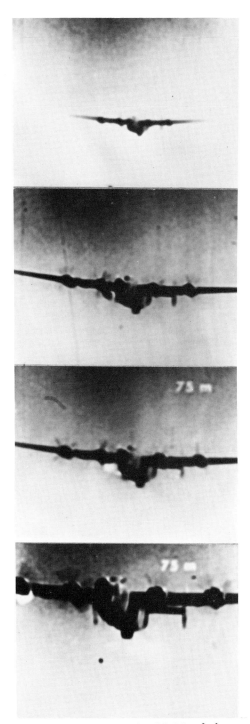

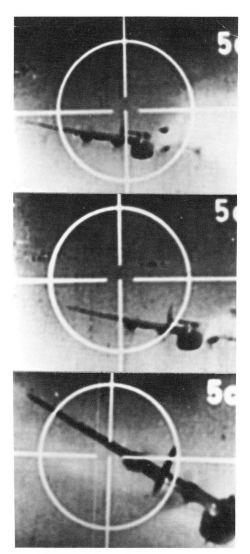

A B-24 "BUYS IT" IN COMBAT: A USAAF B-24 bomber is hit during a pass by a fighter of JG-52 defending the Ploesti oilfields in Rumania. The first two frames of this German gun camera film show hits on #3 and #4 engines of the Liberator. *(Toliver Collection)*

NEAR COLLISION: A JG-52 fighter attacking this USAAF Liberator had a closing speed with the bomber of at least 600 mph. In the top frame the bomber belches smoke from #2 and possibly also #1 engine. The German pilot pulls off his target at the last minute in a near-collision, as witness the bottom photograph in the sequence. *(Toliver Collection)*

NORTH AFRICAN ACE: Franz Stigler was an ace with 28 victories in Edu Neumann's JG-27 in North Africa. Although 28 victories would be considered outstanding in Allied air forces, Stigler was accorded no special distinctions by comparison with such wingmates in JG-27 as Captain Hans-Joachim Marseille with 158 victories. (*Stigler Collection*)

102 WESTERN KILLS: Only a handful of Luftwaffe pilots were able to shoot down over 100 Western-flown aircraft. Major Werner Schroer was one of them. Schroer was one of the top aces of JG-27, with which he spent most of the war. He also downed 26 four-engined heavies in his lifetime score of 114 victories, but had only 12 Eastern Front kills. He was awarded the Swords to his Knight's Cross. (*Toliver Collection*)

STANDBY ROUTINE: Wartime life of fighter pilots oscillates between killing time and frenzied, high-intensity action aloft. Here Sergeant Nocker and a fellow pilot spend their standby time trying to get a ball away from a determined mascot. Fighters can be seen near and in camouflaged hangars in the background. (*Toliver Collection*)

LUFTWAFFE MUSTANG: This captured P-51 of the USAAF, shown shrouded at Brandis in 1943, wears Luftwaffe markings. Germans flew captured Allied fighters of virtually every type, and leading aces of the Luftwaffe flew them in mock combat to discover and explore their combat strengths and weaknesses. Guenther Rall was a high ranking German ace who carried out such evaluations of USAAF and RAF fighters. (*Nowarra Collection*)

14

The Coming of the Jet

"It was as though angels were pushing . . ."
ADOLF GALLAND, describing the Me-262

ADOLF GALLAND was an excited fighter pilot when he stepped down from the Me-262 after his first flight in the new jet-propelled fighter on 22 May 1943. His short test hop from Lechfeld near the Messerschmitt factory at Augsburg remains to this day one of the more memorable experiences of his lifetime. The astonishing speed and climb rate of the jet, and its wide superiority over anything in the world at that time, stood in contrast to the sagging fabric of German air power.

No one was in a better position to appreciate this contrast than Galland. From the time of his succession to the post of General of the Fighters after Moelders' death, he had done his utmost to stem the decline of the German fighter force. Now, the jet fighter offered a real opportunity to restore the situation.

Galland had correctly seen adequate fighter production and pilot training as the hammer and anvil with which German aerial strength could be forged anew. His urgings for action had gone largely unheeded, and he found himself heir to the results of extended and serious derelictions on the part of his superiors. With the jet, all might come right at last.

Galland had not known about the development of the jet fighter until early in 1942. Thereafter, he was kept in the dark concerning its progress until he flew the prototype in May 1943. As General of the Fighters—the officer who would ultimately direct the operations of the new aircraft—he had been given no data on the machine that would have enabled him to include it in his plans and projections for the future.

This in itself exemplifies the intrigue, secrecy, divided loyalties, and mutual mistrust of those who would have to depend ultimately on the fighter pilots of the Luftwaffe for their salvation. Lamentable as this chain of incidents now seems for the Germans, it did have one immediate benefit. The dramatic impact the jet had on Galland was heightened by its earlier quasi-secret development.

The open-cockpit veteran of Spain and Poland, the master tactician and ace of the Battle of Britain stepped not just into the cockpit of a new aircraft, but into a new dimension in aerial warfare. Ten years of technical progress had been compressed into this radical aircraft. The combat advent of the jet fighter could be a decisive blow in the air war. Galland's genius quickly saw the tactical revolution that was within his grasp.

With the Me-262 the Allied bombing could certainly be disrupted, or even made prohibitively expensive to the Allies. Although it was only the spring of 1943, the mounting aerial offensive was of ominous portent for Germany. Unless it was checked, nothing less than physical ruin and total defeat would result. The sleek, propellerless, revolutionary machine was the means by which the bombing offensive might be aborted. No wonder Galland said when asked to describe the Me-262 that it felt like "angels were pushing."

The jet conferred one less measurable but equally important advantage on those who flew it, over and above its technical superiority. The jet pilots would have the decisive edge in morale that is inseparable from possession of a superior weapon. As a fighter pilot, Galland gave due weight to this factor. He understood technical superiority in human terms.

From the moment of his maiden jet flight, Galland's efforts were a central driving force in bringing the jet to operational readiness. Vital and even decisive time had already been wasted in the development of the Me-262, which had come through a rocky history before Galland flew it. These were events in which the General of the Fighters had played no part.

German development of the turbojet for aircraft propulsion had been well in advance of British and American efforts. The Heinkel 178, world's first all-turbojet aircraft, had flown successfully in tests in August 1939. A twin-jet Heinkel fighter, basically a competitive machine with the Me-262, had been test-flown in 1941, so that jet aircraft development was proceeding competitively even at this early date in Germany.

Messerschmitt's Me-262 design was started in 1938. Despite Heinkel's early lead in the field, by 1941 the progress of the Me-262 had outstripped that of the Heinkel twin-jet fighter. The Heinkel organization decided not to further pursue this phase of fighter development, leaving Messerschmitt a clear field.

In the summer of 1941 the Me-262 was test-flown with early-design jet engines. The questionable reliability of these primitive turbojets necessitated the installation of a piston engine in the same test Me-262. The conventional power plant was to guard against destruction of the valuable prototype through engine failure.

The 1941 tests were successful. An elated Willi Messerschmitt reported this substantial progress to both Milch and Udet. The project now ran into really damaging delays. Milch declined to speed up the development of the jet fighter. Udet's flair for development and recognition of the need for new fighters in huge quantities led him to favor pressing forward with the radical aircraft. Unfortunately the old ace was already declining rapidly in influence and prestige, and could not prevail against Milch. The fateful failure to forge ahead with the jet, combined with other pressures, may well have evoked those emotions of despair that led eventually to Udet's suicide. Be that as it may, the Milch decision stood.

Messerschmitt was deeply disappointed; but not a man to be easily put off, he immediately made secret arrangements with BMW and Junkers to continue turbojet development. Power units rather than the airframe were the major problem in bringing the jet fighter to operational status, and as long as engine development continued, Messerschmitt could carry on with his fight for the jet in other ways.

Engine improvements resulting from this *sub rosa* development program were such that by mid-1942 Messerschmitt's brainchild was flown as a pure jet aircraft without any piston emergency motor. Major Rudolf Opitz, the famed test pilot, heard glowing reports about the new fighter from other test pilots. He asked Messerschmitt for permission to fly it.

Messerschmitt agreed. Opitz was deeply impressed by his test hops and conveyed his reactions to Galland. At Messerschmitt's urging,

PROFESSOR DR. WILLY MESSERSCHMITT
(*Messerschmitt A.G.*)

Galland then made his first flight, after which he threw his considerable energies into making the jet fighter operational.

Galland's reports subsequent to his first test flight included the following recommendations:

1. Stop production of the Me-109.
2. Limit single-engined fighter production to the FW-190.
3. Utilize the production capacity thus freed for all-out production of the Me-262.

Galland's enthusiasm and drive infected both Milch and Goering. On 2 June 1943 the decision was made to put the Me-262 into series production. Galland's contention that the aircraft's revolutionary nature justified accelerated development was accepted. The first one hundred machines would serve as practical test craft for subsequent production. They would be "debugged" in combat by selected test commandos.

Hitler killed this proposal. He forbade both mass production and haste. "Nothing will be done with the new fighter until *I* have decided on its merits," he said. He took his time about deciding.

Galland continued to press for the jet, perhaps even beyond the theoretical bounds of his post as General of the Fighter Arm. His importunings and other controversies surrounding the jet finally precipitated Hitler's personal intervention. A new and even more damaging phase in the jet fighter drama now opened.

Contrary to what has been widely believed and frequently written about Hitler's role in the Me-262 affair, he did not begin immediately and strongly with the idea of a "Blitz Bomber." On 2 November 1943 he sent Goering to Messerschmitt's factory at Augsburg to broach the question of bomb clips for the new fighter. The Fuehrer's expectations and demands at this time were extremely modest, and perhaps quite reasonable. He asked only that provision be made for the Me-262 to carry two 154-pound bombs.

Messerschmitt had made no provision at all for bomb clips on the Me-262. When pressed for an answer by Goering, he resorted to obfuscation, and made the impetuous statement that the jet could carry either one 1100-pound bomb, or two 550-pound bombs without difficulty. This statement later had serious repercussions.

By August 1943 the fighter production program as a whole was getting something like the attention it deserved. Milch announced a production goal of four thousand fighters per month. By 1944 it was estimated that this production drive would boost the supply of fighter planes to the level Galland had insisted was necessary to meet the Allied air offensive.

The young General of the Fighter Arm seized this encouraging forecast as an opportunity to again urge mass production of the Me-262. He requested that one of each four fighters produced be jets. His opinion was that one thousand Me-262s were worth at least three thousand conventional fighters. History confirms the general accuracy of this judgment, although the sampling is rather small.

Milch recoiled from this bold proposal. The Fuehrer had ordered caution, he said, and he (Milch) intended to be cautious, even though he personally and privately agreed with Galland. The reaction of Field Marshal Milch exemplified, even as it reinforced, the Technical Office climate of hesitancy and irresolution. Action on the jet was again paralyzed.

Although suspicious because no drawings or designs for the bomb clip installations were available, Goering was satisfied for the moment by Messerschmitt's undertaking concerning the bombs. He would be able to report the kind of thing the Fuehrer liked to hear. The new aircraft could carry over three times the bomb load Hitler had requested.

A special technical commission was set up early in November to oversee the development of the jet. Headed by Colonel Edgar Petersen, of the Luftwaffe Proving Grounds, Rechlin, the commission included Messerschmitt himself, famed engine-builder Franz Jumo, and a coterie of distinguished engineers both military and civilian. Still nothing was done about the provision of bomb clips.

The following month, Hitler was again communicating his urgent need for Me-262s as fighter-bombers, and urging all speed in production of the new aircraft. Hitler's Luftwaffe aide, in a telegram to Goering, formalized the Fuehrer's wishes. The German dictator would regard as "tantamount to irresponsible negligence" any further delays in the jet fighter-bomber program.

The tensions developing in the Me-262 program through its development solely as a fighter while Hitler was assuming it would be a fighter-bomber came to a head in December 1943. The Me-262 was demonstrated at Insterburg in East Prussia to Hitler and his entourage. Galland tells the story in his book, *The First and the Last*.[1]

"Hitler had come over from his nearby headquarters. The jet fighter Me-262 caused a special sensation. I was standing right beside him when he suddenly asked Goering, 'Can this aircraft carry bombs?'

"Goering had already discussed the question with Messerschmitt and replied, 'Yes, my Fuehrer, theoretically yes. There is enough power to spare to carry one thousand pounds, perhaps even two thousand pounds.'"

As Galland emphasizes in his book, this was a carefully formulated answer which from a purely technical viewpoint could not be disputed. A multitude of technical factors nevertheless militated against making the machine into a bomber, but these could not be explained on the spot to Hitler, or any other layman. Nobody got any chance to explain. The lure of "perhaps even two thousand pounds" of bombs had already fired Hitler's imagination. Again quoting Galland's account of the affair:

[1] *The First and the Last* by Adolf Galland, p. 337.

OLD FIGHTER FOES MEET IN PEACE: Lt. General Adolf Galland, left, has become a globe-trotting businessman in peacetime. A visit to Auckland, New Zealand led to this March 1967 reunion with Air Marshal Sir Keith Park, who faced Galland's JG-26 across the English Channel in 1940 as C.O. #1 Fighter Group RAF with HQ at Uxbridge. Galland went on from the Battle of Britain to command the Luftwaffe Day Fighters, and Sir Keith Park became A.O.C. Malta during critical fighter battles that largely determined control of the Mediterranean. *(Toliver Collection)*

"He [Hitler] said, 'For years I have demanded from the Luftwaffe a "speed bomber"[2] which can reach its target in spite of enemy fighter defense. In the aircraft you present to me as a fighter plane, I see the "Blitz Bomber," with which I will repel the invasion in its first and weakest phase.

"'Regardless of the enemy's air umbrella it will strike the recently landed mass of material and troops creating panic, death, and destruction. *At last this is the Blitz Bomber!* Of course, none of you thought of that!'"

Thus was born the Blitz Bomber. Hitler assumed that from this time forward his Blitz Bomber was in preparation. He told Milch in January 1944 of the growing need for jet bombers. Nothing was done nevertheless to modify the design in any way. Work proceeded apace on the fighter version exclusively.

When Hitler learned at a conference in April 1944 with Milch, Goering, and Chief of the Fighter Staff Saur that not even bomb clips had yet been installed on the Me-262, his fury was unbounded. He literally foamed with rage. At the top of his voice he shouted, "Not a single one of my orders has been obeyed." Thenceforth the Fuehrer put his foot down, and he put it down on the Me-262 fighter.

Jet production was to be limited strictly to the bomber. Reference to the machine as anything other than a bomber was forbidden. Fighter activity was to be confined to testing, and there would be no production of fighter versions until all tests were completed and evaluated. The final decision would be made by the Fuehrer.

A steady procession of distinguished personalities, including the Luftwaffe Chief of General Staff General Kreipe, Armaments Minister

[2] Transcripts of Hitler's private conversations verify that he did press for such a speed bomber earlier in the war.

Albert Speer and Adolf Galland among others, sought to have Hitler reverse his disastrous decision. Despite the unanimity of these responsible men, their efforts wrung but one concession from the doomed Fuehrer. Every twentieth Me-262 could be produced as a fighter.

Hitler's permission for full production of the fighter version was withheld until 4 November 1944. The Third Reich was at its eleventh hour. The devastation of the cities and the suffering of the German people had become appalling. Amid this carnage and ruin all efforts to make the Me-262 into a bomber had failed. Hitler's April decision to forbid Me-262 fighter production, taken in vengeful rancor, had denied the Luftwaffe its best possibility for retaliation.

By the end of 1944 some 564 Me-262 fighters had been produced, and in the ensuing three months a further 740 came off the assembly lines. The effort was too late. Allied fighters were sweeping every day into the remotest corners of the crumbling Reich. Just getting the Me-262 into the air from battered and continually harassed airfields was a major undertaking. Many jets were destroyed on the ground or outside assembly plants while awaiting delivery to fighter units.

Tribute should be paid here to the important contribution to the jet program made by Colonel Gordon M. Gollob. The least-known of Germany's fighter ace winners of the Diamonds, he was far from the least in other respects. Austrian-born Gollob was the first German ace to reach 150 victories, a feat as remarkable in its time as was Moelders' conquest of the first century in combat downings. When Gollob scored his 150th victory he was not only the top-scoring ace in the Luftwaffe, but also a leader of quality and renown.

Trained long before the war, and of the same generation as Galland and Moelders, Gordon Gollob was a Destroyer fighter pilot in 1939 with Joachim Hueth's ZG-76. He flew in Poland with this unit, and in the Battle of Britain with JG-3, rising to command II/JG-3 in July 1941 on the Russian Front.

Temporary assignment to the Rechlin test center in early 1942 revealed Gollob's talent for developmental work in fighter aviation. Although he returned later to the Eastern Front as *Kommodore* of JG-77 for a highly successful tour, he was clearly fitted for heavier responsibilities. He became Fighter Leader on the Western Front in October 1942, and in April 1944 became a member of the fighter staff set up under Saur's leadership within the Ministry of Armaments.

On the operational side of these modern fighter projects, Gollob's qualities and skills made substantial contributions to progress. He worked not only in the development of the Me-262, but also with the Me-163 Komet and the He-162. Gollob's responsibilities in this period removed him from fighter combat, although he led the special fighter staff for the Battle of the Bulge, when Hitler hurled the hard-won fighter reserves into close support of the Army with heavy losses.

When Galland was dismissed as General of the Fighter Arm at the end of January 1945, Gollob was his replacement. Gollob survived the

GALLAND'S REPLACEMENT: Colonel Gordon Gollob, seen here getting a handshake from Adolf Hitler, was appointed General of the Day Fighters when Germany's political leaders decided to dismiss Galland in 1944. Gollob had 150 aerial victories, and made outstanding contributions to German aircraft development. Expectations that he would be able to do what Galland considered unfeasible were not realized. Gollob was awarded the Diamonds to his Knight's Cross. (*D. Carlson Collection*)

war. He flew 340 missions in gaining his 150 victories, which include six Western-flown aircraft. He is another who is accorded a much higher place in the fighter pilot hierarchy than his victory tally would suggest. He was one of only nine fighter pilots to win the Diamonds. Gordon Gollob may be fairly characterized as the Oswald Boelcke of the Luftwaffe, and his contributions to superior aircraft and armament were considerable.

Long before the Blitz Bomber fiasco, Galland formed two test commandos of experienced fighter pilots. These tests were in action against daylight reconnaissance Mosquitos of the RAF. The British machines flew unescorted and were therefore ideal for tactical experimentation. The Mosquito had ranged with impunity in daylight

GENERAL OF THE DAY FIGHTERS: Gordon Gollob was elected to replace Adolf Galland as General of the Day Fighters in 1944. With 150 victories, Gollob combined front line experience with a flair for technical development and command. He did a highly creditable job in an impossible situation. (*Boehm Collection*)

up to this time, and the Me-262 was an unpleasant surprise to Mosquito crews.

The first startled Britons to encounter the Me-262 were Flight Lieutenant A. E. Wall and his observer, Pilot Officer A. S. Lobban, the crew of a Mosquito making a daylight photo reconnaissance of Munich on 25 July 1944. The jet quickly overhauled and shot at the speedy Mosquito, which only avoided downing by escaping into a fortuitous bank of clouds. The British aircraft later made a forced landing in Italy.

Many more Mosquitos were attacked and shot down by the speedy jets, which were able to climb and intercept the fast British aircraft. These kills against the hated British bird were conclusive operational proof that the Me-262 was superior to anything in the air. Goering's authority was rapidly draining away by October 1944, but in a last-ditch display of independence for which SS Chief Heinrich Himmler's backing was necessary, he ordered Galland to form the test commandos into a jet fighter wing.

This jet fighter wing, which was later designated JG-7, was to be sent into action in the West against the bomber streams. Hitler's obstructionism had been softened by the increasing availability of the 425-mph Arado-234B jet bomber. For each of these bombers delivered, Hitler released one Me-262 for service as a fighter.

Major Walter Nowotny was entrusted with the formation of the first test commandos, around which JG-7 was later built. He was selected for this critical test assignment because he was one of the Luftwaffe's

258-VICTORY ACE, WALTER NOWOTNY AND PROF. KURT TANK: Major Walter Nowotny pilots an experimental night-fighter from the co-pilot's seat as designer Prof. Kurt Tank sits in the pilot's seat. Nowotny was the first fighter pilot to shoot down 250 enemy airplanes (the 250th on Oct. 14 th, 1943) "Nowi" was killed in action near Achmer on November 8th, 1944 in an Me-262 jet. (*Galland Collection*)

finest young leaders and aces. His assignment to *Kommando Nowotny*, as it became known, crowned a brilliant career.

Walter Nowotny was born in Gmuend, Austria, on 7 December 1920. Adolf Galland firmly believes that the Austrian temperament produces superior fighter pilots, and he quotes Nowotny to this day as an example. Socially gay, professionally serious, intelligent, resourceful, and quick, he was a natural leader and one of the most popular aces in the Luftwaffe.

His career reached brilliance before his 1944 death, but he was a relatively slow starter. Joining the Luftwaffe a month after the outbreak of war and two months prior to his nineteenth birthday, he received a full-length, peacetime type fighter pilot's training despite the war. His training culminated with attendance at the Fighter Pilots' School at Schwechat, near Vienna.

Assigned to JG-54 in February 1941, he flew more than five months on operations before scoring a kill. When he finally opened his account on 19 July 1941 with three victories over Oesel Island, this tyro's triumph set the pattern for his numerous future days of multiple kills. His first victorious day ended wetly. He was shot down in the Baltic and spent three days and nights paddling back to land.

He continued scoring slowly on the Russian Front, and needed more than a year to reach fifty victories. His leadership was already evident, however, and on 25 October 1942 he was given command of No. 9 Squadron of JG-54. He was only twenty-one.

In June 1943 the Nowotny lightning began striking with increasing frequency. In that one month he ran up forty-one kills. In August he was credited with a further forty-nine victories, and he had climbed from obscurity to a place among the top twenty aces of the Luftwaffe. He ranked sixteenth at the time of his 150th victory on 18 August 1943.

"Nowi's" star continued to rise. Forty-five kills in September 1943 put him past the two-hundred-victory mark. He was the fourth German ace to reach this figure. His zenith had still to come. In October 1943 in a ten-day period he sent thirty-two Russian foes crashing to earth, and on 14 October 1943 he was the top-scoring ace of the Luftwaffe with 250 victories. First pilot to reach this stunning total, "Nowi" at least twice scored ten kills in one day.

He reached 250 victories on "only" 442 missions, an achievement which is probably unequalled. Awarded the Diamonds to his Knight's Cross on 19 October 1943, he was the eighth soldier of the armed forces to receive the rare award. He was the fifth of only nine fighter pilots to be so honored.

Nowotny's meteoric Russian Front career was over by mid-November 1943. Not yet twenty-four but already a *Gruppenkommandeur*, he was obviously qualified for the responsibilities of a Wing Commander—testimony to the professional seriousness on which all his contemporaries have remarked.

"Nowi" had added much glory to the laurels of JG-54. The *Schwarm*

he commanded in combat in the 1942–43 period was at one time credited with almost five hundred kills. The pilots of this elite formation were Second Lieutenant Karl "Quax" Schnorrer, "Nowi's" wingman with thirty-five Russian Front kills and nine later in the West; Second Lieutenant Anton Doebele, with ninety-four Eastern Front victories; and Second Lieutenant Rudolf Rademacher, ninety Russian Front victories plus thirty-six kills subsequently in the West. Schnorrer and Rademacher both survived the war—Schnorrer minus a leg. Unfortunately Rademacher was killed in 1953 in a glider crash.

Nowotny's gifts included a marked talent for instructing new pilots. He had contributed to the careful training of Otto "Bruno" Kittel's shooting eye in JG-54, and Kittel went on to score 267 kills in Russia before his death. "Nowi" helped numerous other pilots, and the success of his own *Schwarm* is now history.

"Nowi" was made *Kommodore* of Training Wing 101 in France when he left Russia with 255 victories. The assignment was intended to give scope to his talents as a tutor. He held this training post for five months, and in July 1944 began forming *Kommando Nowotny* for tactical testing of the Me-262. Operating out of Achmer with this unit he scored an additional three Western Front victories before his death.

In his position as General of the Fighter Arm, Adolf Galland saw his country's best pilots and leaders at first hand. His warm admiration for Nowotny has not been dimmed by the years:

"He was the best young man Germany had. He was an excellent fighter pilot, who was qualified well for higher command. He had a certain similarity to Marseille, except that he was more mature, more serious and better educated. Although only twenty-four he was qualified as a Wing Commander. The night before he died I talked with him for many hours. I was pleased to talk to him, and for me in those days that was unusual. I think he was an extraordinarily good man in every sense of the term.

"If he had been given the opportunity to live to the end of the war, I am certain he would be known not only for his big victory record, but also because of his qualifications as an officer, Wing Commander, and man."

The morning following his long talk with Galland, Nowotny took off with his Me-262 squadron to intercept a formation of American heavies. The actual cause of his demise will never be known. Engine failure either as a mechanical factor or as the result of hits brought Nowotny's Me-262 within reach of the Mustang escort.

First Lieutenant Hans Dortenmann[3] was in command of No. 12 Squadron of JG-54, ready nearby for takeoff to assist Nowotny with piston-powered fighters. In a letter to the late historian Hans-Otto Boehm Dortenmann writes:

"Several times I requested permission by radio to take off. I always got the order back from Nowotny to wait. The last words of Nowi were: '...just made the third kill...left jet engine fails...been attacked again ...been hit...'"

Garbled additional communications from Nowotny followed. Flak guns protecting Achmer airfield added to the din and confusion. Knowing that Nowotny would try to nurse his jet fighter back to the field, Galland and his companions, who included Generaloberst Keller, stepped out of the operations room to watch for the returning Nowi.

[3] First Lieutenant Hans Dortenmann. Born 1921. Thirty-eight victories in World War II, including twenty-two on the Western Front. Awarded the Knight's Cross 20 April 1945.

DISCUSSING HISTORY: The later German air historian Hans-Otto Boehm (right) played major role in establishing peacetime contacts between former fighter pilots of warring powers. Here Boehm listens to war and prison experiences of American ace Walker "Bud" Mahurin in Augsburg, Germany in May 1961. Under auspices of German Fighter Pilots Association, which Boehm managed, American Fighter Aces Association made happy and successful visit to Germany to meet their former aerial foes. (Giuliano—USAF)

From above the clouds and overlaying the insistent bark of the flak, the anxious watchers heard the characteristic hammering of 30mm cannons and the roar of machine guns. There was an air battle nearby— undoubtedly Nowotny fighting for his life. With one engine out, his jet would be no match for a covey of Mustangs.

Bursting through the cloud cover, Nowotny's Me-262 came hurtling vertically downward in its death dive. The shrill whistling of the stricken machine ended abruptly in a thunderous roar as it hit the earth at 500 mph. A black pall of smoke climbing slowly into the morning marked the funeral pyre of Major Walter Nowotny. In the wreckage they found one of his hands and a piece of his Diamonds decoration. He had died the classic death of the air hero.

Highly experienced pilots and a well-developed tactical sense were essential for success and survival in combat with the Me-262. Ascendancy was not automatically conferred on the pilot by the jet. Failure to properly apply the performance advantages of the Me-262 over piston-driven aircraft could easily nullify those advantages. Even for the best pilots, combat operation of the jet fighter was not easy.

The Me-262 enjoyed a decisive speed advantage, but the new propulsion method conferring the advantage made new tactics essential. Habits and practices born of generations of piston-powered aircraft had now to be set aside. Dogfighting was out. The large curving radius of the Me-262 meant that any Allied fighter could turn inside it. With high speed came slow acceleration, an innate disadvantage of early jet propulsion due to the design of the primitive turbojets. The throttles had to be opened slowly and with extreme care, or compressor stalls, engine failure, or burnt-out turbines would result.[4]

The high speed of the Me-262 meant reduced maneuverability. This in turn, combined with other factors, made the well-tested *Schwarm* formation of two *Rotten* impractical with jet fighters. The *Schwarm* was hard to keep together. Me-109s and FW-190s kept formation in turns with ease, by appropriate minor adjustment of the throttle by the individual pilots.

In formation with the Me-262, because of the sensitivity of the turbojets to throttle changes, the Germans soon learned to leave them alone. They made formation turns instead by overshooting or cutting inside. Precision formation flying was no longer possible, and was further handicapped by the poor downward visibility from the Me-262. The two large turbojet engines and the unusual width of the lower fuselage obstructed much of the pilot's downward vision.

Accentuating these deficiencies, the short endurance of the jet fighter made rapid assembly after takeoff essential to successful combat operations. In operational service it was found that most fighter runways suitable for jets would accommodate three Me-262s for simultaneous

---

[4] The Luftwaffe very carefully selected the pilots for the Me-262. Experienced wing, group, and squadron commanders, talented flight leaders, and a sprinkling of the most aggressive and promising youngsters were chosen and trained. It was an excellent program.

takeoff, but not four. Once airborne, the jets needed no top cover, so that the mutually protective functions of the *Schwarm* formation were not now essential.

These factors served to oust the *Schwarm* formation from most jet operations. The *Kette* of three aircraft came back into vogue, and proved highly suitable against the bombers. Attacks were usually made in *Staffel* strength, i.e., three *Ketten*. With about three hundred yards between each *Kette* and about 150 yards between the machines in each individual *Kette*, formation turns became more feasible.

In practice, the two rearmost aircraft in turns would pass below the lead aircraft, thus obviating the poor downward visibility and permitting the pilots to keep sight of the machines in their own *Kette* during maneuvers. The arrangement proved a satisfactory substitute for the *Schwarm*.

Attacks against the bomber streams were mounted in *Staffel* strength. Where concentration of several *Staffeln* could be achieved, strikes were made on the bomber streams in successive, *Staffel*-strength waves. With their vast speed advantage and diminished maneuverability, the jets belonged to a new epoch in aerial warfare. Fitting them into the existing dimension was a challenging task. Nowhere was this more evident than in the problem of initiating attacks on the bomber boxes.

From dead ahead, which Georg Eder, Egon Mayer, and other giant-

U.S. ACES ACCEPTING INSIGNIA: American Fighter Aces Association accepted this star and shield emblem as their official insignia and three of America's finest did the honors for the Association. They are from left: the late Eugene A. Valencia of the U.S. Navy with 23 aerial victories; James L. Brooks of the Air Force with 13 victories; and Joseph J. Foss of the U.S. Marines with 26 victories. (*Toliver Collection*)

killers had found a profitable avenue of attack against the heavies, the rate of closure with the Me-262 was about 800 mph. This meant minimum shooting time—not enough to fully exploit the heavy armament of the Me-262. Finding the bombers was no longer a problem. Closing with them and making a telling attack taxed the judgment and experience of Germany's best aces. Even Colonel Guenther Luetzow, distinguished ace and successful tactician, became morose over his seeming inability to correctly initiate strikes against the bombers in the jet. He scored but two kills in the Me-262 to add to his 101 victories in propeller-driven aircraft.

The stern attack proved the most destructive way of attacking a bomber box. From about five miles astern of a bomber formation, with an altitude advantage of five to six thousand feet, the *Staffel* of jets would dive fifteen hundred feet below and fifteen hundred yards astern of the bomber formation. Pulling up into level flight for the final approach, speed would reach 520–540 mph, thus evading the escort fighters.

Successive *Ketten* of jets would then sweep through the bomber stream from stern to leader, the 150-yard separation between the fighters helping divide the defensive fire. With their four 30mm cannons, the jets would rake the bombers with a lethal hail of fire, the rearmost bombers getting the brunt of the action.

Passing tightly against the uppermost bombers in the formation, the jets would pull away in a flat climb, easily outdistancing the fighter escort. The jets could then curve around and repeat their attack. If ammunition or fuel was low, they could make off in a shallow dive back to their base, immune from fighter pursuit.

If there were additional bomber boxes ahead, the jets could easily overhaul them, climbing to the point of vantage behind the bombers and driving home yet another stern-to-leader attack on the whole formation. The great speed with which these attacks were delivered frequently resulted in wide dispersal of the jets in each *Kette*. Reassembly in the classical fashion was not bothered with in most operations, since the individual jets were not as vulnerable to fighter attack as lone FW-190s or Me-109s.

BENT STUKA: What the Russians couldn't do to this tank-busting Stuka of Hans-Ulrich Ruedel's SG-2 *Immelmann*, the plane's own pilot did at Kitzingen, Germany by deliberately ground-looping. Idea was to make the aircraft unusable by the Americans. As the photograph shows, Stuka was "bent" beyond repair. (*Toliver Collection*)

PILOT, PLANE AND GIRL SURRENDER: The pilot of this SG-2 *Immelmann* Stuka had a girl in the dive-bomber's baggage compartment when he flew into Kitzingen to surrender on 10 May 1945. Other pilots of Hans-Ulrich Ruedel's crack tank-busting unit landed gear-up to wreck their surrendered aircraft, but this one came in and safely landed with his lady. *(J. Jackson Collection)*

Limited fuel endurance haunted the Me-262 pilots, and made it important not to waste time observing *traditional* tactics that had only limited application in the new era. The tremendous, devastating punch of four 30mm cannons, and later, the batteries of 5cm rockets fitted to the jets gave the pilots far greater hitting power than they had wielded before. Me-109s, FW-190s, and Me-110s had carried rockets and pods earlier in the war and found them effective against unescorted bomber streams. When the fighters began escorting bombers "all the way," the degradation of German fighter performance inflicted by the rocket pods led to their abandonment until the advent of the jet.

The feeling of superiority and confidence that the Me-262 gave its pilots caused their morale to zoom. The escort fighters, which fell fiercely and in hordes on any Me-109 or FW-190 in sight, could not shake the morale of the man flying the Me-262. Furthermore, the defensive fire from the bombers, while still formidable, was by no means the hazard it was to the pilots of piston-powered German fighters.

Battling Allied fighters, the Me-262 was superior in climb, speed, and firing power to anything sent against it. The jet pilot had to avoid dogfighting, of course. Superior altitude and surprise—the classical primary advantages of aerial combat—usually lay with the jet pilot. He could accept or refuse combat as he chose.

The Me-262 pilot could not only outclimb aggressive Mustangs, but also continue the pursuit of any bomber box in the area while outclimbing the Allied fighters. Me-262s could and often did bounce Allied fighter formations, but they were careful to curve through no more than about half a turn before climbing away. The four 30mm cannons of the jet were designed to hack down the big heavies. Against fighters, 30mm hits were devastating, but the loss of an Allied fighter was much less important than the loss of a bomber, so the Germans saved most of their big shells for the heavies.

The Me-262 pilots did not do all the bouncing. They were themselves sometimes bounced by Allied fighters, particularly when they flew at low altitude looking for the bomber formations silhouetted against high cloud. The Germans could climb and attack the bombers from beneath in the Me-262—a tactic of which the hard-pressed pilots of propeller-driven fighters could only dream.

Allied fighter escorts at these times often were able to bounce the Me-262s from above, their best opportunity for a jet kill unless they happened upon a damaged jet. Scoring a kill over the Me-262 was

PRECIOUS CARGO: Pilot's girlfriend smiles out at ground personnel from baggage compartment of Stuka dive-bomber surrendered to the Americans at Kitzingen on 10 May 1945. *(Toliver Collection)*

one of the most avidly sought honors among Allied fighter pilots.[5]

If the Me-262s were bounced and surprised, so that turning into the attack became impossible, a shallow dive quickly put the Allied fighters far astern. The jets could widen the distance suitably, then turn and attack their pursuers. In the rare cases where jets were surprised from the rear at the same altitude, they could simply accelerate and climb away from their attackers.

The Me-262 was thus a new weapon of multiple virtues. Superbly effective against the bomber streams, its heavy armament, new tactics, and relative immunity to Allied fighters did great physical and morale damage to the enemy. With appropriate tactics, the jet was able to wreak havoc with the previously much-feared fighter escort, thereby exposing the bombers to attack by German propeller-driven fighters. Crowning its virtues, the Me-262 restored and fortified German pilot morale and depressed that of the enemy.

The success of the Me-262 fighter is evident in the victories confirmed to some of the German pilots who became jet aces:

Name	*Jet Kills*	*Kills in Propeller-Driven A/C*
1. Baer, Heinz	16	204
2. Schall, Franz	14	123
3. Buchner, Hermann	12	46
4. Eder, Georg-Peter	12	66
5. Rudorffer, Erich	12	210
6. Schnorrer, Karl	11	35

At least forty-three German pilots scored kills with the Me-262, and there were twenty-two who became jet aces by downing five or more enemy aircraft while flying the jet. Records of the period are necessarily incomplete, since the war ended before many victories were officially confirmed.

[5] In the last ten months of the war, 8th U.S. Air Force pilots claimed 1233 encounters with the Me-262 or other jet and rocket-powered German aircraft. They claimed 146 kills, 11 probables, and 150 damaged aircraft. The 8th Air Force admitted the loss of 10 fighters and 52 bombers to the jets.

AMERICA'S TOP JET ACES: Although the Luftwaffe was using jet fighters and fighter-bombers the last year of WWII, the Allies did not have any jets ready for combat. First jets in combat flown by Americans came during the Korean War. Shown here are the two top American jet aces of the Korean War, Major James Jabara (15 kills) and Captain Joseph McConnell, Jr. (16 victories). *(USAF)*

The foregoing summary of jet tactics has emphasized the positive aspects of jet operations. In actual practice, the German jet pilots had their share of problems. The Jumo-004 engines were underpowered and acceleration for takeoff was long and hazardous. Landing the aircraft was also fraught with danger.

If a pilot came in and was undershooting or overshooting the landing field, necessitating a go-around for another approach, he was in trouble if he had not thoroughly planned his actions. After advancing the throttle very slowly to prevent over temperatures in the hot section of the engine and in the tailpipe, as well as preventing compressor stalls, the pilot had to wait an agonizing fourteen to twenty-five seconds for the engine to generate full power. At a speed of 110–135 mph a lot of ground was being covered at very low altitude. The lowered landing gear further decreased the speed, and heightened the general aerodynamic drag of the airplane.

This meant that the full stall point of the airplane was approaching rapidly while the engine was going through the throes of accelerating. It was a mighty touchy position to be in. Numerous crashes resulted. The United States faced the same problem during the late 1940s and early 1950s and a number of pilots lost their lives in this maneuver.

As the war progressed, the Me-262 pilots faced other problems. Short endurance forced them to return to base and land. Allied fighters would follow them home and shoot them up in the traffic pattern. As a counter, the Luftwaffe assigned FW-190 and Me-109 units to standing patrols—covering the landings of the Me-262s.

When the jets came racing home, the Mustangs and Thunderbolts were usually hot after them, five to twenty-five miles behind. The German propeller-driven fighters would charge into the pack. This rear guard action was usually a sufficient diversion to make the Allied pilots forget the jets, and the precious Me-262s would be safely recovered. But on occasion, a determined Allied pilot would bore straight on through and score a kill over a jet in the traffic pattern.

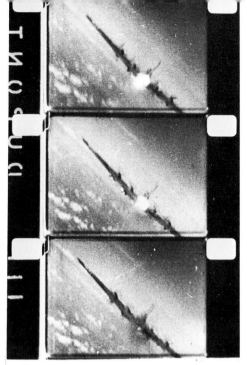

BEGINNING OF THE END OF A FORTRESS: Boeing B-17 takes hits from an Me-262 jet fighter over München. Entire crew bailed out safely, were captured and interrogated at Oberursel where German Luftwaffe maintained their Intelligence and Evaluation Center *(Auswertestelle West)*. *(Boehm Collection)*

The Me-262 was the most effective jet aircraft in Germany's armory, but the Me-163 *Komet* was perhaps even more dramatic since it was rocket-powered—the first such fighter plane in history to become operational.

The Me-163 had its origin before the war, in the activities of the German Research Institute for Sailplanes. Developed from a basic design by Professor Alexander Lippisch, the rocket fighter was pursued under Messerschmitt factory auspices from early 1939 onward.

The actual evolution of this machine has been well described elsewhere, notably in William Green's *Famous Fighters of the Second World War*.[6] The road to operational status for this aircraft was rough, fraught with danger, and demanded outstanding courage on the part

"HEY! QUIT SHOOTING! I'M YOUR BUDDY!!": Allies so dominated the sky over Germany that it was a bigger job to avoid a collision with a friend and more difficult to avoid shooting down one of your own than it was to score a victory if the Luftwaffe could be found. Here, in gun-camera film taken from USAAF Lt. Col. Everett W. Stewart's plane, it is obvious that Stewart almost shot down his buddy Lt. John B. Coleman who got in between Stewart and an Me-110. *(USAF)*

[6] Doubleday & Co., Garden City, N.Y., 1957. Illustrations by G. W. Hermann.

of test pilots. Notable contributions were made to the Me-163 story by Heini Ditmar, Wolfgang Spaete, Rudolf Opitz, Hanna Reitsch, and other test pilots.

The hazards of test piloting in the Me-163 included all the normal difficulties of new aircraft, plus a bundle of completely new problems stemming from rocket propulsion. The fuel was capable of literally blowing the aircraft to bits and more than one test pilot was reduced to jelly by flaming "T-Stoff," as it was called. Testing the *Komet* was no task for the fainthearted.

The career of Rudolph "Pitz" Opitz was typical of these dauntless pioneer rocket pilots. A test pilot before the war with DFS Darmstadt, Opitz was assigned by Udet to Peenemunde in mid-1941. In partnership with Heini Ditmar he did much of the early test work on the Me-163A, which was a pure research aircraft.

The Me-163B followed as a design intended ultimately for combat. The prototype was built in Augsburg in the winter of 1941–42 and flight testing of the airframe started in the spring of 1942 minus engines. The Walther, Kiel, and BMW firms were developing the rocket motors, but delivery of the radical power plants was not expected before fall 1942. Airframe tests were pressed forward independently, with the airframe towed to high altitude to test flight characteristics.

Opitz recounts some of the problems:

"There were numerous questions to be answered to preclude setbacks when this radical new aircraft was scheduled for production. For example, parachutes for flying personnel were to be used only to speeds of 300 mph. The Me-163 was designed for more than twice this speed. Accordingly, the installation of a drag chute was suggested. In case of danger, the drag chute could slow the plane from 600 to about 275 mph for safe bailout.

"The first of these flights really stayed in my memory. The assignment: Towing to fifteen thousand feet, engagement of the drag chute at a certain speed, and measurement of the decelerating force; then blasting the drag chute away with a charge and landing. Completely harmless sort of thing, one would think.

"The chute opened according to schedule. But as I activated the firing mechanism of the ejection explosive, the expected bang didn't occur. The emergency activator, working on a completely separate circuit, also failed to fire the explosive. I could now bail out, or try to land with the opened but not ejected drag chute. That was the choice. the chance of *jumping into* the drag chute when abandoning the aircraft seemed high. Besides, it would be almost impossible to ascertain the cause of the failure if the aircraft were destroyed. I decided to try and land with the chute.

"I went into a steep dive from six thousand feet in order to have enough speed for the critical landing attempt. The landing was smooth, although a few hundred yards from the strip in a beet field."

Later, when the Walther engines were installed, a new series of hazards had to be faced. Again, Opitz tells the story:

"In the fall of 1942, we received the Walther engine for flight testing. In a series of run-ups in the aircraft, which was firmly anchored to the ground, I became familiar with the engine. Then came the first takeoff. Successful, but not without incident. During takeoff and shortly before reaching flying speed, the ejectable landing gear broke. Shortly before reaching the end of the strip, I was able to get the aircraft airborne despite a skidding curve. The engine ran excellently. I went into a steep climb, when suddenly the cabin filled with T-Stoff smoke. Cabin roof, goggles, instruments all became milky white. My eyes burned damnably.

"After about two minutes, the limited supply of fuel which was put aboard for this first flight was consumed. The engine was running at top speed, and quit when the fuel ran out. I went into a glide and made a smooth landing. My mastery of the situation was probably due to having flown the airframe so much without the engine that my experience with its flight characteristics retrieved a precarious situation."

Opitz was knocked about physically in his testing of the Me-163. He took a worse beating than many aces who flew hundreds of combat missions, and like all *Komet* test pilots he could say that The Grim Reaper was his co-pilot.

In making a ferry trip in a *Komet* from Peenemunde to Anklam, the landing skids on his rocket plane failed when he set the little ship down. "Pitz" jarred himself badly, dislocated two vertebrae and tore ligaments in his back. Physicists later calculated that such rough landings as crippled Opitz and others exerted momentarily forces of more than 20 G's. A torsion-sprung pilot seat had to be developed to bridge these 15–30G jolts, which could easily injure or even kill the pilot in an emergency landing.

"Pitz" never abandoned an Me-163 in flight. He rode them all down, despite difficult and unforeseen situations. His last flight was one in which he probably would have been better off to bail out. Near the end of the war he was given command of a group in JG-400. On 7 May 1945 his unit had withdrawn to an airfield in north Germany, and one of the few remaining *Komets* had to be test-flown before it was ready for operations.

Opitz reached six thousand feet on the test hop when ground personnel saw the machine belch smoke and come circling back down in an erratic glide. The aircraft did not return to the field, but disappeared behind some distant trees. A thunderous roar and a pillar of smoke marked the end of the *Komet*.

The fire truck and crash crew went roaring off to the scene of the crash, closely followed by an ambulance, a crane truck, and other vehicles loaded with rescue gear. They expected to pick Pitz up with a spoon. Reaching the scene, the crash crew saw their worst fears realized.

The Me-163 was a blanched pile of smoking metal, flames clawed at

TOO LATE CAME THE AMERICAN JET: While the Germans were slow in getting their Me-262 jets into combat, the Allies were even slower. Lockheed developed the P-80 "Shooting Star" (top photo) and it was flying in 1944. Most amazing is that the plane flew just 143 days after start of design! The XP-80 was powered by a British jet engine. The P-80 never got into combat in WWII.
Lower picture shows a P-38 Night Fighter also developed by Lockheed. This plane did see service in the Pacific Theater of Operations during the final few weeks of the war. (*Lockheed Aircraft Corp.*)

nearby trees, and the stench of T-Stoff hung heavily in the air. Then about thirty yards from the flaming shambles the crash crews saw a white figure stand erect. Uncertain and wobbly, Pitz was alive. His white protective suit had saved him.

"Take cover," he croaked, "the machine is about to explode."

He collapsed and was rushed to a hospital. He had broken several ribs, his collarbone, and an arm. In a few days he could tell the story of his incredible last flight in the Me-163.

Fuel lines became defective during the flight, and the fumes almost overcame Opitz. When he tried to jettison the canopy, the mechanism failed. He took off his safety harness and tried to push the canopy away with his back. No use. The erratic, circular glide observed from the ground had been due to Opitz's efforts to shed the canopy. When the Me-163 went in, the unharnessed Opitz was catapulted out of the doomed aircraft. He married his hospital nurse, so the flight was not without its compensations.

The urgency of the bomber threat eventually led to the abandonment of further testing and the Me-163s were sent into combat as they were. They could fly about four minutes at full thrust on the two metric tons of fuel they carried. After takeoff they could climb and intercept a bomber formation in sixty to ninety seconds. The pilot thus had perhaps two minutes to make his attack.

The rocket fighter was armed initially with two 30mm cannons, firing forward in the conventional way. In the final months of the war, the *Komets* were equipped with a rocket version of the upward-firing Jazz Music cannon batteries which had proved so successful in the night fighters. The tubes pointed upward, and rockets fired automatically when the *Komet* flew under enemy aircraft. The optically guided missiles could shatter the largest bomber.

The first aircraft to be equipped with this installation were not ready until March 1945. Second Lieutenant Fritz Kelb had tested the upward-firing rockets and was a vigorous enthusiast for the new weapons. He brought off one classic interception, and as he flew under the bombers one of them disintegrated from a rocket hit. But as with the Me-262, it was too late. A few weeks later, the Me-163 pilots operating out of Brandis blew up their fantastic rocket fighters as American tanks rumbled along the road to Leipzig.

15

Aces of the Space Age Dawn

"Germany is a country fertile in military surprises."
CHURCHILL

SIR WINSTON CHURCHILL ranked courage foremost among human qualities, and he considered courage the guarantor of individual character. Lieutenant Colonel Heinz Baer,[1] a soldier on the other side, proved in his amazing 1939–45 career that Churchill had uttered a truth about all men. "Pritzl" Baer flew hard from first to last on all fronts. His 220 aerial victories, 124 of them against the Western Allies, place him in the top rank of Germany's fighter aces. Yet he is remembered as much for his considerable personal qualities as for his prowess in the air.

When Baer became Germany's top-scoring jet ace in 1945 it was the climax of a fighting career that would shame the wildest fiction. He flew over one thousand missions between September 1939 and the surrender, tangling with virtually every type of Allied aircraft on the Western Front, in North Africa, the Mediterranean and Russia. At least twenty-one of the big four-engined heavies were shot down by "Pritzl," whose earliest ambition in aviation had been to fly big passenger planes for Lufthansa.

Born in Sommerfeld near Leipzig on 25 May 1913, Baer was a farmer's son whose outdoor youth included practical instruction in gliding. In 1930 he graduated from gliders to powered aircraft and obtained his private pilot's license. His desire to fly for Lufthansa could not be satisfied, however, unless he had all three pilot licenses then issued in Germany.

Financial hardship in the depression years deprived young Baer of

---

[1] The Germans spell his name Bär, and pronounce it like Baer or Bear.

TOP JET ACE WWII: Colonel Heinz Baer was the top jet ace of WWII with 16 confirmed victories in the Me-262 jet fighter. He flew from 1939 to 1945 and was credited with 220 aerial victories. (*Baer Collection*)

his chance to gain civilian instruction, and in 1937 he decided to join the Luftwaffe. His idea was to acquire his additional pilot's certificates during his service training, and then return to Lufthansa. By 1938 he was a sergeant pilot flying fighters, and the die was cast. The worsening European situation precluded his release from the service, and Lufthansa would have to wait.

Sergeant Baer went into action on the outbreak of war, and scored his first victory on 25 September 1939. His victim was a French-flown Curtiss P-36. He flew in the Battle of France and the Battle of Britain with Werner Moelders in JG-51, and as Second Lieutenant Baer emerged from the latter struggle with seventeen kills to his credit. During this period, his career was something other than an uninterrupted series of aerial triumphs.

When the Me-109 pilots first tangled with the Spitfires and Hurricanes, German pilots generally were instructed to dogfight with them. This was a traditional carry-over from the First World War. The Germans soon learned that the Spitfire and Hurricane could out-turn the Me-109, and after heavy losses the German pilots were instructed to hit and run. The way in which Galland and Moelders pooled their talents on this problem has been related earlier in the book.

Baer was one of the Luftwaffe pilots who tried time and again and learned the hard way that an Me-109 does *not* get into a turning battle with a Spitfire. On numerous occasions he got the worst of his encounters with the formidable British fighter. Six times he was barely able to stagger back to France in his shot-up Me-109. On the seventh occasion he was not so lucky.

On 2 September 1940 he was grinding back across the English coast with an overheated engine, his Me-109 riddled and perforated in both fuselage and wings. A lone Spitfire pilot bounced the staggering cripple and administered the *coup de grâce*. The would-be Lufthansa pilot bailed out just before his machine plunged into the Channel within sight of Dover. An exhausting swim of nearly two hours brought him to one of the Channel buoys shortly before dusk. A German patrol boat on its evening rounds later plucked Baer from the drink and brought

POST WAR MEETING OF ERSTWHILE ENEMIES: Stuttgart, Germany in June 1956. Echterdingen Airport served as a meeting place between former enemies. L. to R.: Heinz "Pritzl" Bär, 220-victory ace; Colonel Raymond F. Toliver, Commander of the USAF 20th Tactical Fighter Wing; Erich Hartmann, 352 victory ace; and Major Farley E. Peebles, also of the USAF 20th TFW. Bär flew with JG-1, JG-71, JG-51, JG-3, and JV-44 and his 16 victories with the Me-262 jets is believed to place him first among the jet aces. Bär was killed 28 April 1957 in the crash of a light plane. (*Toliver Collection*)

him home. He was flying again the next day.

As a First Lieutenant and squadron leader he went to Russia with JG-51 and in less than two months ran his victory tally to sixty. He was awarded the Knight's Cross on 2 July 1941 and the Oak Leaves on 14 August 1941. He was clearly now a leader of promise as well as a proficient ace.

Multiple kills were frequent on the Russian Front, and Baer got his share. He downed five Russian planes on 30 June 1941 and topped this one-day bag with six kills on 30 August 1941. He was now the bearer of a sharpshooter's reputation and was daringly aggressive. On 31 August 1941 this aggressive quality led him in pursuit of his foes some fifty kilometers behind the front. He was shot down, and but for his indomitable spirit the Baer legend might well have been stillborn.

Bailing out, he landed heavily. High surface winds dragged him along the ground for a couple of hundred yards before he fought free of his parachute. Badly hurt and half-blind with pain, he began one of the great epics of fighter pilot survival. Hiking and hiding by turns he spent the next two days and nights on a desperate and agonizing journey back to the German lines. When the bruised and battered ace finally reached the sanctuary of German-held positions he was lucky to be alive. His spine was fractured in two places!

After lengthy hospital treatment he returned to the Eastern Front, resumed scoring, and by mid-February 1942 had ninety victories and the Swords to his Knight's Cross. Although the Germans sought to equalize the basis for the award of decorations, one of the anomalies of the war is that Heinz Baer received no further recognition after February 1942. Between the award of the Swords and the end of the war, Baer downed six more Soviet aircraft and 107 additional aircraft of the Western Allies—a feat which surely should have been recognized with the award of the Diamonds.

Leaving the Eastern Front in the spring of 1942, he was assigned to Sicily as *Kommodore* of JG-77. Heavily involved in the struggle to dominate Malta from the air, he also flew in North Africa until the eviction of the Axis from Tunisia. In the Mediterranean and North Africa he piled up another forty-five victories against the Western Allies before returning home to take part in the final defense of Germany.

He was successively *Kommodore* of JG-1 *Oesau* and JG-3 *Udet*, flying combat continually and adding steadily to his victory tally. He was almost as consistently shot down himself, but escaped each time with only minor injuries. Between 1939 and 1945 he was shot down *eighteen times*—enough lives for two cats. He parachuted four times and made fourteen belly landings in pastures, grain fields, and on emergency strips.

On 22 April 1944 Baer scored his two-hundredth kill. Some 104 of these kills were British and American-flown aircraft. Men of Baer's caliber were becoming rare toward the end of 1944. Top-flight ace-leaders like Moelders, Oesau, Mayer, and Muencheberg had been killed. Only the most habile of the remaining veterans would be able to survive the growing hordes of Allied fighters swarming into the German skies every day.

In January 1945 Baer was put in command of the jet fighter school at Lechfeld, near Augsburg. As a consequence, he didn't get to actually fly combat in the Me-262 until late in the war. Nevertheless he got sixteen confirmed kills in the jet to lead all scorers in jet aircraft.[2] He wrote the authors the following:

"Some of these sixteen victories in the jet were with a special model of the Me-262 fitted with a rocket motor from the Me-163 in addition to the jet engines. This special fighter was intended for use against the Mosquito. I was able to down a Mosquito on my first mission. This special Me-262 had a rate of climb of nine to ten thousand meters in three minutes (approximately ten thousand feet per minute) after reaching a speed of 750 kph."

Baer was a Lieutenant Colonel when he became a member of JV-44, Galland's "Squadron of Experts," and he flew with this elite unit until the end of the war. He was appointed to command JV-44 when Galland was wounded and Luetzow was killed on 22 April 1945. He ended the war on an appropriate note—C.O. of the "Squadron of Experts".

His experience of aerial combat was probably longer and more diverse than any other of the "first-to-last" aces and leaders. Baer's twenty-one four-engined kills, some of them while flying the jet, are a considerable achievement. On more than one thousand missions he met every type of Allied fighter on the Eastern, Mediterranean, and Western Fronts. Only the meteoric Marseille shot down more Western-flown aircraft.

On the basis of this experience, Baer told Colonel Toliver in 1955 in Stuttgart:

"Combat against American and British fighters was a highly varied thing, and pilot quality was the great imponderable factor until combat was actually joined. In general, the P-38 Lightnings were not difficult at all. They were easy to outmaneuver and were generally a sure kill.

"The P-47 Thunderbolt could absorb an astounding amount of lead. These aircraft had to be handled very carefully in combat because of the large number of hits they could take with no seeming impairment of their performance.

[2] Top American jet ace in Korea was Captain James McConnell, with sixteen victories.

TOP AMERICAN JET ACE: Captain Joseph McConnell, Jr. scored 16 victories flying jet fighters in Korean War. He is considered tied for jet ace honors with Lt. Colonel Heinz Baer of the WWII Luftwaffe, who also had 16 aerial victories flying the Me-262 jet. *(Toliver Collection)*

"The P-51 Mustang was perhaps the most difficult of all Allied fighters to meet in combat. The Mustang was fast, maneuverable, hard to see, and difficult to identify because it resembled the Me-109 closely in the air. These are my general impressions of Allied aircraft, and of course the quality of the Spitfire needs no elaboration. They shot me down once and caused me at least six forced landings.

"A very good pilot in any of these aircraft was tough to handle, and if he had the tactical advantage he had a good chance to win the fight. You see from my own eighteen experiences as someone else's victory that they often did win. But when we got the Me-262s it was a different story, and they were at a tremendous disadvantage against us.

"The jet was just too much against a single propeller-driven aircraft. We could accept or refuse combat with the Allied fighters. It was our choice. The edge in performance and armament given us by the Me-262 was decisive in fighter combat.

"This assumes, of course, that the Me-262 was functioning correctly on both engines. In the jets we were in real trouble if we lost one engine, and it was a petrifying experience also to be low on fuel, preparing to land, and find that Allied fighters had followed you home."

Baer's views on his fellow aces in the Luftwaffe were also sought. He was asked whom he considered the greatest marksman in the Luftwaffe.

"In my opinion, it was either Marseille or Guenther Rall. I did not know all fighter pilots or get to watch more than a limited number in action. Emil 'Bully' Lang was great, and Erich Rudorffer must be considered among the best too. But Marseille scored the most kills for the fewest rounds fired.

"I think Guenther Rall was the *best*—unsurpassed—at angle-off gunnery. He was fantastic! His wingmen were utterly awed by his ability to shoot across the circle. He seemed to have mastered the art of mea-

SURRENDER OF GERMANY'S MOST HIGHLY DECORATED PILOT, 1945: Hans-Ulrich Rüdel, in light-toned jacket, was awarded a special golden order of the Diamonds by Hitler for his fantastic bravery and courage as Germany's leading Stuka pilot and leader. Rüdel and members of his SG-2 *Immelmann* surrendered at Kitzingen, Germany to American forces based there. Germans landed their Stukas and FW-190 dive bombers "gear up" in most instances to render aircraft unflyable, then surrendered to the Americans. One pilot landed normally—because he had carried a girl friend to safety in his baggage compartment. Defeated but not disgraced, the German pilots are from left, Captain Kurt Lau, 1st Lieutenant Karl Biermann, 1st Lieutenant Schwirrblatt, Rüdel, Major Karl Kennel and Captain Niermann. Date is 10 May 1945. *(Toliver Collection)*

suring precisely the speed and distance to the enemy, and then to aim far enough ahead of him to have the proper lead. He would fire a few shots and *poof!*—no more enemy airplane. Yes, I think Rall was the best."

Baer was also asked whom he considered the bravest and most fearless fighter pilot in the Luftwaffe. His answer required no deliberation:

"That would be 'Bubi' Hartmann. He is a human dynamo, very intense, very quick, and perhaps the best combat flyer I know. He knows just how much he can do and he does it to the very hilt. In the attack he was completely fearless, and in order to be sure he had a kill he would close to *ten or fifteen yards from the enemy before firing*. He ranks with Hans-Ulrich Rudel, the famed Stuka pilot. They are the two most fearless and brave men I know."

Baer thus independently confirmed what Hartmann himself insists was the key to his amazing success record. Close in on the enemy until he fills the windshield and then fire.

Baer's physical appearance made him stand out in any group of men. Head-turningly handsome, his chiseled features and straight, hawkish nose endowed him with a heroic aspect. His sense of humor, sparkling wit, and outgoing personality left an indelible impression on every man who met and knew him. Baer was a man's man and a dynamic natural leader, with the capacity for hard decisions. No pilot under his command was asked to do anything that "Pritzl" had not already done himself—such was the breadth of his experience.

Germany's leading jet ace, a fair and chivalrous man who had wanted nothing in life in the beginning but to fly an airliner, found postwar Germany a harsher challenge than any he had met in the air.

As with Rall, Hrabak, and other German aces we have met in this book, the doors to civilian opportunity were closed to Heinz Baer. "You are a militarist!" was the phrase with which this redoubtable warrior and admirable man was dismissed from interview after interview.

In 1950 he finally got a good break. He was put in charge of engine-powered aircraft in the German Aero Club, supervising sport flying in West Germany. He enjoyed this occupation, which satisfied his un-diminished enthusiasm for flying.

On 28 April 1957 he was demonstrating a light aircraft in Brunswick. The machine spun out from 150 feet and plunged to the ground, killing Baer before the horrified gaze of his family. This volume has cited many examples of the strange ways Fate bears on the lives of fighter pilots, and few have had a more enigmatic end than Heinz Baer. On more than one thousand missions in five and a half years of war he had escaped death at the hands of highly trained Allied pilots whose purpose was to kill him. Twelve years after it was all over, the leading ace of the Space Age dawn fell from the air to his death in a machine designed for safe sport flying.

With fourteen kills in the Me-262 Captain Franz Schall is the second-ranked jet ace of the Luftwaffe. He was a flak gunner early in the war, switched to fighter piloting, and between February 1943, when he first saw air action, and September 1944 ran up 106 kills in Russia with JG-52. He was chosen for the *Kommando Nowotny* in October 1944 and downed a number of Mustangs in combat with the jet.

Transferring to JG-7 shortly before war's end, he continued making kills with the Me-262, although many were not confirmed by the dis-integrating official sources. On 10 April 1945, with the end of hostilities only a few weeks off, Schall made an emergency landing at Parchim Air Base. The cratered runway proved a death trap to this vigorous, dark-haired pilot. His jet dug a wheel into a crater, cracked up and burned, killing the twenty-six-year-old ace.

Three German aces who flew the Me-262 are credited with twelve victories each. They are Major Georg-Peter Eder, whom we met in Chapter Thirteen; short, scholarly looking Sergeant Hermann Buchner, a highly successful ex-tank buster from the Russian Front; and Major Erich Rudorffer, one of the deadliest marksmen in the Luftwaffe, to whom Heinz Baer and other pilots in this book have frequently referred.

A tallish, slender man with a thin, sensitive face and piercing blue eyes, Rudorffer fought a long, grim war, and his career resembles that of "Pritzl" Baer in many ways. With 222 victories Rudorffer is ranked as seventh ace of the Luftwaffe, and Baer with 220 kills is eighth.

Like Baer, Rudorffer flew over one thousand missions between his 1940 start with JG-2 and the end of the war. He fought in Russia with Trautloft's "Green Heart" wing (JG-54) with conspicuous success, in North Africa (twenty-six kills), and in the final defense of Germany flying the jet in JG-7. He rivaled Baer by being shot down himself sixteen

ONE MAN AIR FORCE: Erich Rudorffer flew over one thousand missions between 1940 and 1945. One of the Luftwaffe's deadliest marksmen, he outscored all other German pilots in multiple victories, and once shot down 13 Russian aircraft in one blistering 17-minute aerial battle. The 7th-ranking ace of the Luftwaffe and the world, Major Rudorffer is credited with 222 aerial victories won on all fronts. He scored 12 kills in the Me-262 jet. *(Boehm Collection)*

times, and easily outscored "Pritzl" in the parachuting department. Rudorffer made *nine* jumps, more than enough to qualify him as a paratrooper.

Multiple kills were the undeniable evidence of his marksmanship. While he is generally ranked with Marseille, Hartmann, and Rall as one of the four top marksmen in the Luftwaffe, he outscored all these rivals in multiple victories. In a seventeen-minute engagement on 6 November 1943 he shot down thirteen Russian aircraft—his outstanding feat of gunnery.

He was effective too against the British in Africa. On 9 February 1943 he downed eight American and French flown aircraft (P-40s and P-38s) on one mission, and on 15 February 1943, downed seven US flown P-38s and Spitfires of the 31st Fighter Group in two sorties over Tunisia. His days of two, three, and four kills in Russia are too numerous to list.

In February 1945 Rudorffer was given command of II/JG-7, flying the Me-262. Like many other jet pilots in the waning days of the war, he is believed to have many more jet kills than have been officially confirmed. The jet pilots found themselves fighting alone in nearly every combat, for the reasons outlined in the previous chapter. This meant that they were often widely separated from witnesses to their kills, and wingmen or fellow *Kette* members were rarely around to observe crashes once strikes on the bomber boxes were initiated. Jet combat was taking place at over 500 mph and the Luftwaffe still did not have the robot gun cameras installed in every jet fighter.

Major Erich Rudorffer actually entered aerial combat more than three hundred times on his better than one thousand missions. He survived the war and is today a businessman in West Germany. His marksmanship earned him a permanent place in the history of aerial combat.

Behind Eder, Buchner, and Rudorffer among the jet aces is Second Lieutenant Karl "Quax" Schnorrer, Walter Nowotny's efficient wingman in Russia who followed "Nowi" to jet service after being badly wounded in November 1943. After Nowotny was killed and JG-7 became the operational jet wing, "Quax" continued combat flying until the end of March 1945. He had added eleven jet kills to his thirty-five Russian Front downings when he was shot down over Hamburg. He bailed out, survived the war, but lost his left leg through injury in this final action. He knocked down nine four-engined American heavies with the jet.

As the operational jet fighter wing, JG-7 was built up from the *Kommando Nowotny* nucleus. The first *Kommodore* of JG-7 was Colonel Johannes Steinhoff, and the wing and its staff were organized by him. When Steinhoff was transferred to JV-44 *Galland* in January 1945 he was succeeded by Major Theo Weissenberger, who had made his name in the Far North with JG-5 *Eismeer*, the Polar Sea Wing.

Weissenberger put in two grueling years with JG-5 in the frozen North and later in the invasion battles on the Channel coast. He ran up twenty-five kills against the Western Allies in France in about sixty days following the invasion. A chunky, quick-thinking daredevil, Weissenberger was also an effective leader. He had two hundred kills to his credit when he took over JG-7 from Steinhoff.

Weissenberger is credited with eight kills in the Me-262 scored in the final three months of the war. Here again, he is believed to have made many more kills than this, but without confirmation due to the pressing conditions of the time. After the war, his passion for speed and thrills continued, and he became a motor-racing enthusiast. He was killed while driving in a race at the Nuerburgring on 10 June 1950. He was safer in a jet fighter in wartime.

In the shuffling following Steinhoff's departure from JG-7, III Group was passed to the command of Major Rudolf Sinner, an Austrian-born ace who had served on the Western Front with JG-3, in North Africa with JG-27, in Russia with JG-54, and, again, in the invasion battles with JG-27. Although Sinner scored thirty-two kills in North Africa—all of them fighters and all but one of them British—he was accorded little recognition. He had thirty-six kills when he joined JG-7 and he scored another three victories in the Me-262 before being shot down and wounded on his 390th combat mission, 4 April 1945.

208 VICTORIES: Major Theo Weissenberger carved out a highly successful career with JG-5 in the far north before his recall to the defense of Germany against the Western Allies. He scored 25 victories in two months against the invasion forces in France, followed with 8 more victories while flying the Me-262 jet. He survived the war but was killed in a motor racing accident on 10 June 1950. This photo was taken at Petsamo, Finland in 1943. *(Boehm Collection)*

LITTLE RECOGNITION: Major Rudolf Sinner shot down 32 aircraft in North Africa, including 31 fighters, but never was awarded the Knight's Cross—considered the basic badge of achievement among fighter pilots. With a wartime total of 39 victories Sinner would have been a leading hero in the Allied air forces. He flew 390 missions and entered aerial combat 96 times. He was shot down 12 times and wounded 5 times. After the war, the wounded Sinner was roughly handled by the occupation forces as a hospital patient. 37 of his 39 victories were against fighter aircraft. *(Toliver Collection)*

Now a fire-safety engineer in a chemical works in Linz/Donau, Austria, Major Sinner contributes this account of his final action:

"On April 4 I took off from Parchim on a mission against approaching tactical planes. Before takeoff, enemy fighters were already reported eight thousand meters above the airfield. Their height was tremendously overestimated, judging by the noise of these aircraft. I feel sure that these reported fighters waited right above the cloud cover (8–9/10) at about four hundred meters.

"In one and a half circuits I collected approximately seven of my squadron under the cloud cover, while others remained behind with visual contact [below the overcast]. Through a thin area in the clouds I went up above the clouds and immediately spotted in the sun to the left above me four planes with lanciform wings, which I presumed were Thunderbolts.

"I immediately curved steeply toward the planes, because I didn't have time to engage them due to my inferior speed. The Thunderbolts veered away sharply on a reverse course. When I tried to dive after them, I noticed four Mustangs pursuing a single Me-262. I didn't want to fire my rockets, as it would have been a bad example to my group. When I tried to force the Mustangs away, I suddenly saw to the right above me four more Mustangs attacking in a nose dive.

"I curved through under them, but in the curve I was under heavy fire from behind and below. Evasive action upward or downward or a speeding up were impossible because of the low altitude. I was now under the constant fire of eight Mustangs. When I tried to get into the clouds, I received my first hits.

"I decided to fire off my missiles when I was in the clouds. Two Mustangs followed, but at a distance. My missiles failed to fire. While I worked at the weapon panel, smoke belched into the cockpit.

"I was fired on again, and noticed that the left wing near the root was burning. The fire immediately spread to the cockpit. I could do nothing now to save the aircraft. I decided to bail out. I left the plane at about

700 kph without striking the tail assembly. Immediately I noticed my parachute was torn and my right leg entangled with belts and cords. I was sure the parachute pack had become separated from the harness.

"Since I was close to the ground, I nevertheless took a chance and pulled the parachute handle. To my surprise the parachute, after pulling violently and turning me over three times, began opening. I was tied to the parachute only by a belt on the left. The opening shock was very slight. I landed in a freshly plowed field with one leg and the left arm hanging in the harness.

"Although I pulled the Lyrer plug and opened the lock, I was still entangled in the harness and was dragged about twenty meters to a barbed wire fence. I was now being attacked or fired on by two Mustangs.[3]

"The American machines circled and I kept still as long as I was in their sight. When they circled for another attack, I walked twenty-five paces from my parachute and lay down quickly in a furrow. They fired at the parachute, but their shots were wild. They flew away, probably prompted by the flak from Reddlin airfield, which adjoined the paddock where I had come down."

Rudolf Sinner exemplifies that large number of German aces who fought a long war without achieving any contemporary distinction such as the Knight's Cross. A brief recapitulation of Sinner's achievements will illustrate what was required to win the Knight's Cross. Remember, Sinner didn't win the decoration.

Born in 1915 he was educated at the University of Innsbruck and University of Vienna, and at twenty-one was drafted into the Austrian Federal Army, there to be trained as a mountain artilleryman. He served in a flak unit in the Polish campaign, transferred to fighter piloting in 1940 and was trained in Vienna.

Sinner flew on the Western Front with JG-3 *Udet* and flew in North Africa with JG-27 through the worst of the desert war. In the winter of 1943 he fought on the Russian Front in command of IV/JG-54, staying with this unit until spring 1944. He rejoined JG-27 in France the summer of the invasion before transfer to JG-7 in command of I/JG-7 in the fall of 1944.

He flew 390 missions, joining in aerial combat ninety-six times. All but three of his thirty-nine kills were Western-flown aircraft, and thirty-seven of his victories were over fighter aircraft. He once landed behind the Russian lines, *Dawn Patrol* style, and rescued a downed fellow pilot. He was forced to bail out three times, was wounded five times, and was shot down twelve times, riding his aircraft down to forced landings—three times in enemy territory. This career failed to win Sinner the Knight's Cross. He has his own view of such things:

"All I did during the war was to fulfill my duty as a German soldier,

---

[3] Most American fighter pilots refused to fire upon downed enemy fighter pilots. However, some American commanders ordered the pilots to strafe downed enemy jet pilots so they could not return to fight again. One USAF 8th Air Force ace, with more than seven victories claimed, explained his fetish for strafing downed enemy flyers this way: "It's a rough war!"

AMERICAN ACES WITH AMERICAN LEADER: Captain Robert S. Johnson (left) and Major Richard I. Bong flank USAAF Chief General H.H. "Hap" Arnold in Washington during a wartime stand-down from combat. Johnson was top USAAF ace of European Theater of Operations, with 28 aerial victories, while Bong was the top American ace of WWII with 40 victories in the Pacific Theater of Operations. Johnson survived the war, while Bong died in a California flying accident. Bong flew slightly more than 200 combat missions to attain his 40 victories and Johnson flew 100 combat missions to score his 28 kills. *(USAF)*

and I did not distinguish myself by the number of my victories or other circumstances."

He regards himself as typical of many heretofore anonymous German aces of his generation. There can be no doubt that Sinner's achievements, if they had been accomplished in the USAAF, would have resulted in a plethora of decorations and much distinction.

After the war, he was roughly handled by the occupation forces, although a wounded soldier and a hospital patient. He escaped his tormentors by jumping out of a moving railroad train. His fighting heart brought him through all the adversities of war and peace, but he is not reconciled to American ways and standards as are many Germans today.

He is a loyal and thoughtful German and a fighter pilot who abided by the unwritten rules of sportsmanship and fair play. When in the latter days of the war American fighter pilots strafed civilian refugees from Dresden from the safety of their red-nosed Mustangs, and then strafed descending German jet pilots in their parachutes, Sinner became incensed by the behavior of the victors.

His personal abuse under the occupation and his vividly adverse memories of unchivalrous conduct make it hard for Sinner to admire Americans and what they represent. His analytical mind causes him to believe that Germany would be better off if American standards and customs were not becoming so widespread in his native land.

Sinner has pointed out for historical purposes that JG-7 is actually a misleading designation for the first jet wing, because it never reached full wing strength. "Actually, it was only in the process of being set up," he writes, "and only parts of it were fully ready for combat by the time of the capitulation."

GLIDER PILOT—TESTPILOT—FIGHTER ACE: Oberst Wolfgang Späte, right, trained in gliders before WWII, was a test pilot at Rechlin where he tested the Me-163 rocket fighters, and was a 99-victory fighter ace. Flying the Me-262, he shot down five four-engined bombers. Author Ray Toliver and Historian Hans Otto Boehm pose with the famous pilot. (*USAF-Giuliano*)

Major Wolfgang Spaete took Sinner's place with JG-7 when the latter was shot down. Spaete downed five American heavies with the Me-262 before the war ended, bringing his victory tally to ninety-nine kills. A long-time luminary of JG-54 in Russia, Spaete was a famous figure in German aviation before the war, and was one of his country's leading glider pilots.

Test piloting on the Me-163 *Komet* in 1943-44 brought him further eminence, and he wrote a distinguished record with Test Unit 16 at Rechlin, where the Me-163 was brought to operational status.[4] As a fighter ace in his own right in both piston-powered aircraft and jets, Spaete's long service with the world's first rocket-powered fighter places him in the rank of those who opened the door to the Space Age.

Major Spaete has retired from the German Air Force and is now devoting his time to writing with occasional test flying thrown in to keep his proficiency. In the last seven years he ran a series of flight tests on surface-effect-vehicles (S.E.V.), notably the X-113 Am, another product of the genius of Alexander Lippisch.

"At Peenemunde one day in the spring of 1943 the Me-163A VI stood ready for me—filled with perhaps one thousand pounds of 'T-Stoff' and the proportionate amount of 'Z-Stoff.'

"Heini Ditmar explained a few things. Then he said, 'Just fly off. After all, you are not inexperienced with things of the third dimension. We've even found you a nice parking place. Just to the side, where I have always started, the grass is already corroded and burnt from the Z-Stoff.'

"I was dressed in a white protection suit and let myself be strapped into the pilot seat. After a last quieting sign from outside, I shoved the engine lever forward. At such a first start in a new model one does

[4] Oberst Spaete is still trying to locate some of the last reports from his testing days. These reports, confiscated by the British and Americans, have all been returned to Germany except "Arbeitsberichte of Erprobungs-Kommando 16," numbers 4 through 16 and 18 through 25. History needs them.

not feel too comfortable, even when the aircraft has been well tested by others. But I was happy and without worries. Everyone had spoken to me so reassuringly as if it were the simplest thing in the world.

"The aircraft rolled against a strong wind and gathered speed. After about six hundred feet there was a wave in the ground. Nobody had thought of this wave. It threw my Me-163 into the air sooner than expected. In the wink of an eye I was at thirty feet. 'Like a ripe plum' would be an accurate description of the flight position. Slowly the nose obeyed my full throttle and came forward. Guessing what was going to happen I began to catch it and managed to bring the aircraft into a good three-point on both wheels and the skid sit-down.

"Again the aircraft made a leap into the sky. This time I was able to catch it before it touched the ground again, and then followed a flight which has stayed in my memory even though I later made dozens of engine flights with this model. A forty-five-degree climb into the blue sky. The engine was noticeable only as a light spitting noise in the rear, because of the helmet I was wearing. I had never experienced power like this.

"Then the thrust became uneven, and I was thrown forward against my belt. The fuel was used up. I was at nine thousand feet. In the following glide I found this creation of Lippisch to be an aircraft with flight characteristics so beautifully balanced that I have seldom flown one like it, either before or since this flight.

"After landing I found the reason for the criminal[5] takeoff. The gears were unsprung. Ditmar and Opitz didn't take this so seriously because they had both made dozens of drag takeoffs before the first engine start. Mine was the first takeoff ever made in the Me-163 without prior schooling of the pilot with several drag takeoffs. Immediately I launched a project to see we got a spring gear assembly and a steerable rear wheel or a jet rudder.

"All of us who gave ourselves to the testing of the 'Power-Egg' (a boy from Berlin coined this name for the Me-163) made many criminal flights, as one calls such hazardous flights in pilots' slang. A goodly number of sharp pilots gave their lives in the process. Even the fuel was criminal—84 percent hydrogen superoxide with a mixture of carbon dioxide, hydrogen and mysterious catalysts and ferments. Called T-Stoff and Z-Stoff, these fuels were nothing to fool with. After crash landings, which with normal aircraft would have resulted in no more than broken bones for the pilot, we had to bury pilots who had literally been dissolved through T-Stoff, or reduced to a gelatin-like mass or blown to smithereens because of an explosion.

"My best friend, Joschi Poehs,[6] formerly of JG-54, lost his life in this gruesome manner 30 December 1943, even though just one minute after he crashed at the edge of the field after a false start, the ever-ready

---

[5] The corresponding slang word in American parlance would be "hairy."

[6] Josef Poehs, First Lieutenant, born Vienna 1912. Forty-three victories, including three on the Western Front. Awarded the Knight's Cross 6 August 1941. Germanic spelling of Poehs is Pöhs.

fire apparatus was on the spot and poured thousands of quarts of water over the aircraft. We had protection suits of 'P.C.' fabric, true, but these were not leakproof. Opitz once had only one or two quarts of T-Stoff spilled over his back and hand after a crash landing. Despite P.C. coveralls and P.C. gloves he received burns on the back and on the hand which only disappeared years later.

"Every crash landing meant danger from the fuel, because the fuel tanks were made of pure aluminum only 0.12 inches thick. Every harder or statically firmer material was chemically unsuitable for the fuel. Pure aluminum is known to be soft and not especially resilient. As a consequence, every crash landing had as an almost certain effect the leakage of the tanks.

"Later when we made our test flights at Bad Zwischenahn the engine once quit on me shortly after takeoff. I tried to jettison the fuel load in the tanks, approximately 1.8 tons, with the emergency jettisoning device provided. The device was inoperative, so I had to set down on the slush-covered runway with a heavy surface load and a proportionately high landing speed of about 200 mph. Since we had no skid brake built in at the time, I slid over the whole field at great speed, went through some fences and parking lots, up a little hill and down the other side. There the aircraft stood up on its nose, teetered, and to my relief fell back into normal position. I quickly got out and left all further work to the fire truck. Had I turned over in the 'Power-Egg' I would probably have shared the fate of my comrade Joschi Poehs.

"That same afternoon I made another test flight and couldn't engage the landing flaps. Again I slid with double express-train velocity over the field, and before I reached the end, jumped out of the cabin. At the time the speedometer read 80 mph. The next morning I woke up in the hospital. I had a mighty brain concussion but was otherwise un-damaged.

"With these descriptions I can illustrate the difficulty of our testing work, which didn't scare anyone away but rather drew everyone almost hypnotically to the project. Airframe testing brought us a dozen serious spinal injuries.

"At the end of 1942, during a normal landing in which the skids didn't

AERIAL TERROR: 1st Lieutenant Walter Schuck ended the war with 206 victories, although most German historians say that his unconfirmed victories numbered at least thirty. Schuck is credited with 198 kills against the Red Air Force, plus 8 against the Western Allies while flying the Me-262. Most of his victories were with JG-5 in the far north. Schuck won the Oak Leaves to his Knight's Cross. (Boehm Collection)

function, Ditmar seriously injured a vertebra and was confined to the high bed for a year afterward. Opitz, Kiel, Poehs, Thaler, Hohmann, Olejnik, Roesle, and others spent varying periods in the hospital with wrenched backs."

First Lieutenant Walter Schuck, who made his name with JG-5 *Eismeer* in the Far Northern fighter actions, joined his comrades Theo Weissenberger and Heinrich Ehrler in JG-7 toward the end of the war. The lean, deadly Schuck had 198 kills against the Red Air Force at this time. In the Me-262 he added a further eight victories against the Western Allies—four of them four-engined American bombers.

The aggressive Schuck was another who had difficulty confirming many victories in the jet because of the speed of the machine and the problem of scattered wingmen after high-speed sweeps through the bomber boxes. Schuck is believed to have numerous additional jet kills—some German sources estimating his tally as high as thirty unconfirmed victories. He ended the war with 206 confirmed kills and the Oak Leaves to his Knight's Cross.

110 ENEMIES DOWN: Major Heinrich Ehrler of JG-5 falls into a deck chair at Petsamo, Finland after shooting down his 110th enemy aircraft. Ehrler won the Oak Leaves for his 209 victories in WWII, and ended the conflict flying the Me-262 in defense of Germany. He was shot down and killed by a USAAF fighter on 4 April 1945, and thus just barely failed to survive the war. *(Toliver Collection)*

Major Heinrich Ehrler was a dark-haired, slightly built young man with a resemblance to American screen actor Alan Ladd. With Weissenberger and Schuck he was one of the leading personalities of the war in the Far North. Ehrler rose to command JG-5, and had 204 victories when the *Tirpitz* disaster cast a shadow on his previously unblemished fighting career.

In retrospect, there seems to have been a distortion of his role in the bitter German defeat, the loss of the *Tirpitz*. His court-martial pursuant to this disaster was perhaps a miscarriage of justice in the light of what is now known about the *Tirpitz* affair. History already finds it strange that one lone fighter ace and leader was deemed culpable in such a massive disaster for the Germans.

On 15 September 1944 the RAF sent its crack 617 Squadron (The Dam Busters) to attack the *Tirpitz* in Alten Fjord in Norway. Operating from Yagodnik in Russia, the British Lancasters hit *Tirpitz* with one of Dr. Barnes Wallis's six-ton "Tallboy" bombs, damaging the German giant beyond repair.

Incapable of further operational employment as a warship, the stricken *Tirpitz* was towed two hundred miles south to Tromsø Fjord, there to be used as a fortress. The Germans planned to moor her in shallow water and use her as an unsinkable base for holdout operations after the collapse of the Reich. At this time, a few of the Luftwaffe fighters based in nearby Bardufoss were from JG-5, the wing commanded by Major Heinrich Ehrler.

The German High Command in Norway made a monumental error in their calculations concerning *Tirpitz*. Instead of mooring the hulk in shallow water, they anchored her in about eight fathoms. Frenzied dredging failed to rectify this oversight in time. The 617 Squadron RAF launched another Tallboy attack on the would-be fortress, hit her several times with the deep-penetration earthquake missiles, and as a consequence *Tirpitz* capsized. At least a thousand men died, trapped in her hull.

Heinrich Ehrler was the scapegoat in this disaster.

Fighters from Bardufoss never rose to repel the RAF attack, despite a forty-five-minute radar warning. Ehrler was absent in Oslo, ostensibly seeing a girl friend, and could not be contacted. The battleship Captain radioed in vain for fighter protection to Bardufoss. The RAF escaped unscathed from their mortal blow against the *Tirpitz*.

A court-martial presided over by General Kammhuber sentenced Ehrler to death for dereliction of duty. This sentence was never carried out, probably because of Ehrler's distinguished record as an ace fighter pilot and able commander. He had 204 victories against the Russian Air Force, and was awarded the Oak Leaves to his Knight's Cross in August 1943. He was also nominated for the Swords before the *Tirpitz* disaster.

Stripped of his command, deemed by his superiors to have been responsible for the loss of *Tirpitz* and the deaths of at least one thousand German sailors, the twenty-eight-year-old Ehrler was broken-hearted. He flew thereafter without the purpose and dedication he had previously brought to his combat flying. Since *Tirpitz* was a spent force before she was dragged to Tromsø, it seems strange in retrospect that German leaders in Norway did not see in that first Tallboy hit the shape of things to come. Or that they considered themselves guiltless in the mooring bungle which was the real cause of most of the German deaths.

Ehrler flew the Me-262 with some success, scoring five kills and thus becoming a jet ace, but his comrades knew only too well that the old fire had been burned out of this gifted pilot. On 4 April 1945 he was caught by a gaggle of P-51s over Berlin and shot out of the sky in the ensuing battle. On that day, in the general circumstances of Ehrler's demise, four American pilots claimed victories over Me-262 aircraft. One of them most likely was Ehrler's conqueror. They were:

Captain Raymond A. Dyer	4th Fighter Group
Captain Michael J. Kennedy	4th Fighter Group
Captain Robert C. Croker	339th Fighter Group
Colonel George Ceuleers	364th Fighter Group

JG-7 was responsible for most of the jet downings in the final months of the war, but the jet unit that has clearly claimed history's deepest interest is JV-44, Adolf Galland's "Squadron of Experts." In the colorful history of fighter aviation there has never been a combat unit quite like JV-44, with its rare combination of commander, ace pilots, and revolutionary aircraft.

The designation JV-44 was a backhanded slap at Hitler, and lets the world know that JV-44 was a *pilots'* formation whose personnel was largely contemptuous of the German political leadership. When Galland was deciding on the designation for his squadron, permission for which had been belatedly granted by Hitler, he arrived at 44 as a play on words.

Fighter Wing 88 of the Condor Legion in Spain had been a highly successful operational unit which had paved the way for the early Second World War triumphs of the Luftwaffe. Galland figured that 44 was half of 88, thus establishing a link with the successful past. He also knew that if JV-44 was half as successful as Fighter Wing 88 he would have quite a unit.

The German word for 44 is *vierzig-vier*, pronounced phonetically as "Feartsig-Fear"—the letter "v" in German being sounded as an "f." The two "F's" symbolized *two* Feuhrers. As Galland expressed it. "We decided that we had gone along with one fuehrer for eleven years and it had got us nowhere. We were going to try *two* fuehrers."

Started at Brandenburg-Briest and moved shortly afterward to Riem near Munich, JV-44 quickly proved a magnet for Germany's aerial elite. Colonel Steinhoff, fresh from the organization of JG-7 and its wing staff, took over the retraining of pilots. Colonel Guenther Luetzow, previously banished to Italy as the inciter of the *Kommodores'* Revolt against Goering, returned home to fly combat again with JV-44.

Lieutenant Colonel Heinz Baer left his jet-training job at Lechfeld for one last throw at aerial combat. Major Gerd Barkhorn came from the hospital. These four pilots and their Lieutenant General squadron leader had almost *nine hundred kills between them*. Galland wore the Diamonds, the other four the Swords. And there were others to join them.

Steinhoff combed the hospitals. He retrieved Major Erich Hohagen, a blond-thatched veteran ace, from the clutches of the doctors. He also collected the ebullient Major Walter Krupinski. Hohagen and Krupinski had both been with Steinhoff before, and "Count Punski," as Krupinski was nicknamed, had made his first combat sortie in 1942 as Steinhoff's wingman.

Hohagen had fifty-five kills, thirty-five of them on the Western

JG52s HAPPY-GO-LUCKY "GRAF PUNSKI":
Landing after his 100th victory, Walter
Krupinski tells fellow pilots and his crew
chief all about it. (*Krupinski Collection*)

Front, nineteen of them four-engined heavies. Krupinski with 197
kills was one of the Luftwaffe's greatest fighters. Hohagen wore the
Knight's Cross, Krupinski the Knight's Cross with Oak Leaves. There
were other able but less famous pilots in JV-44.

Second Lieutenant Klaus Neumann was at twenty-one probably
the youngest ace among the tough JV-44 veterans. He had thirty-two
kills when he was assigned to JV-44 from the JG-7 staff. Neumann had
started in combat at nineteen on the Russian Front and his victory tally
included twelve Russian and twenty Western Front kills.

With JV-44 Neumann became a jet ace by scoring another five victories. He was another holder of the Knight's Cross, which Galland
described as the "badge" of JV-44. Neumann survived the war, and
today as a strikingly handsome man in his mid-fifties he flies
American-built jets as a Colonel in the new German Air Force.

First Lieutenant Hans Gruenberg was another habile pilot of long
experience who became a jet ace in the final months of the war. He
flew two and a half hard years, involving over five hundred missions,
with JG-3 *Udet* after joining the wing as a sergeant pilot in May 1941.
He scored his five jet kills as a squadron leader with JG-7 and this led to
his posting to JV-44. He survived the war credited with eighty-two
victories, twenty-one of them on the Western Front. He downed fourteen four-engined bombers.

Other extremely able pilots flew with JV-44 without becoming jet
aces. Tough, slick-haired Second Lieutenant Leo Schuhmacher, a
veteran of the 1940 Norwegian campaign as an NCO Destroyer pilot;
he came to JV-44 after five years of aerial battling. He ended the war
with twenty-three victories against the Western Allies gained in 250
missions. Aristocratic-looking Major Diethelm von Eichel-Streiber
flew from the Battle of Britain to the surrender; he scored ninety-six
aerial victories, all but two of them on the Russian Front. Eichel-
Streiber, after war's end, was working with a church group aiding in
the locating of the bodies of American flyers who had been shot down
over Europe. He met the widow of a P-51 pilot who had come to Germany seeking the body of her deceased husband and a romance was
kindled which culminated in marriage. Deet Eichel, as he is known in
America, emigrated to the USA and lives in Modesto, California raising almonds.

The operational scene at Riem in the closing days of the war was like something out of Dante. Hordes of unmolested Mustangs and Thunderbolts perpetually hovered in the area awaiting the chance to strafe the JV-44 base. Takeoffs were hairy gambles across runways continually plowed up by bombs and patched by relays of half-exhausted workers. Landings after operations were often far more hazardous than combat. To limp back in an Me-262 with perhaps one engine functioning and little fuel remaining, only to find squadrons of Mustangs waiting, was an experience guaranteed to make an old man out of the youngest fighter pilot.

Despite these problems JV-44 struck one last convincing blow against the hated bombers. On 7 April 1945, Me-262s of Galland's squadron, armed with R4M rockets, intercepted a formation of B-17's over Westphalia. This formidable fire power was unleashed from outside the range of the defensive fire from the B-17s. [7] In the span of a few minutes, the long stream of bombers lost between 20 and 30 airplanes, the Me 262 pilots claiming 25 had been downed by their rockets. The psychological impact of the jets and their missiles seemed to have an equally deterrent effect as the bombers appeared to jettison their bombs short of the target area and turned for home. This particular rocket attack rammed home to the USAAF that the Germans had finally discovered the remedy to the massed defensive fire from the Fortresses and Liberators.

The consternation and disquiet created in the Allied High Command by this and other jet and rocket attacks were also an attack in the psychological sphere. Germany's capacity to design and produce jets was wildly overestimated, and Allied intelligence once opined that the Luftwaffe had seven new types of jets in or near production.

These overestimates typified the anxiety created on the Allied side by the tremendous superiority of the Me-262. How serious the consequences might have been for the Allies had Germany been able to organize three or four jet wings in the spring of 1944 does not require much imagination. The jet fighter could have given the air war a decisive turn had the machine been produced and given immediately to the fighter force as Galland urged in 1943.

All came too late. The aces of the Space Age dawn remained a tiny elite. For most of them the final thrill of air superiority after years in the shadows would remain the most memorable experience of their lives.

---

[7] For over two years the USAAF had known that the answer to the four-engined bombers was to equip the German fighters with air-to-air rockets. Fortunately, for the Americans, they came too late.

16

Götterdämmerung

"The history of war can furnish not one single instance in which victory has gone to the markedly weaker of the combatants."

HITLER,
1942

THE fiery chaos of the JV-44 base at Riem exemplified the last days of the German fighter force. Wagner at his imaginative peak could hardly have conceived the real-life drama now approaching the final curtain. Most of its leading characters had already left the stage, or were about to do so.

Adolf Galland lay impotent in a hospital, his knee freshly relieved of enemy steel. Both his fighter-ace brothers, Paul and Wilhelm, were dead. Barkhorn, with 301 aerial victories, was also in the hands of the doctors, after a crash landing in which he was almost guillotined by the slamming canopy of his jet fighter.

Steinhoff lay at death's door, his multiple burns adding desperate physical agony to the pain of years of seemingly wasted effort. "Daddy" Moelders, the brilliant tactician and leader, had gone to his Valhalla, and the upright Luetzow had joined his illustrious ancestors.

Warriors of the memorable quality of Wick, Oesau, Mayer, Nowotny, Kittel, and Philipp had burnished their names in the annals of air history, but they, too, had gone to join anonymous thousands of young German pilots who failed to achieve a single victory before being killed.

Marseille lay in North Africa, his simple tomb standing like the high-water mark of German hopes. Not far away in Tunisia lay Muencheberg, buried on the foreign field where he had fallen.

Lent and Prince Heinrich Sayn zu Wittgenstein, who had found immortal fame in darkness, had both gone to their long night. The records of the night fighter force would also contain the names of hundreds of young pilots who had never scored a kill. History would scarcely know they existed, Their only memorial would be a flying pyre in the night—the fighter in which they had died. The German

Fighter Pilots Asso., in the early 1960's, erected a tall memorial on the banks of the Rhine River at Geisenheim, dedicating it to the Fallen Fighter Pilots of All Nations.

Not all the German aces who had flirted with the gods were dead or wounded. Among the living were those who would find a living death in Soviet prisons. Hartmann the Blond Knight and Hajo Herrmann of the Wild Boar were only two of some eight hundred or more who endured more than ten years of Russian confinement, stripped of every right traditionally possessed by soldiers. By reclassifying prisoners of war common criminals, the Soviets had stripped military prisoners of their only protective rights.

"WILDE SAU" AND RAMMKOMMANDO CREATOR: Colonel Hajo Herrmann, shown here with Ursula Hartmann, wife of top ace Erich Hartmann, on 21 October 1967, was a bomber pilot early in the war (KG-4 and KG-30) and won the Ritterkreuz. Next he founded the Wild Boar night fighter unit using Me-109 fighters. At the end of the war he commanded the "Elbe" Rammkommandos, unit dedicated to bringing down the 4-engine bombers if they had to ram them. Hajo Herrmann was a POW in Russia for nearly eleven years after the war. (Hartmann Collection)

Buehligen, Graf, Hahn, Schoepfel, Grasser, and others would suffer Soviet "hospitality" for lesser periods, but would still find the experience by every measure the worst of their lives. For them the war didn't end in 1945; their late foes continued to punish them long after the guns were stilled.

From their first to their last fight for their Fatherland the German fighter pilots were heroes, even if they were not accorded an unclouded recognition by their own people at the time. A hero is "one who acts with great courage," and on this score the German fighter pilots eclipsed their forebears in aerial warfare. They set standards of courage and achievement unlikely to be excelled now by the pilots of any other nation.

Among German laymen there was a general feeling that the Luftwaffe fighter pilots were responsible for not preventing the cataclysm from the air. The invaders had not been repelled and it was seen in some quarters as a failure of the fighter force. History tells a different story, and the German people owe their fighter pilots a debt.

The German air assault on Britain was a minor event compared with the round-the-clock, years-long pounding administered to Germany by the Allied air forces. While the British pilots who repelled the brief German air offensive have become the "Immortal Few," the German

HARTMANN'S CELL MATE IN RUSSIA: Graf Siegfried von der Schulenberg, seen here with equine companion, was member of German nobility confined with Erich Hartmann in Soviet maximum security prison at Diaterka. Hartmann and "Sigi" von der Schulenberg became fast friends, survived Soviet confinement and served together in the new German Air Force—Schulenberg as executive officer in JG-71 commanded by the Blond Knight. (*Toliver Collection*)

pilots who sought to stem the Allied air assault have remained in relative oblivion.

The RAF won its battle, and the Germans lost theirs, and that accounts partially for the slight recognition accorded the German aces. Hatred of the National Socialist regime further distorted a clear view of history. The resilience of the Luftwaffe was too easily attributed to fanaticism when we now know that the German aces were impelled to their courageous feats by a more rational incentive.

The primary driving force behind the Luftwaffe fighters defending Germany was the desire to diminish, or if possible prevent, the wholesale slaughter of German civilians by the Allied air forces. History is ill served by emotional digressions into "Who started it?" The authors are in no doubt after their research that German airmen drove themselves to and frequently beyond their limits of endurance because of what they saw on the ground.

Nothing was further from their minds than the carping, irrational polemic of the Party. When they climbed into their fighters they were obsessed by one thought—if they could claw down a single bomber they would save perhaps dozens of lives, many of them women and children. Their motives were thus identical with those of the Immortal Few, who sought to deliver the British people from the same fate.

In the Luftwaffe, five hundred fighter missions was commonplace. Not even one British or American fighter pilot reached this level of operational activity. It is doubtful if the most active Allied fighter pilots actually entered aerial combat more than a hundred times. However, there is no doubt in the minds of the authors that some American and British fighter pilots, had they flown 500 to 1000 missions, would have chalked up scores of over one hundred victories, too. By contrast, the leading German ace, Erich Hartmann, survived over eight hundred aerial battles. Hartmann, Barkhorn, and Rall between them shot down at least 928 Allied aircraft.[1] Those machines, if placed together in one park, would cover between ten and fourteen acres of ground, placed as closely together as possible.

[1] Corresponding to twelve fighter groups made up of thirty-seven fighter squadrons. Hartmann alone destroyed fourteen squadrons of enemy aircraft.

SURRENDER: 8 May 1945, pilots await the arrival of Allied troops in order to surrender the Heinkel 162's shown here. The *Volksjäger* fighters never really got into combat in WWII as they were still undergoing flight tests at war's end. This photo believed taken at Lech/Holstein. *(Boehm Collection)*

These brilliant fighting achievements contrasted sharply with the poor performance of the Luftwaffe High Command on the ground. This book has cited numerous examples of the ways in which irrational prejudice, lack of vision, stubbornness, inability to comprehend the real demands of the war, and sheer incompetence on the part of the Luftwaffe High Command undermined the best efforts of the flying warriors. Honesty and competence, insight and strategic clarity, good judgment and superior technical knowledge were abundant in the German air effort, but the bearers of these qualities were heavily hampered in making them effective in behalf of their nation.

Germany's corrupt and incompetent political leadership throttled or misdirected the best thinking and technical achievements. The experience and capacity of Germany's leading aces consequently came to mean little, because the war rapidly developed into a battle of attrition, particularly in the air. Individual brilliance was immersed in mass effects.

The Luftwaffe boasted a number of pilots with over one hundred

WHAT WILL THE ENEMY DO WITH US?: May 1945, pilots of the He-162 *Volksjäger* apprehensively discuss their immediate future as they await Allied troops so they can turn the aircraft over to them. *(Boehm Collection)*

victories against the Western Allies. But for each of these aces the Allies could soon put a hundred fighter pilots in the air,[2] and if they averaged no more than a modest two victories apiece the doom of the Luftwaffe was sealed. On the Russian Front the same situation applied, where the flying Russian hordes became so enormous that they virtually ignored

[2] By 1945 the U.S. Army Air Corps alone had 159,677 trained pilots. In the course of World War II the USAAC (later known as the U.S. Army Air Force) suffered 17,000 pilots killed in action and 6442 wounded, a casualty rate of approximately 15 percent.

the worn-out Luftwaffe fighter units—even when the Germans continued to take a toll of their formations. Numbers won the air war on both fronts.

In the twilight, the German aces could look back on a sequence of events unlikely to be repeated in generations—if ever. Their beloved fighters had risen to pre-eminence in aerial thinking from their secondary prewar role. The Battle of Britain clearly showed that the course and outcome of all the great air battles of the war would depend upon fighters.

The presence of fighters and their success would secure the air for the bombers. Their absence or failure meant an enemy victory. Prior to 1940 the fighter advocate in Germany faced often hostile theorists who had cast their loyalties to the dive bomber. When the new realities were unveiled in 1940 it was the ace-leaders who correctly read the writing on the wall.

The years 1941 and 1942 were literally frittered away by the Luftwaffe High Command, with no adequate effort put behind the fighter force. In 1943 and 1944, the Germans began to act on the clear portent of 1940, by which time Galland and others were hoarse from urging the proper action. The Allied air offensive, which might have been aborted by day and by night with prompt and effective countermeasures, became an unhaltable avalanche.

The German ace-leaders who risked their careers—and their lives—in bitter encounters with Goering and the high command were not only skilled airmen, but also patriots. Galland, Moelders, von Maltzahn, Luetzow, and Trautloff will long be remembered for their ground battles against the irrational leadership. They resisted with all that was in them the ruin to which the incompetent direction of the war was leading their country.

These men were *soldiers*, powerless to remove the political regime but determined to avert or diminish the tragedy that they saw would

SOME PILOTS DO IT DAY AND NIGHT BUT FIGHTER PILOTS DO IT BETTER!: *Mistel;* A fighter pilot flew the Me-109 perched atop the bomber, which was packed with explosives and was supposed to fly by auto pilot after release from the fighter . . . to the target. The bomber missed a few hundred yards but it was a good idea. (*Horst Lux—Mistel Test Pilot*)

"WO IST DER LUFTWAFFE?": The Luftwaffe experimented in WWII and one such was *Mistel,* an idea to attach a fighter plane to a bomber, load the bomber with high-explosives and fly it to the target from the fighter. All tests were not successful. Test pilot Horst Lux, in the fighter cockpit, was drenched with gasoline from ruptured fuel tanks but was rescued unhurt. *(Lux Collection)*

engulf their Fatherland. They were the driving force behind the epic five-and-a-half-year battle put up by the Luftwaffe fighters. In that battle, the fighter force reached the heights and plumbed the depths.

They secured the air for the *Blitzkrieg* triumphs over Poland, Denmark, Norway, Belgium, Holland, and France, and they almost defeated the RAF. Luftwaffe fighters ensured the conquest of the Balkans and the eviction of the British from Greece and Crete. Luftwaffe fighters were the main agency by which the Soviet Air Force was smashed in 1941 and by which it was contained for the next two years. Fighters of JG-27 supported the *Afrika Korps* under Rommel when the Desert Fox fought his way to the very gates of Egypt, there to teeter on the verge of what might have been one of the salient conquests of modern times.[3]

In the spring of 1942, Luftwaffe fighters had the island fortress of Malta ready for conquest by Axis paratroops—a glittering opportunity opened by fighter power and allowed to go begging.

From one experimental squadron, the Luftwaffe night fighters developed into a formidable force feared by the RAF. The night fighters took a heavy toll of British bombers, but numerically and technically they were not equal to the task of halting the night offensive. In terms of courage, however, the night aces were equal to any of the world's soldiers.

In that dolorous chain of events attending the development of the Me-262 fighter, related in Chapter Fourteen, the last great opportunity was cast away. Germany's political leadership ultimately proved unequal even to simple decisions. Germany's most successful aces consequently had to lose the air war while flying the world's fastest fighter.

A longer view of history than is possible at present may well characterize Reichsmarschall Goering as the German airman's worst enemy, but it is certain even now that he squandered the lives of German fighter pilots in a fashion hardly rivaled since the days of Pyrrhus. When Churchill described Goering as "one of the few Germans who has been having a good time in recent years," it was an accurate jibe at the Reichsmarschall's penchant for self-indulgence. And it was from the mire of corruption into which he had sunk that von Richthofen's erstwhile squadron mate uttered his final lines in the Twilight of the Gods.

Around the middle of April 1945 Goering sent for Galland to come to Karinhall. The Reichsmarschall knew his days were numbered, and

[3] Likewise it was the long-range fighters that made it possible for the USAAF bombers to roam and bomb Fortress Europe with near impunity.

he received Galland with a courtesy strange to their relationship in the previous year. He asked about the progress of JV-44, to which he and Hitler had sent the young General with the reasonable certainty that he would be killed.

Then came the admission, awkwardly phrased, subject to innumerable qualifications, that Galland had been right about the Me-262. The machine was a fighter and not a bomber. Galland's recommendations had been correct, the Reichsmarschall now admitted. Galland never saw his old antagonist again, but this final interview at least gave him some satisfaction after the clashes that had led to his dismissal.

Goering once confided to Josef "Pips" Priller that he envied Adolf Galland for his intelligence, quick grasp of every situation, and ability to simultaneously work hard and play hard. "Galland has an uncanny ability to understand his subordinates, to know when they are being honest with him—and he knows how to get the most out of them," the Fat One told Priller. He envied Galland's leadership talent. But to Galland's face he was always the antagonist. The final confrontation of the two men at Karinhall in the last days of the war was as close to making amends as the vain Goering was capable of coming, despite his imminent doom.

The German fighter pilots kept flying against the Allies to the morning of VE-Day, wherever gasoline supplies and runways permitted takeoffs. They fought a long, hard war with courage, chivalry, and fairness. This book has provided the first authentic insight into the character and backgrounds of some of Germany's leading aces to appear in the English language. They are fair and decent men, but it was their misfortune to be lumped historically with the perpetrators of German non-military violence.

As a breed, the German aces lived by the traditional code of soldiers. They observed the bonds that must continue to exist between man and man, both in the air and on the ground, unless every vestige of thought and feeling is to be expunged by war from the human soul—as perhaps the nuclear bomb portends.

Testimonies to the chivalry and good sportsmanship of the German aces are legion from the Allied pilots who flew against them. The Germans regarded such practices as shooting an enemy pilot in his parachute not as fighting, but as murder, and from this policy they never departed. As a consequence, their soldierly conduct in wartime stands untarnished. They lost the war, but they did not lose their souls, and in the aftermath they have helped build a better Germany.

German ace Major Rudolf Sinner has expressed precisely the views of the authors when he writes from Austria:

"It is reassuring for both parties when, after combat, the visor is opened and the faces of real, decent men among the enemy peer out of the helmets. If one were to look into faces distorted by fanaticism, then one could not as a victor be proud of any superiority over apes. And the man who was overcome in single combat must feel doubly humiliated."

The German fighter pilots never betrayed the traditions of manhood, and it is as men that they wrote one of the most colorful and incredible chapters in the history of arms.

FIGHTER PILOT MEMORIAL: This magnificent memorial to the fallen fighter pilots of WWII was erected at Geisenheim in the Rhineland by the German Fighter Pilots' Association. Every October, during the October Festival, fighter pilots hold memorial services for their fallen comrades. Visiting Allied pilots are made welcome. *(German Fighter Pilots Association)*

GENERAL STREIB RETIRES: General Werner Streib retired on March 23, 1966 at Porz Wahn near Köln. Shown here offering best wishes to Streib are civilian Adolf Galland and Colonel Erich Hartmann. *(Hartmann Collection)*

FOES MEET AS FRIENDS: The American Fighter Aces Association was invited to visit Germany as guests of the German Fighter Pilots Association in 1961. This visit initiated strong friendship ties between men who once fought in the air. From left, the gathering includes: Colonel Edu Neumann, USN ace Gene Valencia, "Pips" Priller, Jim Brooks, with "Hub" Zemke kneeling. *(USAF Photo)*

FROM ONE EAR TO ANOTHER—ONE NATION TO ANOTHER: Lt. General Robert M. Lee, USAF, and Lt. Colonel Erich Hartmann of the Bundesluftwaffe examine a model of the F-104 fighter at Colorado Springs, Colorado in June 1961. As the all-time top-scoring fighter ace of the world with 352 victories, Erich Hartmann has been a frequent visitor to the U.S. since his 1955 release from illegal Russian confinement. He was selected to be Kommodore of JG-71, Germany's first jet fighter wing in the Bundesluftwaffe, which he raised and trained. *(USAF Photo)*

CHIEF OF THEM ALL: The Germans hold a fascination for the American Indians and Erich Hartmann is no exception. On a visit to Colorado Springs in 1961, the author introduced Hartmann to Chief Lone Eagle, a white who was said to have been found by Indians as a baby, raised by them as one of their own and eventually became Chief of the tribe. *(Toliver)*

PLAYBOYS FOREVER: Fighter pilots are often called the "playboys of the air" and they almost never lose the tendency. This photo, taken in Augsburg at the home of "Pips" Priller in 1962, shows Priller wearing a portion of antique armor, Cdr. Eugene Valencia wearing a *pickelhaube* helmet and holding Priller's Kommodore's Baton and epaulets, while wearing the icebucket for a helmet is none other than ex-Kommodore of the AFRICA BOYS himself—Edu Neumann. *(Toliver Collection)*

ERSTWHILE ENEMIES—NOW FRIENDS: In 1961 the American Fighter Aces Asso. sent a delegation to Germany to join the German Fighter Pilots Asso. in the dedication of the Memorial To The Fallen Fighter Pilots erected on the banks of the Rhine River at Geisenheim. At Büchel Airbase they met with new-Luftwaffe pilots as this photo attests. (l. to r.) Col. Gerhard Barkhorn (301 vics.); USN Cdr. E.A. Valencia (23); Lt. Col. Erich Hartmann (301); Col. R. F. Toliver. *(Toliver Collection)*

AGING EAGLES REMEMBER: Wolfgang Falck on the right has grey plumage nowadays to replace his black wartime feathers as the Happy Falcon, and he reminisces with Lt. General Herbert Wehnelt, center, and Hans-Joachim Jabs at a 1976 meeting of German Fighter Pilots' Association. General Wehnelt had 36 victories in WWII, and former Lt. Colonel Jabs was one of the leading personalities among night fighter pilots. Jabs flew 710 missions, and scored 22 day and 28 night victories in winning the Oak Leaves to his Knight's Cross. Falck is now president of the German Fighter Pilots' Association, and Wehnelt and Jabs are 1st and 2nd vice presidents respectively. (*Jagerblatt*)

TRAGER DES GOLDENEN EICHENLAUBS MIT SCHWERTERN UND BRILLIANTEN ZUM RITTERKREUZ DES EISEREN KREUZES: Stuka-Colonel Hans-Ulrich Rudel, wearer of Germany's highest decoration for bravery in WWII, meets with author Raymond F. Toliver at the Los Angeles International Airport March 25th, 1977. Motorbuch-Verlag/Stuttgart has recently published a most informative book *Stuka Oberst Hans-Ulrich Rudel* by author Günther Just which portrays most effectively the life and tribulations of Rudel. (*Photo by Trevor J. Constable*)

Tops and Firsts—Luftwaffe, World War II

Top Ace
  Major Erich Hartmann   352 victories
Top Night Fighter Ace
  Major Heinz Schnaufer   121 victories
Top German Ace of Spanish Civil War (1937–1938)
  Lieutenant Werner Moelders   14 victories
First German Ace
  Major Hannes Gentzen
First Ace to exceed Baron Manfred von Richtofen's
 World War I score of 80
  Captain Werner Moelders
First to score 100 victories
  Major Werner Moelders   15 July 1941
First to score 150 victories
  Major Gordon Gollob   29 August 1942
First to score 200 victories
  Captain Hermann Graf   2 October 1942
First to score 250 victories
  Major Walter Nowotny   14 October 1943
First to score 300 victories
  Captain Erich Hartmann   24 August 1944
First to score 350 victories
  Major Erich Hartmann   8 May 1945
Most kills scored in a single day
  Major Emil Lang   18 victories
Most kills on a single mission (sortie)
  Major Erich Rudorffer   6 November 1943
            13 victories
Most kills scored on the Western (includes
 Mediterranean) Front
  Captain Hans-Joachim Marseille 158 victories
Most kills scored on the Russian Front
  Major Erich Hartmann   352 victories
Best kill average per sortie flown (day fighters)
  Lieutenant Guenther Scheel 70 missions 71 vic-
         tories (Russian Front)
Top Fighter Ace for number of four-engined aircraft shot
 down (day fighters)
  Lieutenant Herbert Rollwage 102 victories
     (44 of them four-motor bombers)
Top four-engine killer (night fighters)
  Major Heinz Schnaufer   121 victories
       (mostly four-engine)
Top Jet Ace (Me-262)
  Major Heinz Baer   16 victories

Luftwaffe Aces with One Hundred or More
Aerial Victories

	Name	Rank	Victories	
1	Hartmann, Erich	Maj.	352	262 single engine, 90 twin
2	Barkhorn, Gerhard	Maj.	301	
3	Rall, Guenther	Maj.	275	
4	Kittel, Otto	1st Lt.	267	
5	Nowotny, Walter	Maj.	258	
6	Batz, Wilhelm	Maj.	237	

	Name	Rank	Victories	
7	Rudorffer, Erich	Maj.	222	13 on one mission
8	Baer, Heinrich	Lt. Col.	220	
9	Graf, Hermann	Col.	212	
10	Ehrler, Heinrich	Maj.	209	possibly 252
11	Weissenberger, Theodor	Maj.	208	8 with Me-262
12	Philipp, Hans	Lt. Col.	206	
13	Schuck, Walter	1st Lt.	206	
14	Hafner, Anton	1st Lt.	204	
15	Lipfert, Helmut	Capt.	203	
16	Krupinski, Walter	Maj.	197	
17	Hackl, Anton	Maj.	192	
18	Brendel, Joachim	Capt.	189	
19	Stotz, Max	Capt.	189	
20	Kirschner, Joachim	Capt.	188	
21	Brandle, Werner	Maj.	180	
22	Josten, Guenther	Lt.	178	
23	Steinhoff, Johannes	Lt. Col.	176	
24	Reinert, Ernst-Wilhelm	1st Lt.	174	
25	Schack, Guenther	Capt.	174	
26	Schmidt, Heinz	Capt.	173	
27	Lang, Emil	Capt.	173	18 in one day
28	Adameit, Horst	Maj.	166	
29	Wilke, Wolf-Dietrich	Lt. Col.	162	
30	Marseille, Hans-Joachim	Capt.	158	17 in one day
31	Sturm, Heinrich	Capt.	157	
32	Thyben, Gerhard	1st Lt.	157	
33	Duettmann, Peter	Lt.	152	
34	Beisswenger, Hans	1st Lt.	152	
35	Gollob, Gordon	Col.	150	
36	Tegtmeier, Fritz	1st Lt.	146	
37	Wolf, Albin	1st Lt.	144	possibly 176
38	Tanzer, Kurt	1st Lt.	143	
39	Mueller, Friedrich-Karl "Tutti"	Maj.	140	
40	Gratz, Karl	1st Lt.	138	
41	Setz, Heinrich	Maj.	138	
42	Trenkel, Rudolf	Capt.	138	
43	Schall, Franz	Capt.	137	
44	Wolfrum, Walter	1st Lt.	137	
45	Dickfeld, Adolf	Lt. Col.	136	
46	von Fassong, Horst-Guenther	Capt.	136	
47	Foennekold, Otto	1st Lt.	136	
48	Weber, Karl-Heinz	Maj.	136	
49	Muencheberg, Joachim	Maj.	135	
50	Waldmann, Hans	1st Lt.	134	
51	Grislawski, Alfred	Capt.	133	
52	Wiese, Johannes	Maj.	133	
53	Borchers, Adolf	Maj.	132	
54	Clausen; Erwin	Maj.	132	
55	Lemke, Wilhelm	Capt.	131	
56	Ihlefeld, Herbert	Lt. Col.	130	includes 7 in Spain
57	Sterr, Heinrich	1st Lt.	130	
58	Eisenach, Franz	Maj.	129	
59	Dahl, Walther	Col.	128	
60	Doerr, Franz	Capt.	128	
61	Obleser, Friedrich	1st Lt.	127	

	Name	Rank	Victories	
62	Rademacher, Rudolf	Lt.	126	
63	Zwernemann, Josef	1st Lt.	126	
64	Hoffmann, Gerhard	1st Lt.	125	
65	Hrabak, Dietrich	Lt. Col.	125	
66	Oesau, Walter	Lt. Col.	125	includes 8 in Spain
67	Ettel, Wolf-Udo	1st Lt.	124	
68	Tonne, Wolfgang	Capt.	122	
69	Marquardt, Heinz	Sgt.	121	
70	Schnaufer, Heinz-Wolfgang	Maj.	121	all at night
71	Weiss, Robert	Capt.	121	
72	Leie, Reich	Maj.	118	
73	Beerenbrock, Hans	Lt.	117	
74	Birkner, Hans-Joachim	Lt.	117	
75	Norz, Jakob	Lt.	117	
76	Wernicke, Heinz	Lt.	117	
77	Lambert, August	1st Lt.	116	17 in one day
78	Moelders, Werner	Col.	115	includes 14 in Spain
79	Crinius, Wilhelm	Lt.	114	
80	Schroer, Werner	Maj.	114	
81	Dammers, Hans	Lt.	113	
82	Korts, Berthold	Lt.	113	
83	Buehligen, Kurt	Lt. Col.	112	
84	Lent, Helmut	Lt. Col.	110	102 at night
85	Ubben, Kurt	Maj.	110	
86	Woidich, Franz	Lt.	110	
87	Seiler, Reinhard	Maj.	109	includes 9 in Spain
88	Bitsch, Emil	Capt.	108	
89	Hahn, Hans "Assi"	Maj.	108	
90	Luetzow, Guenther	Lt. Col.	108	
91	Vechtel, Bernard	Lt.	108	
92	Bauer, Viktor	Capt.	106	
93	Lucas, Werner	Capt.	106	
94	Galland, Adolf	Lt. Gen.	104	
95	Sachsenberg, Heinz	Lt.	104	
96	Grasser, Hartmann	Maj.	103	
97	Freytag, Siegfried	Maj.	102	
98	Geisshardt, Friedrich	Capt.	102	
99	Mayer, Egon	Lt. Col.	102	
100	Ostermann, Max-Hellmuth	1st Lt.	102	
101	Rollwage, Herbert	1st Lt.	102	44 four motor
102	Wurmheller, Josef	Maj.	102	
103	Miethig, Rudolf	1st Lt.	101	
104	Mueller, Rudolf	F/Sgt.	101	
105	Priller, Josef	Col.	101	
106	Wernitz, Ulrich	Lt.	101	
107	Daehne, Paul-Heinrich	1st Lt.	100	

Luftwaffe Aces with Fifty or More Night Victories

	Name	Rank	Victories	
1	Schnaufer, Heinz-Wolfgang	Maj.	121	
2	Lent, Helmut	Col.	102	plus 8 day
3	zu Sayn-Wittgenstein, Prince	Maj.	83	
4	Streib, Werner	Col.	66	

5	Meurer, Manfred	Capt.	65	
6	Radusch, Guenther	Col.	64	
7	Roekker, Heinz	Capt.	64	
8	Schoenert, Rudolf	Maj.	64	
9	Zorner, Paul	Maj.	59	
10	Raht, Gerhard	Capt.	58	
11	Becker, Martin	Capt.	57	
12	Herget, Wilhelm	Maj.	57	plus 14 day
13	Francsi, Gustav	1st Lt.	56	
14	Kraft, Josef	Capt.	56	
15	Struening, Heinz	Capt.	56	
16	Frank, Hans-Dieter	Capt.	55	
17	Vinke, Heinz	Sgt.	54	
18	Geiger, August	Capt.	53	
19	Luetje, Herbert	Lt. Col.	53	
20	Drewes, Martin	Maj.	52	
21	Hoffmann, Werner	Maj.	52	
22	zu Lippe-Weissenfeld, Prince	Maj.	51	
23	Welter, Kurt	1st Lt.	50	
24	Greiner, Hermann	Capt.	50	

Partial List of Day Fighters Downing Four-motor Bombers

NOTE: Information is not available on types of aircraft shot down by night fighters at this time. This day fighter list is not complete.

Confirmed Victories

Rollwage, Herbert	44	
Dahl, Walther	36	
Eder, Georg-Peter	36	(plus 32 probables)
Hackl, Anton	32	
Bauer, Viktor	32	
Welter, Kurt	30	
Frey, Hugo	26	
Hermichen, Rolf	26	
Schroer, Werner	26	
Staiger, Hermann	26	
Gerth, Werner	25	
Mayer, Egon	25	
Borngen, Ernst	24	
Buehligen, Kurt	24	
Loos, Walter	22	
Weik, Hans	22	
Baer, Heinrich	21	
Glunz, Adolf	21	
Karch, Fritz	21	
Kirchmayr, Rudiger	21	
Kociok, Josef	21	
Lemke, Siegfried	21	
Ehlers, Hans	20	
Kientsch, Willi	20	
Koenig, Hans-Heinrich	20	
Mertens, Helmut	20	
Piffer, Anton-Rudolf	20	

German Jet Aces of World War II

	Name	*Rank*	*Victories*
1	Baer, Heinz	Lt. Col.	16
2	Schall, Franz	Capt.	14
3	Buchner, Hermann	Sgt.	12

4	Eder, Georg-Peter	Maj.	12
5	Rudorffer, Erich	Maj.	12
6	Schnorrer, Karl	Lt.	11
7	Buttner	Sgt.	8
8	Andreson, Lorenz	Oblt	8
9	Lennartz, Heinz		8
10	Rademacher, Rudolf	1st Lt.	8
11	Schuck, Walter	1st Lt.	8
12	Wegmann, Guenther		8
13	Weissenberger, Theodor	Maj.	8
14	Galland, Adolf	Lt. Gen.	7
15	Mueller, Fritz		6
16	Steinhoff, Johannes	Col.	6
17	Baudach	Sgt.	5
18	Ehrler, Heinrich	Maj.	5
19	Grunberg, Hans	1st Lt.	5
20	Heim	C.W.O.	5
21	Neumann, Klaus	Maj.	5
22	Schreiber	Lt.	5
23	Spaete, Wolfgang	Capt.	5

Partial List—The Luftwaffe Fighter Aces

*Knight's Cross; **Oak Leaves; ***Swords; ****Diamonds

Lt. = Lieutenant (Leutnant); Maj. = Major; Capt. = Captain (Hauptmann); Lt. Col. = Lt. Colonel (Oberstleutnant); Col. = Colonel (Oberst); W.O. = Warrant Officer; Sgt. = Sergeant
(Note: There are over 5000 Luftwaffe Aces. This is a partial list.)

Decoration	Name	Last Wartime Rank	Combat Unit	Victories
	Adam, Heinz-Gunther	Lt.	26	7
**	Adameit, Horst	Maj.	54	166
*	Adolph, Walter	Capt.	27, 26	28 (1 in Spain)
*	Ahnert, Heinz-Wilhelm	Sgt.	52	57
	Ahrens, Peter	Lt.	26	11
	Aistleitner, Johann	Capt.	26	12
*	Albrecht, Egon	Capt.	ZG76	25
	Andel, Peter	Lt.	26	6
	Andres, Ernst	1st Lt.	NJG2, 4	28
	Arnold, Heinz	Ofw	5	40
	Artner, Rudolf	Fw	5	20
*	Augenstein, Hans-Hermann	Capt.	NJG1	46 (all at night)
*	Baagoe, Sophuu	1st Lt.	ZG76	14
*	Baake, Werner	Capt.	NJG1	41 (all at night)
	Babenz, Emil	Sgt.	26	24
*	Bachnick, Herbert	Lt.	52	80
*	Badum, Johann	Lt.	77	54
	Bahnsen,	Lt	27	8
*	Bahr, Gunther	Sgt.	NJG6	37 (36 at night)
	Bahr, Hans-Joachim	Lt	5	7
**	Balthasar, Wilhelm	Capt.	27, 2, 3	47 (7 in Spain)
***	Baer, Heinrich	Lt. Col.	51, 77, 1, 3	220 (21 four motor, 16 with Me-262)
*	Bareuter, Herbert	Lt.	51, 3	56
***	Barkhorn, Gerhard	Maj.	52, 6, 44	301
*	Bartels, Heinrich	Sgt.	5, 27	99

Decora-tion	Name	Last War-time Rank	Combat Unit	Victories
*	Barten, Franz-K	Capt.	51	53
	Bartz, Erich	W.O.	51	30
***	Batz, Wilhelm	Maj.	52	237
**	Bauer, Viktor	Capt.	3	106
**	Becker, Ludwig	Capt.	NJG1, 2	46 (all at night)
*	Becker, Martin "Tino"	1st Lt.	NJG1, 6, 58	31 (all at night, 9 kills one night)
	Becker, Paul	Lt.	27	20
*	Beckh, Friedrich	Lt. Col	51, 52	48
**	Beerenbrock, Hans	Lt.	51	117
	Beese, Artur	1st Lt.	26	22
*	Beier, Wilhelm	Lt.	NJG1, 2	36 (all at night)
**	Beisswenger, Hans	1st Lt.	54	152
*	Bellof	Sgt.	NJG2	25
*	Belser, Helmut	Capt.	53	36
*	Bendert, Karl-Heinz	1st Lt.	27	54 (9 four motor)
*	Bennemann, Helmut	Lt. Col.	52, 53	92
*	Benning, Anton	Lt.	106, NJG1, 301	28 (18 four motor)
	Benz, Siegfried	Lt.	26	6
*	Bergmann, Helmut	Capt.	NJG4	36 (all at night)
*	Berres, Heinz-Edgar	Capt.	77	53
	Berschwinger, Hans	Sgt.	NJG1	10
	Bertram, Gunther	1st Lt.	NJG100	35
*	Bertram, Otto	Maj.	2, 100, 6	21 (8 in Spain)
	Beth, Arthur	Fw	5	16
*	Beutin, Gerhard	Sgt.	54	60
*	Beyer, Franz	Maj.	3	81
	Beyer, Georg	Capt.	26	8
	Beyer, Heinz	Sgt.	5	33
	Bierwirth, Heinrich	Sgt.	26	8
	Beulich, Erich	Ofw	5	7
	Birk, Heinz	Ofw	5	14
*	Birkner, Hans-Joachim	Lt.	52	117 (Hartmann's wingman)
*	Bitsch, Emil	Capt.	3	108
	Blazytko, Franz	Sgt.	27	29
*	Blechschmidt, Joachim	Lt. Col.	ZG76	17
*	Bleckmann, Gunther	Capt.		27
	Bloemertz, Gunther	Lt.		10
	Blume, Walter	Maj.	26	14
*	Bob, Hans-Ekkehard	Maj.	3, 51, 54	59
	Boehm-Fettelbach, Karl	Maj.	234	40
*	Boewing-Trueding, Wolfgang	1st Lt.	51	46
	Bohn, Kurt	Sgt.	26	5
	Bohn, Paul	Oblt	NJG2	5
*	Bolz, Helmut-Felix	Maj.	JG105	56
*	von Bonin, Eckhart-Wilhelm	Maj.	NJG1	39
*	von Bonin, Hubertus	Maj.	26, 52, 54	77 (4 in Spain)
*	Borchers, Adolf	Maj.	51, 52	132
*	Borchers, Walter	Lt. Col.	NJG5, 51	63
*	von Boremski, Eberhard	1st Lt.	3	90
*	Borngen, Ernst	Maj.	27	45 (24 four motor)

	Name	Last Wartime Rank	Combat Unit	Victories
	Borreck, Hans-Joachim	W.O.	26	5
*	Borris, Karl	Maj.	26	43
	Bozicek, Franz	Uffw	5	5
	Brandis, Felix-M.	Oblt	5	14
**	Brandle, Werner-Kurt	Maj.	3	180
*	Brandt, Paul	1st Lt.	54	34
*	Brandt, Walter	1st Lt.	51, 3	57 (11 four motor)
	Bremer, Peter	Sgt.	54	40
**	Brendel, Joachim	Capt.	53, 51	189
*	Bretnuetz, Heinz	Capt.	53	37 (2 in Spain)
*	Bretschneider, Klaus	1st Lt.	53, 300	40 (14 at night)
	Brewes	Capt.		18
*	Broch, Hugo	Lt.	54	81
*	Brocke, Juergen	Lt.	77	45
*	Broennle, Herbert	Lt.	54	57
	Bruekel, Wendelin	Lt.		14
*	Brunner, Albert	Sgt.	5	53
*	Buchner, Hermann	Sgt.	4	58 (12 four motor with Me-262)
*	Bucholz, Max	1st Lt.	3, 5, 101	30
***	Buhligen, Kurt	Lt. Col.	2	112 (24 four motor)
*	von Bulow-Bothkamp, Harry	Lt. Col.	NJG101, 2, 77	? (+6 in WW I)
*	Bunzek, Johannes	Lt.	3, 52	75
*	Burckhardt, Lutz-Wilhelm	Capt.	77, 3	58
*	Burk, Alfred	1st Lt.	53	56
	Burschgens, Josef	Capt.	26	10
	Busch,	Lt	JG-51	20
	Busch, Erwin	1st Lt.	26	8
	Busse, Heinz	1st Lt.	51	22
	Buzzi, Bruno	Fw	5	9
*	Carganico, Horst	Maj.	5	60
*	Cech, Franz	Sgt.	52	65
*	Christl, Georg	Lt. Col.	ZG26, JG10	19 (test pilot)
	Christof, Ernst	Sgt.	26	9
	Claude, Emil	1st Lt.	27	27
**	Clausen, Erwin	Maj.	51, 11	132 (14 four motor)
	Clerico, Max	Haupt.	54	7
	Conter	Lt.	NJG100	15
	Cordes, Heine	Lt.	54	52
**	Crinius, Wilhelm	Lt.	53, 27	114
	Crump, Peter	Lt.	26	31
*	Daehne, Paul-Heinrich	1st Lt.	52	100
**	Dahl, Walther	1st Lt.	3, 300	128 (36 four motor)
*	Dahmer, Hugo	Capt.	26, 5, 54	57
	Dahms, Helmut	Sgt.	NJG100	24
	Dahn, Friedrich	Lt	5	26
*	Dammers, Hans	Lt.	52	113
*	Darjes, Emil	Lt. Col.	54	82
*	Dassow, Rudolf	Lt.	ZG76, 6	22 (12 four motor)
	Demuth, Erich	Lt.	JG-1	16
*	Denk, Gustav	1st Lt.	52	67
**	Dickfeld, Adolf	Col.	52, 2, 11	136 (11 four motor)
*	Diesing, Ulrich	Lt. Col.	ZG1	15
	Dietze, Gottfried	Lt.	26	5
*	Dinger, Fritz	1st Lt.	53	67
	Dipple, Hans	Capt.	26	19

Decora-tion	Name	Last War-time Rank	Combat Unit	Victories
	Dirksen, Hans	Sgt.	26	5
	Dittlmann, Heinrich	Sgt.	51	57
*	Doebele, Anton	Lt.	54	94
*	Doebrich, Hans-Heinrich	Sgt.	5	70
*	Doering, Arnold	Lt.	KG53, NJG300, 3	23
*	Doerr, Franz	Capt.	77, 5	128
	Doerre, Edgar	Sgt.	26	9
*	Dombacher, Kurt	1st Lt.	51	68
	Dortenmann, Hans	1st Lt.	26	38
	Dreisbach, Heinrich	Ofw	5	16
**	Drewes, Martin	Maj.	ZG76, NJG1	52 (43 at night)
*	Druenkler, Ernst	Capt.	NJG5, 1	45
	Dueding, Rudi	Sgt.	NJG100	18
*	Duellberg, Ernst	Maj.	1, 27, 76	50 (10 four motor)
*	Duettmann, Peter	Lt.	52	152
	Ebbinghausen, Karl	Capt.	26	7
*	Ebeling, Heinz	1st Lt.	26	18
*	Ebener, Kurt	Lt.	3, 11	57
	Ebersberger, Kurt	Capt.	26	27
*	Eberspaecher, Helmut	Capt.	NJG1	7
	Eberwein, Manfred	1st Lt.	52, 54	56
**	Eckerle, Franz	Capt.	54	59
*	Eckardt, Reinhold	1st Lt.	NJG1, 3	22
**	Eder, Georg-Peter	Maj.	51, 26, 1	78 (plus 40 prob-ables, 36 four motor)
	Edmann, Johannes	Sgt.	26	5
*	Ehle, Walter	Maj.	ZG1, NJG1	36 (33 at night)
	Ehlen, Karl-Heinz	Lt.	26	7
**	Ehlers, Hans	Maj.	3, 1	52 (20 four motor)
*	Ehrenberger, Rudolf	Sgt.	53, 77	49
**	Ehrler, Heinrich	Maj.	77, 5	209 (possibly 220, 5 with Me-262)
	Eichhorn, Günter	Lt	5	7
*	von Eichel-Streiber, Dieter	Maj.	1, 26, 51 27, 44	96
	Eickhoff	1st Lt.	26	5
	von Einsiedel, Graf Heinrich	1st Lt.	3	35
*	Eisenach, Franz	Maj.	54	129
	Ellenrieder, Xaver	Lt.	26	12
	Elles, Franz	Lt	27	5
*	Engel, Walter	Capt.	NJG1, 5	25
*	Engfer, Siegfried	Sgt.	3, 1	58
	Espenlaub, Albert	Lt	27	14
**	Ettel, Wolf-Udo	1st Lt.	3, 27	124
*	Ewald, Heinz	Lt.	52	85 (Barkhorn's wingman)
*	Ewald, Wolfgang	Maj.	52, 3	78 (1 in Spain)
*	Falck, Wolfgang	Col.	ZG1, NJG1	8
*	von Fassong, Horst-Gunther	Capt.	51, 11	136
	Fast, Hans-Joachim	W.O.	26	5

Decoration	Name	Last Wartime Rank	Combat Unit	Victories
	Feiser, Walter	Ofw	5	11
*	Fellerer, Leopold	Capt.	NJG1, 5, 6	41 (39 at night)
	Fengler, Georg	1st Lt.		16
*	Findeisen, Herbert	Capt.	54	67
*	Fink, Gunther	Capt.	54	46
	Fischer, August	Capt.	NJG100	10
*	Fleig, Erwin	Lt.	51, 54	66 (Moelders' wingman)
*	Flogel	Sgt.	NJG1	25
*	Fonnekold, Otto	1st Lt.	52	136
	Förster, Hermann	Lt	27	13
*	Fözö, Josef	Maj.	51, 108	27 (3 in Spain)
*	Francsi, Gustav	Lt.	NJG100	56 (top night fighter on Russian Front)
**	Frank, Hans-Dieter	Capt.	ZG1, NJG1	55 (all at night)
**	Frank, Rudolf	Lt.	NJG3	45 (all at night)
*	Franke, Alfred	Lt.	53	59
*	Franzisket, Ludwig	Maj.	26, 27, 1	43
	Frese	Lt.	3	44
*	Freuworth, Wilhelm	Sgt.	52, 26	58
*	Frey, Hugo	Capt.	11, 1	32 (26 four motor)
**	Freytag, Siegfried	Maj.	7, 77	102
*	Friebel, Herbert	Lt.	53, 51	58
*	Friedrich, Gerhard	Maj.	NJG4, 6	30 (all at night)
*	Frielinghaus, Gustav	Capt.	3	74
	de Fries, Heinz	Sgt.	NJG100	10
	Frohlich, Hans-Juergen	Sgt.	26	5
	Fuchs	Sgt.	51	22
*	Fuchs, Karl	Sgt.	54	67
*	Fuellgrabe, Heinrich	1st Lt.	52, 11	65
	Fuhrmann, Erich	Sgt.		5
	Furch	Lt.	51	30
*	Fuss, Hans	Lt.	3, 51	71
	Gabl, Pepi	Sgt.	51	38
*	Gaiser, Otto	Lt.	52, 51	74
****	Galland, Adolf	Lt. Gen.	27, 26	103
	Galland, Paul	Lt.	26	17
*	Galland, Wilhelm-Ferdinand	Maj.	26	55 (8 four motor)
*	Gallowitsch, Bernd	Maj.	51, 7	64
	Gartner, Josef	Sgt.	26	6
	Gath, Wilhelm	Maj.	26	14
	Gayko, Werner	Oblt	5	13
**	Geiger, August	Capt.	NJG1	53 (all night)
**	Geisshardt, Friedrich	Capt.	26, 77	102
	Gentzen, Hannes	Maj.	JG102	18 (first German ace of WW II)
	Gerhard, Dieter	1st Lt.	52	8
	Gerhard, Gunther	1st Lt.	52	18
	Gerhardt, Werner	Sgt.	26	13
	Gerlitz, Erich	Oblt	27	20
*	Gerth, Werner	Capt.	3, 300, 400	30 (25 four motor)
	von Gienanth, Eugen	Lt.		10
**	Gildner, Paul	1st Lt.	NJG1, 2	48 (44 at night)
	Gleuwitz, Gerhard	Olt	JG52	12

Decora-tion	Name	Last War-time Rank	Combat Unit	Victories
	Glöckner, Rudolf	Oblt	5	32
**	Glunz, Adolf	1st Lt.	26, 7	71 (21 four motor)
*	Goetz, Franz	Maj.	53, 26	63 (5 four motor)
*	Goetz, Hans	Capt.	54	82
*	Golinski, Heinz	Sgt.	53	47 (in 2½ months of combat)
****	Gollob, Gordon	Col.	3, 77	150
*	Goltzsch, Kurt	1st Lt.	2	43
	Gomann, Heinz	Sgt.	26	12
*	Gossow, Heinz	Sgt.	300, 301, 7	70 (9 four motor)
	Gottlob, Heinz	Capt.	26	6
*	Grabmann, Walter	Maj. Gen.	ZG76, 234	12 (includes 6 in Spain)
****	Graf, Hermann	Col.	52, 11	212 (10 four motor)
**	Grasser, Hartmann	Maj.	1, 51, 76	103 (2 four motor)
*	Grassmuck, Berthold	Sgt.	52	65
*	Gratz, Karl	1st Lt.	52, 2	138
**	Greiner, Hermann	Capt.	NJG1	50 (46 at night, 4 four motor by day)
*	Grimm, Heinz	Lt.	NJG1	27 (26 at night)
**	Grislawski, Alfred	Capt.	52, 1	133 (18 four motor)
*	Grollmus, Helmut	Lt.	54	75
*	Gromotka, Fritz	Lt.	27	27 (8 four motor)
*	Gross, Alfred	Lt.	54, 26	52
*	Groth, Erich	Maj.	ZG76	18
	Gruber, Viktor	Lt	27	10
*	Gruenberg, Hans	1st Lt.	3, 52, 7, 44	82 (14 four motor, 5 with Me-262)
	Gruenlinger, Walter	Sgt.	26	7
	Grumm, Josef	Lt.	27	5
	Helms, Bodo	Lt.	5	6
	Grzymalla, Gerhard	Sgt.	26	7
	Guenther, Joachim	Lt.	26	11
	Guhl, Hermann	Lt.	26	15
	Guttmann, Gerhard	Sgt.	26	10
*	Haas, Friedrich	Lt.	52	74
*	Haase, Horst	Capt.	51, 3	82
*	Hachfeld, Wilhelm	Capt.	ZG76, JG51	11
*	Hachtel, August	1st Lt.	JG400	5
	Hacker, Joachim	Lt.	51	32
***	Hackl, Anton	Maj.	11, 26, 300	192 (32 four motor)
*	Hackler, Heinrich	Lt.	77	56
*	Hadeball, Heinz-Martin	Capt.	NJG4, 6	33 (all at night)
**	Hafner, Anton	1st Lt.	51	204
*	Hafner, Ludwig	1st Lt.	3	52
*	Hager, Johannes	Capt.	NJG1	48 (47 at night, 8 one night)
*	Hahn, Hans	Lt.	NJG2	20
**	Hahn, Hans "Assi"	Maj.	54, 2	108 (4 four motor)
*	von Hahn, Hans	Maj.	3, 53, 103	34
*	Haiboeck, Josef	Capt.	26, 52	77
	Halstrick, Heinz	Fw.	5	13
	Hamer	Lt.	51	30
*	Hammerl, Karl	Sgt.	52	63
	Handrick, Gotthardt	Col.	26	20

Decoration	Name	Last War-time Rank	Combat Unit	Victories
	Hanke, Heinz	Lt.	1	9
*	Hannack, Guenther	Capt.	27	47
**	Hannig, Horst	Maj.	54, 2	98
	Harder, Harro	Capt.	53	22 (includes 11 in Spain)
**	Harder, Juergen	Maj.	53, 11	64 (9 four motor)
	Hartwein, Hans-D.	Oblt.	5	16
	Hartigs, Hans	1st Lt.	26	6
	Hartl	Sgt.		11
****	Hartmann, Erich	Maj.	52	352 (world's top ace)
	Hartmann, Ludwig		2	10
*	Haugk, Helmut	Capt.	ZG76, 26	18 (6 four motor)
*	Haugk, Werner	Lt.	ZG76	20 (8 four motor)
	Hauswirth, Wilhelm	Sgt.	52	54
*	Heckmann, Alfred	1st Lt.	3, 26, 44	71
	Heckmann, Gunther	Lt.	51	20
	Heidl, Alfred	Olt.	27	8
	Heeger, Günther	Hptm.		90
	Heimann, Friedrich	Sgt.	51	30
	Hein, Kurt	Sgt.	26	8
	Heinecke, Hans-Joachim	Capt.	27	28
*	Heiner, Engelbert	Sgt.	ZG76, NJG1	11 (possibly several more)
*	Heller, Richard	Lt.	ZG76, 26, 10	15
*	Hennig, Horst	Capt.	KG77, NJG3	5
	Henrici, Eberhard	1st Lt.	26	7
**	Herget, Wilhelm	Maj.	ZG76, NJG3, 1, 4	72 (57 at night)
	Hermann, Kurt		NJG2	9
**	Hermichen, Rolf	Maj.	26, 11, 104	64 (26 four motor)
***	Herrmann, Hajo	Col.	KG4, 30, JG300	9 (9 four motor)
*	Herrmann, Isken	Col.		56
	Heuser, Heinrich	Sgt.	26	5
*	Heyer, Hans-Joachim	Lt.	54	53
	Hilleke, Otto-Heinrich	Lt.	26	6
*	Hirschfeld, Ernst-Erich	1st Lt.	300, 54	45
*	Hissbach, Heinz-Horst	Capt.	NJG2	34
*	Hoeckner, Walter	Maj.	52, 77, 26, 1, 4	68 (5 four motor)
*	Hoefemeier, Heinrich	Capt.	51	96
	Hoerschelmann, Juergen	1st Lt.	3	44
*	Hoerwick, Anton	Sgt.	NJG2, 7	27
	Hoffman, Friedrich	Olt.	27	11
*	Hoffmann, Gerhard	Lt.	52	125
**	Hoffmann, Heinrich	Sgt.	51	63
	Hoffmann, Hermann	Sgt.	26	8
*	Hoffmann, Reinhold	Lt.	54	66 (6 four motor)
*	Hoffmann, Werner	Maj.	NJG3, 5	52 (51 at night)
*	Hofmann, Karl	Lt.	52	70
*	Hofmann, Wilhelm	1st Lt.	26	44 (5 four motor)
*	Hohagen, Erich	Maj.	51, 2, 27, 7, 44	55 (13 four motor)
	Höhn,	Ofhr.	5	6

Decoration	Name	Last Wartime Rank	Combat Unit	Victories
	Holl, Walter	Sgt.	26	7
	Holler, Kurt	Maj.		18
	Holtz, Helmut	Sgt.	51	56
*	Homuth, Gerhard	Maj.	27, 54	63
	Hoppe, Helmut	Capt.	26	24
**	Hrabak, Dietrich	Lt. Col.	54, 52	125
**	Hrdlicka, Franz	Maj.	77, 2	96 (indefinite—could be 45)
*	Hubner, Eckhard	Lt.	3	47
*	Hubner, Wilhelm	Lt.	51	62
	Huebl, Rudolf		1	16
	Huebner, Werner		JG-51	7
	Hulshoff, Karl	Lt. Col.	NJG2	24
*	Huppertz, Herbert	Capt.	51, 2	68 (possibly 76)
*	Husemann, Werner	Maj.	NJG1, 3	32
**	Huy, Wolf-Dietrich	Maj.	77	40
***	Ihlefeld, Herbert	Col.	77, 52, 11, 1	130 (7 in Spain, 15 four motor)
*	Isken, Eduard	Sgt.	77, 53	56 (17 four motor)
**	Jabs, Hans-Joachim	Lt. Col.	ZG76, NJG1	50
	Jackel, Ernst	Sgt.	26	8
	Jakobi, Alfred	Lt.	5	10
	Javer, Erich	Sgt.	26	12
	Jenisch, Kurt	Lt.	27	9
*	Jenne, Peter	Capt.	300	17 (12 four motor)
*	Jennewein, Josef	Lt.	26, 51	86
	Jessen, Heinrich	1st Lt.	26	6
	Johannsen, Hans	Lt.	26	8
*	Johnen, Wilhelm	Capt.	NJG1, 5, 6	34
**	Joppien, Hermann-Friedrick	Capt.	51	70
**	Josten, Guenther	Lt.	51	178
	Jung, Harald	Capt.	51	20
*	Jung, Heinrich	Capt.	54	68
**	von Kageneck, Erbo Graf	Capt.	52, 27	67
	Kaiser, Emil	Olt.	27	13
*	Kaiser, Herbert	Lt.	77, 1, 44	68
*	Kalden, Peter	1st Lt.	51	84
**	Kaldrack, Rolf	Capt.	ZG76	21
	Kalkum, Adolf	Sgt.	53	57
*	Kaminski, Herbert	Maj.	ZG76, JG53	7
*	Karch, Fritz	Capt.	2	47 (21 four motor)
	Kaross, Eberhard	Lt.	NJG100	10
*	Kayser, August	Lt.		25
	Kehl, Dietrich	1st Lt.	26	6
	Keil, Georg	Sgt.	2	36
	Kelch, Guenther	Capt.	26	13
	Keller, Hannes	W.O.	51	24
*	Keller, Lothar	Capt.	3	20
*	Kelter, Kurt	Lt.	54	60
	Keppler, Gerhard	Olt.	27	12
*	Kemethmueller, Heinz	Lt.	3, 54, 26	89
*	Kempf, Karl-Heinz	Lt.	54	65
*	Kennel, Karl	Maj.	ZG1, SG2	34
	Kiefner, Georg	1st Lt.	26	11

Decoration	Name	Last Wartime Rank	Combat Unit	Victories
*	Kiel, Johannes	Capt.	ZG26, 76	20
**	Kientsch, Willi	1st Lt.	27	52 (20 four motor)
*	Kirchmayr, Rudiger	Capt.	1, 11, 44	46 (21 four motor)
**	Kirschner, Joachim	Capt.	3, 27, 53	188
***	Kittel, Otto	1st Lt.	54	267
	Klager, Ernst	Olt.	53	10
*	Klein, Alfons	1st Lt.	52, 11	39
	Klein, Erich	Ofw.	5	5
	Klein, Hans		52	10
*	Klemm, Rudolf	Maj.	54, 26	42 (16 four motor)
*	Kloepper, Heinrich	1st Lt.	51, 1	94
**	Knacke, Reinhold	Capt.	NJG1	44
*	Knappe, Kurt	Sgt.	51, 2	54
	Knauth, Hans	Capt.	51	26
*	Knittel, Emil	Sgt.	54	50
*	Knoke, Heinz	Capt.	1, 11	44 (19 four motor)
*	Koall, Gerhard	Capt.	3, 54, 51	37
	Koch	1st Lt.	26	9
	Koch, Harry		JG-51	13
*	Kociok, Josef	Lt.	ZG76, NJG1	33 (21 at night)
*	Koehler, Armin	Maj.	77	69 (13 four motor)
*	Koenig, Hans-Heinrich	Capt.	ZG76, JG11	24 (20 four motor)
*	Koeppen, Gerhard	Lt.	52	85
*	Koerner, Friedrich	1st Lt.	27	36
*	Koester, Alfons	Capt.	NJG2, 3	25 (all at night, possibly 29)
*	Kolbow, Hans	1st Lt.	51	27
*	Kollak, Reinhard	Sgt.	NJG1, 4	49 (all at night)
*	Korts, Berthold	Lt.	52	113
	Koslowski, Eduard	Sgt.	26	12
	Kosse, Wolfgang	1st Lt.	26	11
	Kothmann, Willi	Olt.	27	13
	Kowalski, Herbert	Lt.	27	5
*	Krafft, Heinrich	Capt.	51, 3	78
	Kraft, Georg "Schorsch"	Sgt.	NJG1	14
**	Kraft, Josef	Capt.	NJG4, 5, 6, 1	56 (all at night)
*	Krahl, Karl-Heinz	Capt.	2, 3	19
	Krainik, Erich	Olt.	27	12
*	Krause, Hans	Capt.	NJG101, 3, 4	28 (all at night)
	Krenz, Herbert	Olt.	27	11
	Kroh, Hans	Lt. Col.		22
*	Kroschinski, Hans-Joachim	Lt.	54	76 (1 four motor)
	Krug, Heinz	1st Lt.	26	9
**	Krupinski, Walter	Capt.	55, 11, 26, 44	197
	Kuehlein, Elias	Lt.	51	36
*	Kuhn, Alfred	Capt.	NJG7	25 (all at night)
	Kuken	Sgt.	51	45
	Kunz, Franz	1st Lt.	26	12
	Kunz, Josef	Lt.	5	15
*	Kutscha, Herbert	Capt.	3, 27, 11	47
*	Lambert, August	1st Lt.	SG2, 151, 77	116 (17 in one day)
*	Lang, Emil	Capt.	52, 54, 26	173 (18 in one day)
*	Lange, Friedrich	Lt.	26	8
*	Lange, Gerhard	Capt.	6	5

Decoration	Name	Last Wartime Rank	Combat Unit	Victories	
*	Lange, Heinz	Maj.	26, 54, 51	70	
	Langer, Hans-Joachim	Hptm.	51, 44	58	
*	Langer, Karl-Heinz	Maj.	3	30	(possibly 68)
*	Laskowski, Erwin	Sgt.	51, 11	46	(14 four motor)
*	Lasse, Kurt	1st Lt.	77	39	
*	Lau, Fritz	Capt.	NJG1	28	(all at night)
	Laub, Karl	Sgt.	26	7	
	Lausch, Bernhard	Sgt.	51	39	
*	Leber, Heinz	Lt.	51	54	
*	Lechner, Alois	Maj.	NJG100, 2	43	(all at night)
*	Leesmann, Karl-Heinz	Maj.	52, 1	37	(5 four motor)
	Leibold, Erwin	Sgt.	26	11	
*	Leie, Erich	Maj.	2, 51, 77	118	
	Leiste	Lt.	54	29	
*	Lemke, Siegfried	Capt.	2	96	(21 four motor)
**	Lemke, Wilhelm	Capt.	3	131	
****	Lent, Helmut	Lt. Col.	NJG3	110	(102 at night)
*	Lepple, Richard	Maj.	51, 105, 6	68	
	Lesch, Heinrich	Oblt.	5	8	
	Leuschel, Rudolf	Capt.	26	9	
	Leykauf, Erwin	1st Lt.	26	33	
	Liebelt, Fritz	Lt.	51	25	
	von Lieres, Carl	1st Lt.	27	31	
*	Liesendahl, Frank	Capt.	53, 2	50	
*	Lignitz, Arnold	Capt.	51, 54	25	
	Lillenhoff, von Rolf	Fhr.	5	6	
	Lindelaub, Friedrich	Sgt.	26	5	
	Lindemann, Theodor	1st Lt.	26	7	
*	Lindner, Anton	1st Lt.	51	73	
*	Lindner, Walter	Lt.	52	64	
*	Linke, Lothar	1st Lt.	NJG1, 2	28	(25 at night)
*	Linz, Rudolf	Lt.	5	70	
**	Lipfert, Helmut	Capt.	52	203	
*	Lippert, Wolfgang	Capt.	53, 27	29	(4 in Spain)
**	zu Lippe-Weissenfeld, Prince Egmont	Maj.	NJG2, 1, 5	51	(all at night)
*	Litjens, Stefan	Sgt.	53	38	(5 four motor)
*	Loos, Gerhard	1st Lt.	54	92	
*	Loos, Walter	Sgt.	301	38	(22 four motor)
*	Losigkeit, Fritz	Maj.	26, 1, 51, 77	68	
*	Lucas, Werner	Capt.	3	106	
	Lübking, August	Ofw.	5	28	
	Lüdecke, Friedrich	Lt.	5	6	
	Lüder, Rudolf	Hptm.	5	6	
*	Luecke, Max-Hermann	1st Lt.	51	81	
*	Lueddecke, Fritz	Sgt.	51	50	
	Lueders, Franz	Sgt.	26	5	
**	Luetje, Herbert	Maj.	NJG1, 6	53	(51 at night)
***	Luetzow, Gunther	Col.	3, 44	108	(5 in Spain)
*	Lutter, Johannes	Sgt.	ZG1, 76	12	
	Lutzka,	Uffz.	5	5	
	Luy, August	Ofw.	5	35	
	Maak, Ernst	Olt.	27	12	
*	Machold, Werner	Capt.	2	32	
	Mackenstedt, Willy	Sgt.	26	6	
*	Mader, Anton	Lt. Col.	ZG76, JG2, 77	86	

Decora-tion	Name	Last War-time Rank	Combat Unit	Victories
	Mahikuch, Heinz	Oblt.	77	16
*	Mai, Lothar	Lt.	51	90
*	Makrocki, Wilhelm	Maj.	ZG76, JG26	9
**	von Maltzahn, Guenther	Col.	53	68
*	Marquardt, Heinz	Sgt.	51	121 (12 in one day)
****	Marseille, Hans-Joachim	Capt.	52, 27	158 (17 in one day)
*	Matern, Karl-Heinrich	Capt.	ZG1, 76	12
*	Matoni, Walter	Maj.	27, 26, 2	44 (14 four motor)
	Matzak, Kurt	Lt.		18
	May, Lothar	Sgt.	51	45
***	Mayer, Egon	Lt. Col.	2	102 (25 four motor)
*	Mayer, Hans-Karl	Capt.	53	38 (8 in Spain)
	Mayer, Otto	Capt.	27	22
*	Mayer, Wilhelm	Lt.	26	27 (6 four motor)
*	Mayerl, Maximilian	Capt.	51, 1	76
*	Meckel, Helmut	1st Lt.	3, 77	25 (possibly 50)
*	Meier, Johannes-Hermann	Lt.	26, 51	77
*	Meimberg, Julius	Maj.	2, 53	53
*	Meister, Ludwig	Capt.	NJG4, 1	41 (all at night)
	Meltzer	Sgt.	52	35
	Menge, Robert	Lt.	26	18 (4 in Spain)
*	Mertens, Helmut	Capt.	3	97 (20 four motor)
	Methfessel, Werner		LG-1	8
**	Meurer, Manfred	Capt.	NJG1	65 (all at night)
	Mecke, Erhardt	Fw.	5	12
	Mendl, Arthur	Uffz.	5	9
	Mentnich, Karl	Lt.	27	8
	Meyer, Conny	Maj.	26	16
*	Meyer, Eduard	Lt.	ZG26	18
	Meyer, Walter	1st Lt.	26	18
*	Michalek, Georg	Maj.	54, 3, 108	59
**	Michalski, Gerhard	Lt. Col.	53, 4	73 (13 four motor)
*	Miethig, Rudolf	Capt.	52	101
**	Mietusch, Klaus	Maj.	26	72 (10 four motor)
*	Mink, Wilhelm	Sgt.	51	72
	Mischkot, Bruno	Lt.	26	7
*	Missner, Helmut	Sgt.	52, 54	82
*	Modrow, Ernst-Wilhelm	Capt.	NJG1	33 (all at night)
****	Moelders, Werner	Col.	51, 53	115 (14 in Spain)
*	Moritz, Wilhelm	Maj.	51, 3	44
*	Mors, August	Lt.	5	60
**	Mueller, Friedrich-Karl "Tutti"	Maj.	53, 3	140
*	Mueller, Friedrich "Nose"	Maj.	NJG11, 300	30 (all at night)
*	Mueller, Hans	Capt.	NJG10	30 (all at night)
	Mueller, Kurt	1st Lt.	26	5
*	Mueller, Rudolf	Sgt.	5	101
	Mueller, Wilhelm	Sgt.	26	10
	Mueller-Duhe, Gerhard	Lt.	26	5
***	Muencheberg, Joachim	Maj.	26, 77	135
*	Muenster, Leopold	Lt.	3	95 (8 four motor)
*	Muetherich, Hubert	1st Lt.	51, 54	43

Decoration	Name	Last War-time Rank	Combat Unit	Victories
	Munderloh, Georg	W.O.	54	20
*	Munz, Karl "Fox"	Lt.	52, 7	60
	Nabrich, Josef	1st Lt.	NJG1	18 (17 at night)
*	Nacke, Heinz	Lt. Col.	ZG76, NJG3	12
*	Naumann, Johannes	Maj.	26, 6, 7	34 (7 four motor)
*	Nemitz, Willi	Lt.	52	81
	Neu, Wolfgang	Capt.	26	12 (7 four motor)
*	Neuhoff, Hermann	Lt.	53	40
	Neumann, Eduard	Lt. Col.	27	13
*	Neumann, Helmut	Lt.	5	62
*	Neumann, Karl	Lt.	5, 7	75
*	Neumann, Klaus	Lt.	51, 3, 7, 44	37 (5 with Me-262)
	Ney, Siegfried	Sgt.		11
	Niederhöfer, Hans	Olt.	27	12
**	Nordmann, Karl-Gottfried	Lt. Col.	51	78
*	Norz, Jakob	Lt.	77, 5	117
****	Nowotny, Walter	Maj.	54, 7, 101	258 (2 with Me-262)
	Oberlander, Horst	Uffz.	5	9
*	Obleser, Friedrich	Lt.	52	127
***	Oesau, Walter	Col.	3, 2, 1	125 (8 in Spain, 10 four motor)
*	Ohlrogge, Walter	Lt.	3, 7	83
*	Olejnik, Robert	Maj.	2, 3, 1, 400	41
*	Omert, Emil	Capt.	3, 2, 77	70
*	Osterkamp, Theo	Lt. Gen.	51	6 (32 in WW I)
***	Ostermann, Max-Helmuth	1st Lt.	54	102
*	Patuschka, Horst	Capt.	NJG2	23 (all at night)
*	Peterburs, Hans	Sgt.	ZG76, 1	18
*	Petermann, Viktor	Lt.	52, 7	64 (4 after losing his left arm)
	Peters, Erhard	Capt.		22
	Pfeiffer, Karl	Sgt.		10
*	Pflanz, Rudolf	Capt.	2	52
	Pfueller, Helmut	Sgt.	51	28
***	Philipp, Hans	Lt. Col.	54, 1	206
*	Philipp, Wilhelm	Sgt.	26, 54	81
*	Pichler, Johannes	Lt.	77	75 (16 four motor)
*	Piffer, Anton-Rudolf	Lt.	JG1	26 (20 four motor)
*	Pingel, Rolf	Maj.	26, 53	26 (4 in Spain)
	Plucker, Karl-Heinz	1st Lt.	1, 52	34
*	Pohs, Josef	Lt.	54	43
	Polster, Wolfgang	Sgt.	26	5
	Pragen, Hans	Lt.	26	23
*	Preinfalk, Alexander	Sgt.	77, 51, 53	76
***	Priller, Josef "Pips"	Col.	51, 26	101 (11 four motor)
	Pringle, Rolf-Peter	Lt.	2	22
	Preisler, Bela	Uffz.	5	6
*	Pusch, Emil	Sgt.	NJG2	30 (possibly more, all at night)
*	Puschmann, Herbert	Capt.	51	54
*	Puttfargen, Dietrich	Maj.	KG51	5
	Putzkuhl, Joseph	1st Lt.	NJG100	26 (all at night, 7 on one mission)
*	Quaet-Faslem, Klaus	Maj.	53, 3	49
	Quante, Richard	Sgt.	51	44

Decoration	Name	Last War-time Rank	Combat Unit	Victories
*	Quast, Werner	Sgt.	52	84
*	Rademacher, Rudolf	1st Lt.	54, 7	126 (10 four motor, 8 with Me-262)
*	Radener, Waldemar	1st Lt.	26, 300	36 (16 four motor)
**	Radusch, Guenther	Lt. Col.	NJG1, 2, 3, 5	64 (63 at night, includes 1 in Spain)
**	Raht, Gerhard	Capt.	NJG3, 2	58 (all at night)
***	Rall, Guenther	Maj.	52, 11	275
*	Rammelt, Karl	Maj.	51	46 (11 four motor)
*	Rauch, Alfred	Lt.	51	60
*	Rauh, Hubert	Maj.	NJG1, 4	31 (all at night)
*	Redlich, Karl-Wolfgang	Maj.	27	43 (2 in Spain)
	Reiff	Sgt.	3	48
***	Reinert, Ernst-Wilhelm	1st Lt.	77, 27	174 (2 four motor)
	Reinhard, Emil	Sgt.	54	42
	Reischer, Peter	1st Lt.	26	19
*	Remmer, Hans	Capt.	27	26 (8 four motor)
*	Resch, Anton	1st Lt.	52	91
*	Resch, Rudolf	Maj.	52, 51	94 (1 in Spain)
*	Reschke, Willi	Sgt.	300, 301	26 (18 four motor)
*	von Rettberg, Ralph	Col.	ZG26, 2	8
	Reuter, Horst	Hptm.	27	21
	Richter, Hans	Lt.	27	22
*	Richter, Rudolf	Lt.	54	70
	Roch, Eckhard	Lt.	26	5
**	Roedel, Gustav	Col.	21, 27	98 (12 four motor)
*	Roehrig, Hans	Capt.	53	75
**	Roekker, Heinz	Capt.	NJG2	64 (63 at night)
*	Rohwer, Detler	Capt.	3, 1	38
**	Rollwage, Herbert	1st Lt.	53	102 (44 four motor)
*	Romm, Oskar	1st Lt.	52, 3	92
	Rosenberg, Heinrich	Olt.	27	12
*	Rossiwall, Theodor	Lt. Col.	ZG76, NJG4	17
*	Rossmann, Edmund	Lt.	52	93
	Rost, Wolfgang	Lt.	5	12
	Roth, Willi	Lt.	26	20
*	Ruebell, Guenther	Capt.	51, 104	47
****	Ruedel, Hans-Ulrich	Col.	SG2	11 (2530 sorties!)
***	Rudorffer, Erich	Maj.	2, 54, 7	222 (13 on a single mission, 10 four motor, 12 with Me-262)
*	Rueffler, Helmut	Sgt.	3	70 (8 four motor)
*	Ruhl, Franz	1st Lt.	3	64 (12 four motor)
*	Rupp, Friedrich	Lt.	54	53
	Russ, Otto	Uffz.	53	27
	Rysayy, Martin	1st Lt.	26	8
*	Sachsenberg, Heinz	Lt.	52	104
	Salwender, Florian	Ofw.	5	24
*	Sattig, Karl	Capt.	54	53
	Sawallisch, Erwin	Sgt.	27	38
***	zu Sayn-Wittgenstein, Prince Heinrich	Maj.	NJG2	83 (all at night)
**	Schack, Guenther	Capt.	51, 3	174
*	Schact, Emil	1st Lt.		25
*	Schalk, Johannes	Col.	ZG26, NJG3	21

Decora-tion	Name	Last War-time Rank	Combat Unit	Victories
**	Schall, Franz	Capt.	52, 7	137 (14 with Me-262)
	Scharf, Ludwig	Uffz.	5	12
	Schaschke, Gerhard	Hptm.	5	20
	Schauder, Paul	Capt.	26	20
*	Scheel, Gunther	Lt.	54	71 (70 missions, 71 kills)
	Scheer, Klaus	Lt.	NJG100	24
*	Scheffel, Rudolf	Capt.	ZG1, 26	7
*	Schellmann, Wolfgang	Lt. Col.	2, 27	26 (12 in Spain)
**	Schenck, Wolfgang	Maj.	ZG1, SG2, KG515	18
*	Schentke, Georg	1st Lt.	3	90
*	Scherfling, Karl-Heinz	Sgt.	NJG1	31 (all at night)
	Scheyda, Erich	Lt.	26	20
*	Schiess, Franz	Capt.	53	67
*	Schilling, Wilhelm	1st Lt.	54	50
*	Schleef, Hans	1st Lt.	3, 4	98
*	Schleinghege, Hermann	Lt.	3, 54	96
*	Schlichting, Joachim	Maj.	27, 26	8 (5 in Spain)
	Schlossstein, Karl-F.	Oblt.	5	8
*	Schmid, Johannes	Maj.	26	41
*	Schmidt, Dietrich	1st Lt.	NJG1	39 (all at night)
*	Schmidt, Erich	1st Lt.	53	47
	Schmidt, Gottfried	1st Lt.	26	8
**	Schmidt, Heinz "Johnny"	Capt.	52	173
	Schmidt, Johannes	1st Lt.	26	12
*	Schmidt, Rudolf	Sgt.	77	51
*	Schmidt, Winifried	Capt.	3	19
****	Schnaufer, Heinz-Wolfgang	Maj.	NJG1, 4	121 (all at night, 9 in one 24-hour period)
*	Schneeweis, Wolfgang	Capt.	NJG101	17 (all at night)
	Schneider, Gerhard	Lt.	51	41
	Schneider, Walter	1st Lt.	26	20
*	Schnell, Karl-Heinz	Maj.	51, 44	72
**	Schnell, Siegfried	Maj.	2, 54	93
	Schmidt, Heinz	Lt.	27	6
	Schneider, August	Lt.	5	11
	Schneider, Bernd	Otl.	27	23
	Schneider, Hugo	Lt.	27	9
*	Schnoerrer, Karl "Quax"	Lt.	54, 7	46 (9 four motor)
*	Schob, Herbert	Capt.	ZG76, 26	28 (6 in Spain, 10 four motor)
**	Schoenert, Rudolf	Maj.	NJG1, 2, 5, 6	64 (all at night)
*	Schoenfelder, Helmut	Sgt.	51	56
*	Schoepfel, Gerhard	Maj.	26, 4, 6	40 (3 four motor)
	Schöfbock, Erich	Otl.	27	12
	Scholz, Günter	Oblt.	5	22
**	Schramm, Herbert	Capt.	53, 27	42 (3 four motor)
***	Schroer, Werner	Maj.	3, 27, 54	114 (26 four motor)
*	Schroeter, Fritz	Maj.	2, SG10, 4	50
	Schubert, Hans		1	8
**	Schuck, Walter	1st Lt.	5, 7	206 (8 with Me-262)

Decora-tion	Name	Last War-time Rank	Combat Unit	Victories
*	Schuhmacher, Leo	Lt.	ZG76, JG1, 44	23 (10 four motor)
*	Schulte, Franz	Sgt.	77	46
*	Schulte, Helmuth	Capt.	NJG5	25 (all at night)
*	Schultz, Otto	1st Lt.	51	73 (8 four motor)
	Schulwitz, Gerhard	Lt.	26	9
*	Schulz, Otto	1st Lt.	27	51
	Schumacher, Werner	Uffz.	5	10
*	Schumann, Heinz	Maj.	51, 2, SKG10	18
*	Schwaiger, Franz	Lt.	3	67
	Schwanecke, Günther	Oblt.	5	10
	Schwartz, Gerhard	Sgt.	51	20
	Schwarz, Erich	Sgt.	26	11
	Seckel, Georg	Lt.	77	40
	Seegatz, Hermann	Capt.	26	31
*	Seeger, Guenther	1st Lt.	53, 2	56 (8 four motor)
*	Seelmann, Georg	1st Lt.	51	39
	Segatz, Hermann	Hptm.	5	31
	Seidel	Sgt.	51	20
	Seidel, Alfred	Otl.	53	10
*	Seifert, Johannes	Lt. Col.	26	57
**	Seiler, Reinhard	Maj.	54, 104	109 (9 in Spain)
*	Semelka, Waldemar	Lt.	52	65
*	Semrau, Paul	Maj.	NJG2	46 (all at night)
*	Sengschmitt, Fritz	1st Lt.	ZG76, 26	15
**	Setz, Heinrich	Maj.	27	138
*	Siegler, Peter	Sgt.	54	48
*	Sigmund, Rudolf	Capt.	NJG1, 3	28 (26 at night)
	Simon	Sgt.	51	22
*	Simsch, Siegfried	Capt.	52, 1, 11	95
	Sinner, Rudolf	Maj.	27	39
*	Sochatzky, Kurt	1st Lt.	3	38
	Soffing, Waldemar	Lt.	26	33
*	Sommer, Gerhard	Capt.	11, 1	20 (14 four motor)
	Sommer, Hermann	Hptm.	NJG2	19
**	Spaete, Wolfgang	Maj.	54, 400, 7	99 (5 four motor with Me-262)
**	Specht, Guenther	Lt. Col.	ZG26, JG11	32 (15 four motor)
**	Spies, Wilhelm	Maj.	ZG26, JG53	20
	Spreckles, Robert	Capt.	11, 1	21 (6 four motor)
*	Sprick, Gustav	1st Lt.	26	31
	Stadek, Karl	Sgt.	51	25
**	Stahlschmidt, Hans	1st Lt.	27	59
*	Staiger, Hermann	Maj.	51, 26, 1, 7	63 (26 four motor)
	Stammberger, Otto	1st Lt.	26	7
*	Stechmann, Hans	Sgt.	3	33
	Stedtfeld, Gunther	1st Lt.	51	25
*	Steffen, Karl	Sgt.	52	59
	Steffens, Hans Joachim	Lt.	51	22
***	Steinbatz, Leopold	Lt.	52	99
*	Steinhausen, Guenther	Lt.	27	40
***	Steinhoff, Johannes	Col.	26, 52, 77, 7, 44	176 (6 with Me-262)
*	Steinmann, Wilhelm	Maj.	27, 4, 44	44 (6 four motor)
	Steis, Heinrich	Lt.	27	21
*	Stendel, Fritz	Maj.	51, 5	39
	Stengel, Walter	1st Lt.	51	34

Decoration	Name	Last Wartime Rank	Combat Unit	Victories
	Sternberg, Horst	Capt.	26	23
**	Sterr, Heinrich "Bazi"	1st Lt.	54	130
	Stigler, Franz	1st Lt.	27	28
	Stolinberger, Hans		SG-1	10
*	Stolle, Bruno	Capt.	51, 2, 11	35 (5 four motor)
	Stolte, Paul		JG-1	43
*	Stolte, Paul-August	Capt.	3	5
**	Stotz, Maximilian	Capt.	54	189
*	Strakeljahn, Friedrich-Wilhelm	Capt.	5, SG4	18
*	Strassl, Hubert	Sgt.	51	67 (15 one day, 30 in 4 days)
***	Streib, Werner	Col.	NJG1	66 (scored 1st night fighter victory)
**	Strelow, Hans	Lt.	51	68
	Stritzel, Fritz	Sgt.	2	19
	Strohecker, Karl	Sgt.	NJG100	10
**	Struening, Heinz	Capt.	NJG2, 1	56 (all at night)
	Stückler, Alfred		JG-27	10
*	Stumpf, Werner	Sgt.	53	47
*	Sturm, Heinrich	Capt.	52	157
	Surau, Alfred	Sgt.	3	46
*	Suss, Ernst	1st Lt.	52, 11	70
*	Szameitat, Paul	Capt.	NJG3	29
	Szuggar, Willy	Sgt.	26	9
	Tabbat, Adolf	Sgt.	26	5
*	Tange, Otto	Lt.	51	68
	Tangermann, Kurt	Lt.	54	60
*	Tanzer, Kurt	Lt.	51	143 (4 four motor)
	Tautscher, Gabriel	W.O.	51	55
**	Tegtmeier, Fritz	Lt.	54, 7	146
*	Teige, Waldemar	Sgt.	NJG6	11 (9 at night)
	Tetzner, Hans	Oblt.	5	20
*	Teumer, Alfred	1st Lt.	54, 7	76
*	Theil, Edwin	Capt.	52, 51	76
*	Thierfelder, Werner	Capt.	ZG26	27
	Thimmig, Wolfgang	Lt. Col.	NJG1, 2, 4	24
**	Thyben, Gerhard	1st Lt.	3, 54	157
*	Tichy, Eckehard	Capt.	53, 3	25 (all four motor)
*	Tietzen, Horst	Capt.	51	27 (7 in Spain)
**	Tonne, Guenther	Maj.	ZG1, 26	15 (possibly 20)
**	Tonne, Wolfgang	Capt.	53	122
**	Traft, Eduard	Maj.	ZG26	37
*	Trautloft, Hannes	Col.	51, 54	57 (4 in Spain)
*	Truenkel, Rudolf	Capt.	77, 52	138 (bailed out 5 times in 10 days)
**	Uben, Kurt	Maj.	77, 2	110
*	Udet, Hans	Lt.	26	20
	Ulbrich	Sgt.	51	33
	Ulenberg, Horst	Lt.	26	17
*	Unger, Willy	Lt.	3, 7	22 (19 four motor)
	Unzeitig, Robert	Lt.	26	10
	Vandeweerd, Heinrich	Sgt.	26	6
*	Vechtel, Bernhard	Lt.	51	108
*	Viedebantt, Helmut	Maj.	ZG1, SG10	23

Decoration	Name	Last Wartime Rank	Combat Unit	Victories
**	Vinke, Heinz	Sgt.	NJG1	54 (all at night)
	Vinzent, Otto	1st Lt.	54	44
	Vogel, Ferdinand	Capt.	27	33
*	Vogt, Heinz-Gerhard	1st Lt.	26	48 (8 four motor)
	Vollett, Hans	Lt.	5	11
*	Wachowiak, Friedrich	Lt.	52, 3	86 (possibly up to 40 more)
*	Wagner, Edmund	Sgt.	51	57
*	Wagner, Rudolf	Lt.	51	81
**	Waldmann, Hans	1st Lt.	52, 3, 7	134 (2 with Me-262)
	Walter, Horst	1st Lt.	51	25
	Wandam, Siegfried	1st Lt.	NJG1	10
*	Wandel, Joachim	Capt.	54	75
**	Weber, Karl-Heim	Capt.	51, 1	136
*	Wefers, Heinrich	Sgt.	54	52
*	Wehmeyer, Alfred	1st Lt.	ZG26	18
	Wehnelt, Herbert	Maj.	2, 51	36
*	Weik, Hans	Capt.	3	36 (22 four motor)
	Weinitschke, Dietrich	Fw.	5	18
**	Weiss, Robert	Capt.	54	121
**	Weissenberger, Theodor	Maj.	5, 7	208 (8 with Me-262)
*	Weissmann, Ernst	1st Lt.	51	69
**	Welter, Kurt	1st Lt.	300, NJG11	60 (30 four motor)
	Weneckers	Sgt.	1	9
*	Werfft, Peter	Maj.	27	26 (12 four motor)
*	Wernicke, Heinz "Piepl"	Lt.	54	117
*	Wernitz, Ulrich	Lt.	54	101
*	von Werra, Franz	Capt.	3, 53	21
**	Wessling, Otto	1st Lt.	3	83
	Westphal, Hans-Juergen	Capt.	26	22
	Wettstein, Helmut	1st Lt.	54	34
*	Wever, Walter	1st Lt.	51, 7	60
**	Wick, Helmut	Maj.	2	56
	Wiegand, Gerhard	Lt.	26	32
	Wiegand, Heinfried	Fw.	5	9
	Wienhusen, Franz	Hptm.	5	12
**	Wiese, Johannes	Maj.	52, 77	133 (+75 probables)
***	Wilcke, Wolf-Dietrich	Col.	53, 3, 1	161
*	Willius, Karl	1st Lt.	26	50 (11 four motor)
	Winkler, Max	1st Lt.	27	21
*	von Winterfelt, Alexander	Lt. Col.	2, 77	9 (fighter pilot of WW I also)
*	Wischnewski, Hermann	W.O.	300	28
	Witzel, Hans	Lt.	26	14
*	Woehnert, Ulrich	Lt.	54	86
*	Wohlers, Heinrich	Maj.	NJG6	29
*	Woidich, Franz	1st Lt.	27, 52, 400	110
**	Wolf, Albin	Lt.	54	144 (possibly 176)
*	Wolf, Hermann	Lt.	52, 11, 7	57
	Wolf, Robert	Lt.		21
*	Wolfrum, Walter	1st Lt.	52	137
	Wollmann, David	Lt.	5	21
	Woltersdorf, Emil	1st Lt.	NJG1	10

Decora-tion	Name	Last War-time Rank	Combat Unit	Victories
	Wuebke, Waldemar	Capt.	54, 101	15
	Wuensch, Karl	Lt.	27	25
	Wuenschelmeyer, Karl	1st Lt.	26	16
*	Wuerfel, Otto	Lt.	51	79
***	Wurmheller, Josef	Maj.	53, 52, 1	102 (13 four motor)
	Zeller, Joachim	Sgt.	26	7
*	Zellot, Walter	Lt.	53	85
*	Zimmermann, Oskar	Lt.	51, 3	48 (14 four motor)
	Zink, Fuelbert	Capt.	26	36
	Zirngibl, Josef	Sgt.	26	9
**	Zorner, Paul	Maj.	NJG2, 3, 5	59 (all at night)
	Zoufahl, Franz-Josef	Sgt.	51	26
*	Zweigart, Eugen-Ludwig	1st Lt.	54	69
**	Zwernemann, Josef "Jupp"	1st Lt.	52, 11	126
*	Zwesken, Rudi	Sgt.	52, 300	25

The Order of the Iron Cross, World War II

The Order of the Iron Cross is awarded in the following sequence:
1. The Iron Cross, 2d Class
2. The Iron Cross, 1st Class
3. The Knight's Cross to the Iron Cross
4. The Knight's Cross to the Iron Cross with Oak Leaves
5. The Knight's Cross to the Iron Cross with Oak Leaves and with Swords
6. The Knight's Cross to the Iron Cross with Oak Leaves and Swords and Diamonds
7. The Knight's Cross to the Iron Cross with Golden Oak Leaves and Swords and Diamonds
8. The Great Cross of the Iron Cross

NOTE The #3 award, The Knight's Cross, was won by approx. 7500 military men.
The #4 award, The Oak Leaves, was won by 860 military men.
The #5 award, The Swords award, was won by 154 military men.
The #6 award, The Brilliants (or Diamonds), was won by 27 military men.
The #7 award, with Golden Oak Leaves, was won only by famed Stuka pilot Hans Ulrich Ruedel.
The #8 award, The Great Cross, was issued only to Reichsmarschall Hermann Goering.
Approx. 1730 Luftwaffe personnel won The Knight's Cross.
192 won The Oak Leaves.
41 won The Oak Leaves and Swords.
10 won The Oak Leaves, Swords and Diamonds.
1 won The Golden Oak Leaves, Swords and Diamonds (Ruedel).
1 won The Great Cross of the Iron Cross (Goering).

The German Luftwaffe Fighter Aces

KNIGHT'S CROSS with OAK LEAVES, SWORDS, and DIAMONDS
Germany's Highest Military Award

Galland, Adolf	104 Victories	
Gollob, Gordon	150	,,
Graf, Hermann	212	,,
Hartmann, Erich	352	,,
Lent, Helmut	110	,, (102 at night)
Marseille, Hans-Joachim	158	,,
Moelders, Werner	101	,, (+ 14 in Spain)
Nowotny, Walter	258	,,
Ruedel, Hans-Ulrich	11	,,
Schnaufer, Heinz	121	,, (all at night)

Knight's Cross *with* Oak Leaves *and* Swords
The Second Highest Award

Baer, Heinz	220 Victories	(16 with Me-262 jet)
Barkhorn, Gerhard	301	,,	
Batz, Wilhelm	237	,,	
Buehligen, Kurt	112	,,	
Hackl, Anton	192	,,	
Herrmann, Hajo	9	,,	
Ihlefeld, Herbert	130	,,	(includes 7 in Spain)
Kittel, Otto	267	,,	
Luetzow, Guenther	108	,,	(includes 5 in Spain)
Mayer, Egon	102	,,	
Muencheberg, Joachim	135	,,	
Oesau, Walter	123	,,	(includes 8 in Spain)
Ostermann, Max Helmut	102	,,	
Philipp, Hans	206	,,	
Priller, Josef	101	,,	
Rall, Guenther	275	,,	
Reinert, Ernst Wilhelm	174	,,	
Rudorffer, Erich	222	,,	
Sayn-Wittgenstein, Prince zu	83	,,	(night)
Schroer, Werner	114	,,	
Steinbatz, Leopold	99	,,	
Steinhoff, Johannes	176	,,	
Streib, Werner	66	,,	(night)
Wilcke, Wolf-Dietrich	162	,,	
Wuermheller, Josef	102	,,	

Glossary

A-20: Twin-engined Douglas attack bomber, also known as a "Boston" or "Havoc."

Abort: Turn back from an aerial mission before its completion.

Acceptable Loss: Combat loss judged not to be high for results obtained; within the limits of affordable cost.

Aerial Combat: Combat between or among hostile forces in the air.

Aileron: Control surface on wing of an airplane.

Airacobra: Nickname for the Bell P-39 fighter airplane.

Air Strip: Generally a landing field for aircraft.

Ammo: Ammunition.

Anchor: Apply air brakes, flaps, etc., in an attempt to slow down rapidly in flight. "Throw out the anchor"—reduce speed as rapidly as possible.

Angle-off: The angular measurement between line of flight of an aerial target and line of sight of an attacking aircraft.

Anoxia: Absence of oxygen in the blood experienced by pilots while flying at high altitudes.

Attrition: The process of permanent loss of aircraft due to enemy action or other operational or defined causes.

Auger-in: A slang term meaning to crash in an airplane.

Ausbildungsabteilung: Training Branch.

Ausbildungsstab: Training Staff.

AVG: American Volunteer Group. American volunteers under the command of Claire Chennault who aided the Chinese against the Japanese 1941–1942.

B-17: Four-engined bomber by Boeing. The "Flying Fortress."

B-24: Four-engined bomber by Consolidated. The "Liberator."

B-25: Two-engined bomber by North American. The "Mitchell."

B-26: Two-engined bomber by Martin. The "Marauder."

Bail or Bailout: The action of parachuting from an airplane. Sometimes written as "bale out."

Bandit: Pilot slang for an enemy aircraft.

Barrel Roll: An aerial maneuver in which an airplane is caused to make a complete roll about a line offset but parallel to the longitudinal axis, as the chamber of a revolver revolves about the barrel. Sometimes called a "slow roll," but the two are slightly different.

Belly-land: To land an airplane on its underside without the benefit of the landing gear. A skidding landing with no wheels, due to their having been shot away in combat or the lowering mechanism rendered inoperative.

Big Week: 20–25 February 1944. A maximum effort by Allied bombers against Germany.

Bird: An airplane is a bird to a pilot.

Bird Dog: A radio direction-finder used in aircraft.

Blind Approach: Approach to a landing under conditions of very low visibility made with the aid of instruments or radio.

Blitz, Blitzkrieg: Highly mobile form of warfare introduced by the German Army, featuring close cooperation between fast-moving armored forces and air power. Old-style army units could not cope with these new techniques, which led to rapid victories. Literally, "flash war"; generally, lightning war.

Blue Max: Top German decoration of World War II, officially the Pour le Mérite.

B.O.B.: Battle of Britain.

Bogey: First sighting of an unidentified airplane in flight.

Bounce: To attack an aircraft or target on the ground from another aircraft. Especially applied to catching an enemy pilot unawares.

Break!: "Break right!" or "Break left!" was a signal to an airborne comrade to make an instantaneous turn in the direction indicated, a maneuver designed to avoid being shot down by an attacking enemy aircraft.

Buck Fever: The tension and excitement experienced by a fighter pilot in his first few combat missions. "Buck fever" usually leads to wild firing and missed targets. A fighter pilot no longer so afflicted is said to have conquered his buck fever.

Buzz Bomb: The German V-1 pilotless missile, so named because of the buzz-like noise of its pulse-jet engine.

CAP: Combat Air Patrol.

Ceiling Zero: Atmospheric condition when cloud height or ceiling above ground is less than fifty feet to its base.

Chimney: Code name for German radar station; also called "Wassermann."

Chop Up: To shoot up an aerial or ground target, the bullets tearing the target to pieces.

Christmas Trees: Colored flares used by the British Pathfinders to mark ground targets at night for the bomber streams.

Clobber: To crash an airplane; to destroy or damage an area or airplane with gunfire.

Cockpit: The pilot's seat and controls in an airplane.

Condor Legion: A volunteer Air Force made up from the Luftwaffe to gain experience in Spain in supporting General Franco, 1936–39.

Controlled Interception: Friendly aircraft are directed to the enemy aircraft or target by radio from a ground or air station.

Control Tower: A radio-equipped facility at an airfield manned by trained personnel to control air and ground traffic on or above the field.

Court-martial: To try or judge a person in a military court.

Damaged: As claimed in combat, an aircraft claimed as partially destroyed but subject to repair.

Day Fighter: A fighter airplane designed for use when the target can be seen in daylight.

Deck: The ground, the cloud level, or the deck of an aircraft carrier.

Deflection Shot: The angle of a shot in gunnery measured between the line of sight to the target and the line of sight to the aiming point.

Ditch: To force-land an airplane in the water with intention of abandonment.

Dogfight: An aerial battle between opposing fighter aircraft.

Dry Run: A practice exercise or rehearsal.

Eagle Squadrons: Three RAF squadrons composed of American volunteer pilots during the early years of World War II.

Ejector Seat: A seat designed to catapult at sufficient velocity to clear the airplane completely.

ETD: Estimated Time of Departure.

ETO: European Theater of Operations.

External Store: Any fuel tank, bomb, rocket, etc., attached to the wings or fuselage of an airplane.

Fat Dog: Luftwaffe expression for large bombers loaded with bombs. Sometimes called "fat target"—a target of considerable value.

Feldwebel: Flight Sergeant.

Flaking: Loss of members of a flight of aircraft as they turn back homeward before reaching the target.

Fliegerdivision: An Air Division.

Fliegerhorstkommandant: Airfield Commandant.

Fliegerkorps: Air Command Office (Operational).

Flivo: Abbreviation of *Fliegerverbindungoffiziere.* A Luftwaffe liaison officer with Army units, coordinating close-support air action.

Forced Landing: A landing forced upon an aircraft through mechanical failure or any other reason.

Four-motor: A four-motored bomber. In World War II these were generally the British Halifax, Stirling, Lancaster, and Lincoln; American four-motors were the Boeing B-17 Fortress and Consolidated B-24 Liberator.

Fuehrerhauptquartier: Fuehrer Headquarters.

Fuerungsstab: Operations Staff.

Full Bore: Full throttle or full speed ahead.

FW-190: The Focke-Wulf single-engined fighter plane.

Gaggle: A number of aircraft flying in loose formation.

Gear: Short for landing gear, the wheels of an airplane.

General der Jagdflieger: General of the Fighter Forces.

General der Kampfflieger: General of the Bomber Forces.

Generalstab: General Staff.

Geschwader: The largest mobile, homogeneous formation in the Luftwaffe. A Wing. In the Luftwaffe a Fighter Wing *(Jagdgeschwader)* consisted of three *Gruppen.* Thus:

> A Wing consisted of three *Gruppen* (Groups)
> A *Gruppe* ,, ,, ,, *Staffeln* (Squadrons)
> A *Staffel* ,, ,, ,, *Schwarms*

Each *Schwarm* consisted of four aircraft, and was divided into two *Rotten.* The *Rotte* of two aircraft was the basic tactical element.

Geschwaderkommodore: The Wing Commander. Usually a Colonel or Lieutenant Colonel; sometimes a Major; very rarely, a Captain.

Glycol: A thick alcohol $C_2H_4(OH)_2$ used as a coolant in liquid-cooled aircraft engines.

Ground Loop: Loss of lateral control of an airplane on the ground resulting in the aircraft making a sudden turn, a sudden change in direction. Usually a wheel or gear strut on the outside of the turn will break and the aircraft suffers considerable damage. A nose-over or a somersault on the ground is not a ground loop.

Gruppe: A Group. Usually consisted of three Squadrons. Largest (thirty-six aircraft) individual operational unit of the Luftwaffe fighter force.

Gruppenkommandeur: Group Commander. Usually a Major, sometimes a Captain.

Hack: To tolerate something; also to accomplish something, or shoot another aircraft down, especially a big bomber.

Hauptquartier: Headquarters.

Havoc: Nickname for the A-20 attack bomber.

Head-on: A frontal attack.

Heavies: Bomber aircraft of the four-engined type.

Hedgehop: Sometimes called "contour chasing." Flying very low over the ground, rising up over trees, houses, hills, etc.

Horrido!: The victory cry of the Luftwaffe fighter pilots. Also a greeting and parting word among friends and comrades of the Luftwaffe.

Hun: A derogatory word for a German.

Hyperventilation: Excessive ventilation of the blood induced by rapid or deep breathing, often experienced by pilots while flying at high altitudes.

Hypoxia: Insufficient oxygen in the blood at high altitudes.

Inspekteur der Nachtjaeger: Inspector of Night Fighters.

Inspekteur der Tagjaeger: Inspector of Day Fighters.

Jabo: Abbreviation for fighter-bomber.

Jafü: Abbreviation of *Jagdführer*, Fighter Leader. Separate fighter commands in each *Luftflotte*. Originally assigned a policy-regulating and observing role, Fighter Leaders later controlled operations and handled considerable administration.

Jagdgeschwader: Fighter Wing. Usually consisted of three or four *Gruppen* of pilots and aircraft. From 108 to 144 aircraft made up the establishment of a Wing. Some were larger. See under *Geschwader*.

Jagdstaffel: Fighter Squadron.

Jagerblatt: Fighter News. A periodical published by the German Fighter Pilots' Association.

Jink: To jerk an aircraft about in evasive action.

Jockey: To fly or pilot an airplane. Slang name for pilot.

Joy Stick: Slang for control stick of a fighter airplane.

Jump: To attack an enemy aircraft.

Jump Sack: Parachute.

Kadetten Korps: Cadet Corps.

Karinhall: Goering's estate on the Shorfheide, about twenty-five miles north of Berlin.

Kette: Basic three-ship element used in early Luftwaffe fighter tactics, the counterpart of the RAF's three-ship "Vic" formation. Replaced in the Luftwaffe before World War II by the *Rotte* and *Schwarm* formations; returned with the Me-262.

Kettenfuehrer: Flight Commander.

KIA: Killed in action.

Kill: A victory in aerial combat. Destroying an enemy aircraft in flight. Does not refer to the death of an enemy pilot.

Kommodore: Abbreviation of *Geschwaderkommodore*. C.O. of a Wing.

Kriegie: One who was a prisoner of war in Germany in World War II.

Kriegsliederung: Battle Order.

La: Lavochkin La-5. A fighter plane employed in Russia.

Lagg-3: A single-engined Russian fighter plane designed by Lavochkin, Gorbunor, and Gudkov.

Lancaster: A British four-engined heavy bomber developed by the AVRO Company.

Lead (rhymes with heed): The action of aiming ahead of a moving target. See "deflection shot."

Lehrgeschwader: Training, tactical, and experimental Wing.

Lehr-und-Erprobungskommando 24: 24th Training and Testing HQ.

Leutnant: Lieutenant.

Lightning: The Lockheed P-38, a single-seat twin-boom fuselaged fighter aircraft.

Lufbery Circle: A formation in which two or more aircraft follow each other in flight in circles in order to protect one another from enemy aircraft. Named for Major Raoul Lufbery, American ace who developed the tactic in World War I.

Luftflotten: Tactical and territorial air commands. Literally, Air Fleets.

Luftflottenkommando: Air Fleet HQ.

Luftgaue: Administrative and supply organizations of the Luftwaffe.

Luftwaffe: Air Force. The name of the German Air Force from 1935 through 1945.

Lysander: A British two-place single-engined high-wing monoplane extensively used for Army cooperation.

Macchi: An Italian fighter plane manufactured by the Macchi Co.

Mach: The speed of a body as compared to the speed of sound, which is Mach 1.0.

Marauder: Popular name for the U.S.-built Martin B-26 medium bomber.

Mayday: International radiotelephone signal of distress.

Me-109: Officially known as the Bf-109, Germany's most famous single-engined fighter. Originally designed by Bayerische Flugzeugwerke A.G. at Augsburg. Called Me-109 in this book because it is so known by most Americans and is so referred to by virtually all German aces. The term Bf-109, while historically correct, is relatively unknown in the United States.

Me-262: The Messerschmitt twin-engined jet fighter.

MIA: Missing in Action.

Mission: An air objective carrying out a combat air mission; a number of aircraft fly x number of sorties (number of aircraft committed) to carry out a mission.

Nachtjagdgeschwader: Night Fighter Wing, abbreviated as NJG, followed by the number of the Wing, e.g., NJG-6.

Night Fighter: A fighter aircraft and crew that operates at night, the aircraft being provided with special equipment for detecting enemy aircraft at night.

Nose Over: An airplane moving on the ground noses over, tips over on its nose and propeller, damaging nose and prop. Sometimes it somersaults over on its back. This is *not* a ground loop, which is merely directional loss of control of an airplane on the ground.

No Sweat: Slang for "without difficulty."

Oberkommando der Luftwaffe: Referred to as OKL, the Luftwaffe High Command.

Oberkommando des Heeres: Referred to as OKH, the Army High Command.

Oberleutnant: First Lieutenant. Not to be confused with *Oberstleutnant,* Lieutenant Colonel.

Oberst: Colonel.

Oberstleutnant: Lieutenant Colonel.

O'clock: Position of another airplane sighted in the air was called out by its clock position from the observer, twelve o'clock being straight ahead, six o'clock high directly behind and above the observer, nine o'clock horizontally ninety degrees left of the observer.

OKH: Army High Command.

OKL: Luftwaffe High Command.

OKW: High Command of the Armed Forces.

Open City: A city of a belligerent power declared by that power to be non-combatant, and made so in order to avoid bombing or shelling from any of the combatant forces.

Overshoot: In air combat, to fly over or past the enemy plane when following through on an attack.

Pathfinder: A highly trained and experienced bomber crew that preceded the bomber formation to the target and marked it with flares or smoke bombs for easy location and attack by the main force. The RAF frequently used Mosquito fighter-bombers in the Pathfinder role.

Perch: Position of tactical advantage prior to initiating an attack on an enemy airplane.

Personalamt: Personnel Office.

Photo Recce: Photographic reconnaissance.

Port: The left side of an airplane facing forward. The right side is Starboard.

POW: Prisoner of War.

Prang: Slang for crash or collision of airplane, also to crash-land. Also in RAF slang to down an enemy airplane or accurately hit a target, as in "wizard prang"—meaning a successful operation.

Probable: An instance in which a hostile airplane is probably destroyed. With a "probable" it is not known whether it actually crashed, but it is considered so badly damaged as to make its crash probable. USAAF claims in aerial combat listed three categories: 1. Confirmed destroyed. 2. Probably but unconfirmed destroyed. 3. Damaged.

Prop: An abbreviation for propeller.

PTO: Pacific Theater of Operations.

Rack: To make a sudden, violent maneuver in a fighter plane.

RAF: Royal Air Force.

Recce: Abbreviation for reconnaissance.

Recip: Abbreviation for reciprocating engine.

Red Alert: An alert that exists when attack by the enemy is or seems to be imminent.

Red Line: A red mark on the airspeed indicator showing the safe maximum speed of the airplane.

Reef It In: To change direction of flight violently.

Rev: To increase the rpm of an engine; to rev it up.

Rhubarb: A dogfight or the harassment of ground targets by a flight of aircraft. A German term for aerial combat.

RLM: *Reichluftfahrministerium*, the Air Ministry.

Robot: A mechanism, device, weapon, etc., that operates automatically. Trade name of a well-known German camera used to make sequence exposures of aerial combat and synchronized with the fighter aircraft's armament.

Rotte: A two-plane formation. Smallest tactical element in the Luftwaffe fighter force.

Rottenflieger: Wingman.

Rottenfuehrer: Leader of a *Rotte.* Loosely, an element leader.

R/T: Radiotelephone.

Schiessschule der Luftwaffe: Luftwaffe Gunnery School.

Schlachtgeschwader: Ground Attack Wing, or Close Support Wing.

Schwarm: Two-*Rotte* formation, four or five aircraft acting in a single flight. Three *Schwarms* flying together made up a *Staffel,* or Squadron.

Schwarmfuehrer: Leader of a *Schwarm.*

Scramble: The action of getting fighter aircraft into the air quickly.

Scrub: To cancel a flight, sortie, or mission.

Snake Maneuver: A Soviet tactic developed to get the IL-2 *Stormovik* fighter-bomber home when attacked by German fighters. The IL-2s would enter a Lufbery Circle, then descend to a few feet above the ground and work their way home using the snake maneuver, a weaving, follow-the-leader maneuver for mutual protection.

Snaking: The tendency of an airplane to yaw in flight from side to side at a certain frequency.

Sortie: A flight or sally of a single airplane which penetrates into airspace where enemy contact may be expected. While a single plane or any number of aircraft may go out on a mission, each aircraft flying is actually making a sortie. One mission may involve any number of sorties.

Split-ess: A high-speed maneuver in which the airplane makes a half-roll onto its back and then dives groundward, leveling off going in the opposite direction at a much lower altitude.

Stabs-Schwarm: A headquarters flight of three to six aircraft, usually of the same type that make up the *Geschwader.* The Wing Commander and his Adjutant normally fly in the *Stabs-Schwarm.*

Staffel: A Squadron. Consisted of three *Schwarms,* made up of from twelve to fifteen aircraft. Three or sometimes four *Staffeln* made up a *Gruppe.*

Starboard: Right side of an aircraft facing forward. The left side is Port.

St. Horridus: The Savior Saint of the Luftwaffe fighter pilots and origin of the victory cry *"Horrido!"*

Strafe: To dive at and machine-gun targets on the ground. Sometimes spelled "straff."

Strip: An aircraft landing field.

Tallyho!: A code expression called over the radio by a fighter pilot when he sights the enemy target. Derived from the traditional English hunting cry.

Throttle-jockey: Slang name for a pilot.

Thunderbolt: Popular name for the Republic P-47 fighter airplane.

Tiger: Eager pilot; eager to fight.

Tiptank: A fuel tank carried on the wingtips of a fighter aircraft.

Tommy: A British soldier.

Tour: A period of time or course of duty performed by a serviceman at a given assignment or place.

Tracer Bullet: A bullet containing a pyrotechnic mixture to make the flight of the projectile visible.

Undershoot: To land short of the runway; to shoot under a target in aerial combat.

Unteroffizier: A rank equivalent to a US Army Sergeant or a USAF Airman First Class. This rank is above the German Obergefreiter (Senior Corporal) *and below the rank of Unterfeldwebel* (Staff Sgt.). *Unteroffizier* is the lowest non-commissioned officer rank, hence "Under Officer."

Verbandsfuehrer: Unit Commander.

Verteidigungszone West: Western Air Defense Zone.

Vic: A vee formation of three airplanes.

Waffengeneral: Technical Service General.

Wetterkuendigungstaffel: Weather Reconnaissance Squadron.

Wilco: Radiotelephone word of acknowledgment. Abbreviation for "Will comply" or "Will cooperate."

Wilde Sau: Literally, Wild Boar, name of a German night fighter unit operating without radar aids in single-engined fighters.

Window: Metal foil strips that cause a reflection on radar scopes corrupting radar information. Also called "chaff."

Windscreen: An airplane windshield.

Wingco: Abbreviation for Wing Commander.

Zerstörer: Literally, Destroyer. The name chosen for the long-range, twin-engined Me-110 fighter.

Zerstoerergeschwader: Destroyer Wing. Fighter Wings consisting of Me-110s, expressed as ZG-26, ZG-1, etc.

Index